*H*in*d*sights

the autobiography of an unknown artist

Stan Erisman

Hindsights

Published by Stan Erisman
Publishing partner: Paragon Publishing, Rothersthorpe
First published 2021

© Stan Erisman 2021

The rights of Stan Erisman to be identified as the author of this work have been asserted by him in accordance with the Copyright, Designs and Patents Act of 1988.

All rights reserved; no part of this publication may be reproduced, stored in a retrieval system, or transmitted in any form or by any means, electronic, mechanical, photocopying, recording or otherwise without the prior written consent of the publisher or a licence permitting copying in the UK issued by the Copyright Licensing Agency Ltd.
www.cla.co.uk

ISBN 978-1-78222-891-2

Book design, layout and production management by Into Print
www.intoprint.net
+44 (0)1604 832149

Cover illustration: *Mais il faut cultiver notre jardin*, oil painting #84, by Stan Erisman, 1979-81.

The Foreword to the *Hindsights* series can be found in Book 1, *Natural Shocks*.

To be, or not to be, that is the question:
Whether 'tis nobler in the mind to suffer
The **slings and arrows** of outrageous fortune,
Or to take Arms against **a Sea of troubles**,
And by opposing end them: to die, to sleep
No more; and by a sleep, to say we end
The heart-ache, and the thousand **natural shocks**
That Flesh is heir to? 'Tis a consummation
Devoutly to be wished. To die, to sleep,
To sleep, **perchance to Dream**; aye, there's the rub,
For in that sleep of death, what dreams may come,
When we have shuffled off this mortal coil,
Must give us pause. There's the respect
That makes Calamity of so long life:
For who would bear the Whips and Scorns of time,
The Oppressor's wrong, the proud man's Contumely,
The pangs of despised Love, the Law's delay,
The insolence of Office, and the spurns
That patient merit of the unworthy takes,
When he himself might his Quietus make
With a bare Bodkin? Who would Fardels bear,
To grunt and sweat under a weary life,
But that the dread of something after death,
The undiscovered country, from whose bourn
No traveller returns, puzzles the will,
And makes us rather bear those ills we have,
Than fly to others that we know not of.
Thus conscience does make cowards of us all,
And thus the native hue of Resolution
Is sicklied o'er, with the pale cast of Thought,
And enterprises of great pitch and moment,
With this regard their Currents turn awry,
And lose the name of Action.

– William Shakespeare, Hamlet's soliloquy
from *Hamlet*, act III, scene I

Perchance to Dream

Book six in the Hindsights series

Stan Erisman

CONTENTS

Chapter 1: Paradox 1

How I struggled with the sorrows of having to give up painting; how Lena's hostility towards me turned to outright hatred, partially offset by the joyous prospect of parenthood; and how I came to be a middleman in Bob's flirtation with a woman named Carmen.

Chapter 2: Bornholm and beyond. 11

How we spent four days with friends on the Danish island of Bornholm, and how a warm friendship, a toxic home environment and an excess of alcohol led to unforgiveable desires; how a brother-in-law's financial shenanigans added to our distress; and how buoyed I continued to be by approaching fatherhood.

Chapter 3: Waiting 22

How I marveled at pregnancy; how alarmed I was by Bob's Parkinson's and how little he was; how my pulmonary problems put me in the hospital; how much there was to prepare for a new family member, and how much I hoped it would bring harmony to our home.

Chapter 4: A new world 32

How the traumatic birth of Jenny focused me; how determined I was to overcome my problems; how Jenny's birth caused an outpouring of the religious fervor of others, which I refused to suffer in silence; how we enjoyed a few months of domestic peace.

Chapter 5: Generations and degenerations 50

How I dealt with my mom's strange visit and interactions with us, Jenny, Bob and others; how a friendship with a Norwegian family developed; how the debates between me and my brothers continued; and how I was awed by the daily development of our infant.

Chapter 6: For the sake of argument 69

How Lena's disgust and hostility towards me grew and developed into threats of divorce; how she incongruously suggested that we should have a second child; how she conceived, yet soon threatened abortion; how I was unable to do anything right, and was being screamed at almost daily; how Lena expressed her aversion to Bob; how my depression was returning and how I loved caring for Jenny.

CHAPTER 7: Joyful desperation 96

How Sally was born (November 1985) and how fascinated I was by sibling interaction; how the murder of Sweden's Prime Minister shocked and saddened us; how we spent a summer vacation on the island of Gotland; how Bob and I came to realize that we'd become Europeans; how my work from home enabled me to care for Jenny and Sally; and how a visit from my mom led to valuable confrontations.

CHAPTER 8: Delamination 114

How Lena's return to work (January 1987) meant a new phase in our lives, with me as the primary caregiver for our girls; how we returned to Gotland during our summer vacation and made a bizarre visit; how vicious Lena had become towards me except in the presence of others; how Lena began to live another life and subject me to her growing rage.

CHAPTER 9: Derailment 129

How I hid Lena's hostility from Bob; how I struggled to understand cause and effect; how the kids came to enjoy Mozart's opera *The Magic Flute*; how I began taking notes more systematically in order to understand the chaos; how Elsa (my old Swedish teacher) returned to my life; and how misery was coming to a head.

CHAPTER 10: Destruction 141

How I pressured Lena into admitting her affair (March 10th, 1988), how she announced she was leaving me, and how I fought the despair that was overwhelming me; how I feared the detrimental consequences to my girls and how I used writing – and careful note-taking – to bring order to the chaos in my world and in my mind; how Lena pretended to respond to mediation and how I saw through the sham.

CHAPTER 11: Damage control 166

How I gave up trying to rescue a marriage that only I wanted to rescue and instead salvage what I could for the sake of my girls; how my old Swedish teacher helped me save my house; how three months of forced cohabitation and my careful documentation enabled me to stabilize instead of plunging into the abyss; how Lena's moving day (May 15th) ended up giving me a huge sense of relief.

CHAPTER 12: Deliverance 185

How I quickly overcame the disorientation of a single-parent life; how improbably I met Karin two days after Lena's moving day; and how quickly a casual fling turned into something far deeper than either of us had ever experienced; how excited yet cautious we both were about how this could possibly be for real.

Chapter 13: At last………………………………………………209

How our wonder quickly blossomed and grew into a wonderful relationship; how on one extraordinary day (December 3rd, 1988) I said goodbye to one family and was warmly welcomed by another; how pleasant Karin's first meeting with my girls went, and how thrilled and delighted Bob and Karin were to meet each other.

Afterword …………………………………………………227

Here I have sought to tie up a number of loose ends concerning the narrative of my journey from Dallas to Glendale to Oak Park to San Francisco to Vancouver to Malmö to Glimminge, and to fill in some further developments up to October 2021.

Appendix: Drawings of our homes …………………………281

CHAPTER 1

Paradox

"Mrs Erisman, you're pregnant!"

The doctor's words shot like tiny darts from the phone into my left ear, on to my brain, my heart, my adrenal glands, through my legs, to my fingertips. I erupted in joy. I was resurrected from bleakness. The call from the doctor on May 10th, 1983, brought us the news that an embryo had begun her nine-month journey to become our daughter. (Actually the call didn't bring us news about the gender part, but that was of no importance.) It also restored another kind of hope in me: that Lena, at long last, would no longer vacillate about returning my love.

Jeanette hadn't want to bring children into the world because she felt the world was too hostile an environment for them. Her arguments convinced me. Besides, I didn't feel I needed children I'd never known – but I did need her. She was my life for more than 12 years, from our first meeting in San Francisco in early October 1964 until her suicide in late March 1977. She was my muse, my inspiration, the enabler of my art. In what appeared to be her final note to me, she pleaded, "*Teach art to the world to help us all.*"

Her death nearly killed me. Had I found it reasonable, even plausible, to believe in a hereafter, I wouldn't have hesitated to join her. But my inability to believe in the pipedream of a life after death saved the rest of my real one. I didn't kill myself; I had a vasectomy. If I couldn't have children with Jeanette, I thought, I would not have any at all. For a long time, pain defined me. Nothing mattered.

And then, a year later, with the indefatigable help of Bob (my one incredibly close friend) and a few other well-meaning ones, as well as a serendipitous catharsis brought on by writing, I burst out of a suicidal, alcohol-drenched stupor that first anesthetized, then fed, my deep depression. In March 1978 I decided to live again. Although I was still wobbly, my natural optimism began flowing back overnight. Was I grabbing a bull by the horns? Or just clutching at straws?

Lena, the most beautiful girl I'd ever seen, totally bewitched me, swept me away, blew me away, blasted me away. I lost all control of my feelings. I was unable to temper my emotions with reason. My desire for her to love me in return blinded me; I refused to admit that she didn't share my feelings and might not ever do so; there was no rational reason to suppose that she ever would. But neither of us reckoned with my tenacity, nor with her paradoxical pattern of pushing me away, over and over, yet never allowing me to *get* away. She always reeled me back in with glimpses of affection. After a couple of years of seesawing, we got married in June 1980, but our relationship remained a one-way street; we both loved one person: the same person.

My efforts to win her love were continuous – and continually rebuffed. I tried to keep on painting, but with no active encouragement from my muse (and with active *dis*couragement from Lena) my courage to paint eroded and left me. I did, however, channel a great deal of creative energy into the completion of the great work that Jeanette and I had come close to completing: the renovation of a 19th-century house – now Lena's and my home – at Korngatan 12 in the Kirseberg ("Backarna") neighborhood of Malmö, in the province of Skåne, in southernmost Sweden. I had two operations to reverse my vasectomy, the second of which proved successful, as evidenced by the doctor's phone message that day, May 10th, 1983.

We were expecting the doctor's call, but we hadn't dared to expect the life-changing news. Lena answered. I leaned in with my left ear. On hearing the message, I let out a whoop and tried to hug Lena. I was close to jumping up and down, trying to breathe, trying to work off the flood of adrenalin, trying to control my emotions without wanting to or seeing any need to. I was delirious with joy. When I saw that the only outward expressions of euphoria were coming from me, however, I realized I'd better tone them down or channel them elsewhere.

Remembering our pledge to each other (that we'd both quit smoking the moment we got confirmation of pregnancy), I rushed gleefully from room to room gathering up all our cigarettes, butts and packs, and threw them into the garbage bag that hung on the inside of the cupboard door beneath the kitchen sink, a few meters from where Lena was still standing next to the wall-mounted phone just inside the door to our atrium yard and garage. She looked at me with some alarm and irritation. I was thinking to myself, "*Now she'll love me – I'll always be the father of her child!!*" [*Was she thinking, at that moment, "Now I'm trapped – he'll always be the father of my child"? But of course I couldn't know what was going on in her head. Not then, not ever.*]

Instead of supporting my destruction of our tobacco, she hissed at me. "*What the hell do you think you're doing?!*" I was confused. We'd *both* agreed that the moment we found out that she was pregnant, we'd get rid of *all* of it. I reminded her. She responded angrily: "*Oh no, not like that! I'm not going to quit just like that, and don't think you get to tell me otherwise!*" I tried to present rational arguments for taking this opportunity to quit, but to no avail. Her irritation was building up like a pressure cooker; I eventually went out and bought a three-pack of cigarettes. The next day I did the same, then a whole pack. Within a matter of days, however, Lena's hormones changed in a way that made the taste of tobacco repulsive to her, but the psychologically right moment for me to kick the addiction had passed. I continued smoking a pack a day – *mea culpa* – my own fault! The blame for that rested *entirely* on my shoulders (or lungs). Now I'd have to find a new "perfect moment" to ambush and finally overcome my goddamn craving nicotine addiction.

She permitted more of my hugs than usual that day, but returned them lamely and initiated none. She smiled at my jubilation and tears of joy. She listened patiently to my outpourings of love and endearment – all the behaviors I expected such a life-changing announcement to bring to *both* of us. It wasn't that she wasn't thrilled at the prospect of motherhood. But little of *her* thrill seemed to be about *us*. I was perplexed. Her disdain for me took no more than a brief nap; when it awoke again, my anxiety grew greater than ever.

Some changes were almost immediate. Less than two months earlier, Lena had finally agreed to make a month-long trip with me to the States in July. Before we met, she'd been to the US several times to see Larry, her former fiancé in Sacramento. The last of those trips was to make wedding plans, but she got cold feet. *We'd* never been to the States together. [*In fact, I <u>never</u> succeeded in arousing her interest in seeing photos from my childhood. Not once!*] My mom had generously insisted on paying for our trip. (At Christmas, Mom sent presents for everyone in Lena's family, including every one of Lena's nieces and nephews!) Now, on May 10th, I had to phone Mom to tell her we had to cancel our trip; the doctor advised Lena not to make such a trip unless it were absolutely necessary, in view of her miscarriage six months earlier. Considering how much effort I'd had to put into persuading her to make the trip with me in the first place, perhaps she felt relieved to have a good excuse not to go. Mom, however, was bitterly disappointed. It took some weeks for her delight at the reason for the cancellation to outweigh her letdown.

I wrote Bob that same day, instead of phoning him. I knew his initial reaction would be powerful, and I suspected that he'd prefer to process it on his own first. That turned out to be the case. On May 13th he replied: "*Now that was a letter among letters which came this morning! When I saw the news about your pregnancy, a pulse of warmth flooded my senses, then I cried like a small child."*

On the practical level, from our perspective, the pregnancy added urgency to Lena's brother Lars' promise to buy his siblings' shares of the summer house in Eket "during the summer". We badly needed a new car; we no longer felt certain that our old Datsun could be relied on to get us to the maternity ward when the time came. Moreover, the constant repairs were a drain on our budget.

Bo and Peter, our textile-designer next-door neighbors, had offered to lend Lena their large loom so she could weave rag-rugs for our kitchen and hallway. In late April, Lena took them up on their offer. Five days after we got the Big News, Bo helped Lena set up the loom in the east end of my now-defunct studio. Lena began weaving rag-rugs a few days later. [*She would later claim – repeatedly, for decades – that I'd never "allowed" her to have rugs on our kitchen floor. Photos and videos reveal otherwise – but the fact that I failed miserably in* wanting *to have rugs there apparently outweighed the fact that we* had *them!*]

The prospect of my having, at last, a proper studio had been one of the principal reasons Jeanette and I bought the house in the first place. While the studio was theoretically big enough to accommodate my table and easel as well as her loom, Lena repeatedly made it clear that she didn't want to see any more of my damn art on our walls.

Within days of getting our joyful news, both Lena and I experienced marked increases in our nightly dreams and correspondingly greater tiredness during the days. Jeanette and I had noticed a similar type of tiredness during our first month or two in Sweden, when every little thing was just sufficiently different to escape conscious recognition of its differences from what we'd been used to in North America. But the sum of all the trivial differences was significant – and mentally tiring.

I'd heard that many women experience increased mood swings in the early stages of pregnancy, such as sudden crying spells or outbursts of temper. For Lena it was almost exclusively the latter. I sometimes struggled to keep on a mask of bravery; it was unacceptable to her for me to appear hurt by her behavior towards me, even when she screamed at me, her *goddamn idiot* husband.

But in the presence of others she continued to treat me decently, sometimes even nicely. Consequently, I wanted us to have company as often as possible. We socialized regularly with Ole and Birgitta, Maj and Lars, Charlotte and

Kent, Øivind and Gunilla, Bo and Peter, as well as several other neighbors and acquaintances and family members (Marie-Louise, Jan and Eva). I also had my pupils. All those people were friendly towards me and seemed to enjoy my company. With all of them I could converse more or less freely, laugh and have fun. I couldn't understand why Lena was the only exception.

Bob's bizarre "relationship" with Carmen Heusser (the recent widow of a colleague of his, and whom he usually referred to by her initials, CH, in his correspondence with me) was lurching along. I sent her a note on returning to Sweden from Basel in early April, thanked her for her hospitality and the lovely dinner she hosted for Bob and me, and in general terms expressed a wish to return the favor some day. (I never went behind Bob's back, but always informed him of the contents of letters in either direction.) She responded as if I'd sent her a specific invitation, and wanted to know whether it was our intention to invite Bob at the same time. I replied that it would be for them to decide. She continued writing frank letters to me, claiming that she was only looking for Bob's companionship, nothing more. Bob made it clear to me that if he were looking *only* for companionship, it wouldn't necessarily be hers. I didn't know how to handle the awkward role of go-between I'd stumbled into, and tried to let Bob know I was uncomfortable mediating his "pursuit" of this flirtatious woman who seemed to want no more than to play the coquette.

 As an outsider, I'd been struck by the mismatch from the start. Carmen was a privileged, well-to-do defender of upper-middle-class values, traditions, everything Swiss, and her husband's memory (which included the wheelings and dealings of the chemical and pharmaceutical industries in general and the Swiss versions of those industries in particular), yet she seemed fascinated by reaching across the invisible divide to Bob. Although Bob adopted some of the trappings of Swiss social formalities (like written invitations and cultivated [or stilted] forms of address), in many other respects he defied placement in any social role. He was, apparently without realizing it, a disrespectful maverick, at least by Swiss standards. His dress was too informal, his humor far too satirical, his respect for convention way too lacking, and his speech too outlandishly *ausländig* (alien). Worst of all, he was full of contempt for greedy capitalists in general and the Swiss pharmaceutical industry in particular.

 Yet Carmen was also a warm person who didn't deserve to be cast aside – I emphatically agreed with Bob on that. But the issue of Carmen led to one of the only sober disagreements Bob and I ever had, at least the only one that gave rise to noticeable irritation. Fortunately, it was temporary and extremely mild compared to the irritation I was now facing at home on a more-or-less daily basis.

We told Bo and Peter our good news and they were thrilled on our behalf, much more thrilled than I expected them to be. And yet I thought I detected a trace of melancholy in their vicarious delight, the kind of melancholy I'd seen in the eyes of involuntarily childless couples – or was I just projecting my imagination? I'd seen a few recent articles in newspapers and magazines on the controversial issue of gay adoption, but I'd never previously given it a thought in terms of anyone I knew personally.

A slowly decreasing majority of those articles were negative: *"Think of the child, think of the social stigma."* More like think of the bullshit! Or why not think of firmly anchoring one's values in the Middle Ages? Bo and Peter were caring people, compassionate, intellectually active, and highly creative. I was convinced that they would have made excellent, devoted parents. Even though homosexuality in itself is no qualification for being responsible and loving parents, neither is heterosexuality! But their chances of being allowed to adopt – even in Sweden in 1983 – were miniscule. Why? Despite Sweden's exceptional secularism and general abandonment of the theological aspects of religion, many of the traditions of religion remained intact, like stubborn, intractable stains on the social fabric.

The Church of Sweden was still the country's official religion, and would remain so until 2000. All other Protestant churches were known as "free churches", a distinction that remains in the minds of most Swedes to this day (2021), even though the Church of Sweden is now just as "free" as any other (in theory)! In 1983, most Swedes belonged to it more or less automatically, whether they were believers or not. The regent is not only required to be a member, he or she is the titular head of the Church. And traditional religious doctrines continue to regard homosexuality as an "abomination", in accordance with the Bible – the same Bible that commands people to stone to death anybody who works on the Sabbath and a host of other "abominations", the same Bible that condones slavery, massacres of children, torture, treachery, deceit, cheating, and all the other behaviors that lead so many people to view the Bible as the ultimate bastion of morality.

As for what society would think: more bullshit. Society *doesn't* think! It doesn't have a brain. It's not an organism. "Society" is a rather abstract something for people to hide behind when they're disinclined to think for themselves and decide for themselves what's *really* right or wrong. Treating people badly is what's really wrong, and society tends to be pretty good at that.

Swiss social conventions were becoming obstacles in the development of the relationship between Bob and Carmen. One of the more Byzantine conventions involved what form of address to use with each other. Bob told me she always addressed him as Herr Krause, while he always addressed her as Frau Heusser. When I wrote her that thank-you note, I wrote "Dear Mrs Heusser". To my surprise (and to her credit) she replied "Dear Stanley" (so I wrote "Dear Carmen" after that).

Some years earlier (mid- to late-1970s), Bob told me that he occasionally exchanged visits with a retired colleague named Werner Felsenmeier, three or four times a year. They always had a meal (lunch or dinner) a different restaurant in the Basel environs. Bob and Meier (as Bob referred to him to me) always addressed each other formally. These restaurant visits were normally the consequence of written invitations to each other, even though they lived only minutes apart and had phones. Meier always picked the places, and they took turns picking up the tab.

In the autumn of 1982, Meier invited Bob to a special dinner for a special occasion: *"Duzis"* – the Swiss-German term for a formal meal at which the elder of the two (Meier) proposed to the younger (Bob) that they should begin addressing each other informally (with first names and with the informal version of the second-person-singular pronoun). To me it sounded hilariously stilted, cramped, claustrophobic, antiquated and anachronistic. But I wasn't Swiss – whatever my ancestors may have been.

I wrote to Carmen to ask about this incomprehensible custom, and how I should approach it with her. Her reply was straightforward: "'Carmen' is OK, of course!" Then she commented that she didn't like these customs much.

> *As to your cousin and myself, we met somewhere in the sixties and if we address each other formally it is just because we are used to it for years. I know that it is up to me – following Swiss customs, for more than one reason – to change it. But why should I change something so special and precious only because everybody else would probably do it? [?!] And besides, Mr Krause has enough personality to change it himself, if he thinks it is necessary.*

What she didn't seem to realize was that Bob by *no* means had the right personality to change it himself. Although he was delighted that my correspondence with Carmen gave him a parallax view of her, he remained strangely and unnecessarily bound by certain Swiss customs, carefully cherry-picked by himself. Nobody who ever met Bob would have found "conventional" to be a salient characteristic. Nor did anyone seem to expect conventional behavior from him. The fabric of Swiss social customs was far more convoluted than Bob perceived, which meant that the few customs he followed stood in strange contrast to the many he didn't (like someone who might wear a tux and flip-flops). Yet the customs he felt obliged to follow caused him a great deal of anxiety, effort and pain (which I endeavored to minimize).

On May 24th, Lena had her first ultrasound scan, standard Swedish procedure quite early in the pregnancy when there'd been a miscarriage before. Seeing the fetus nearly made me faint with excitement, as did the now-graphic prospect of parenthood. I hoped the prospect alone would assuage my unrequited love, my frustration (sex was now off limits *all* the time instead of *most* of the time), and my loneliness (guess why). The due date was estimated at January 4th, but based on his medical experience, Bob suggested revising this date to sometime between the 4th and the 18th. And I had many small projects to finish around the house before then.

Bob was coming (alone) to spend two weeks with us starting July 23rd. Just before that, Lena and I were going to spend four days on the Danish island of Bornholm together with Ole and Birgitta (they'd be leaving their little girl Sara with Birgitta's mother). Time spent with others would again provide me respite from Lena's barrages of verbal abuse.

I could do nothing right. If I made dinner, Lena would scream at me "*Why are you always making dinner?!*" If I didn't make dinner, she would scream at me "*Why do I have to do all the cooking around here!?*" I felt my heart would fall apart the first time she screamed at me, "*Why the hell did I ever want to have a child with someone like you?!*" Such outbursts of loathing and hate from the woman I loved, my wife, hurled my body into an empty, howling cavern from which I could see no escape. I fought furiously to hold off resurgent feelings of suicide. Then her furor would abate, as if (to *her*, apparently) nothing had ever happened, i.e. no need to apologize, much less to make amends.

But when anybody else joined us, her voice went silky. She was *instantly* sweet and demure, the very picture of charm. Nobody could have known, or even guessed, that her charm was not ever-present. [*Nor did I guess it when I was in the process of falling in love with her!*] Now I tried telling myself that it was her hormones due to the pregnancy, even though the post-conception differences in her comments were more quantitative than qualitative.

For some time now, my work for Perstorp entailed having up to three pupils per week at home, one pupil at a time, for a whole day of speaking English, nine to five. But sometimes I went several weeks at a time with no pupils at all, to compensate for all the extra hours I'd put in. Our library was my classroom, which left the big house to Lena when she wasn't working, except at lunchtime.

At around noon, my pupil and I would go across the small yard to the kitchen, where we would continue speaking English while I cooked. Many of my pupils told me they came for the food as much as for the lessons. I made a lot of Asian-style dishes (and no boiled potatoes!). In our own domestic life, Lena left more and more of the cooking to me, for ourselves and for our guests as well. I got lots of praise (some, but not much, from Lena). Bob sent me an electric wok which I would continue using for decades. [*I'm still using that same wok, now, in 2021!*]

The main reason I did so much of the cooking was simply because Lena didn't – it became my task by default. Yet she resented it. Why? Why was she always angry with me? She'd say, "*You always have to be right!*" She expressed it as an accusation, not an observation. What did she mean? That I should *try* to be wrong sometimes? That every other day I should claim that two plus two is five?! I *could* have said something like "If you were right, I'd agree with you," which was quite true, but it would have set off a bomb. She couldn't seem to understand that to me it didn't matter whether *I* was right, as long as *we* found the right answer. Whoever came up with the old saying that it takes two to make a quarrel was never married to her.

One Saturday afternoon we were relaxing in the living room. I was half slumbering, half watching football on TV. Lena was reading or sewing or something like that. Suddenly she burst out harshly, "*What's the matter with you?!*" Semi-awake, I replied that nothing at all was the matter, why did she ask? "*Don't you tell me nothing's the matter!!*" she shot back furiously. Dumbfounded, I wondered how she could possibly think anything was the matter. "*Then why were you smiling?!!*" I was so flabbergasted by this exchange that I left the room to draw a comic strip of the incident – and to try to figure it out (or figure *her* out).

The most gut-wrenching incident that spring was the first time she screamed at me "*I hate you!!*" ("*Jag hatar dig!!*"). It felt as if my body had been hurled from a height of 10 stories and splattered all over the concrete below. I wanted to die, to disappear, to evaporate. Eventually I became numb and went to sit down and calm down in our library. After an hour or so, she entered, looked at me, and wondered what I was moping about. *No form of apology! Just pretend it never happened!*

I was beginning to sense a connection: that the only way to assure that wouldn't scream at me was to agree – fully and enthusiastically – with *whatever* she said. Had she been like this all along and I just couldn't or wouldn't see it – in the best "*love is blind*" tradition? When her rage towards me boiled over and she spewed out her bitterness at having allowed me to be the father of her child, my defenses against depression began falling apart.

Nobody else saw those incidents. I didn't dare even to hint at them to anyone (including Bob – *especially* Bob) for fear that they (or he) would look at Lena in a different way and she would know, and then she'd become more furious than ever. I'd *almost* convinced myself that when the baby came, all would be well, that new hormones and buckets of serotonin would prevail, that my willingness to help would be appreciated, and that I would win her heart.

CHAPTER 2

Bornholm and beyond

On Thursday, June 9th, Ole and Birgitta invited us for dinner and to discuss our upcoming four-day, three-night trip to Bornholm the following month. I think they said it would be their first trip on their own since the birth of Sara. We had a great time that evening. Lena was affectionate towards me – even when we were alone on our way home.

The four of us got to talking about work. Lena would soon be starting a new job as a "special teacher" (for special-needs children); Ole always had interesting tales of horticulture to tell from the university campus in Alnarp, where he worked; and Birgitta, like Lena, was a schoolteacher, and was now on maternity leave. During our conversation, I mentioned my work for Frigoscandia and a guy called Leif. Birgitta, who was from Helsingborg, turned out to have been a babysitter for that same Leif's little boys while she was a girl still living with her parents. I wondered to myself whether Leif had tried anything on with her.

It was things Leif said that made me wonder, although nothing about Birgitta. Leif was an almost stereotypical marketing manager: the gold Rolex, the big BMW, the fast talker. He knew marketing, and I learned a great deal from him about writing market communications, but he knew enough about manipulating people to make me wince. He did a lot of traveling and bragged about having women wherever he went. He took great pleasure in telling me about one young Brazilian lady who could administer the most amazing hands-free internal massage (presumably the Singapore grip) and other tricks. He didn't limit the tales of his trysts to his overseas travels; he claimed to have regularly banged his secretary *in* his office in Helsingborg on their lunch hour! Sometimes they met at her apartment. Nobody seemed to be off his radar. That's why I wondered.

Leif was a hunter in the literal sense as well. He asked me if I liked venison; I said I loved it. He frequently offered to supply me some, but he never did [*not in 30 years of collaboration*]. He kept telling me he would introduce me to Alf, the founder and head of Frigoscandia's latest advertising agency, whose work I was constantly rewriting as Leif's ghost writer. It would take decades before I finally met Alf. I enjoyed my work as a copywriter, and was grateful for Leif's confidence in me to do it, but I kept plenty of salt on hand for the many grains I would have to take with his comments.

My work with Leif typically went something like this. When Frigoscandia was preparing to launch a new freezer, Leif would brief the agency. The agency would then plan a campaign, complete with drafts of brochures, product data sheets and PowerPoint presentations, as well as press releases, an article or two for the trade press and accompanying advertisements. Leif would then come to Korngatan, drafts in hand, and ask me to edit them or rewrite them extensively (sometimes completely), bringing them up to his level of satisfaction.

Sometimes I also invented slogans for the campaign in question. I rewrote nearly everything the agency drafted, often with Leif sitting opposite me in my home office. Then he'd take the new drafts back to Helsingborg, present them to Alf and tell him *he'd* edited them. I'm sure Alf didn't believe him for a second, but the customer is always right, right?

The agency would often rewrite my revisions, then Leif would bring them to me to *re*-rewrite them. There might be several rounds like this, stretching both the timeline and the budget a lot more than if I'd sat down with Alf in the first place and worked it out directly. It costs money and takes time to re-re-re-re-rewrite. I suggested this to Leif, but he showed no interest in working that way. The only explanation I could imagine was that he enjoyed behind-the-scenes intrigues and playing the spider in the web.

I eventually began to grow weary of that game – especially one time, after many years of collaboration, when he accused me of padding the bill. Perhaps he thought the endless rewrites he demanded took no time and should therefore not cost anything. Since I had no way of proving my working hours, even though I knew I had in fact charged *less* than for the hours the rewrites required, I backed down. But it took a great toll on my enthusiasm for working with him. [*When he accused me a second time of overcharging, many years later, I lost all remaining interest in having anything to do with him.*]

As soon as summer vacation began, Lena and I made several trips to the seaside in Höllviken together with Ole and Birgitta. Like me, Ole had little interest in sedentary hours on the beach, so we brought along a Frisbee for our amusement while our wives soaked up the solar radiation. Then Ole and I noticed a guy renting windsurfing boards. Ole was curious and eager to try it. I told him I'd windsurfed quite a bit in the summer of 1977 and thought I'd probably remember how. The water off the beach in Höllviken remains knee- or thigh-deep quite a long way out, which makes it ideal for a first-time windsurfer; if you're blown off the board, you just step back up onto it. (In deeper water you first have to haul yourself up onto the board, in a nearly prostrate position, then try to stand up while maintaining your balance even when waves are rocking the board violently.)

I showed Ole the basics, and after many tries he began to get the hang of it. There was a strong offshore breeze that day, and when we got going, the wind whipped us along, away from the beach. Ole found it exhilarating. I enjoyed it too, but many of my memories from the awful summer of '77, when I'd first learned how to windsurf, gave me mixed feelings.

We were rapidly getting farther out to sea. I shouted to Ole that we'd better start heading back to shore. He *understood* the technique of tacking (I think he had some sailing experience), but he didn't know how to apply those techniques to windsurfing. I stayed with him for a while, but he was getting blown farther and farther from the shore, and I didn't know how to get both him and myself back. The north coast of Poland was probably less than a week away. I hurried back to the beach (as fast as I could hurry when tacking) and sent the renters out in a powerboat to tow Ole back in. (I think they'd been keeping track of him with their binoculars.) We had a good laugh about it that evening, but it still made me nervous (probably Ole too!).

Our trip to Bornholm (July 19th-22nd) was wonderful on many levels. Small islands always seem to me to have a special atmosphere – greater freedom than the mainland despite (or because of?) their isolation from it. Although Bornholm is part of Denmark, it's much closer geographically to Sweden (and even a bit closer to Germany and Poland than to the rest of Denmark) in the windswept southwestern Baltic Sea. We explored the ruins of Hammarshus, (a 13th century castle), the charming villages of Gudhjem and Svaneke, and a couple of small 12th century "round churches", before reaching the vast, wild, nearly deserted sandy beach at Dueodde in the southeasternmost corner of the island.

There were lots of waves out in the Baltic that Ole and I couldn't wait to plunge into, which we did the moment we'd helped spread out the blankets and picnic baskets, and our wives were settling into their conversation and sunbathing. There was a stiff but warm offshore breeze, and the waves were breaking diagonally against the shore. Ole and I raced out into them until it was waist-high, then dove in headfirst. We could still walk on the bottom and went farther out, diving into the breaking waves again and again. Although the current was strong, we failed to notice it because we were heading in the same direction.

When we finally looked back towards the shore, we realized we'd been carried quite far west from where Lena and Birgitta were talking and soaking up the sunshine.

We tried to turn back, but the powerful undertow wouldn't allow us to move eastward by walking on the seabed. We tried swimming instead. Although we were both pretty good swimmers, the current was stronger, and our efforts only took us farther and farther from our goal. We tried again to walk eastward, leveraging our feet against the sandy bottom to try to achieve some forward progress in the now chest-high water. That too was a losing battle in the now-powerful current. Finally, we found that we could gradually get closer to the shore by walking on the seabed diagonally north*west* towards it. When at last we reached the shore, we collapsed, panting and exhausted. Our wives were no longer in sight. Some forces of nature are just too strong to resist.

Even though they missed their daughter, Ole and Birgitta seemed to enjoy having time both on their own together, and with us. I envied them. Lena was civil towards me when they were around, but once we'd gone to our separate rooms for the night, the party was over for me. I was just glad when Lena wasn't mean; passion was far too much to expect. I dreaded going home again, but I kept up my defensively cheerful façade, my brave face.

The day after we got back, July 23rd, Bob arrived for a two-week visit. For once, I had no building project to distract me. I did, however, have stomach cramps, fever and coughing, so I went to the clinic for tests, but got no real answers. Bob encouraged me to insist on further tests, and to keep insisting until the clinic found it easier to test me than not to.

Lena's pregnancy, now slightly visible to the trained eye, was enough to launch a wild variety of flights of my imagination: from scenarios of marital and familial bliss to cataclysmic upheavals of misery. But I left Bob entirely in the dark about the raging anxiety within me. Thanks to his preoccupation with Carmen, it was no problem for me to divert his attention from signs of friction or tension between Lena and me.

The week after Bob returned home, the doctor phoned to tell me I'd somehow contracted a relatively rare infection called *yercinia*. I'd never heard of it, nor did I have any idea how I might have acquired it. By the time the doctor phoned, I had no further symptoms, but he prescribed an antibiotic called *pivmecillinam* anyway, three pills a day for 10 days. I experienced no side-effects, nor any recurrence of the symptoms, so I thought no more about it. But my coughing persisted.

On Sunday, August 14th, Lena told me she felt the first movement of our child-to-be inside her. I was instantly rapturous, which only seemed to irritate Lena [*WTF?!*]. Maybe neither of us could help whatever we did or didn't feel – about anything, about each other, about the future. Or was I longing for harmony that simply wasn't there and would never be?

I was lonely, terribly lonely. And I was *starving* for affection. That scared me, made me feel vulnerable. How would I ever be able to resist a kind word, let alone an affectionate one? Was Lena aware of this? She continually rebuffed me, and did so with withering disdain. Was she trying to provoke a break-up? Was that what she needed, and if so, was she aware of it? I kept coming back to Sonja's dreaded truth: *"you can't make someone love you!"*

I kept asking myself if it was just about sex for me, although I was certain it wasn't. Had Lena been ill and couldn't, but loved me anyway, I was certain it wouldn't have been a problem for me. Her constant *contempt* was the "disease", and I couldn't deal with it. The lack of sex was just a symptom. Sex was the mortar, love was the brick wall. The latter doesn't stand firmly without the former. And without either, there's no wall at all.

Ole and Birgitta invited us to a crayfish party at their place on Friday, August 19th. I don't remember many things about that party, probably because the things I do remember are things I remember far more clearly than I want to.

Crayfish parties, held in August, are a Swedish cultural institution. They were originally based on the time of year when the crayfish in Swedish lakes and rivers were at their prime. Strict laws once regulated the fishing season for crayfish, although not when they could be eaten. When demand overtook supply, crayfish were imported in great quantities from places like Turkey, the US (especially Louisiana) and China. And once freezers were commonplace in Swedish households, the consumption of crayfish was no longer limited to August. But the traditional August crayfish parties endured.

These crustaceans look like miniature lobsters. In Sweden they are cooked with dill umbel and served with liberal quantities of aquavit and beer. A crayfish tail has about as much meat as a fairly large prawn, but extracting the small morsels of meat from the claws takes a long time and can be frustrating, especially if one is hungry. Other foods (garlic bread, Västerbotten cheese pie, etc) prevent hunger from outpacing one's ability to extract the tiny bits of the goddamn crayfish meat. The crayfish is first broken in half, then slurped (even noisily is not impolite). The hard shell is twisted, pinched and peeled away to get at the delicious tail. Nutcrackers may come in handy for breaking open the small claws, where the bits of meat are so small that they wouldn't be worth the effort if tradition didn't dictate otherwise. More aquavit, more beer. (Lena's pregnancy ruled out all alcohol for her that evening, but not for me.)

Lena was grumpy towards me even before we left home to walk to the party venue. It was a balmy summer evening. I don't remember how many of us there were (at least a dozen, possibly more). Our hosts had set up tables in their beautiful back garden, with candlelight and lanterns for when darkness followed dusk, making it wonderfully cozy. People were laughing, singing traditional Swedish drinking songs, and telling jokes (I could always be counted on for quite a few of those). The atmosphere was thoroughly friendly, apart from Lena's frequent scowls in my direction.

In keeping with another Swedish tradition, guests were assigned seats at the table in a way that prevented husbands and wives from sitting next to each other. I'd been placed next to Birgitta, whose enjoyment of that fact became increasingly apparent to me as the evening and night progressed. She made it quite clear that she enjoyed my company, enjoyed hearing my voice, my jokes, my laughter. And the more I drank, the prettier she got. As the dew was beginning to fall along with inhibitions at around midnight or a bit later, people began drifting away from the yard and into the house. Birgitta and I, still seated next to each other at one of the garden tables, were oblivious to what was going on. We were wrapped up in a lovely warm haze of alcohol and pleasant chatter, until we realized that we were all alone, but had no idea how long we'd been that way. We were both pretty soused – and aroused.

We were laughing as if we'd had too much to drink, which indeed we had. We leaned in closer, as if starving for affection, which I (at least) was. I was seeking warmth, a kind word, a caress, anything that would make me feel I had any value left as a human being. Through our boozy haze, our lips met and parted and met again. We embraced softly, passionately. She showed me all the affection and attraction I'd been longing for – and missing – from Lena for so terribly long. When my brain finally realized it, I nearly cried.

"*You goddamn sonofabitch, you rotten piece of stinking shit!!!*" Lena was standing right behind us, bellowing. Neither Birgitta nor I had seen or heard her coming. "*How could you?? How <u>could</u> you?!*" I staggered to my feet. Lena continued to swear, outraged that I could do such a thing to her, she being pregnant and everything. I was the world's worst human being, if indeed I *was* a human being. She screamed that she was going home and that I needn't bother to join her. She stormed away cursing my vilely; her shrill shouting attracted a few curious faces from the house. I was too drunk to register whose or what or why.

The agony of the situation slammed into me like a speeding bus. I lurched across the street into Beijer's Park. I didn't know where to go or what to do. I staggered and collapsed on the black ground beneath the old beech trees. Horrendous scenarios crashed over me like breaking waves, pulling me out to sea like the undertow in Dueodde. I was in utter drunken despair. If Birgitta and I hadn't been interrupted, would we have wanted to stop? Perhaps wouldn't have. At the same time I was [*and am*] convinced that if Lena had been the least bit interested in showing me the slightest affection (or even a bit less hostility), the whole thing would never have happened. Although I was in no way blameless – I certainly felt all kinds of guilt and remorse – it did constitute an answer to her outraged question: that was *how* I could do it, even though I well knew that that didn't make it right. *The fact that I was totally <u>starved</u> for love was an explanation, not an excuse.*

I lay there in the night hoping my head would stop spinning, hoping I could wake up and shake off the nightmare of my own making. I have no idea how long I lay there on the dark ground. I heard a few residual sounds of the party from across the street, but didn't want to go back or encounter anybody on my way home. Nor could I begin to imagine what I would face once I got there. My brain was intoxicated, numb, in a state of total confusion, yet in a special mode of self-preservation. I have no memory of whether I came home to a dark house or a barrage of condemnation or both. I don't remember where I slept, except that it was indoors, in our home. I must have passed out as soon as I found a flat surface.

The next morning, Lena's fury was unabated, but more in the form of smoldering than exploding. I apologized profusely and sincerely. I groveled and pleaded for forgiveness. Her undiminished rage seemed to me to contain a note of triumph, as if my groveling apologies were feeding her fires of vengeance. Did she now have me where she wanted me? Was she – or was I, or were both of us – subconsciously trying to create a scenario that would provide an excuse to terminate a failed marriage? Among the many things she claimed to hate about me was my propensity to analyze everything, and here I was analyzing this. Didn't *she* need to understand?! Or were her own feelings the only ones she felt to be worthy of consideration?

[*Something that didn't occur to me at this time (but should have) was <u>why</u> I was trying desperately to understand her feelings, her sense of betrayal, her general sense of disgust with and contempt for me, as expressed frequently and explicitly many time a week long before this "Birgitta incident". Did I have any reason whatsoever to suppose that she might have any interest at all in understanding me, my feelings, my visceral sense of betrayal and frustration and loneliness, my general sense of desperation and being unloved? Where was the reciprocity?!*]

In the late morning, Ole phoned to see if we were OK (!). I apologized deeply and wretchedly to him as well, but he merely chuckled and said that such things happen, that it was nothing serious, that Birgitta and I were just expressing sympathy for each other, which he found perfectly understandable. I couldn't believe my ears. Was he aware of how Lena was responding? Had he seen signs of her contempt for me when we were together on Bornholm? Did he sense the nature of the maximum-security doghouse I was now in? In any case, he said he'd be right over to talk about it with Lena too. Minutes later, he was at our door.

Ole's equanimity and good-humoredness seemed to take the wind out of Lena's sails (at least during the half an hour or so he remained at Korngatan). Was she disappointed that he didn't come after me with an axe? Who knows? But *she* certainly wasn't about to bury the hatchet, at least not deep enough that she couldn't quickly dig it up whenever she needed strong grounds for starting a new quarrel with me on any subject at all. As a result, for the next four years Lena would add castigation for kissing Birgitta to whatever else she chose to castigate me for at the time – even though she didn't express any objections to our continued socializing with Ole and Birgitta [*?!?*]. Neither they nor I ever brought the incident up again with each other. After a brief hiatus, the four of us resumed seeing each other with unaltered frequency. As far as I could tell, Lena didn't mention the incident to her mother or her sister for years. And I didn't mention it to Bob or anyone else. But the additional scorn and hatred Lena so often expressed to me was gradually breaking down, undermining and disintegrating my bulwarks against depression.

Lena's new job as a special-needs teacher meant providing in-class tutoring to children with special learning difficulties, and assistance to the ordinary class teacher (her pupils were kids in their early teens). I admired her willingness to take on the extra challenge that this daunting task entailed; the extra pay involved was good, but didn't really match the extra difficulty. Moreover, her position was at one of Malmö's more problematic schools. But the challenges inspired her, drove her, and she was enthusiastic about her work. (I'd have gladly offered her another prodigious challenge: the clearly daunting task of finding anything worthwhile about me!)

For a time, she was a bit nicer to me. At least that's how I chose to see it, but it may have been that she was simply less hostile, or that the hostility stopped increasing for a while. Did it have to do with greater job satisfaction in her new position? Or hormonal changes with the advancement of pregnancy? Or something else? Was "the Birgitta incident" some sort of wake-up call for her after all?

School was back in session for the autumn. Lars had failed to deliver on his promise to pay out Lena's share of the mosquito-infested cottage in Eket "during the summer". (To be fair, he never actually specified which year!) The delay, he wrote, was because he discovered that waiting would be of financial benefit – to *him*. We could hardly believe the arrogance of it! Instead, payment would be made "by the end of November". We just shook our heads and sighed. Although that would cut it pretty close, we'd still have time to replace the Datsun before Junior arrived in January.

In the meantime, I started taking a closer look at the car market. We wanted something new (a criterion passed on to me by my dad, who feared that used cars would likely mean inheriting somebody else's problems), yet within our modest budget, and small enough for good fuel economy and easy urban parking (and preferably able to fit into our small garage). But it also had to be spacious enough to accommodate baby paraphernalia. We boiled it down to a little five-door Daihatsu. We went to the dealer's to have a look and confirm our choice. Payment wouldn't be due until 30 days after the purchase date, so we said we'd come back at the end of October. (We could, of course have had an installment plan, but I'd always had a strong aversion to debt; the loan on the house was my only exception.) We hoped that no more major repairs would be needed on the Datsun in the meantime, and that we'd still be able to pay in full when the money from Lars came through in late November.

My mom was showing signs of getting her engines revved up for the birth of Junior, unfortunately in the form of increased evangelizing. Did she want to succeed with Junior where she'd failed with me? It was easy to ignore her forays into religion when they came in envelopes. It would be trickier to deflect those delivered in person, which was likely if she came to visit soon after Junior's arrival.

Marie-Louise, on the other hand, was very much present. Although I always liked her – loved her – there seems to be something about the imminent birth of a grandchild that makes some grandmothers feel not only entitled but obliged to turn on the preaching machine. In Lena's mother's case, her preaching was limited to christening; she regarded it as an absolute and self-evident necessity. Marie-Louise was not, however, motivated by the religious aspect of it, nor could she have defended her case for christening on her own theological grounds. For her, it was all about *tradition*, particularly the what-will-people-say-if-you-don't variety. I told her kindly, but in no uncertain terms, that I had no intention whatsoever to start my child's life with a *lie* by promising in the name of the Father, the Son, and the Holy Spirit that I would raise my child in a faith I did not have and considered fallacious. Thinking of the earlier deception (in which she co-conspired against her eldest son and how that contributed to ruining his marriage), I added that I would not permit it. After a few weeks of sighing, she found it best to let the matter rest.

Junior had now passed the halfway mark of embryonic development and was kicking his or her way around the womb to remind us that he or she was in there. Lena's diatribes against me abated further. Screaming at me was no longer a daily event, but was reduced to once or twice a week. [*Was this due to a temporary surge of warmth towards me, or because I was getting better about keeping any divergent tastes or views well concealed from her?*] Perhaps she was fearful of two great unknowns: delivery and motherhood. And perhaps her mother knew what she was talking about when she told Lena that I might be the right one to hold onto in a storm.

My approaching role as a father seemed to be appearing out of nowhere, popping up like a daffodil from the still-frozen ground in February. I sang and hummed Mozart to Lena's bulging abdomen. I crooned Evert Taube's soothing lullaby *Nocturne*, as well as Brahms' *Lullaby*, to that little fighter in there. I began reading books on parenthood and searching for documentaries. I could be intense at times.

As soon as we heard our good news in May, I informed Sverker Hellsten and Bo Husberg, the two surgeons who reconnected my *vas deferens* (although I'm well aware that "vast difference" has great pun potential here, I refuse even to mention it!) and thus enabled procreation. With Junior now kicking away, I phoned them again in late August and invited them to drop by and see for themselves. They did so on Monday, September 5th, and were rewarded with two bottles each: a single malt and Champagne. Good things cry out to be celebrated.

CHAPTER 3

Waiting

Bob's accounts to me of his inner turmoil concerning Carmen, Tante Lore, occasionally his brother Charles, memories of his dysfunctional relations with his parents, his ex-wife Sigrid, and his ex-boss Theiss (i.e. Sigrid's ex-husband), seemed to indicate that difficulties were again piling onto him (too), gaining control, threatening to overthrow his hard-won balance. I was both puzzled and alarmed. He'd told me that Jeanette and I had been instrumental in helping him to clamber out of his deep depression back in the early 1970s (in time for him to help me through mine in the end of that decade; we both had experience in the field). Was he (too) now in danger of sliding back into that quagmire?

Seeing the clear signs of his current inner conflicts made it both natural and necessary for me to reach out to him more than ever before. I came to surmise, after years of knowing him, that he was a deeply emotionally sensitive person, perhaps more than I was. Unlike me, however, he nearly always kept this side of himself well hidden – consciously (but perhaps not voluntarily), and most of his outward behavior was expressed in a highly intellectual and dispassionate manner.

How much of his own sensitivity was he aware of? Only rarely did emotions alone seem sufficient to justify a course of action. Instead, his emotional response appeared to trigger a search for intellectual justification, and only when that search was successful would he take action – if indeed his resolve hadn't lost the name of action by that time. While many others seemed to act impulsively (often *entirely* on their emotions), and might have benefited from some intellectual reflection prior to action, Bob seemed to have had an overdose of the latter, with paralyzing effects on his ability to act. Perhaps before he dared to express himself emotionally, he needed to assure himself that it wouldn't lead to exploitation, and such assurance is seldom available – except in hindsight.

When I expressed my thoughts on this subject to him in one of my letters, he replied:

> *I was moved so deeply by your understanding of my chief burden – the "intellectualizing" compulsion which is not recognized by me because automatic, I suppose since childhood – that I could scarcely believe my eyes.*

We not only loved and cared for each other, we also observed each other, critiqued each other, challenged each other, respected each other, and helped each other to understand and grow. I can never know what Bob chose to withhold from me (nor did he know what I'd withheld from him, except after the fact). Whatever it may have been, I can be pretty sure it was only because he didn't want to assail me with details.

[*My only reason for knowingly withholding anything from Bob was not because I didn't want to or feel that I could confide in him, but because I wanted to spare him the great anxiety I'm sure it would have caused him. While that may have been true, a case could be made for my failure to trust him enough. After all, in the deepest of crises, he always seemed to have a reserve of energy and wisdom that might have benefited all concerned.*]

Even though I'd found myself unable and/or unwilling to confide in him fully, Bob nevertheless turned out once again to be my "catcher in the rye", helping to keep me from thoughts or actions that might overwhelm me and drop me back into my own chasm of deep depression. I wished I knew how to do likewise for him. I gritted my teeth and hoped that all my problems with Lena would evaporate once Junior arrived.

On October 14th, it was time for the next chapter in the saga of Lena's piano. When she moved in with me in Malmö in June 1979, she chose the living room as the right location for her upright black beauty. But she hardly ever went near it because she said she felt too self-conscious, too exposed to the eyes and ears of passersby in the street outside. As a result, some 16 months later we had it moved (pushing the limits of the possible) to the newly refurbished room in the downstairs of the little house. But it continued to just stand there, in its new location, as unplayed as ever (except when Øivind came to visit). I asked her why she still never played. She said the downstairs room was too dark and confined, but if we could move it *up*stairs, into the new library, *then* she would play.

So once again, three piano movers arrived, took measurements, looked at the steep staircase, then scratched and shook their heads. They strongly doubted that it would fit. Since I made it a point of order and honor not to rely on belief without evidence, I took new measurements and quickly removed the bannister, adding valuable centimeters to the width of the stairway opening. Then I measured the height of the piano and the height of the overhead clearance, and found that there were just under six centimeters of disparity. The piano was supported by four removable castors that lifted it four centimeters off the floor. I looked at the joist that formed the overhead beam across the opening of the stairway and felt I could sacrifice three centimeters (one for good measure) without jeopardizing the integrity of the support for floor above it. I hurriedly grabbed a crosscut saw, a hammer and a chisel from the garage, feverishly whacked away at the beam, and finally convinced the reluctant movers that the move could now be achieved after all.

With mover's straps slung over their necks and shoulders, one of the movers started backing up the steps. He pulled and lifted, while the other two stood behind the piano, pushing and shoving from below. After managing to get the entire piano angled upwards onto the stairway with about five millimeters to spare all around, they were wheezing and grunting and swearing and turning red in the face, their cheeks distended like trumpet players' at the end of a long night's gig. And then, halfway up the stairs, they solemnly announced that they could move no more. They declared that it was just too damn heavy and unwieldy to budge any further.

I spotted an extra moving strap, grabbed it and raced across to the big house, up the stairs, across the garage roof to the library, where I joined the lone exhausted guy to help pull from above, so that we were now two on each end. With a final series of coordinated tugs, literally step by step, we made it to the top, all four of us sweating and gasping. They said it was both the shortest and the toughest piano move they'd ever done.

And still she didn't play.

I was naturally curious about how children learn language, particularly in bi- and multi-lingual families. My mom's parents, who were born in the US to Swedish immigrants, grew up bilingual; they spoke Swedish in their home and English everywhere else. It wasn't a problem managing the two languages side by side. Bob's mother, the eldest of the six Larson girls (my mom was fourth), also learned quite a lot of Swedish, but for some reason, my maternal grandparents abandoned teaching their kids Swedish long before it was my mom's turn to be born, so she never learned more than a few words of her ancestral language. (She did, however, "mis-learn" much more than she learned!)

I knew several couples in Sweden whose children were bilingual, the result of one parent speaking English with the kids and the other Swedish. Their kids spoke both languages without mixing them up, an ability apparently enhanced by *consistency*. (I also knew some native speakers of English living in Sweden who didn't bother to keep the languages separated. They threw in lots of Swedish words when speaking English, and vice-versa. As a result, some of them turned out not to be bilingual, but *semi*-lingual; they spoke both languages poorly.) Everything I read and everyone I talked to supported the idea that consistency was the way to go. I resolved to speak nothing but English to Junior, and Lena would speak nothing but Swedish.

During much of the autumn, Lena's aggression towards me seemed to have largely disappeared. While she never initiated any affection or displayed any passion, the mere absence of hostility was a welcome relief, like the game of "headache" (repeatedly hitting oneself on the head with a hammer because it feels so good when one stops). The *relative* harmony was wonderful. I didn't reflect on it much at the time, or perhaps I would have concluded that this was as good as it was going to get. But our lives were now totally focused on the pregnancy, the longed-for arrival of Junior and our rapidly approaching parenthood. In these matters we were fortunately in agreement on nearly everything, and pulled together (in the same direction) like never before.

On Monday, October 17th, we went to our first meeting with a midwife to set up a program of prenatal care. (All pre-natal, maternity and post-natal care was free in Sweden, including 12 months' maternity leave with pay, and the right to return to one's job. While American politicians love to *talk* about America's "family values", the Swedes strangely seemed to *do* something to establish them for everyone, regardless of income.) Now it was for real, and yet if felt more *sur*real than ever. Parenthood! Lena carrying *our* child!

There was so much stuff I didn't know. Worse, I now *realized* that I didn't know much about all that I realized I *had* to know. Vital questions jostled with curious ones: about fingerprint formation, whether feeding times should be regular or on demand, how the hell to identify the causes of crying, expectations of eye contact with a newborn, how the hell to change a diaper, names, registration, citizenship, rashes, keeping warm but not too warm, protection from infections, protection from the nastiness of the world, whether the infant should lie on its stomach or back, how to prepare a nursery, how to keep a level head, and how and when to say goodbye to the person I used to be and the routines I used to have (although I didn't realize that yet).

We were aware of the months of waiting and we weren't particularly patient. When we focused on the goal – Junior's arrival – time seemed lethargic, endless.

But as we gradually became aware of all the changes and adjustments that had to be made before that happened, time flew swiftly, like watching a slow-motion film of a cheetah sprinting.

The midwife used a Pinard horn to listen to Junior's heartbeat. (A Pinard horn is something like a small wooden trumpet that was used instead of a stethoscope – I had to look the word up too.) When she looked up from Lena's belly, smiling and nodding, our hearts beat a few extra times as well. How can such a simple experience – probably shared by billions worldwide for many centuries – feel so unique? Lena and I were at last *sharing* a period of joyful anticipation, a warm and gentle wave of hope. She wasn't yelling at me. She even stopped playing "the Birgitta card"; I hoped it would never return.

By late October, with two and a half months to go, Lena's discomfort was increasing, her legs were swelling, her back ached, and her sleep was disrupted. But she took it in stride, almost sailed through it, and her mood swings leveled out to a great extent. I, however, continued to cough.

Bob's Parkinson's was advancing at an alarming pace. His gait, never buoyant by any definition in all the years I'd known him, had slowed to a geriatric shuffle. [*Now, in 2021, I'm starting to learn how that feels!*] His manual dexterity was at once cramped, stiff and tremulous; he found it hard to grasp objects and to let them go once he'd clamped onto them (he would eventually have to use one hand to pry open the fingers of the other in order to release things). Strangely, while the loss of manual dexterity was painfully obvious in his manipulation of things like cutlery and buttons, he was still able to churn out multi-page, single-spaced typewritten letters to me as often as three times a week. His mental and intellectual dexterity remained intact.

Thus he had no difficulty in grasping new ideas or letting go of previously held beliefs once he found that evidence contradicted them or otherwise warranted modification. In his mind he was as agile as a mountain goat, and he flatly refused to feel sorry for himself, despite his many all-too-real infirmities. Instead of bemoaning the advances of his disease, he rejoiced that it had enabled his early retirement, and that he could still derive intense pleasure from books and music, as well as effervescent and vicarious joy regarding the pending arrival of Junior. (He was already hoping there'd be a Junior 2, 3, etc.) And he still hadn't begun taking "the hard stuff", the last line of medication, the strongest available.

Bob kept opening new doors for himself. He read incessantly about the latest developments in physics, medicine, biology, chemistry, religion, classical music, Elvis, Dylan, cosmology, global politics, opera, local politics (in as many localities as he could obtain information about), operetta and philosophy. To my considerable surprise, he even took a great interest in watching professional tennis. And he became an avid follower of the Formula One racing circuit! When he read a book that gave him particular pleasure, he often sent me a copy, both to share his pleasure and to enable us to discuss it. He was my true mentor. And he would have been highly critical of me if I failed to be critical of him.

My mom informed us that she was planning to come and see us in the spring, after we'd had a little time to get settled in with Junior. She also wrote that she wanted to visit Bob. When I told him, he was alarmed. Since his arrival in Europe back in the 1950s, he'd had no visits from family members, apart from the time my parents and I visited him for two days in May 1971. He preferred to keep it that way. (He didn't count me as family – we always considered our familial ties to be purely coincidental – that our close relationship was more in spite of than because of our being cousins.) He nearly panicked at the thought that having my mom there might open floodgates to waves of unwanted visits from his brother Charles, various nieces and nephews, cousins, and – most abhorrent of all – his father Harold.

Yet he was very curious about another meeting with my mom. So I proposed that he come to Sweden at the beginning or end of Mom's visit, in order to let him limit the number days with her, and be able to fall back on the constant availability of a new Chief Distractor: Junior. This arrangement thrilled him.

One of my most urgent prenatal projects was to convert the room at the top of the stairs in the big house into a nursery. Since Lena was currently using it as her study, it meant that I also had to set up a desk for her at the far end of my former studio, which still also contained the loom. We acquired a few big items (e.g. a crib and a baby buggy) from Eva and other friends whose kids had outgrown them. I also built in a worktop and some drawer cabinets to support it in the downstairs bathroom, to be used as a changing table for Junior.

Now that the piano was no longer in the downstairs room in the little house, I converted that room into my work-from-home office. I moved the old black leather sofa and armchair back into my old studio as well. My ouster from my studio was now complete.... For my office I acquired some additional old floorboards from a demolition company and turned them into bookshelves and a cabinet for the fax. Perstorp supplied an extra phone line and a proper office chair (they were only too happy not to have to provide me office space in Perstorp). I even got them to fund the installation of an intercom system so we could monitor the nursery from downstairs – or from my office in the little house.

As October was drawing to a close, I was feeling pretty run-down. My cough was getting worse. I finally decided to see a doctor about it, so I made an appointment for Friday morning, November 4th, at 9 o'clock. I had a full-day pupil the day before, a friendly young man (eight years younger than me) named Peter. When he arrived in the morning, we went straight to the library in the upstairs of the little house, and began speaking English – and smoking. We carried on with both all morning until we went to the kitchen (downstairs in the big house), where we continued speaking English while I made lunch, but took a break from the smoking for Lena's sake.

After lunch we returned to the smoke-filled library. Peter smoked around 30 cigarettes a day, and I just over 20. While filling the ashtray, we'd already covered a lot of different topics in our conversation, especially on matters related to his work. At about 3 PM, as we continued talking about work and English grammar, I reached for my almost empty pack of cigarettes. I took the last one and lit it, commenting that I was planning to quit smoking the day Junior arrived; it would be my new and long-awaited psychologically right moment to quit. Peter began to laugh. I didn't understand his mirth; I asked him why. He explained that he had a daughter, now 11 months old, and that he'd also vowed to quit smoking the day she was born, but that the days leading up to and following the delivery made him so nervous that he found himself smoking more than ever.

I was stunned. I knew there was a huge risk that my response would be similar. I thought of my doctor's appointment for the next morning – for a cough, no less. I would either have to quit *right now* or go out to buy a new pack. So I finished my last cigarette and *quit*. Just like that. [*I never smoked again, apart from a single puff on a Cuban cigar that a colleague of mine was smoking while we were attending a conference in Thailand in around 1997; I'd always been so curious about the taste of a Cuban cigar.*]

The next morning, the doctor listened to my lungs and calmly asked me if I smoked. I calmly replied *no*. He looked a bit surprised and asked me if I *used to* smoke. I said *yes*. Then he asked me when I quit, and I said *yesterday*. When he began laughing, I protested that I really, really *had* quit, for good. "*All right,*" he said, "*but you shouldn't have waited so long. You have a problem.*" He prescribed an antibiotic regime for 14 days and scheduled a chest x-ray for me on November 28th. He suspected some form of bronchitis.

The next evening, Lena and I went to Björn and Isobel's for dinner and a horrible evening. They traded insults with each other and put each other down the entire time. There was no British jocularity underlying their brutal, painful and crude war of words. It sounded more like a fight to the death, with no winners and three losers (the third being their son Patrick, now six).

On Monday, November 21st, we picked up our new 5-door Daihatsu Charade, a tiny white car with a surprisingly spacious interior. It was possible to fold down the seats in such a way as to have room for a buggy or a refrigerator or lots of lovely building materials. It offered good fuel economy, but its lack of power became evident on the way to and from Barkåkra. Climbing the uphill grade at Glumslöv felt like we were missing a pulley or a cogwheel or an engine or something that actually had some *power*; despite having my foot on the floor and downshifting, the car gradually slowed down, more and more, all the way to the peak of the modest hill.

With payment from Lars imminent (he'd promised – after several long delays – "the end of November"), we'd purchased the Daihatsu on a down payment of five thousand kronor, with the remaining 35,000 to be paid in full within three weeks, well after the Eket deal was to have gone through. At the end of November, however, Lars sent his siblings another letter, announcing that it would be beneficial – again *for himself only!!* – to wait until late January to complete the deal, and that was therefore what he would do. He didn't *ask* us, he *told* us. It was another unilateral, egocentric decision, with no consideration shown.

While the delay might have put a few extra kronor into his pocket, for us it meant a painfully large extra cost of taking a short-term bank loan to cover the outstanding balance on the Daihatsu. But I was confident that getting such a loan would be an easy matter. I'd used the same bank (originally Skandinaviska Banken, then Skandinaviska Enskilda Banken after a merger, now SE-Banken) since I came to Sweden and I'd never defaulted on any payment. The amount we needed to borrow was relatively modest, and I had only a small mortgage on a house that was now worth many times more than the value of the mortgage.

It turned out that credit was tight, they said, and my part-time income failed to impress the bank's assessors, or whatever titles of non-cooperation they had.

There would be no loan. My confidence was blown away. Jeanette and I originally chose that bank solely on the basis of the convenience of its location to where we lived. We kept it when we moved to Korngatan out of loyalty to a supplier of services who'd never failed us (not that we'd ever needed many services). Now my loyalty to them was every bit as blown away as my confidence in them. Instead, I turned to Sparbanken, the bank at our little square (Kirsebergstorget) where I sometimes went to cash checks, which they always did for me out of good neighborliness, despite my not having an account there. My request for the loan to pay for the car was granted instantly. We transferred our accounts to Sparbanken without hesitation.

At around this time, Lena had the third of her pregnancy's three ultrasound scans. Our excitement at the new glimpse of Junior was tempered only by our concerns for what pain Lena might have to endure at delivery; the scan also revealed that Junior was likely to weigh in at four kilos. Lena gulped. I gulped.

We attended a series of prenatal classes to practice breathing exercises and get information about what to expect. We could now almost grab Junior's foot through Lena's stomach wall when Junior kicked. I continued softly humming Mozart, Brahms and Taube to Junior while lying next to Lena. Bob was also becoming restlessly excited, as was Mom – and Bo, our neighbor.

Lena and I began playing around with possible names for Junior. Our first criterion was that the name had to work in both English and Swedish (there are a few that don't!). For a boy, we both liked "Carl" well enough, but since my mom's uncle Carl was still living, and since he murdered my ducks when I was young and more vulnerable, I didn't want to risk his finding out about it and drawing the greatly mistaken conclusion that I was honoring him by giving my son his name. I think we decided to wait and see. For a girl, it was easy: "Jenny" not only worked well in both languages, but was a silent way for me to honor Jeanette (whom I occasionally called "Jenny", as did her mother). Lena said that Jenny must have the same middle name – "Marie-Louise" – as all the females in Lena's clan: her mother (whose first name was Sigrid), Lena herself, Eva and Lina.

The day after we picked up the new car, I visited the doctor again. The two weeks of antibiotics hadn't worked, so I was prescribed a week's regime of a different antibiotic, as well as sulfa and terbutaline pills. There was still no improvement. My coughing was bad and my breathing was laborious. On Sunday, December 4th, we visited Marie-Louise in Barkåkra for a belated celebration of her 65th birthday (three days earlier). During the course of the afternoon my breathing became disturbingly difficult and remained so during our drive back to Malmö and throughout the night.

The next morning I phoned the doctor, who asked me to come to the clinic at once. After listening to my lungs, he sent me to the emergency clinic at the Malmö Hospital. I was admitted, put on an infusion of theophylline and cortisone and held for observation. The doctors were uncertain as to whether I had bronchitis or asthma and whether I would be released in one day or two. A spirometry test revealed that my lung function was *below 40%* of what a person of my age and height should have. I ended up spending a whole week in the hospital (December 6th-13th) and left with prescriptions for three different kinds of pills and two different inhalators. And I still found breathing difficult. I was advised to engage in strenuous exercise to try to push the limits of my reduced lung capacity.

Bob arrived for a 12-day Christmas visit on December 22nd. This time, Lena was also happy to have a doctor in the house for a couple of weeks. I had long since stopped being astonished by the vastness of Bob's knowledge, so his grasp of obstetrics merely gave me a mild surprise and gave Lena a lot of reassurance.

Bob asked me a lot of probing questions about my health, and was alarmed to find that the doctors who'd been treating me and prescribing antibiotics apparently hadn't run any cultivations to determine precisely what kind of bacteria lay behind my pulmonary infection. Bob urged me to make demands on them to find out. As he explained it, although ordinary infections can often be treated with a broad-spectrum antibiotic, unusual infections may not respond, making it necessary to pair the type of antibiotic with the specific bacterium. I promised to make myself a nuisance if I didn't get answers.

When Bob got to feel Junior's kick, tears came to his eyes, his big brow wrinkled, he forced his lips into a tight smile to keep from dissolving into a sob. Having children had been his greatest wish; now, vicariously, it was about to come true.

CHAPTER 4

A new world

Lena's contractions began late in the evening on Sunday, January 8th. We phoned the hospital, described her status, and were told to wait at home. Just after midnight, the contractions were coming a bit more frequently and she began bleeding a little, so we did as instructed and went in right away. Bo rushed out to see us off. He appeared more flustered than me. I was surprised by my composure, but I had to be a rock for Lena. Our Daihatsu got us to the hospital without a hitch. I remember thinking that this was no charade, no dress rehearsal – this was *it*.

Lena was admitted, and quickly changed into hospital clothing. She was then examined for cervical dilation. They found that dilation was still too minor to warrant calling in "the team", but they said they'd keep her there for the night. I kept asking her if I could do anything for her or get anything for her or read to her or adjust for her – until I saw her rising exasperation with my fussing, so I tried to shut up.

At around 2 AM, a nurse told me that Lena would most likely have a long way to go before delivery, that she'd need to get a few hours (at least) of sleep in order to have as much strength as possible to be able to face what was to come. They suggested (their way of giving orders) that if I wanted to be helpful during the delivery, I should go home and get some hours of sleep myself, and not return before 8 AM. That advice made good sense to me so I took it. I parked on Källargatan in the middle of the night. Bo spotted the car in the morning and hurried over to see if the baby had arrived. His empathy clearly came from the genuine kindness of his heart. I explained the current (as of last night) status to him and said I'd be returning to the hospital as soon as I'd had a quick breakfast.

It turned out that we still had many long hours of waiting ahead of us. Sometimes a nurse would enter the room to listen to Lena's abdomen or take her blood pressure or pulse. Sometimes a team of nurses and doctors scurried into the room and fussed about before scurrying out again. Sometimes we were alone facing this momentous event. Lena's acceptance of my support moved me. If I'd known how, I'd have lifted her into my arms and carried her safely to the other side of the pain she had before her. Instead, I brought her some tea and held her hand and chattered away.

At around 4 PM, the obstetrician decided it was time for Lena to have epidural anesthesia. Her pain vanished almost instantly – a respite that lasted for about four hours, after which its pain-relieving powers started to dwindle. After a further hour or two the pain began returning with a vengeance. At half past 10 PM, the obstetrician removed the epidural and transferred Lena to a delivery bed, even though dilation was not yet complete. I squeezed her hand and she squeezed back. She was in great pain. I was trying to remember what type of breathing pattern we'd been instructed to use at what stage, but the nurses knew better and kept us informed. We breathed together. I wiped her forehead. The doc kept popping in and out of the room for a look and a quick word, his brow increasingly furrowed (he was handling other births that evening as well). He was a big, muscular man with a kind face. When he thought that the hour was at hand, he sat down on a small stool, strategically placed, and watched for Jenny's head to appear. Between contractions, I tried to see for myself, but found that Lena's need to grab onto me for support was considerably greater than my need to satisfy my curiosity.

It was slow going. At this point, the only pain relief they could offer Lena was puffs of nitrous oxide gas, also known as laughing gas. But she wasn't laughing. She was suffering horribly and soaking wet with sweat. My pain of being unable to do anything but stand by and watch was nothing by comparison. I caught enough fragments of the conversations among the staff to understand that the doctor felt that the birth had already passed the point of no return for an emergency cesarean.

After some unknowable and almost unbearable lapse of time, the doctor was softly issuing firm commands to the closest members of the team, while the rest of the team were scurrying. Lena was agonizing and I was being pulled apart by confusion. I heard the curtly spoken words "baby in distress" and felt panic rising through me, lifting me off the floor. But I couldn't let Lena see how I felt, I had to be calm for her. Just after midnight, the doctor sat down on his stool once again. This time he was holding what I correctly guessed to be a suction cup, mounted on one end of a stick, with some kind of lever-type handle on the other end. I craned around to see what he was going to do with it. I couldn't see exactly how he went about it, but deduced that he'd placed the cup on the baby's head, which was still only partially out. Then he grabbed the other end of the device firmly and started pulling, gently at first, then gradually increasing his force until he was pulling with all his might. His mounting urgency was echoed by the staff. Lena was writhing in agony. She was terrified. I was hugging her and caressing her and trying to say soothing things, while casting an eye down to the foot of the bed.

The doctor was also sweating now, flexing his muscles, clenching his jaw. He placed one foot on the frame of the bed for leverage and seemed to be pulling on that suction device so hard that that he would literally pull the baby's head right off before falling backwards off his stool, holding the head at the end of his stick.

Instead, Jenny was born, half an hour into January 10th, 1984.

I'd never before experienced such intense, soaring, overwhelming, debilitating, exhilarating, heartbreaking joy. I also felt new levels of gratitude (to Lena for her valiant and victorious struggle), relief (that Jenny was healthy and hearty despite the terrifying finale), confusion (about what to do next and where to go from here), exhaustion (due to more than 24 hours of tension, anxiety, empathy and awe) and hope (against all reasonable grounds for optimism) that a certain someone would, at long last, love incorrigible me.

I began to weep. Lena lay collapsed in total exhaustion, but with a wan, almost beatific smile on her weary face. While the nurses were sponging her off, I watched as the staff wrapped beautiful little Jenny up in some soft cloth, stuck a tiny knit cap on her head to hide the alarming bump from the suction cup, and brought her over to Lena. We both looked back and forth from Jenny to each other. We laughed and cried without inhibition as waves of emotion cascaded off us. Jenny was so sweet, so adorable, so precious, so fragile and so tiny. Yet so tough.

She was about the size of a somewhat deflated American football; I could have balanced her in one cupped hand. Her foot was shorter than the length of my little finger. The distance from her hip to her heel was equal to the span of my hand. She'd instantly created an entirely new chamber in my heart, one with an endless capacity for loving her, yet without diminishing one iota my capacity for loving Lena. I never saw it coming. The bump on her head looked like she had half a tennis ball under her little cap. Seeing the alarmed expression on my face, the staff hastened to explain that the bump would soon recede, in a day or two, and that Jenny was healthy in every way. (Apart from the temporary bump, she certainly was *beautiful* in every way!!)

Everyone else seemed to know exactly what they were doing, which was fortunate, because Lena and I were totally dazed and worn out. They also seemed to know what we were thinking and anxious about, which was also fortunate, because we didn't. Lena had lost blood, required stitching, and definitely needed rest. *She seemed to need me too!*

I got to hold Jenny for a few minutes. An hour or so earlier, I might have been afraid of crushing her, thinking she might be as fragile as a soap bubble. But after I'd seen the muscular doctor pulling so hard on that suction cup for so long, all such fears were gone. A senior nurse approached me and said she had to take Jenny. She told me that it was high time for me to go home and get some sleep so I could make myself useful in the morning. After hugging Lena and bidding my family – *my family!* – good night, I drove off into the darkness to Korngatan.

I don't remember the drive, only that my body arrived at my destination intact. My head and heart were still back at the hospital. Despite the late hour, Bo came rushing out of the house next door to hear the news. He was incredibly excited, even though his excitement was no match for mine this time. He had loads of questions, of course, but our conversation had to be cut short. In spite of my euphoria, Bo could see how exhausted I was – I was hardly able to stand up – so he kindly advised me to go get some sleep.

Before sleep, and to give myself a chance to calm down, I phoned my mom (the nine-hour time difference made it early evening at her place) and told her the good news. Her gut reaction was one of joy, incongruously adulterated by Biblical references and aphorisms about Jenny being in peril of eternal damnation if she failed to choose the "right" path. (*Jesus Christ, Mom, get real!!*) Sensing that she had derailed my attention, Mom quickly got back on track by backtracking, and ceased preaching. Poor Mom, I thought, she just couldn't help herself. Her perverted sense of obligation to "witness" arose from a lifetime of indoctrination. But even though the brainwashing seemed to have blocked her faculties of critical thinking, it failed to extinguish her humanity.

Still filled with euphoria and with thousands of thoughts and a great sense of the monumental change that was already happening in my life, the sleep of exhaustion came easily to me that night. I was in a state of pure bliss. Wonder and awe had me by the throat. (Yes, yes, I know. It's not unique. Practically every parent feels that way. By the way, I pity the child whose parents don't feel that their very own particular children are the most special ever. Because they are – or should be – to those particular parents!) And after that internal morality lecture, I slept.

Humanely early the next the morning I phoned Marie-Louise and Eva. They were both thrilled, as expected. I sensed that they shared my hopes that having a baby would bring forth Lena's love for me as well. I saved Bob for last because I was uncertain about how well he would be able to manage his own emotional reaction. When I phoned him before leaving for the hospital in the morning, he was overjoyed. Then he went silent. I knew he was crying because he was overwhelmed. He told me a year or so before that one of the side-effects of his Parkinson's medication was to make him weepy. I'm sure he didn't need that excuse this time. After briefing Eva, Marie-Louise and Bob, I went next door to give a fuller briefing to Bo and Peter, who seemed to feel nearly as involved as anyone else.

I was hyperactive that morning, but after my three phone calls and a lot of rushing about the house tidying up (we'd left in a hurry, and I was feeling tons of self-inflicted pressure to see that everything was up to the highest standards), I'd half worn myself out again. In other words, I'd worn off most of my hyperactivity and could behave more or less normally. Lena was actually happy to see me when I arrived. I paused in the doorway to catch my breath at the sight my wife and my daughter. She was feeding Jenny. She was looking at me lovingly. I was overwhelmed. [*What?! Were you, dear reader, expecting me to growl and flex my muscles like some mucho macho type on steroids? You haven't been paying much attention, have you?!*]

Little Jenny, with cap on, eyes closed, and suckling vigorously, was the picture of exquisite delight. The feeling of seeing her, seeing *them* like that, was far, far beyond what I'd imagined it could be like. This was my first day of class in a course called Advanced Happiness. Dreamer optimist that I am, I thought this was *it*, this was my future.

I got to hold Jenny a lot during those first days at the hospital. Lena was still exhausted and in quite a lot of pain after her valiant ordeal. And who was this new little person who captivated my attention, exploded my curiosity, fired my imagination, created a whole new part of my brain and my heart, motivated me to learn to change diapers, support her head when I lifted her, rock her gently when she whimpered, watch her every movement for hours? Could anything *be* this wonderful?!

I had no intention of being a passive parent, lurking like a silent presence in the background. The nearness I felt to Jenny, our child, my child, was intoxicating. I just wanted to care for her and for Lena and be part of everything they did or needed or wanted.

When Lena and I got married three and a half years earlier, Bo and Peter presented us with a magnificent wedding present: a textile patchwork portrait of our home. A couple of weeks after Jenny arrived, they came over to give us an equally exquisite little quilt, of a size suitable for Jenny's crib, every stitch done meticulously by hand by Bo and Peter, their original design. They'd been working on it for months. The quilt only needed a few finishing touches to be complete with Jenny's name and date of birth beautifully stitched in. That's how involved they felt.

Bob's prenatal excitement had apparently rubbed off on Carmen as well. Bob told me that every time they talked (which was several times a week), her first questions were about the status of Lena's pregnancy. Carmen told Bob that her travel agent offered her an excellent deal on some trips. When Bob asked her where she might go, she replied, *"Why, to Sweden, of course, to see Stanley and Lena and the baby! Where else?"*

Bob was pleased that their conversations had begun moving beyond talk of Roche and her late husband, and in the direction of greater substance, such as what they did or didn't believe, and why or why not; in other words, what they perceived to be true, and why. He wrote me, in his elegant manner, that Carmen *"seemed genuinely surprised to discover that unbelief as I represent it is not a denial of all that is positive, merely of all that is inauthentic."* Is there a better way of putting it?!

The staff at the hospital were magnificent. They were reassuringly attentive to both Lena and Jenny, giving them all the care and comfort they needed. Jenny lay in a small, transparent Plexiglas bassinet beside Lena's bed, at a height where Lena could lie down to rest while looking at Jenny. Lena looked joyful, yet still rather exhausted. I gave her a huge but cautious hug, asked how she was doing, then picked Jenny up and held her while sitting on the edge of Lena's bed. This was a new world – for all three of us.

Due to the difficult delivery and the extensive healing Lena required, they were allowed to stay a full week at the hospital so Lena could regain her strength (two or three days was normal hospital procedure at that time). Breast-feeding came naturally to both of them. The bump on Jenny's head was receding rapidly. The fantastic staff at the hospital made everything super-convenient. We were even shown how to change diapers – and free disposable diapers were provided.

Between trips to the hospital that week, I put the finishing touches on the nursery, prepared a bassinet to have next to our bed for the initial months, made sure we were all caught up on the laundry, bought the groceries and our first bale of diapers, vacuumed and tidied the whole house until not a carpet fringe was out of place.

Carmen visited Bob for the evening on the 13th, bringing with her a bottle of pink Champagne to celebrate Jenny's birth. The next day, Bob wrote:

> *I got to thinking the other day of ages and dates and realized to my shock that only 16 years are left to the change of millennia, a circumstance which, although not of primary relevancy, reminds me that my chances of seeing [Jenny] grow to adulthood are not such as to make plans about, so I'll follow her progress all the more intently while she is growing up.*

> [Full disclosure: I wept when I re-read Bob's letter some 30 years later when writing *Hindsights* – at a place in my life where I now find myself in a position a bit similar to Bob's where my own grandchildren are concerned.]

Lena and Jenny came home on January 17th. It was difficult for both of us to grasp. Jenny didn't yet need to grasp much, even though she seemed to try. This little piece of humanity that could hardly open her eyes had already begun to change our routines, our priorities, our lives, our anxieties, hopes, wishes, dreams (and some of our sleeping patterns) *forever*. We still got a decent total number of hours of sleep, although it was broken into some unaccustomed segments. It didn't take more than a day to realize that caring for our precious little girl was going to be a full-time job, but one filled with unprecedented fascination and stimulation.

There was nothing more delightful to me than just sitting there watching her sleep, thinking of what awaited her in the first few years of life, when consciousness and intellect are at their lowest and a child's personality and psychology begin to form. And then all the years it can take to understand this formation and sometimes try to guide it, channel it, correct it, repair it and build on it without ever stopping. There was a great deal going on (or what I imagined might be going on) inside that tiny girl, some of which I convinced myself I could perceive through careful observation, but admittedly in a most enigmatic form.

I didn't make wild promises to the walls or the sky about how her future would be, since I couldn't possibly know. But I did pledge one thing to myself: *I will never lie to this little girl.*

I relished the thought of relieving Lena from as many household duties as she would allow me to. My love for her knew no bounds, and her pain was mine vicariously. Cooking, dishwashing, laundry, doing the shopping, paying the bills, vacuuming: these were all things I gladly undertook. (I was admittedly worthless at ironing, but I started learning.) Lena took my help in stride and didn't complain. [*Nor did she praise.*]

I'd never before reflected on what a tidal wave of stereotypes the birth of a child could elicit. Pink soon inundated our house – as powder blue would certainly have done if Jenny had been a boy – most of which was given to us by well-meaning, but tradition-bound family and friends. "Even in *Sweden*," I thought to myself. It wasn't that I found anything *wrong* with pink (or blue) *per se*; but after all, I was still an artist at heart, and wasn't about to let any stereotypes, political movements, social orders, favorite sports teams, fads or fashions seize exclusive rights to *any* parts of the spectrum or the color charts. The worst aspect to me was the haughtiness that a few people displayed: *of course* she has to have pink, she's a *girl!* I vowed to do my utmost to prevent Jenny's choices in life from being limited in such foolish biases.

[*When Jenny was around five years old, I asked her what she thought she'd like to do when she was grown up. She said, without hesitation, that she wanted to be a nurse. I said that sounded fine, helping others and all, but had she considered being a doctor? She looked at me incredulously and said, "But Daddy, I'm a girl!" I was gobsmacked. "Who on earth told you that you couldn't be a doctor if you're a girl?!" She grinned sheepishly and said she didn't know. "Of course you can!" I told her. "I can?!* she answered, grinning. *A week or two later, I had to visit my doctor for an asthma check-up. I made certain to bring Jenny along (my doctor was a woman).*]

Lena, for two wonderfully obvious reasons, was totally in charge of feeding Jenny, and did a terrific job of it. I tried to make myself useful in caring for Jenny in every other way: changing her diapers whenever Lena allowed me to, burping her (Jenny) after feeding, and rocking her to sleep in my arms while singing or humming softly to her.

Although Lena seemed pleased to have my help, for some possibly subconscious reason she began treating me as though I were one of her youngest pupils, strangely tacking on phrases like "don't you see?" or "you understand" in unmistakably patronizing tones when telling me how to do things I'd already been doing repeatedly and well. I noticed it, but I refused to let it bother me, at least when she was stating the obvious. But when she stated what to me was *not* obvious, or obviously *not* the case, I *had* to comment (I'm like that), momentarily forgetting that any such comments could and therefore would be taken as criticism. And *postpartum* Lena didn't take criticism lightly either; that would probably never change. So I tried to bite my tongue.

Perhaps I saw (and perhaps I was mistaken) a correlation between my mom's aggressive assertions and insertions of her religious nonsense into every aspect of life – as long as I let her get away with it – and my own failure to push back when unfounded opinions were presented as Truths. This failure only seemed to fuel my mom's zeal to up the ante, to raise the bar. But I was accustomed to pushing back when my brothers' claims of truth failed to convince me or stand up to scrutiny.

Congratulations began trickling in during the week or two after Jenny was born. Carmen sent a teddy bear and a handcrafted jigsaw puzzle, to our surprise (especially Lena's, who'd never met her). Just about all our friends and immediate families got in touch, with the exception of Lena's brother Lars. Instead, after about 10 days of silence following his kid sister's very difficult delivery, Lars sent his siblings yet another "white paper" (mercifully his last), announcing that payment was being effected forthwith. But he also announced that he was deducting a substantial chunk for "various costs", carefully itemized, all of which were incurred during the period *after* his siblings had already agreed to the sale and the amount, and after which he alone visited the property, and he alone benefitted from the improvements made! There were deductions for the paint he bought during the summer to repaint *his* house – *and* even for the wages he paid to his kids to do the job! Unbelievable! (Obviously, there was no reimbursement to *us* for the extra costs for the loan *we* had to take due to his many unilateral postponements of the agreed date.)

I asked Lena what she thought of it. She was outraged. I asked if she wanted me to phone Lars and ask him *What the hell?!* She said I should perhaps phone the other siblings first, to see whether they had another interpretation, so I did. Eva was also flabbergasted and irritated by Lars' brazenness, but was afraid of incurring Lars' wrath by questioning him. Lars' brother Jan was so pissed off with Lars' shameful behavior that he couldn't be bothered to speak to him, but welcomed my offer to phone on everyone else's behalf.

It was the first, last and only time I would *ever* phone Lars. I was expecting him to begin with some belated words of congratulation to us on the birth of Jenny, and some concerned questions about how his kid sister was doing. Instead, the *instant* he recognized my voice, after I'd only had time to say, "*Hi Lars, this is Stan*" (not a word more!), he began screaming furiously: "*You bastard, you goddamn bastard, you're always making trouble!*" I was totally ambushed and puzzled about what kind of trouble I'd ever conceivably caused him in the past. I asked him what he was talking about. "*You always want to question things, you have to question my figures, I wrote everything down and that's the way it is, and I'm not going to listen to any shit from you!!*" Then he hung up on me – slammed down the phone. I never even had time to *mention* the house, the payment, or anything else. He never congratulated us on Jenny nor did he show any interest in Lena's welfare. I was hurt and outraged, but Lena told me not to bother about him: "*That's just the way he is sometimes, so just ignore him.*" [*Which is exactly what I did. The few times we or I ever encountered Lars in the years that followed, I ignored him. I figured that any future conversation between us needed to begin with him saying the words "I'm sorry." But that was never going to happen. It wasn't until Marie-Louise's funeral in December 2006 that I had a precious few formally polite words with him. And he has, as of 2021, never seen fit to apologize for behaving like a rectal orifice.*] A few days later, the money (less deductions!) arrived in Lena's bank account and she had to use nearly all of it to pay off the short-term loan for the car, plus the interest.

On January 25th, I went to the hospital for my second spirometry. I was told that the result was inconclusive, but was reminded that I ought to undertake vigorous physical activity to expand my lung capacity, which was still hovering just below 40% of what was considered normal for a person of my height and age. I found jogging and gyms so *utterly* boring, but I'd always loved ball sports. My favorite ball sports – American football, basketball and baseball – were in those days about as rare in Sweden as curling was in 18th century Uganda. But I still played a little tennis, and I knew a few guys whom I could ask.

The problem was that I only felt free to play at a time when my help was least needed at home, which ruled out everything except early Saturday or Sunday mornings. That, in turn, ruled out most of my potential tennis partners. Then I asked Ole, even though I had no reason to think he played tennis. He didn't. But he said he'd be happy to play *badminton* with me at seven o'clock on Saturday mornings, at Aura, a dedicated badminton hall comprising 14 courts with proper lines, regulation nets and everything. I was hesitant. *Badminton*?! Was that really a sport? Wasn't it just a *game* people played while relaxing in backyards and on beaches (like horseshoes), not a sport that would require any real exertion to help my lungs? He grinned, shaking his head. I said we could try.

Within five minutes of stepping onto the court, Ole had me springing, twirling, lunging, backpedaling, diving and swinging my racket all over the place, while he seemed to be standing almost still, either hitting the shuttle hopelessly beyond my reach or smashing it back at me so fast that I felt it hitting my chest before I saw it. I was wheezing like a broken steam engine, gasping for breath, red in my face, unable to speak, and had to sit down (collapse) on the floor while fumbling frantically for my inhalators. But after a few minutes, we were at it again. For most of the rest of our hour, Ole kept me running and wheezing, with frequent breaks for spraying. I loved it.

At first, I was trying to hit the goddamn shuttle like a tennis ball, which made my shots ill-timed and ineffective. It also threw me off balance for the return, which seemed to come as fast as if two tennis players were smashing at each other while both were standing one meter from the net. My backhand was non-existent, so I found myself looping around to be able to hit obvious backhand shots with my forehand, thus exposing most of the court to a return that was far out of reach. A shuttle has roughly the same trajectory as a ball – for the first half of its arc – but then the arc suddenly tapers off. My ball-tuned eye kept telling my brain that Ole's long shots would be way too long; I was chagrined time after time when the shuttle dropped well within the baseline. I was never in position, but went racing and sprawling for shots, only to watch the returns sail over my head (and land inbounds as I lay gasping on the floor. But I wouldn't give up. Whether I'd ever learn this _sport_ well was of secondary importance to me. It was extremely fun, fast and challenging. And since I was determined to boost my lung capacity, this seemed to be a great path forward.

Ole and I agreed to play badminton for an hour every Saturday morning we could. Unless tennis players are reasonably well matched, neither will have fun. Fortunately this doesn't apply to badminton. Within a few weeks, I was beginning to pick up enough of the technique and strategy to be able to give Ole a *bit* of a workout and some fun too, even though he still beat me easily every time, and I required frequent short breaks with my inhalator.

My spirometry having been inconclusive, I was sent to an ear-nose-throat specialist on February 3rd, for an x-ray and ultrasonic scans of my sinuses. In addition to my two inhalators, I was taking three kinds of airway-dilating medications, and seemingly endless rounds of antibiotics.

I was at that time still one of the many people who felt that modern medical science could do anything, that all one should need to do is stand before a doctor and demand "*Cure me!*", and if he or she doesn't, it might well be a question of malpractice. Only later in life would I grasp the amount of guesswork involved in making a correct diagnosis. [*The excellent TV series* House, *with the outstanding Hugh Laurie in the title role, gave a lot of insight into this.*] One major reason for diagnostic difficulty is that widely differing diseases can present nearly identical symptoms that require entirely different treatments. (Fortunately, a high percentage of those guesses are intelligent ones. That's what medical school is for.) And then there's the little fact that a correct diagnosis doesn't necessarily mean that there is a cure, or that there ever will be a cure, or that a cure that will be anywhere close to 100% effective. But I've observed that patients aren't the only ones who sometimes lack humility. I've met doctors who don't see their patients as human beings, but merely as a sore shoulder or an aching ear. Some of those doctors are unable or unwilling to offer a consoling word or even make eye contact. Perhaps those few should be working in labs and keep patient contact to a minimum?

As I write this, over three and a half decades later, I sometimes need to remind myself of certain aspects of life that have vastly changed the way we do things. I'd been taking photos of Jenny, Jenny and Lena, Lena and Jenny, on a 36-shot roll of film. It required (with our kind of budget) some care and discretion in the selection of motifs so as not to waste film. I had to take all 36 shots before mailing the roll to a budget-rate processor to be developed and returned to me as prints about a week later – the first time I could see the outcome of any picture. As a result, it took some time before I could send the first photos of Jenny to Bob and my mom. When I finally did, Bob wrote, "The pictures of Jenny so overwhelmed me I almost forgot there was a letter in the envelope too."

During a visit to Garmisch at around this time, Tante Lore was determined to introduce Bob to her 30-year-old *Naturheilpraktikerin* (homeopath) to cure an ailing shoulder Bob had been suffering from for some time. He wrote:

I was easily charmed by her without feeling attracted to her medical notions. I let her massage my shoulder and then inject the area with various "natural" assortments of molecules according to the homeopathic principle (you put a tiny amount of the stuff in an injectable fluid, then dilute it; the most effective dilutions are those which have none of the substance left, the injected solution carrying with it the "spirit" of the original molecule). Whether due to my unbelief or to excessive dilution, my shoulder got worse and worse, and that promptly after each treatment. She said we must remain steadfast and I did, but after the fourth treatment with the same result she said the treatment was evidently unsuitable and should be broken off, to which I agreed eagerly.

Jenny was changing every day – numerous, tiny, incremental changes that added up to a not-so-tiny total. She would look straight into my eyes for a few seconds and then, as the memory of something familiar appeared to register, she would get all excited and start waving her arms about, kicking as though she were trying to start an invisible motorcycle, before finally breaking into a full-face grin accompanied by a squeal of delight. Lena's and my division of labor meant that Lena fed her (always, due to anatomical constraints) and I put her to bed (usually). As an apparent result, when Jenny looked at Lena she'd start smacking her lips, and when she looked at me she'd start yawning.

And I thought: *this is all the immortality I'll ever want – or need, or get.*

On Sunday, February 12th, Eva invited us to Lund to celebrate Jan's 42nd birthday. His sister Ninni and his mother Gun (two examples of Swedish names that don't work so well in English) were also there. Jan's parents divorced under conditions of considerable animosity many years earlier. His father met another woman and left his wife, which was why Jan's father was never allowed to join any family gathering when Gun was present. Those sores never healed, and Jan became extremely allergic to divorce, so much so that he avoided it for himself by flatly refusing to marry Eva, even though she clearly wished for them to be married, and occasionally said so out loud.

This was something I found impossible to understand. What the hell was the matter with him? Eva was lovely! She was like the sister I'd never had (forget the *-in-law* bit!). I'd been told that she and Jan had some real screaming sessions, which sounded to me like a fabrication. But I realized there was something called "personal chemistry" and something else called "what goes on behind closed doors...."

Gun was either a posh elderly lady or was merely eager to be perceived as such, or both. She allowed herself a couple of obligatory and restrained *oohs* and *aahs* upon seeing Jenny, then looked at me and asked, "*What will her name be?*" I was puzzled by her choice of verb tense and answered, "*Her name is Jenny.*" Gun raised her eyebrows and asked with some astonishment, "*Has she already been christened?!*" I replied that she wasn't going to be. Gun flinched, then scowled, then demanded to know why not. I replied that we saw no reason to start Jenny's life with a lie, a promise to raise her to believe something we didn't believe ourselves. Gun acted as though I'd insulted her. Then her scowl turned into a sneer as she turned away, shaking her white coiffed head.

On Saturday afternoon, February 25th, my boss Stig Troell stopped by with his wife to see Jenny and her proud parents. Thanks to the many hours in my "pot" of extra working time, I'd been able to devote myself full-time to caring for Jenny and Lena. When they were both asleep, I could easily deal with the translation and editing jobs that came my way. Although I hadn't set foot in Perstorp for ages at this point, and didn't even have a pupil at home until March 7th, Stig had no complaints. As far as he was concerned, I'd been a cash cow for his Education Department (which consisted of him and me) for more than five years, and would be again, all in due course.

By March 8th I was on my fifth round of antibiotic regimes, with no end (or relief) in sight. Actually, I'd had a stretch of 16 days without antibiotics in there somewhere, but with no apparent effect one way or the other. Starting with my initial contact with the doctor at the local clinic on November 4th, 1983, I'd now had two chest x-rays, a sinus x-ray (due to swelling), a sinus ultrasound, a hearing test, an ear pressure test, about 30 stethoscopic examinations (asthma- or bronchitis-like sounds), about 30 ESR (sedimentation rate) tests, two blood tests for allergies, three ear-nose-throat examinations, an invasive flushing of my sinuses, a tooth-root x-ray, two cultures taken from my nose, a culture taken from my throat, at least two spirometries, a test of arterial blood for oxygen content, about a dozen urinalyses, countless blood pressure tests, countless temperature readings, four days of infusion of theophylline and cortisone (as well as three injections of same), and my home medications (two inhalators four times a day, one three times a day, as well as theophylline pills twice a day. And I'd never been one to take any medication at all!

With Jenny at home, new routines began developing quickly and naturally. Jenny slept rather well, with only a few short feeding breaks during the night.

What required some adjustment was that, by her definition, night was *over* at about 4.30 AM. I'd always been an evening person: whenever possible, I'd stay up till 2 AM, then sleep till 10 AM. Since that didn't change much on the *evening* end of things, I simply got fewer hours of sleep. And that became my new normal. (I theorized that I'd learned to sleep more efficiently, by entering and leaving deep sleep more rapidly, thus retaining the number of hours of deep sleep I needed.) [*My theory might be bullshit, but it seemed to work for me a few years later when I was revving up my career while being a single parent at the same time, all the way into my 60s. But at one point, after three straight months of 70-hour working weeks, I felt a need to slow down, and did.*]

The realization that my mom was already targeting Jenny for indoctrination gave me one more urgent reason to resume my struggle against religion and other superstitions. I should mention that I get rather sick of people telling me something along the lines of "*You're probably anti-religion only because your religious upbringing was so extreme.*" True, I was raised on a force-fed diet of it for the first 18 years of my life and my family continued to shove it under my nose against my will until I was well past 60. Yes, it is conceivable that if my upbringing had been "mainstream Christian" (whatever that means at any point in history), I might never have found sufficient cause to rebel. But I did. Until I left home, I read – *had* to read – the *whole* Bible, from cover to cover, several times over (and selected parts countless times); I had to go to church ("Meeting") an average of five times a week; I had to participate in family Bible readings, hymns and prayers on a daily basis. So that once I began to question certain teachings, I took a hard look at the Bible itself in terms of its role as the "Christian Constitution". My anti-religion views are based on knowing what religion is actually about, what the Bible actually says, not merely casual church attendance and a cherry-picked verse now and then. What did I find there? A god who is the all-time champion of genocide: the entire population of the earth except for Noah and his immediate family, for starters, in the Old Testament; nearly everybody still standing at the end of the world, in the New Testament. And tons of mayhem and murder in between, all ordered by the same "good, righteous," first-order psychopathic god.

How, then, can anyone seriously consider that the 10 Commandments can be the foundation of human morality?! Apart from the likelihood that very many people preach adherence don't even know what they are! So here's a little review: The first is only about having no other god than Jehovah. But since the Abrahamic religions claim to be monotheistic – there *is* just one god – thus there can't be any others anyway, so what's the problem, apart from the description in the biblical god being one of a psycho?

The second says "no graven images" or any likenesses of *anything* on earth, in the sky or under the sea. Goodbye to most non-abstract art! And Jehovah admits he's so jealous that he'll be punishing your *progeny* for up to four generations for what *you* do! Do you find that fair or humane or moral? I certainly don't!

The third commandment is kind of interesting: "Thou shalt not take the name of the LORD thy God in vain." In that case, OMG would not be OK, but WTF would be just fine (and "May the devil take you!" wouldn't break that commandment). I can live with that. The question is, can all those who believe in this stuff live with it?

The fourth says to keep the Sabbath day holy. The three Abrahamic religions can't even agree what day of the week that is. Muslims, Friday; Jews, Saturday; Christians; Sunday. But not even allowing the cattle to do any work?! And "the stranger that is within thy gates"? Does that really have to do with morality?

The fifth is the only one based on a promise, not an order: "Honour thy father and thy mother: that thy days may be long upon the land which the LORD thy God giveth thee." What if you have abusive parents? What about parents honoring their children? (By the way, my dad, who lived to be only 61, apparently didn't do too well here…. I'm sure glad I didn't have to honor *his* father!)

Number six ("Thou shalt not kill") and number eight ("Thou shalt not steal") are pretty straightforward requirements for any society to function at all. The interesting thing about these commandments, however, is that *in the biblical context* they were clearly meant only to tell one Jew how to behave towards other Jews – not other peoples. On the contrary, God *commanded* them to kill the Midianites and all the other –ites he could find. Kill them, rape their women and plunder their villages – that was god's message to His people! Great pillars of morality!

As for the seventh, "Thou shalt not commit adultery", what about David and Bathsheba? Solomon's 300 wives and 700 concubines?! How is adultery even possible?

Number nine, "Thou shalt not bear false witness…" is basically "Don't lie!" except for the tag, "…against thy neighbor"! Again, lies to Hebrews are not OK. Everyone else? Sure, why not?

Finally, number 10: "Thou shalt not covet thy neighbour's house, thou shalt not covet thy neighbour's wife, nor his manservant, nor his maidservant, nor his ox, nor his ass, nor anything that is thy neighbour's." This one isn't about anything you *do*, it's about what you *think*! Suddenly George Orwell's Thought Police are the basis of morality?!

The progress of civilization seems to correspond roughly to the rate at which religious beliefs are discredited and made irrelevant. Scientific discovery has been continually closing the gaps in our knowledge, leaving fewer and fewer superstitions to refute. And yet: the *emotional* chokehold religion has on billions of people *prevents them from questioning and understanding* the origins of their beliefs and what they entail.

It is undeniable that the history of Western culture, including American culture – the culture of my roots – is closely linked to, intertwined with Christianity. Religion has inspired (or at least financed!) centuries of artists, writers and composers. But that doesn't make religious beliefs *true*! *People do actually choose to believe just about anything, whether it's true or not!* The Church, with its vast power and wealth over many centuries was often the only source of livelihood for great artists. But it was also a principal source of coercion and forced allegiance.

I've never knocked on people's doors to tell them what to believe or not to believe, like the Jehovah's Witnesses and Mormons have done at my door. I've never accosted people at airports or on street corners like Catholics and Evangelicals have done to me. That doesn't mean that I'm going to roll over, cede the floor to them, or give them the first, last and only say on what life is or isn't about. If they want to believe nonsense, so be it. But if they shove their nonsense in my face, or claim that their nonsense is *true*, I feel entitled (and sometimes compelled) to respond, to defend my non-belief – even though my defense often leads to an accusation that I'm the one doing the attacking, that I'm a "militant atheist". I've never bought that. I still don't buy that.

Throughout my life, I've been fortunate never to have had too little money to eat and have shelter, and equally fortunate never to have felt compelled to amass money, nor to let my life be driven by an unquenchable desire for more.

A lot of people talk about the need for taking personal responsibility. I agree that personal responsibility is very important. But according to what definition? In my view, if a person perceives his or her responsibility as a human being as being limited to oneself, they will (and do) create societies that are *ir*responsible, because they are based on egocentricity, greed and selfishness. In the real world, people suffer misfortune, failure, illness and disaster well beyond their control. And they need help.

Is charity the answer? Perhaps, but it's not without problems. A wealthy or well-off person may perform the charitable act of buying a needy person a meal. That's good. The wealthy or well-off person may then feel good about him- or herself for weeks, but the needy person is hungry again in a matter of hours. *Charity is not good enough*. What is needed is a social framework in which the fundamental needs of life are assured for everyone: *a charitable society*, one in which those fundamental needs are viewed as rights, not privileges. A charitable act is about sharing one's prosperity that another may live under decent conditions. A charitable society is about a social structure in which enough wealth is shared so that *all* others may live decent lives.

Nobody can *choose* to start life from the bottom of the ladder. It's much easier to preach personal responsibility from a position higher up on the ladder. But not all people are given the same chances in life, the same starting points, the same intelligence, skills, talents, wealth or educational opportunities. Is anyone on the upper rungs entitled to scorn those below, or simply look the other way? Conversely, should anyone with any capacity to contribute to the greater good be excused from doing so?

Could there be a truly *moral* commandment in there somewhere, a *realistic* foundation for a *good* society?

CHAPTER 5

Generations and degenerations

Bob spent April 2nd to 8th (Monday to Sunday) with us. Mom arrived on April 6th and stayed until the 22nd. She and Bob had met only once since his mother's funeral in the 1950s. It was when my parents came to Europe in May of 1970 to visit Jeanette and me, which also turned out to be the only time we would see Dad after we moved to Sweden. He died in July 1973, at a time when I could not safely revisit the US.

Initially, Bob was much more nervous about meeting my mom than vice-versa. The big fear for him was her possible reactions to his now-obvious Parkinson's, because he abhorred the thought of her pity and sentimentality – and that of others whom she might inform about his condition. His fear was uncharacteristically irrational and exaggerated. He had moments when he was afraid that meeting Mom would lead to a stream of transatlantic visitors knocking unbidden on his door. I asked him whether he thought that scenario – which I found far-fetched – more likely or more compelling than his real opportunity to satisfy the great curiosity he said he had about meeting my mom.

Bob's first look at Jenny generated such a profound effect that I thought I'd have to hold on tight to prevent him from wafting straight up to the ceiling and banging his head on it. He couldn't speak. Tears came to his eyes. I suggested that he might like to sit in his favorite corner of the sofa, from where he'd be able to survey the living room, the entrance hall, and on into the kitchen dining area. Then I brought Jenny over to him and let him hold her. His intellect was put on hold. Decades of longing for fatherhood now came to unexpected and powerful vicarious fruition. It was a triumph over years of deep depression, later followed by the long period of desperate anxiety he endured as a result of my deep despair. He trembled, but maintained a façade of outward, wordless calm. I saw through it.

As I observed him observing Jenny, I thought of his selfless and unflagging efforts to pull me back from the brink of the abyss. Without his efforts there would have been no Jenny, no joy. Then Jenny squirmed a little and Bob looked up anxiously to be rescued. I took her back with a smile to match his and gave her to Lena for a feeding. Once he and I were alone together, his face radiated euphoria.

He had us to himself for four full days prior to Mom's arrival, which turned out to be a perfect solution. In spite of his astounding intellectual agility – his ability to weave coherency from threads of history, music and scientific developments, philosophical schools and global politics – when it came to social adjustment, his lack of spontaneity was always a problem for him. He relied on (and sometimes hid behind) habits and routines, including those we'd developed during all his previous visits to Malmö. With Jenny around, everything was different: mealtimes were often interrupted, bedtimes were earlier, priorities and focus of attention were drastically altered, noise levels were both higher (Jenny's vocal disapproval of something) and lower (music and TV), laundry times were nearly always, and drinking habits were curtailed. With every little thing and every big thing unpredictable, Bob was forced to respond more spontaneously than ever. And he loved it.

Mom arrived on the Friday morning. She'd turned 71 just nine days earlier (making her then several years younger than I am as I write this). As I recall, Jenny was sleeping at the time I brought Mom home from the hydrofoil terminal, so the first "new" face for Mom would have been Bob's (their first encounter in 13 years). There was a brief period of awkwardness, jockeying for positions and topics, astutely avoiding the herds of elephants that popped up in every corner of the room, reciting polite phrases and neutral aphorisms, smiles, and lots of *"well, well, well"*. Jenny, of course, played the unwitting role of conversation restarter and attention magnet every time she entered the room on Lena's or my arm.

The brevity of Bob's meeting with Mom was fortuitous. Although Bob had pre-meeting jitters, he quickly found his poise and tried to speak with her as one adult to another. There was time to see how Mom interacted with Jenny, and how Bob ignored Mom's baby talk. He witnessed her in preaching mode on several occasions and refrained from comment at the time. Much of what the two of them spoke about occurred when they were on their own, while Lena and I were tending to Jenny (or had gone to bed). But Bob wrote a lengthy letter (addressed to her at our place) as soon as he got back to Binningen; he sent me a copy.

He said that meeting her was "great fun and very useful at the practical level," since their common language (linguistically and generationally) required far less explanation than he usually required with others he encountered. The relative ease of communication emboldened Bob to be surprisingly direct in his letter to her. He asked her point-blank, why her relations with me, which

> ... though excellent in general terms as a result of mutual love and trust, are burdened, as I see it, by your sudden swings into biblical analysis and interpretation? You surely realize that [Stan's] only responses to them are negative. [...] I wonder, though, how you yourself interpret this apparent compulsion to irritate Stanley in this way. My only speculation is that you feel yourself the object of a heavenly assignment to bear witness to your beliefs.

Bob's departure had no discernable effect on Mom's conversation. It was as if he hadn't been there. She didn't show me his letter to her, nor did she give any indication as to its contents or any effect it might have had on her. As soon as I handed the envelope to her, she opened it in my presence and, with a blank face, read the contents to herself, then buried it in her handbag without comment. This was in contrast to a very different letter she received from her sister Maxine during her stay with us. She chose to read Maxine's preachy, cliché-filled letter aloud to us, with drama. It seemed to provide Mom a pulpit for her own religious messages, while affording her a disclaimer, because the words were Maxine's, albeit drawn from the same antiquated glossary.

She turned her attention entirely to Jenny, who was no more than obliquely aware of being the object of Mom's fervent love, while remaining blithely unaware of Mom's occasional outbursts of religious fervor. I was only aware of the tail ends of them – snippets I would catch on entering the room whenever Jenny was alone with her. Since Jenny was pre-lingual, I saw no direct harm in her being the brunt of these onslaughts, but I didn't like or appreciate the intimations of a role Mom might be assuming for herself in the future life of our precious daughter.

Mom brought with her a cute little white wooly lamb for Jenny, dressed in a pink (!) outfit that Mom had crocheted. Shortly after Bob's departure, while I was showing the lamb to Jenny (Mom was in the bathroom), I discovered a winder buried in the wool on the lamb's lower back, well hidden by the pink yarn. I wound it up to see what would happen. It began playing the tune of "*Jesus loves me, this I know*" – one of the most common children's hymns of my childhood, a veritable icon of my indoctrination. I was too flabbergasted to know what to do. I explained the ramifications to Lena, and she just shook her head and wrinkled her nose. Then we heard Mom approaching, so I hid it away until I could decide what to do about it.

Mom reminded us that each of her grandchildren had hitherto spent a week with her (and Dad while he lived) prior to their 10th birthdays. The ostensible reason was to get to know each other better. But Mom always had an agenda (I'd spent something like 970 weeks with her). I said nothing, but shuddered at the thought of her fervor unleashed on Jenny for an entire week. I promised myself I would not allow my daughter to be subjected to brainwashing attempts.

Bo and Peter were eager to meet Mom. My efforts to describe to them what she was like baffled them, amused them and aroused their curiosity. They knew of her religious fanaticism – her broad-spectrum disapproval of everything from TV, movies, theater and dancing, to alcohol, homosexuality, swearing and most activities tainted with pleasure, unless it were made clear that the pleasure in question were of a pious, chaste nature.

Bo and Peter were outstanding cooks; every visit to their home was bound to be a gastronomical delight. They said they'd like to have us over for dinner during Mom's stay with us, and suggested, in view of the complexities of bringing Jenny to their place, that they could prepare the meal in our kitchen instead. We were banned from the kitchen during the final stages of the process, which they were clearly enjoying fully. (They'd done most of the peeling, marinating etc in their own kitchen.) The meal was *incredible*. The starter was baked goose-liver pâté with an unfamiliar but delicious sauce. When Mom spontaneously exclaimed – with undoubted honesty – that it was the most *scrumptious* thing she'd ever eaten in her entire life, their eyes shone and they grinned broadly (at least after I'd explained the meaning of the word Mom reserved for the pinnacle of deliciousness). The rest of the three-course meal proceeded in the same overwhelmingly delicious fashion, and Mom even asked for – *demanded* – the recipe for their sublime and artistic apple-and-almond-paste dessert creation.

When we met them a week or so after Mom left, Bo and Peter could scarcely contain their mirth as they explained to us that their pâté had been *drenched* in cognac; the main course had been marinated in sherry; and the dessert had been liberally doused in calvados. They knew that she condemned their homosexuality, and they weren't about to let her moral indignation at who they were go unrewarded!

During one of the first days of her visit, Mom provided Lena with a few demonstrations of her manipulative skills. One day we all took a drive to Torups Slott, a small castle or manor on the edge of Malmö. It was surrounded by a large park with beautiful walks in beech woods. Spring was just revving up, with snowdrops and winter aconite blooming bravely, and bulging leaf pods and cherry blossoms beginning to burst. Just before we left the house, Mom said she presumed we'd be giving Jenny a bath that afternoon when we got back. Apparently Mom "knew" that infants should be bathed at least once daily. We'd been told by our post-natal caregivers that daily baths were likely to do considerably more harm than good, due to the risk of dry skin and the removal of beneficial skin bacteria. Following the advice of our domestic childcare experts, our routine for Jenny was a bath about once every three days. When we told Mom about it, her eyes widened. She involuntarily shook her head slightly, but said nothing.

As we were pulling into the castle parking lot, we heard Mom in the back seat telling Jenny, in a loud stage whisper, "*Ooh, Jenny, you've been such a good little girl, maybe Mommy and Daddy will let you have a bath tonight!?*" Lena and I looked at each other, rolled our eyes and repressed our sighs. Mom would bring up her bathing advice more than a dozen times during her stay, each time with equal subtlety, and each time (except for once every three days) ignored by us.

On Sunday, April 14th, Eva and her family came by for the afternoon to meet Mom. They brought Marie-Louise with them. One aspect of Mom's endearing fun side was that she could be a real showboat. (Her fun side was on full display most of the time during the rest of her stay with us, except for a few occasions when she felt obliged to mount her high religious steeds. Did Bob's letter to her find fertile ground?) Whenever Jenny slept, Mom became the center of attention. First she showed our guests her ability to count in Swedish, firing off the figures 1-20 at high speed and with perfect Swedish pronunciation. (When she came to number 18, however, she used the archaic *aderton* instead of the current *arton*, a shortened form which hadn't yet caught on when her ancestors left the Old Country.) Everyone was mightily impressed, and she rode the wave as they chuckled and smiled and nodded in approval.

Then my pious little mother announced that as a child she'd also learned a Swedish nursery rhyme. Before anybody could urge her to recite it, she was off: "*Ria, ria, runka, hasten heter blunka....*" Everyone gasped a little, eyes widened, jaws dropped, until a ripple of nervous chuckling disintegrated into embarrassed laughter. Nobody wanted to make fun of her! Everyone was *squirming*! Mom mistook the irrepressible mirth for appreciation and repeated it, "*Ria, ria, runka....*" I quickly changed the subject, trying desperately to distract Mom from further demonstrations of her "Swedish" prowess. It wasn't that anyone there was a prude; it was just the absurdity, the hilariously embarrassing incongruity of my Bible-thumping mom talking like a drunken sailor.

The next day, Mom and I took a walk in the park nearest to us (Garnisonsplanteringen, but known locally only as "Tjuvaparken") with Jenny in the buggy. I cautiously advised her to check her "Swedish" with me before turning it loose on unsuspecting Swedes. Mom, like most Anglophones (and monolinguals) I know, seemed to feel that words (even swear words) in other languages "don't count". Thus she dismissed my concern: *"It doesn't matter, they understand what I mean."* I replied that while that was probably true, they might also understand what she *said*. Again she dismissed the importance of her mistake and said there was no need to check anything with me first. "OK, Mom," I said in exasperation. "<u>You</u> tell <u>me</u> *if it matters. You said, 'Ria, ria, ...*" She interrupted me with a triumphant "*Runka!*" I looked at her. "No, Mom, it's "'R<u>a</u>nka', not '*R<u>u</u>nka*'!" She almost sneered at me. "<u>That</u> *doesn't matter!*" she exclaimed with a chuckle, as if the mere use of an incorrect vowel should bother anyone. I thought of giving her a few examples in a language she understood: *shit* instead of *shoot*; *fuck* instead of *fake*; *cunt* instead of *can't*. But she'd already gotten the picture. (So have you.)

Instead, I sighed. "<u>You</u> tell <u>me</u> *if it matters, Mom, 'Runka' means masturbate!*" (Since "runka" is the crude word for it, "jack off" would have been a more accurate translation, but I wasn't certain that Mom would have understood "jack off".) She stopped in her tracks, turned slightly pale, looked down at her feet and mumbled "Oh, dear!" a couple of times. We discussed it no further. [*At least for the time being. She would, however, repeat the very same mistake at least two more times, more than a decade later.*]

Lena and I drove with Mom and Jenny up to Barkåkra to meet Marie-Louise one afternoon. The language barrier was fortunate. Since Lena's mom was the widow of a vicar, Mom apparently felt entitled to start playing the religion card for all it was worth, but in doing so, she drifted into her King-James-English-cliché mode, all but incomprehensible to Marie-Louise, who was thus spared the brunt of Mom's sermonizing. Marie-Louise had a relatively loose, non-dogmatic, tradition-based association with religion which was almost certainly equally difficult for Mom to understand, albeit for different reasons. Mom said she'd written a poem on the occasion of Jenny's birth. (Fortunately, she didn't have it on hand to recite. I'd seen it and knew it to be an effusively religious poem, full of spiritual aspirations for getting Jenny on the One True Path.) Marie-Louise said she'd also written a poem for Jenny, quickly located it, and read it aloud in Mom's presence: "*May the fairies of the fairy tales watch over your bed and give you the peace of the world,"* or some utter silliness (yet full of good intentions) to that effect. It was, however, dead *wrong* in terms of Mom's worldview, and it burst so many of the illusions she may have been harboring about Marie-Louise being a True Christian (according to Mom's narrow definition), that I almost felt sorry for *both* of Jenny's grandmothers. Instead, I was delighted with Marie-Louise. The topic of religious conversion would now almost certainly be off the table; Mom realized she'd have to abandon her sermonizing and get down to the more human business of grandmothering a darling little girl.

While I was helping Marie-Louise in her kitchen (Mom, Lena and Jenny were in the living room, out of earshot), Marie-Louise challenged me on my anti-religious views. Didn't I think my mom at least got some comfort from her religion?, she asked me abruptly. I thought about it for a moment, and for the first time it struck me that she *didn't*, not at all. On the contrary, I saw lots of evidence that her religion was perhaps the only anxiety- and agony-creating, dehumanizing thing about her, an otherwise only slightly neurotic, kind-hearted person. But her religion was so deeply rooted in her that the very thought of letting go of her superstitious nonsense would terrify her – a great pity for all concerned, especially herself. *Discredophobia*!!

There is, perhaps, a real danger for a thoroughly indoctrinated person to shed the beliefs on which he or she has based his or her entire life. I liken it to what might happen to a person who for whatever reason has mistakenly been confined to a wheelchair since birth and is later in life asked to stand on his or her own two feet. [*In some languages, including English and Swedish, the current forces of political correctness would call for – or insist on – new, "gender-neutral" pronouns instead of "his or her" in this paragraph. I feel that recognizing both genders is preferable to recognizing neither.*]

Leif stopped by one afternoon during Mom's visit. As a slick, smooth-talking marketing man, Leif was eager to impress the hell out of whomever he met, but he got nowhere with Mom. She got nowhere with him either. She saw in him the personification of a Lost Soul and resorted again to King James English. He was totally baffled and turned to me with a pleading look to be rescued from this house of mirrors so I could help him edit some texts (i.e. rewrite some texts for him) for a couple of hours. But he was also eager to see Jenny, and made an interesting suggestion: that Lena and I should use a video camera to keep a record of this early time in Jenny's life. That planted a seed.

On the whole, Mom's stay with us was wonderful. Although she was in many ways far out of her element – linguistically, culturally, philosophically, generationally – my love for her and hers for me nearly always seemed to ease the way forward. She and Lena appeared to get along all right; and during her entire stay, Lena had no flare-ups at me at all, which made Mom an even more welcome guest from my point of view.

Mom largely refrained from further evangelizing after the incident with Marie-Louise, but when I took her to the airport, it came gushing out like some major gastrointestinal disorder: When the Lord returns to the earth in judgment, she abruptly declared for no apparent reason, Sweden will be Number One on His Divine hit list for retribution, for "*having turned from the Light!*" She *knew* this. Fire came into her eyes, she clenched her teeth and swung her arm viciously through the air at the thought of her god destroying the wicked (basically everybody) in my adopted country. And she seemed eager for that day to arrive. Her unfounded, unbounded certainty and uncharacteristic maliciousness sickened me.

Where did her bloodlust come from? Why did her beliefs turn her into a murderous savage? And what made her think that America was any better? (And was there a better example of how it takes religion to make good people do bad things?) I invited her to compare. I told her that many Americans I'd met took great pride in telling me how charitable they were as a nation; yet Sweden contributed around seven times more *per capita* to foreign aid. My former countrymen often talked about their country's "Christian moral values". I reminded her that the biblical Jesus emphasized (almost to the point of nagging) that caring for the sick, the elderly and the poor were the true cornerstones of morality (cf. Matthew 25:32-46), yet America was the only Western society that steadfastly refused to support universal healthcare and assure decent living conditions for the poor and elderly. When I pointed out these discrepancies to Mom, and added that Sweden didn't go around invading other countries either (at least not *since* turning from the Light!), she winced and tried a completely different approach.

She reminded me that in the afternoon on the day Jeanette died, she (Mom) was on a train and saw a rainbow, which she *knew* to be a *sign* from God that "*all is right!*" I tried to control how livid this made me. I had strong impulses to puke, scream and simply abandon my own mom halfway to the airport. Instead I pointed out the nine-hour time difference between Sweden and her land of rainbows. It didn't occur to me that I could have pointed out that the biblical rainbow in question was the finishing touch of a god who had just destroyed every man, woman and child on the planet (apart from eight adults), making him the all-time psychopathic mass-murderer – the same god Mom and her fellow religionists claimed to be the source of all morality and goodness. (There are those who protest that the story of the Flood needn't be interpreted literally; fair enough, but *please* provide a *metaphorical* interpretation of mass infanticide that makes it moral!!) No wonder the world is so fucked-up! I was bitterly disappointed that the final hours of Mom's visit degenerated so grotesquely and ended on such a sour note.

As soon as I got home, I picked up the lamb Mom had brought for Jenny and wound it up. Apparently I wound it too far; it never played again. *Whoops!*

Lena and I thrived in our parental roles. I was only too happy to assume as many duties as Lena would allow; Jenny was my only "project" now. I leaped at the opportunity to change her diapers, put her to bed when she was sleepy, rock her when she was upset, sing to her, talk to her – always in English. And Lena (who consistently spoke Swedish with Jenny, of course) left more and more of the cooking and vacuuming to me. Since I also always cooked lunch for my pupils, I knew my way around the kitchen quite well by this time. I liked to experiment; I might read some recipes to get general ideas about good combinations of ingredients, but improvisation was my method, and the results were usually pretty good.

There was nothing I could directly put my finger on in Lena's behavior towards me that was a problem during this time, apart from talking at me as if I were three years old and keeping a chokehold on our sex life (or lack thereof). Although much of the time she seemed to be genuinely mitigated that I was on hand to help out with everything, my subservience to her wishes (and total avoidance of criticism) was a prerequisite for harmony. And there was so much condescension! I didn't know, didn't understand a thing, did I? *She* did, however, even when she didn't. I held my tongue as best I could and did as she wished, and kept any dissention to myself, far from view.

Seeing Lena in the role of loving mother to my little girl only increased my frustration about why she so very reluctantly displayed any affection for me. At best, I could hope that she would accept mine. Unfortunately, that didn't change with the arrival of Jenny. I struggled to hide how profoundly sad it made me.

(*Not* hiding it would have been a flagrant form of criticism!)

During the spring, Leif's visits to Malmö became more frequent, and my copy-editing work seemed to please him more and more. It was definitely turning into a question of copywriting; very little of the original text was left by the time I was done with it. And Leif kept coming back for more. Each time he came by, a moment with Jenny was compulsory. He said that Frigoscandia had a number of video cameras and promised that we could borrow one soon.

One of my new pupils that spring was a guy who'd recently transferred to Perstorp from the company's facility in Trelleborg (where our laminated kitchen countertops and cupboard doors had been bonded to board material). His name was Hans-Åke (Åke is pronounced OAK-eh). He worked with finance and was one of the most affable people I've ever met. His wife was seriously ill with cancer, and he found he could talk to me about his anxiety – which would soon turn to grief. I told him about my long ordeal after losing Jeanette, and how writing about her death gave me a lot of insight and eventually helped me overcome the deepest depths of my depression. We spent many hours discussing that subject and came back to it often during his many visits. He entreated me to share my writing with the public, because there were surely plenty of others out there who could benefit from feeling less alone with their own intense grief.

I thought again of Jeanette's injunction – "*teach art to the world to help us all*" – an injunction I'd attempted to follow and failed. I thought of something William Walsh, the professor of my first-ever university course, had said back in 1964, about all the arts being related. I was aware that the more I'd been painting, the less abstract I was becoming; my art was moving more in the direction of literature. Now I thought, now that all my desire to paint had been crushed, that maybe someday I would try again, not as a painter, but as a writer. [*Which is what I'm endeavoring to do now.*]

Our frequent visits to and from Ole and Birgitta continued, and Ole and I played badminton every Saturday morning from seven to eight. I was picking up some of the techniques – snapping my wrist more than just swinging my arm, allowing for the queer non-symmetrical trajectories of the shuttle, and learning to position myself strategically immediately after each shot. Our play soon became faster, less one-sided, and more exciting. Ole was starting to get a real workout too. The fiercely competitive side of my nature also began to manifest itself. I tried to curb it so as not to make myself obnoxious. But above all, my need to take inhalator breaks was decreasing despite playing harder; this exercise *worked*, therapeutically, and it was fun! Moreover, since the game was so fast, it was impossible to think of other things while playing. Brooding about my one-way street of a marriage might get me a return smash in the face.

The doctors were still perplexed by my pulmonary infection, and I (emboldened by Bob) began making noise. I'd been on antibiotics for months without any clear relief, yet they'd never taken any cultivation of the crap I was coughing up to help discover exactly what kind of bacterial infection I had, so they couldn't know whether the antibiotics they were treating me with were those that capable of defeating the bacteria in question. They said that their suspicions of asthma were becoming stronger, but I'd never been given a thorough allergy test, and they seemed in no hurry to do so. I began nagging about that, too. (I would finally get a patch test during the summer, but it revealed no specific allergens either.) Bob felt there were other basic tests that should have been conducted long ago. It bordered on dereliction of duty, he claimed, and that some of those people ought to lose their licenses to practice. But I felt obliged to bear in mind that he might have found it somewhat difficult to maintain clinical objectivity where I was concerned.

The arrival of balmier weather in May brought with it the prospect of spending more time outdoors with Jenny. Our relatively new cobblestone courtyard, with its little stream and fishpond, looked beautiful, but we realized that it was the product of our priorities at a time when the prospect of parenthood remained purely theoretical. The fishpond and the cobblestones clearly had to go. So I dug up all the cobblestones and filled in the pond (the goldfish got a free trip to the much larger pond in Beijer's Park – a solution I would later learn was not such a great idea). We bought a truckload of topsoil, and Ole arranged for us to get some sod to create a tiny lawn that was just big enough for Jenny to crawl about on.

Bob was greatly disappointed with my mom. After sending him a thoughtful response to the letter he'd written her at our place, Mom's "dark side" took over. She felt it her place to inform Bob how much his sadistic father "loved" him, which didn't go down at all well with Bob. Then she sent him not one but three books by someone called Janette Oke, an author who specialized in the genre of "Christian fiction" (isn't that a tautology?), with syrupy novels aimed at pubescent girls who feel no particular need to use their brains. Bob addressed his response to the insulting stimulus in a letter to me instead (June 8th), perhaps mercifully, posing a hypothetical question to god (although it could just as well have been aimed at his father or my mom):

> *You sonofabitch, how can you claim to be interested in what happens to me when my whole life long you have polluted my sources, twisted the thoughts and affections of those on whose good will I depended, where did you get your infantile notions of guilt, sin and the like, why do you insist on blind obedience when you put in people's skulls an organ providing them with both the means of analytical thought and, independent thereof, of emotional reactions independent of the analytical capacity and then arrange everything to punish those who use the first part for any purpose except perhaps for that of making armaments and similar things which appease your bloodlust?*

In mid-June, Perstorp granted me my first electric typewriter (I'd hitherto been using a manual portable), which multiplied my productivity. It also increased my output of letters to Bob, who took great interest in every report of Jenny's progress. She was now able to sit on her own.

Bob and I continued to examine the double standard our brothers applied to "communication" with us. Since Bob faced roughly the same thing from his brother Charles (and my mom), we agreed that we needed to level the playing field by telling them, in effect: *sure, correspond on any subject, but know that liberties you take in expounding your ideologies will be met in kind. Dish me your crap only if you want to be told that that's what I think it is.*

I wrote to Bob that anyone who has decided to espouse an immutable belief in something without having a sound and rational reason for doing so is not about to be interested in rational arguments against it. They may venture to put forth a pseudo-rational argument, but when it starts coming apart at the seams, they immediately retreat behind a wall of "*I don't need any rational arguments anyway because I have my proof and my proof is in my heart and the Lord knows and His ways are not our ways, blah, blah, black sheep!*"

Their approach didn't seem fair to Bob and me, but "fair" implies broken rules, and they used no such rules; their Lord pre-empted them. Bob added that "<u>He</u> *was invented for the purpose of having ways other than ours, and would immediately be thrown out of office if <u>He</u> didn't live up to expectations in this regard.*"

No approach worked. My brothers' Teflon coating was impenetrable, although it generally required them to ignore whatever arguments I'd taken the trouble to formulate, and whatever questions of theirs I'd taken the time to answer. I felt that the playing field would never be level. I didn't know how to respond, nor was I inspired to. Yet I *did* want to. Despite all the highly frustrating non-communications I received from them, I loved my brothers deeply, like they were embedded in some kind of magnetic field in my marrow.

I spent a lot of time that summer helping Bo and Peter on a major revamping project next door. They paid me for my work, and we needed the extra money for the deluge of baby items we'd never thought of. Our neighbors' main house was an A-frame construction (like mine had once been, long before Jeanette and I bought it), and they wanted to adopt the same solution: change the roof slope in the yard-side of the upstairs to achieve more floor space, many more windows, and thus more light. Basically, their northern façade would be elevated by more than two meters along its entire length of 10-11 meters. Their wish for windows would require a large arch. (I had already built them an arch more than three meters wide to enable them to open up their living room downstairs. The new one upstairs would be even bigger.) It also meant reconfiguring the A-frame roof beams. It was a huge job, but by this time I'd acquired a number of hard-won skills that I was no longer using, so I was glad to have the opportunity to help them out. My role in the project would last well into August.

In late June, Jenny developed her first real cold. Although Lena and I needed to provide some extra care, Jenny remained as good-natured and happy as ever. She conveyed her desire for extra fluid quite easily, but invariably did so with a huge grin and a squeal of delight, as if to make up for putting us to the trouble. Ironically, perhaps, Lena's spontaneous affection for and loving care of Jenny highlighted (by contrast) her lack of those qualities for me, and made me agonize over why she should find that impossible. But I dismissed such thoughts from my mind as quickly as I could.

We socialized with Øivind and Gunilla (whose daughter Anna was 10 months older than Jenny) quite a bit despite their having moved to Vä, a small town on the edge of Kristianstad, about an hour's drive northeast of Malmö. Øivind seemed to have a posh job, and they now had a pretty posh house and a posh car. Those things seemed to be their priority, and if it worked for them, why not? Øivind showed great pleasure in flaunting material things. I was happy for him that he was able to do it so well, but also a bit sorry for him.

Lena and I had been pretty much out of touch with Øivind's brother Jan and his family for a couple of years because they'd moved from Oslo to the southwest of Norway, where Jan took a job in hospital administration – a major advance in his career. The move more or less doubled the already long (seven hours or more) travel time between us. Our contact was reduced to Jan's and my somewhat irregular correspondence during this period. They moved back to Oslo in early 1984, to a new, even better job for Jan. They were currently living in temporary quarters in an apartment while their large, brand-new home was being constructed in an affluent neighborhood on the slopes of Holmenkollen. (Jan and Øivind's epic fraternal rivalry in status symbols seemed to alternate between inspiring them and obsessing them.)

We drove up to Oslo to visit them for a couple of days in mid-July. Jan was of course eager to impress us with the construction site. I enjoyed playing with Preben and Carl-Victor, now about nine and seven respectively. There'd always been a deep and instant rapport between me and those boys, despite the considerable language barrier. It usually took a couple of days before I could understand a word of what they said (and never when they spoke to each other), in Norwegian, of course. I had the same language problem with Grete. Jan, however, spoke a more Scandinavian-neutral version of Norwegian with us that we could easily follow.

Jan's big new house would enable him to invest in ever-bigger and more powerful stereos, since he could disregard possible objections from neighbors regarding the volume. (Objections within the family apparently didn't matter to him.) His taste in music was broad and exquisite. Although Bob's knowledge of Classical was probably far greater, Jan's music tastes included Classical, but also all the way up to young people's favorites of the 1960s, 70s and early 80s. [*Jan introduced me – and Jenny and Sally – to performers like Elton John, J.J. Cale, ELO, Charley Pride, John Fogerty, Traveling Wilburys and others by giving us audio cassette tapes we could listen to in the car on long trips like those to Oslo.*]

The only problem with Jan's love of music was that the volume he seemed to require to achieve full personal enjoyment was usually a number of decibels above what causes pain in mere mortals and above what allows conversation without shouting. Perhaps this contributed to my prankish communications with the boys – non-verbal gestures that made them roar with spontaneous laughter before they shot a nervous glance at their father's less-than-amused glare. The boys seemed to love having me around, but at the time I didn't reflect much on why that might have been.

Several other quirks struck me as odd. Since Jan and his family were the only Norwegian family we knew (apart from Jan's expatriate brother), I presumed that everything about him and them was typically Norwegian, to be accepted as different (and sometimes silly) but not wrong. [*I hadn't learned much since Bruno, the Typical Swede, had I?*][1] One such thing was Jan's obvious supreme and unquestionable authority in the family and in his home, the unabashed Lord of the Manor.

On one of our visits, as soon as we'd entered the house, Grete showed us into the living room and asked us to sit down while she fetched us each a glass of wine to enjoy after our long highway journey. I took a seat in the first comfortable-looking armchair I came to. Moments later, I felt Jan standing next to me, over me, staring down at me, scowling, with arms folded across his chest. He glared sternly, without saying a word. I assumed he was joking, playing some sort of game. I laughed and asked, "*What, did I sit in your chair?*" He didn't crack a smile, just nodded sharply. I got up so he could take his "rightful place". (I thought, "*Are you serious, man?!*") At dinner (one of Grete's fabulous meals, such as leg of lamb with garlic and rosemary that had been very slowly roasting in the oven for half a day), Jan always sat at the head of the table, and Grete always served him everything *first*! I figured that not serving guests first was simply the Norwegian way. [*I've since learned it's not.*]

At the table, if the boys behaved like boys, he glared at them sternly and they instantly desisted. But when I behaved like the boy I still was to some extent, he was perplexed, particularly at the obvious delight with which his sons responded to my antics (as did Grete!). I usually managed to cajole him and get him to loosen up for a while. They came down to visit us for a few days just a week or so soon after we returned to Malmö.

Al, Nancy, Andrew (now in his late teens) and Amy (now 10) came to stay with us for six days in mid-August. Al had a rental car (seven in our Daihatsu would have been physically impossible). One sunny day, Lena suggested that we all go to the beach in Höllviken (surprise?!), so off we went in two cars. The beach was sparsely populated by Mediterranean standards, but fairly crowded for being in Sweden, which was where we were. Nancy seemed to be a bit agitated by the sight of the many nude bathers – all of them children under the age of five

---

1 See *No Traveller Returns*, chapter 2.

which was perfectly normal for Sweden. She seemed to be in a quandary about how to shield her family's eyes from the sight of that awful toddler nudity. I had totally forgotten about the extent of American prudery.

Al, Andrew and I brought along a Frisbee and/or a football to throw around. They found the water too cold for a swim. Andrew and I began wrestling on the beach, and I soon discovered that my knee didn't appreciate being bent sideways as I tried to brace myself in the soft sand. I felt a tearing, searing wrench, but little pain. The pain began in earnest an hour or two later, and during the evening my knee began to swell. By morning I couldn't walk. Al had to drive me to the orthopedic clinic of the hospital. Nothing was broken, but there were torn ligaments; I was given ibuprofen to ease the pain and the swelling. Over the next two days, the ibuprofen triggered an asthmatic reaction, and I had to return to the hospital for several hours for an emergency infusion of cortisone and theophylline.

Andrew was a real magnet for teenage girls. At the beach, at the store, in town, wherever he went, he seemed to find himself suddenly surrounded by girls lurking nearby, staring longingly at Andrew. Even Lina was in awe of him. Andrew was extremely fashion-conscious and had adopted a certain very modern, aloof style which, in combination with his natural good looks, apparently gave him irresistible charm to which he pretended to be indifferent (also part of the image). But he and I had some interesting talks and he asked me one probing question after another about what my teenage years were like.

Al related something hilarious that had happened to them just before coming to see us in Malmö. They'd visited Amsterdam and decided to take one of the many canal boat tours offered there. They picked one at random and went aboard. When the quota of twenty or so passengers was filled, the guide went around to find out where they were from, then announced that she'd be conducting the tour in English, French, German and Spanish. An obese and extremely American tourist lounging sloppily by the side railing barked in irritation at the guide, "*Why don't ya just speak English?!*" Al said that he and his family were deeply ashamed to be Americans at that moment. Andrew quickly turned his backpack around to display a small Canadian flag he'd sewn on one side.

I understood from Al that he and John had been discussing what to do about their baby brother. Al claimed that the core of the problem was the difficulty of dealing with someone (me) who always had to prove that he was right. I pointed out the (il)logical unfairness and paradoxical nature of such an accusation: defending myself against it would oblige me to do the very thing he was accusing me of. But getting my brothers (among others...) to see that I was equally interested in proving myself *wrong* was another matter. I didn't want to prove *myself* right: I wanted to determine *what* was right, even if it were a different view from my own, one that obliged me to change my mind (I've never succeeded in making this distinction clear to some people...). Bob always pushed back whenever I advanced an idea that didn't stand up to scrutiny; I was grateful to him for that too.

In one sense, John was eager to have it both ways: he wanted to keep many of his straight-laced beliefs, while at all times appearing to be "cool". He convinced himself that he was "evangelical", while at the same time not restraining himself from doing what he felt like anyway. (John had come to prefer "evangelical" to "fundamentalist", an esoteric distinction made primarily by evangelicals who regard the term "fundamentalist" as pejorative, although most dictionaries equate the two terms.) He practiced a kind of pragmatic, cherry-picking fundamentalism guided by do-it-yourself devoutness, drive-in divinity, a buffet-style belief in pious prosperity, with a buy-now-pray-later Lord-and-Mastercharge.

Cherry-picking what is to be regarded as literal or figurative also happens to be the case with the interpretation of the Koran by fundamentalist and non-fundamentalist Muslims, or the Torah by ultra-orthodox, orthodox and non-orthodox Jews. Yet, as far as I know not one of these religious groups (including Christians) has ever mustered up the intellectual honesty or emotional courage to define exactly what it is in the Bible (Koran, Torah, etc) that they take literally and what exactly is to be taken figuratively. Nor is it conceivable to me that even the most figurative interpretation of the biblical God's many psychotic acts of genocide could offer anything remotely related to a foundation for morality.

I'm astounded whenever religious people claim that religion is a prerequisite for goodness, or that their particular brand of god defines "good". Some even profess astonishment that non-believers might have any basis whatsoever for morality! Good god, what a fallacy! Their holy books portray psychotic gods, butchers of mankind, treacherous, fickle and vengeful. The fact that these holy books can and must be cherry-picked to glean any good, or to make any rules you want, only makes me wonder why all the cherry-picking hasn't led to some serious editing. Christianity's "justification" for centuries of persecution of homosexuals, *for example*, is based on a very few obscure yet unambiguous biblical verses (such as Leviticus 20:13: "*If a man lies with a male as with a woman, both of them have committed an abomination; they shall surely be put to death*"). Yet just before that quote, in the same Bible, the same book (Leviticus), the same chapter (20), verse 9, offers this juicy command: "*For every one that curseth his father or his mother shall be surely put to death.*" Why highlight one obscure text while dismissing an equally obscure text? It's called cherry-picking. Is this the foundation of morality?

Much of today's religion-based charitable work comes with strings attached: anything from subtle image-building to outright bribery (listen to our sermons and we'll give you a meal). Religion adulterates people's natural desires to do good by tying them to religion's self-serving manipulation to strengthen the organization. Not really moral, as I see it.

Both of my brothers strayed "far" from their Plymouth Brethren roots – but the "far" part was only from their Plymouth Brethren perspective. From my perspective, because they refused to question or seriously challenge their first premises as to why on earth anyone should believe in any god in the first place, let alone the biblical one, they still appeared deeply mired in it all. Their only questioning seemed to me to come from what was allowed by any of several Christian Apologist authors they trusted, those who were "approved" by the guardians of their new, non-Meeting religious affiliations.

In 1979, the American League in baseball introduced the "designated hitter" – someone who would bat for the pitcher, since pitchers were generally presumed unlikely to be able to hit for themselves. My brothers seemed to me to have found their "designated *thinkers*". Why did they seem to find it so hard to grasp that I was unable to believe in "God" when they were equally unable to believe in Zeus or Mars or Thor – or why not Zonk? Change the name of the god and they had no problem at all not believing. They might even find ludicrous the very notion of such a god.

Lena was on paid maternity leave for the rest of the year. Since I worked almost entirely from home, I was also able to participate fully in Jenny's infancy (everything but the breast-feeding, which came to an end in August). My days of full-time painting were over, and my first thoughts of replacing brushes with a typewriter had only just begun to form. Since we needed the money, in the early autumn I asked my boss whether I could increase my working hours from 50% (20 hours per week on average) to 75% (30 hours). He readily agreed. It wasn't because I *wanted* to work more. I'd already been working at least 30 hours a week for some time, and I thought it could be good to secure a higher *fixed* income during the autumn (and possibly beyond) before Lena returned to work after New Year's. Despite taking so much time off since November, I still had 15 weeks of accumulated comp time and felt I might as well get paid for it. Lena and I were also discussing how we might find a way – if she worked 75% as well – to manage the care of Jenny between us with no or minimal need for external childcare services. We found that with the help of a sitter just half a day per week, we could manage on our own just fine.

It wasn't that we were against day-care centers in principle; far from it. Sweden had a good and comprehensive system of affordable childcare, but we were both reluctant to turn our little girl over to the care of strangers *provided* that we could work it out to be with her and give her our love instead. For the social contact, we had access to an open day-care center where I took Jenny a couple of times a week to interact with other small children and play with new toys.

Jenny's pace of learning accelerated daily on so many levels. But I realized it was unlikely that Jenny would remember *any* of the things that utterly fascinated Lena and me at that moment. My own earliest memory, for example, was from an incident that took place several months before my fourth birthday.[2] Jenny clearly *recognized* things – including us – but is recognition the same as memory?

I speculated (and shared with Bob) that all impressions and learning that predate language development (i.e. non-verbal memory) are necessarily filed haphazardly in the brain (not by topic or keywords or verbal associations) and thus become difficult (if not impossible) to retrieve later on. I further wondered whether such memories might be drowned out or superseded by verbal memories once those begin to be filed in a more orderly way. I had no answers to these questions, but it was fun to ask them!

---

2 See Book 1 (*Natural Shocks*), chapter 1 (Glendale), Kathy Fiscus.

CHAPTER 6

For the sake of argument

For reasons I may never fully understand, the end of summer weather – and with it the autumn's slow, inexorable slide into Nordic darkness – brought an end to what remained of our familial harmony. Lena's relentless hostility towards me went into overdrive. If I expressed opinions that deviated from hers, or questioned her wisdom, she claimed I was starting an argument. That, in turn, seemed to make her feel entitled to scream nasty things at me. Once again, I was ugly, I smelled bad, I had an irritating voice, I was an irritating person, a goddamn idiot, too sensitive, too *in*sensitive, an impossible person to live with, ridiculously eager to learn (she *said* that, as if that were a defect!!), and hopelessly unable to think like her. I found it strange that not one other person ever said similarly awful things to me (or, as far as ever reached my ears, about me).

It was not enough if I *agreed* to do what she wanted; I had to *want* to do what she wanted. Her wish was *literally* to be my command. I not only had to quench every objection, I also had to suffocate my own desires and questions. Lena's approach was to repeat her wishes or opinions, many times, louder and louder, especially things I didn't agree with. Because if I still didn't agree with them after she'd said – screamed – them repeatedly, I couldn't possibly have heard them, could I? After all, her opinions were facts, weren't they? And my failure to agree enthusiastically was proof that I was an asshole.

What on earth had happened?! I was both dumbfounded and devastated. Had I done anything to bring about this change in her? Immediately and automatically, I looked for the cause in myself; my self-confidence had been eroding constantly, but too slowly for me to realize it. Or was the harmony we'd once enjoyed a mere aberration, and hostility was the norm, the default mode? I refused to think that an answer that hopeless could be true. I tried not to dwell on the fact that she'd never relented on discounting as having any possible importance anything in my past. It was of no interest to her, and thus it was banned from discussion.

In any case, she was back to dismissing my views as nonsense without allowing me to explain them. And that was before her rage set in, the rage that inevitably followed attempts to defend myself, the rage that caused her to say the hurtful and hateful things for which she didn't apologize after each outburst subsided. Her renewed hostility took on a chilling new dimension: *she began talking about divorce* on the grounds of extreme incompatibility (Swedish: "*lång och varaktig söndring*", literally "long and permanent disintegration"), something she would reiterate with increasing frequency over the next few years.

And still I loved her! I tried my utmost to convince myself she'd just had a poor night's sleep, a trying day, a tough week, a difficult month, a hard year. She was, after all, the mother of my child. But I was ill-equipped to deal with her aggressive attacks; they cut deeply into my heart; they made me panic, put me on the defensive, and perhaps blinded me to the possibility of other explanations for her behavior. Years later, I came to wonder whether her intolerance of criticism might be due to some deep-seated (possibly sub-conscious) insecurity of her own? But even if I'd known that to be the case, would it have helped? What could I have done about it, given the fact that my every suggestion to get counseling was viewed as criticism and thereby only fueled the fire?

One of my pupils that fall was transferring to the company's office in Singapore for several years at least. Perstorp also sent his wife Anna to have five days of English lessons with me, with a week or two between each full-day session. Anna was beautiful in a gracious, ethereal way, and she seemed to find me a pleasant and amusing person. We got along well. There wasn't a trace of flirting involved, but spending a few days with a beautiful woman who bore no hostility whatsoever towards me made me aware of how much I was longing for something that was sorely missing in my life. It was not a happy feeling.

Bob found out that his ex-mother-in-law (Tante Lore's sister-in-law) had died in the early part of 1984. Bob had never had much contact with her, and none at all after divorcing Sigrid. I suggested several times that he should mention Sigrid's mother's death to his lawyer. Bob resisted the idea initially, but when he finally did, she (the lawyer) told him it could indeed constitute grounds for reviewing and reassessing Bob's punitive alimony payments. The initial divorce settlement only required him to pay a high rate during the first few years, but had Bob inexplicably continued, probably to appease Tante Lore, who'd commanded Bob to "fix this", regardless of the considerable financial burden on him.[3]

It was ridiculous and incomprehensible to me. Sigrid's first ex (Theiss, Bob's despised ex-boss) was scraping by with his penthouse and Ferrari; Sigrid's family – including the filthy rich Tante Lore and her husband – could have provided

---

[3] cf. Book 3, *No Traveller Returns*, chapter 6

any additional support Sigrid might need without even noticing it, but chose instead to let *Bob* "fix this". It made me furious on Bob's behalf. He refused to see that he was being exploited.

But I – and Bob's lawyer Irène – finally got through to him. If Bob simply stopped the absurd alimony payments, Irène told him, Sigrid would be obliged to reopen the settlement, in which case she would also have to disclose the scope of her inheritance from her late mother. Irène felt certain that Sigrid would prefer to accept cessation of alimony from Bob than to make that disclosure. So Bob stopped paying in the early autumn, and there was no reaction from Sigrid. He was off the hook.

In addition to my Saturday morning badminton sessions with Ole, I was now also playing badminton with a number of my pupils, which meant that I sometimes played three hours a week. The effect was remarkable; I'd now achieved above 80% of normal lung capacity, up from my low-water mark of below 40%.

During the autumn I underwent three or four types of allergy tests, including my first patch test. They all came up negative. The doctors were still unable to diagnose my pulmonary condition. Then I read that a long-term pulmonary infection – which I had – could *cause* asthma. If the doctors had persisted in taking cultivations of my mucous from the start, to be able to use the right antibiotic, might they have prevented my infection from becoming chronic? Even though it was unproven, that thought left a bitter feeling.

On Sunday, December 16th, three days before Bob came for his two-week Christmas visit, Jenny took her first steps. It was nearly a month before her first birthday, a fitting reminder of everything amazing about 1984. Jenny dazzled Bob with her progress – her responsiveness, her nuanced facial expressions, her walking and natural curiosity, and her efforts to communicate by making noises that she seemed so impatient to craft into words. He was determined to see that we improved our image-capturing technology, whether by means of single-reflex or video or both. He was also convinced that Lena and I and Jenny formed the most harmonious and happy family he'd ever experienced. I wished like hell that it could be true – and I refrained from disabusing him of that pleasant thought.

Almost every trip Bob made to Malmö included at least one side trip to Lund. At first, back in the early 1970s, he was intrigued by the atmosphere of the venerable university town. On one of those first trips, he discovered Gleerups, a bookstore diagonally across the street from the cathedral and the university. Bob and I spent a couple of hours among its eclectic selection of English-language books on science and philosophy each time Bob came to see us. The store provided comfortable chairs to enable a more thorough perusal of the books. They were repaid by Bob's extensive purchases every year.

After his departure on January 3rd, 1985, with no "chaperone" left in the house, Lena's hostility towards me roared back. She screamed that I was "*ett mjäkigt mähä*" (roughly "a worthless weakling") – her linguistically creative summation of my existence. But apparently even she found this description a bit over the top, because the next day she broke her own rule by apologizing!! Jenny's first birthday was celebrated in peace and joy.

Lena returned to work again in early January, after the Christmas break, but not full-time. She had every Wednesday off, as well as Friday afternoons. Since I could easily fill my quota of working hours for Perstorp by having just two pupils per week (Wednesdays and Fridays), we needed the services of a sitter on Friday mornings only. I thus became Jenny's primary caregiver and loved every minute of it – but now I began to notice signs that Lena *resented* me for all the care I gave Jenny! Why did she have to turn the care of our darling daughter into a contest between us?!

It wasn't long (January 18th) before Lena announced, after yelling at me for disagreeing with her on some trivial point: "*I'm moving out to have a life without you, and I'm taking Jenny with me!*" I turned pale and had to sit down. I felt physically ill, like I'd been struck hard in the solar plexus. Nothing could be more terrifying to me. She didn't apologize. We were back to "normal". I didn't breathe a word of such outbursts and attacks to anyone, especially not to Bob. I was hurting badly, but hid it well. My only "therapy" was to make careful notes of what was said, by whom and when.

As usual, my brothers' Christmas greetings consisted of a printed card and a copy of a circular letter – a chronicle of the salient events in their families' lives for the past year, spiced with pious declarations of their faith and devotion to the Lord. Since I invariably reacted to such declarations, they knew full well what kind of responses they would get from me, yet they always blamed me for reacting. The unwritten scenario might have gone like this: "*We <u>know</u> that Stan will react heatedly if we send him this stuff, but we'll send it anyway, then we can accuse him for reacting the way we know he will.*" No level playing field here!

The Christmas '84 card from Al and Nancy, however, included a lengthy and surprising letter to me from Nancy in which she expressed (to *me*!) her concern about the disturbing nihilism in Andrew's recently adopted "New Wave" lifestyle. She wanted to know how my views on nihilism had changed since 1977.

Naturally, I responded willingly. In my letter to her of January 12th, I wrote that in any discussion of abstractions and philosophies, I had all too often found that people use different definitions of the key concepts, which precludes meaningful exchanges. As a starting point I therefore quoted my Random House dictionary's definitions of nihilism:

1. *total rejection of established laws and institutions;*
2. *extreme skepticism, esp. with regard to value statements or moral judgments;*
3. *total and absolute destructiveness toward the world at large and oneself.*

Although I had to varying extents embraced all three definitions in the year following Jeanette's death, I pointed out that my current position had undergone some major modifications. Regarding definition 1, I had changed from "total rejection" to "certain questioning". I still subscribed to definition 2, but I now saw definition 3 as *"the cancer in the lot, the one that is self-defeating and disturbing, to say the least."*

I told Nancy that if Andrew's position mirrored my current one, I would have to take my hat off to him.

> *What I really would consider disturbing is if he didn't sense the slightest grounds for questioning the kinds of established [American] values that allow people to vehemently oppose abortion on one hand while sanctimoniously supporting capital punishment on the other. [I knew that Al and Nancy strongly opposed abortion while largely supporting the death penalty.] Any value can be questioned and any value that is held to be true without a reason for doing so is not worth very much in my book.*
>
> *I truly hope that I will never come to hold any point of view which, if challenged or questioned, would produce in me a feeling of resentment or fear. I love living, but I don't feel it is necessary to run around holding things sacred, whether they be flags or virgins or ghosts – holy or otherwise.*

In her next letter, Nancy replied that she would need a separate sheet of paper to reply to my comments. She never sent that sheet of paper....

Looking at nihilism again in connection with responding to Nancy's letter got me thinking about it again in the light of Bob's former attraction to it, in the context of my own self-destructive path that serendipitously led to a catharsis, and in view of rethinking my worldview while creating *Jardin*. Prior to my catharsis, prior to painting about it in *Jardin*, I realized that I'd always been searching for meaning – meaning as an entity *out there* to be discovered or at least pursued – thinking and assuming I could find meaning in one or several or many *external* sources. And yet the total ruin and collapse of my life that led up to my catharsis *was* the total disillusionment that I could *find* meaning. Instead, I had to *create* meaning. We have *zero* evidence for supposing that our lives, the earth, the universe have any purpose or meaning apart from what we fabricate about them.

My working hypothesis was now that there is no fate or destiny that is not of your own creation and fantasy, except insofar as you have chosen to believe in the creations and fantasies of others.

Is this assertion jolting? It certainly undermines any delusions of grandeur! It makes you responsible for your own "destiny" – that what you will be or strive to be is up to you. And *in your mind* you can be the person you want to be – and more importantly, be the person you would like others to be – even though your actions will be limited by the people, structures and circumstances around you. Further, you are not compelled always to follow a fixed destiny, but may change your course (even if only in your mind!) at any time.

The universe doesn't give a shit about you or me. Get over it. Get over yourself. The universe is just there, without a purpose or meaning, but as a result of processes we're only beginning to understand, a little bit more than mankind has ever done. The same applies to the microworld, to the mitochondria, to the sub-atomic particles. Some of their hugely complex processes are predictable, others are chaotic. All of them happen, but as far as we know, they happen for no discernable *reason* (except for the laws of physics, chemistry and quantum mechanics), and with no discernable *purpose*.

Does that leave us without value? No! It leaves us with the freedom to create value, to cultivate our garden! Wouldn't that mean total anarchy and selfishness? No again. Almost everything in human history and pre-history suggests that *homo sapiens* is a social species to some extent; we have survived and thrived by interacting. For interaction to work, certain principles naturally emerge that facilitate interaction and benefit the group. No society would survive if people went around murdering each other. We don't need imaginary creatures to tell us that, to command us. We are not moral because our gods and goddesses order us to be. And as societies become more complex, so do the principles that facilitate our interaction.

I think that few people, if any, will gain lasting happiness through seeking their own; greater happiness results from seeking to contribute to the happiness of others, with one's own happiness emerging as a by-product, and in a form that is more profound and enduring. Such morality doesn't follow dictates blindly, doesn't bow in fear to fantasies. It comes from within, with the greatest possible awareness.

Whether by coincidence or for some other reason, a few weeks after returning to work, Lena stopped screaming at me. Instead, she began talking about the importance of Jenny having a sibling, because being an only child would be problematic for Jenny. (Lena also allowed a resumption in our sex life, if only temporarily.) Although I'd never heard of any or believed in any such correlation, I said nothing (being keenly aware that she would interpret it as criticism of her). In fact, I *welcomed* the idea of Lena not yelling at me. I also welcomed the idea of a second child – Jenny had primed me well! – *and* Lena's unexpected tolerance of renewed intimacy was most welcome!

A few weeks of something resembling harmony followed. My depression was shrinking daily. Entire days went by without Lena screaming at me. Jenny was laughing and squealing and running. Was this just a hiatus? Could it possibly last? Apparently not. [*Many years later, I would put two and two together and understand that this window was only open long enough to ensure conception.*] The next diatribe came on February 21st: "*I despise you so goddamn much, you don't appeal to me one bit!*" A week later came the next: "*You're so goddamn ugly, disgusting, dirty – always, always!*" What brought this on?! What had happened?! I'll probably never know.

In January, I received a call from a guy at Perstorp's facility in Trelleborg. He had a subordinate named Jörgen who had been promoted to a new role in the company that required him to use far more English than he could manage. The boss was desperate to see whether I could bring Jörgen up to speed quickly. I said I would try, and we booked six full-day courses at Korngatan over the coming two months.

When Jörgen arrived at my door for the first of those six days, in mid-

February, I casually asked him whether it had been difficult to find a parking space. First he stared at me in total silence, then rolled his eyes about as he searched and searched for words in the air around me. After about 20 (twenty!) seconds, he blurted, "No." I thought to myself that this pupil was a *complete* beginner. I asked him (with the greatest enunciation possible), "<u>Where did you park your car?</u>" He gave me a look of pain, stood there silently, his brow wrinkling. Finally he grunted and pointed in the direction of the square. "*Up at the square?*" I asked. He nodded in relief. But since the main purpose of my question was to get him to speak, not to learn where he'd parked his car, his non-verbal reply disappointed me.

We crossed the yard to the little house and I led the way up the stairs to my classroom in the library. I continued asking simple questions and waited impatiently for his monosyllabic replies, uttered only after he'd fretted and festered for a while in complete and excruciating silence.

This went on for a couple of hours. I was ready to tear my hair out when it suddenly occurred to me that he had, in fact, *eventually* answered every question in a way that indicated he'd understood it. I decided to see what he would do if I skipped to something *much* more advanced: an article from a recent issue of Time. I asked him to read it to himself (while I took an urgent break to recover my sanity!) and to underline words he didn't understand. Did he understand the assignment? He nodded. I was expecting him to underline just about every word.

When I returned to the library, I saw that he'd underlined only about half a dozen words in the entire article. I was astonished and asked him, incredulously, if the few words he'd underlined were the only words he didn't understand. He nodded. I had to let this sink in. The prospect of six days of monosyllabic answers and hours of silence was daunting. I would have to try a new approach.

I abruptly stopped speaking English to him and switched to Swedish. I told him that I didn't see how I could possibly teach him English – a *spoken* language, after all – if he refused to *speak*! What was going on? Why wouldn't he speak? He'd obviously understood everything I said?!

He seemed ashamed of himself, and told me (in Swedish) that he understood everything, but couldn't find the words when he came to speak, because he'd only ever *read* English, he'd *never* spoken it before in his life. "*But surely you've spoken it when you've travelled abroad?!*" I asked. No, he answered, he'd never been abroad (he'd always been a guy). I could hardly believe it. It was most unusual for Swedes (especially in southern Sweden) not to travel abroad, to other European countries at least. He told me that he'd read technical books, magazines and manuals, lots of them, and could do so without difficulty, but he'd simply never uttered a word of English, never had a conversation in English, nor ever spoken with English-speaking visitors.

I suddenly thought of Sonja, who once told me that when she had to rehearse a role for a theatrical performance, it was vital for her to do so out loud. I thought of deaf people whose speech is often difficult to understand, not because of anatomical problems with their vocal cords or larynxes or tongues, but because they can't hear the sound of their own voices. I already had personal experience, when reading stories to Jenny, of how dramatically easier reading aloud became with each new reading. Then I took a wild guess.

"*Here's what I want you to do,*" I told Jörgen. "*Every day between now and when you come here for your next lesson, go into a room by yourself, close the door, and read <u>aloud</u> for at least 20 minutes. Do this every day. Read with exaggerated drama, as if you're reading a story to your child, so your speech doesn't quickly degenerate into mumbling. Promise me you'll do this! In fact, if you don't do this every day, then maybe you shouldn't bother coming back!*" I said that last bit with a wink and a smile to soften the harshness of my ultimatum. He promised he would.

On February 27th he was back. I was dreading the meeting. When I opened the door, I asked him, "*How was the traffic from Trelleborg today?*" He looked me in the eye and said, in English, without hesitation, but slowly and timidly at first, "It was not too bad most of the way, and I had no problem to find a parking place." As he spoke, a grin spread across his face. My hair stood on end. Throughout the day, I got clear and developed answers from him to every question, and he asked a few of his own. It was the most dramatic teaching breakthrough I would ever experience, and it made everything seem worthwhile. A few weeks later, his boss phoned me and asked what on earth I'd done with Jörgen – he was a changed person; he was amazingly more communicative, even in Swedish! And I hadn't known what I was doing – it was all a hunch, a wild guess!

Based on that experience, whenever one of my courses was over, and my pupil would ask what he or she could do on their own to maintain the language skills they'd acquired, I thought of my incredible experience with Jörgen. I would relate the story and tell my pupils how to benefit from it: *Read out loud, with exaggerated drama, every day. Don't pick a text only because it's in English. Pick one you find interesting. It's that simple – if you have the self-discipline to see it through.*

On a visit to me in early March, Leif brought one of Frigoscandia's video cameras for us to borrow for a couple of days. It was a big unwieldy thing. It *could* be supported on one's shoulder, but it gave the best results when mounted on a tripod. After I'd filmed a complete cassette – mostly Jenny, of course – and we'd watched it a few times, I sent it to Bob. He was thrilled and showed it to Carmen. Her interest in visiting us was immediately revived. In a letter to us shortly thereafter, she announced that she'd like to spend four days with us in mid-May. I thought that Lena would object, but she said it would be fine.

On March 27th, we received confirmation regarding a question that had arisen due to a missed period: Lena was pregnant again. The due date was in mid-November! I was both overjoyed (at the prospect of another wonderful child), and apprehensive (at the memory of Lena's fairly terrifying mood swings, especially during the first trimester). My initial thought was to excuse Lena's most recent diatribes by ascribing them to her hormones talking (or screaming). Then I tried to figure out how to fasten my marital seat belt for the bumpy ride ahead. At that point, Lena didn't seem all that pleased about the news of her pregnancy, which worried me considerably.

That weekend we started a major project to organize all our papers – receipts, insurance documents, tax forms, building permits, etc – in the drawers in the library. Most of the work fell to me. On Sunday, March 31st, Lena decided to become outraged with me because she felt the task needed to be finished *immediately*. I felt we needed to do it carefully and logically so that we could find things once the job was done. I thus committed the fatal error of questioning her, and the screaming began. I had to do it her way, and her way only. And it had to be done *now*!

Lena was at home for the Easter vacation week. On Monday morning she asked me what I thought we'd be doing that day. She'd said before that *she* wanted to go shopping in town on her own, so I replied that that would be fine with me – I certainly didn't mind staying at home with Jenny. Then she changed her mind; she wanted us to come along. I knew she wanted some stylish new clothes for herself, and I realized I would have to bite my tongue so as not to arouse her ire in case I might fail to hold my tongue about what I thought of the latest attempts of the boys in Paris to prey on the gullibility of the fashion-conscious.

I had become fairly good at biting my tongue, but I was still sorely deficient in expressing enthusiasm for things that were not at all in my taste. While we were shopping for her, she *insisted* on hearing my opinions – yet she berated me for the ones I had. I didn't offer advice or disapproval. It was enough that I avoided outright lies. She was furious. "*I made a horrible choice when I married you!*" she snarled.

Doing something wrong – something that can be pointed out, realized, admitted, rectified, atoned for – is one thing. But *being the wrong person* or *thinking the wrong thoughts* is a dead end. I felt a huge wave of depression looming over me. Jenny's growing restlessness gave me an excuse to take her home. Jenny wasn't the only one becoming tired and upset. I told Lena to take her time, enjoy shopping, stay as long as she liked, it would be no problem at all. I handed her the cash equivalent of my annual clothing budget to contribute to buying whatever clothing she wanted for herself. She took it and grumbled.

As soon as Jenny and I got home, she needed changing. She was still a bit upset, so I read her some stories. She wanted a snack so I prepared one for her. We'd only been at home for an hour when Lena returned, tired, having bought nothing. She was immediately furious with me for not having taken Jenny for a walk to the park – after we'd walked all the way home from town! I asked Lena why she hadn't enjoyed a cup of coffee at a café or something. "*Why didn't you suggest that before?!*" she railed. I thought to myself that if I had, she might have accused me of bossing her around.

Then she claimed I was trying to take over the care of Jenny (see my earlier conjecture). Exasperated, I said I'd get back to sorting our papers, something that had been so bloody urgent the day before. That was wrong too, and she grew furious again. I literally didn't know which way to turn.

When it was time for Jenny's supper, Lena was back to "normal," while I felt like a wrecked train trying to hide in a tunnel. Unconsciously, I sighed audibly. Lena demanded to know why I'd sighed. Her demand was stated in a tone of voice sufficiently normal to fool Jenny, but not me. I felt (but didn't say) that I had just seen a similarity between her and her brother Lars – the inability to apologize for eruptions that cause real pain and injury. Her "normal" mask on such occasions was awfully difficult for me to swallow, since I'd learned to identify the rage and contempt that lurked behind the mask. I knew that if I were to reveal such thoughts, she would *explode*! I didn't have the strength to face more of that, nor did I wish to subject Jenny to the sights and sounds it would entail.

Jenny was overtired and upset. It was well past her bedtime. Lena and I took turns rocking her, reading to her, without success. Finally, on one of my turns, Jenny fell asleep at last.

Lena also seemed exhausted (who wouldn't be, having to put up with an asshole like me?), so I suggested that she turn in. She did, but not before firing off a parting round: *"Are you trying to get rid of me or something? I'll have you know, I don't want this baby* [indicating her abdomen], *not with you. But I'll keep Jenny if we get divorced!"* – as if that were the self-evident outcome.

I repeatedly asked Lena, in all kinds of contexts, whether there were *anything* I could do for her, help her with, make for her, buy for her, make her happy with. She *never* asked me any such questions. Just one, just once, might have been enough: *"What can I do to make you happy, Stan?"* But it *never* happened. She just told me she'd chosen the wrong man. I tried to suggest that we get help, counseling, talk with Eva or Marie-Louise? *"Absolutely not!!"* she thundered. Or a psychologist? *"Never!"* Couldn't we record our "discussions" to try to figure out what made them derail? *"No way, don't you even dare to think about it!"* Then she stormed off to bed.

I couldn't sleep. While she slept, I wrote down all that had been said and done that day to try to get some clarity for myself at least. I suspected that someday it might be important to know what was actually said, before memory could polish it up or smear it or distort it. I needed to calm down as well; I was close to the edge, to the void.

Bob was probably the most knowledgeable person I would ever meet. And one of the wisest, as evidenced by his exceptional ability to combine his knowledge with sharp analytical skills and solid, defensible, humane values – as well as remarkable empathy. He maintained a healthy skepticism concerning everything that smacked of superstition – including religion. Those attributes gave him an abundance of wisdom in every respect but one: on the emotional level he was gullible. He had trouble reading people. Like most people (myself included!), he had blind spots. He sometimes displayed a fierce loyalty to strangers who used and exploited him, because erroneous premises made him draw false conclusions.

A case in point was the surly woman at his local laundry, to whom he'd been bringing an average of around five shirts a week for longer than I'd known him. When I first accompanied him to that laundry on the Hauptstrasse in Binningen, near Kroenenplatz, on our way into town in 1970, I was astonished to witness her open disdain for him, her cringing at his broad American accent, despite Bob's politely handing her an accumulation of nearly 30 shirts' worth of business. In the early 80s, as Bob's degenerative medical condition began to affect his movements and voice, that bitch's disdain turned to rudeness. I saw that she was cordial to other customers, but treated Bob as if he were drunk. (I would definitely have intervened on his behalf, but I didn't speak German, let alone *Baseldeutsch*, and Bob would have been horrified.) I asked him why he persisted in giving her his business. He said he had no option. When I told him I'd found another laundry even closer to his home, and a lot cheaper, he summarily dismissed the information.

By the mid-80s it had become extremely difficult – painstaking – for Bob to button and unbutton shirts (and nearly all his shirts had button-down collars with tiny buttons). Then the witch (Notice the rhyming degeneration? In reality it was worse!) proclaimed to Bob that all shirts left in her care must henceforth be completely unbuttoned or she would not wash them. And clean laundry would not be returned with rebuttoned collars. He still refused to change. So every time I arrived at Bob's place, one of my first tasks was to unbutton all the buttons in his accumulation of dirty shirts, then fill a large sack of them to take to the witch. We would then pick up a large parcel of washed and wrapped shirts for me to unwrap and rebutton the collars.

Experiences like that were part of Bob's daily life. I wanted to do everything I could to ease his pain and help him function. Thus I felt it would be cruel to destroy his illusion that Lena and I lived in a relationship of joy and well-being. His vicarious enjoyment of this illusion seemed too important to his own well-being for me to disabuse him of it. When I wrote him on April 4th to tell him that we were expecting Junior II, it was all sweetness and light. In late April, I commented to Bob on the joys of spring:

> *Spring is springing, bounding, leaping and occasionally stumbling (like yesterday when we had snow flurries). Daffodils began blooming in our garden last weekend, trees and bushes everywhere are waiting for the first really warm day in much the same way I wait with my thumb on the champagne cork for the stroke of midnight on New Year's Eve. Jenny is out and bounding about in her first springtime bounding ever. When life IS so bloody marvelous, it makes you wonder why so many spend so much time trying to make believe that life is something it isn't, so they can then be miserable that it isn't what it isn't.*

Those sentences were my attempt to disguise the anguish I felt over Lena's tirades at me, which continued throughout April, and included such things as:

She'd never, ever been happy with me; she'd never had such an awful life; she loathed me and detested me; she should never have had a child with the likes of me; she was going to have an abortion; she was going to leave me and take Jenny. She actually said (or screamed) all these things at me.

Several times I suggested to Lena that I wanted to use a small tape recorder to try to figure out how it came about time after time, when a simple conversation rapidly degraded into a bitter fight, with her becoming furious and livid. Whenever I tried to recapitulate what was said, she inevitably denied it and claimed "I never said that!" or "It wasn't that way at all!" So I persisted, and she finally agreed to a tape. On April 12th, she announced that she was going to a tanning parlor. I may have smiled, I may have involuntarily rolled my eyes, or questioned her need for artificial tanning. Whatever the trigger, I suspected that I was about to get a first-rate tongue-lashing, and was fortunate to have the small tape recorder close enough at hand to be able to trace how the dialogue developed:

> Lena [*angrily*]: You ridicule everything I want about heat and sun. You think it's all ridiculous.
> Stan [*defensively*]: No, the only things I find ridiculous are the *pills* to make you tan, and the solariums.
> Lena [*sneering*]: You just can't accept that I have a different point of view; you find it so hard to put yourself in someone else's shoes.
> Stan [*pleading*]: Lena, I've never said that nobody has the right to like solariums, I just expressed my own view about it.
> Lena: Yeah, but that's the problem. [*Her voice becomes patronizing.*] You always have to question. You damn idiot! You're so damn mean to me!
> Stan [*confused*]: What?! You get to have your opinion, but I don't get to have mine? Am I a "damn idiot" for wanting to have my own opinion? Does that make me "so damn mean" to you?!
> Lena [*sneering*]: Of course you can. But I said one can experience heat in different ways, and you can't just say that a solarium is the same as a sauna!
> Stan [*defensively*]: But I *didn't*! And you've never even been to a solarium, I have.
> Lena [*sneering*]: And that's the same as a sauna, huh?
> Stan: No, but I bet…
> Lena [*starts to scream and sob*]: No more! I'm getting a cramp in my stomach! Which doesn't matter to you! All this about having a baby, I understand now that it's all up to me!

Stan [*with exasperation*]: What do you want me to do? You get upset if I say nothing or at whatever I say. *What am I supposed to do?!*
Lena [*now hysterical*]: We can't get anywhere! Don't you see?! I have to talk with my mom about this, I'm so....
Stan [*struggling to remain calm, and pleading*]: <u>Please</u> talk with her!! Or your sister!! [*Lena is now sobbing.*] Shall I phone Eva?
Lena [*sobbing and snarling*]: *You just dare*!!!
Stan [*pleading*]: Why won't you speak with someone outside?
Lena [*furiously*]: *Get outta here! You <u>cruel</u> person!!*

My only relief was her absence (from home) three full days a week, when I could devote myself to the joy of Jenny and teaching her words in English. She was like a tape recorder and would faithfully (and surprisingly clearly) repeat nearly every word I said. I was absolutely thrilled by her ability. Her mind was like a blotter, and my thrills were her encouragement to learn faster and faster.

As usual, to gain some breathing space from Lena's ill will towards me, I tried to fill our weekends with visits to and from our circle of friends and family, in whose presence Lena's mask of pleasantness seldom slipped a millimeter. In addition to Øivind and Gunilla, Mai and Lars, Charlotte and Kent, and Ole and Birgitta, we were now also seeing more of Dave and Christina. Dave was a Scotsman born in London. He'd been a colleague of mine at Hamedi's language school. Christina was a teacher. They'd been neighbors of Björn and Isobel – and of Lena and Larry. (Coincidences like these often lead people to conclude "It's a small world!" But nobody I know ever sits in an airport watching thousands of total strangers pass by and exclaiming "It's a big world!" each time one more passes by....)

Dave and Christina had two small children, which meant that we had certain experiences in common. During one of our evenings together, they suggested that we jointly rent a country house for a week in the summer. We agreed and decided to rent a place on Öland, a long, narrow, windswept island off the east coast of southern Sweden, connected to the mainland at Kalmar by a bridge completed in 1972. None of us had been there before.

We'd been talking with Mom about visiting her (and possibly my brothers) for a few weeks in the summer as well. Lena and I had still never been to the States together, having had to cancel our planned trip in 1983 due to Lena's pregnancy. Now we had to scrap our plans again, for the same reason. But neither Lena nor

I seemed to feel terribly disappointed about that. I hadn't been to the US in six years and didn't miss it. (And a trip to visit my family in the States was unlikely to include sunbathing.)

Mom and Bob had been carrying on a nearly constant skirmish by letter since they met at Korngatan the year before. She would write a warm and pleasant letter that Bob would become enthusiastic about and he would respond in kind. Then she would write a letter full of religious fervor, hawking her loving and vengeful god to him, thus enraging him, and he would respond in kind. But Bob's replies were invariably couched in highly academic and convoluted wording, giving Mom an excuse to ignore what he said and respond instead to what she "knew" he meant (which she didn't). All their communication disintegrated into misunderstandings and non sequiturs. Bob usually sent me copies of her letters and his draft replies, but he kept trying to achieve something that would never happen as long as she remained in preaching mode.

Following a phone call to Bob on May 15th, the day before Carmen arrived, I explained to Lena a possible itinerary for Bob's tentative summer visit. Her reaction left me so flabbergasted that I found it necessary to draw a comic strip (for my eyes only):

> Stan: *Bob had some problems coming here in July, so I suggested the last week in June and the first week in July.*
> Lena [scowling]: *What?! Am I supposed to be tied down here for 14 days doing nothing?!*
> Stan [confused]: *What do you mean "nothing"? I can get done what needs to be done on the house while he's here!*
> Lena [accusatory]: *And leave me with everything for 14 days?! You might have asked me first!!*
> Stan [astonished]: *What was I supposed to say to him? And hadn't we <u>agreed</u> on 14 days?!*
> Lena [angry]: *We agreed on <u>10</u> days!! And I'm not about to sit here tied up for 14 days! In that case I'll go away somewhere with Jenny!*
> Stan [trying to appease]: *OK then, I'll write him that he can come for 10 days instead!*
> Lena [smoldering]: *I'm not going to waste two weeks this summer being tied down!*
> Stan [exasperated]: *All right! I <u>said</u> I'd write <u>10</u> days!!*
> Lena [continuing to rage] *14 days!!! Never in a....*

Stan [becoming pissed off]: *I said I'd change it to 10 days....*
Lena [seething]: *Oh how you piss me off.*
Stan [resigned, leaving the room while Lena growls]: *Sigh!*
Lena [yelling angrily after me]: *You're so goddamn... ruining the entire summer!*
Stan [angry at last]: *All right! I'll write and tell him we'll cancel the whole thing!!*
Lena [charging furiously away]: *Oh, you... You don't understand me at all!*
Stan [sitting alone, upset, to himself]: *No, I really don't!*

This exchange *should* have made it clear to me right then that Lena considered having Bob around to be a waste of her time. But it didn't occur to me, not right then; I was doing a lot of filtering. Although she always added a flamboyant signature to the letters I wrote to him, she never read them. And she never more than skimmed his letters to us, even though they normally contained paragraphs that Bob had specifically addressed to her.

What happened?! I thought (presumed) that after three visits to Bob, including his extremely generous gifts of a trip to Jungfrau and two weeks in the Engadine, plus his generous hospitality in Basel and his unassuming, undemanding, giving stays with us in Malmö, that Lena had some feelings of friendship towards him! His praise of me might have been a problem. Perhaps it had become *the* problem? (I had to guess *something*!)

Carmen arrived on Thursday evening, May 16th, and stayed with us until Monday afternoon, May 20th. She was gracious, elegant, and surprisingly enthusiastic about our growing little family. She brought several lovely gifts for Jenny and something sweet for Lena. For me she brought a white chef's hat (she said she'd heard a lot about my cooking from Bob). Across the forehead, in red letters, was emblazoned, "KISS THE COOK". I hoped that Lena might be tempted to comply. She never did, even though she remained on her best behavior during Carmen's stay. She seemed a bit in awe of Carmen's elegance; Carmen seemed enchanted by Lena's charm, but she kept her distance.

It was a bit strange having Bob's non-girlfriend, frequent conversation partner and disinterested romantic interest staying with us for four days. Lena had never met her; I'd only met her a couple of times under circumstances more formal than I was used to, and she was less relaxed using English than Lena was. Neither Lena nor I were in any way fluent in German. As tourists we had no major problems, but deep conversations had to remain off the menu. Yet we had a reasonably, improbably pleasant time.

I'd no sooner returned to Korngatan after seeing Carmen off on the airport bus at the central station when Lena launched into me, for no apparent reason whatsoever. She screamed, "I've never been worse off than I am with you!" Instead of following up those kind words with an apology the next day, she hit me with a new round of screaming; *"I HATE you – just so you know!! I detest you, you're an old goat! I'm getting an abortion! I'm going to divorce you! You can take care of Jenny till then and then I'm taking her!!"*

That was a thought – a threat – I could not *bear*. Jenny had wound herself so completely around my heart, I couldn't entertain for more than a split-second the thought of being without her without shuddering in horror and gasping for breath. As for the threat of abortion, I'd always felt that it was a woman's right to choose – it was her body, after all. But Lena's stated – screamed – *reason* for wanting an abortion hurt like a white-hot branding iron on my back.

Al and I occasionally debated the subject of abortion, an extremely complex topic, which many people, eager to avoid complexity, see only in terms of black and white. I didn't believe that "you're a Catholic the moment dad came."[4] Nor did I favor abortion on demand near the end of pregnancy – unless it was a question of saving the mother's life or perhaps a fetus with extreme birth defects. The tricky part was all the gray areas in between.

Al was working from a premise that even an embryo (the first 11 weeks after gestation) constitutes a human life. Based on that premise, it might be valid to conclude that abortion is morally wrong. (Remember that logic only tells you what conclusions may validly be drawn from your premises, not whether the premises themselves are valid!) Many opponents of abortion make exceptions for an ectopic pregnancy (a dangerous pregnancy in which the embryo/fetus develops outside the uterus lining). Some say that an embryo is not yet a human life, that life doesn't begin until birth. Others say it only becomes a human life once the fetus would be viable outside the womb, yet modern medicine is pushing back the age at which a fetus can be incubated and survive. So who determines when acceptable becomes immoral? The doctor? Some clergyman in a dress? Why not the mother?! Ultimately she's the one, more than anyone else, who'll have to live with her decision, one way or the other.

---

4   From the song *Every Sperm Is Sacred* in the film *Monty Python's Meaning of Life*, released in 1983

Jenny was so *funny*. She would run around with her arms held stiffly behind her as though imitating a peregrine falcon in a nose dive, then stop to emit a laugh that seemed to come from her toes – not a guffaw, but a long, drawn-out, intense, impishly gleeful, audible grin. And she loved reading books. She would grab a book (preferably whatever one Lena or I was reading) and start turning the pages *in earnest*, reading aloud, "*den mo-et bitt watt bah soo-ess deee!!*" She could go on and on like that for several minutes, then she'd run off joyfully to do something else.

As she was increasingly using recognizable words in her verbal ramblings, Jenny always addressed me in English ramblings and Lena in her Swedish *svada*. Sometimes, if the three of us were in the same room, she'd say something to me in English, then turn to Lena and repeat it, but this time in Swedish. When we were out driving, she loved it when I pointed out things we saw and I told her what they were called in English. She was unstoppable. I showed her the electrical power station at the end of the E6/E22 freeway into Malmö, and she would repeat after me, "e-lec-tri-cal trans-for-mers", getting it almost right. There was only one word that she inexplicably couldn't say. Often when we were driving on the freeway to Lund, we passed a striking windmill on a nearby hilltop (*Kronetorps mölla*). I'd say "windmill"; she'd say "veem-low". Then I'd say "wind-mill", enunciating clearly, and she'd say "veem-low", with corresponding emphasis. I'd laugh and ask her to say "wind". She said it perfectly. Then I asked her to say "mill". She repeated that perfectly too. Then "windmill", and again she'd proudly say "veem-low".

I loved reading her bedtime stories, numerous children's books. I read them all in English to her, even if the book in question was in Swedish. She soon got to know them by heart and would protest if I skipped a word. Sometimes I would hesitate before saying the last word in a sentence or on a page, and she would quickly finish with the right word. We had a little book with pictures of animals from all over the world, and soon she'd be repeating after me names like "Rocky Mountain goat", "capybara", "hippo" and dozens of others. (It wasn't long before she could say all the names when I merely pointed at the picture of the animal in question.)

Following his first meeting with Carmen after her return to Basel from Malmö, Bob reported that she expressed general satisfaction and pleasure with her stay with us, but to Bob's great surprise, she offered few details and quickly changed the subject. A few days later, she gave Bob a number of photos she'd taken at our place, but she sent none to us. Bob found that inexplicable. I immediately wondered (to myself only) whether the good lady was more observant of the subcutaneous trouble and strife at Korngatan than I'd supposed, and that she didn't know how to deal with it or didn't want to get mixed up in it. It was the only conclusion that seemed to fit. [*I could speculate that Lena may have told Carmen what she really thought of me, but since I can never know one way or the other, I'll refrain from mentioning it at all.*]

One of my character defects, according to Lena, was that my desire to please her had limits, especially when others I cared about were adversely affected. Bob didn't *deserve* to be treated as if he were wasting our time. He was kind and generous towards us in countless ways. He never even allowed me to get away with *giving* him a painting. He either insisted on paying me well for it or he would pay me back through gifts bordering on the extravagant, as well as my air fare to come and help him. [*It didn't occur to me at the time that not all people are like Bob in this respect.*] He genuinely *loved* us and *needed* our company from time to time. I loved him. Jenny already clearly loved him. Lena didn't *have* to have sole possession of the limelight *all* the time, did she? – even if she found Bob boring or irrelevant to her ego. I rebelled.

I *knew* how badly he wanted to visit us again. It was also safe to assume that he was once again finding it hard to keep up with his accumulation of paper at home – a task I'd been helping him deal with since Jeanette's and my first visit to Binningen in 1970. Lena and I visited him – and partook of his extreme generosity – in 1979, 80 and 81. Then she lost interest and never visited him again. I continued my trips to Binningen on my own, but it became more and more difficult. There were accusations of "*So you're leaving me to deal with everything?!*" But I came to prefer those accusations to the countless other mindless accusations I faced almost daily at home. I thus revisited the summer plans and suggested to Bob that he come to Malmö – for *nine* days (June 25th to July 3rd) – *and* that I would accompany him back to Basel for a week to get his paperwork sorted out. Lena expressed no objections to that, as far as I recall.

The day before Bob arrived, I must have done something (or failed to do the same thing), because Lena felt that whatever I had done or failed to do gave her just cause to scream at me: "*I can't stand you! Get the hell out of here! I never want to see you again!*" These outbursts didn't happen every hour of every day, but they were frequent. A conservative estimate would be an *average* of one hostile outburst per day. And because she never saw any need to apologize, they left wounds and scars. She sometimes claimed – even on seeing me hurt by what she'd said – that fighting was *good* for a marriage! I wasn't buying it. Hurtful words can't be unsaid. A spoonful of strychnine added to a vat of soup cannot be retrieved. Even if someone apologizes for bad behavior, repetition of that behavior revokes the apology, renders it hollow, insincere and meaningless, like the "sincere" apologies of a chronic wife-beater.

Had I not returned to Basel with Bob, he might have wondered about the abbreviated invitation to Korngatan – nine days instead of the usual 14 – but since our total time together was longer (16 days), he didn't seem to notice, and was most grateful for my willingness to take time off from my family to provide much-needed help getting his apartment back in order. At our home, Jenny's progress dominated Bob's thoughts and perceptions, and Lena never revealed her dark side in his presence, at least never to an extent that Bob found impossible to ignore.

Bob's apartment had again descended quite far into chaos since my last visit. Mail, packaging, newspapers, clothing and whatnot were strewn liberally on every flat surface, including the floor. We arrived in the late afternoon. I made a visual assessment, but said nothing, and cleared only enough space to allow us to sit down, have a meal, and give me a place to lie down that night. There was no need to ask Bob what I could throw out and what he needed to deal with; we'd established the ground rules years before.

As soon as he retired late that evening, I went to work – silently – on the living room and had it in fairly tidy shape before flopping on the sofa cushions several hours later. Early the next morning I tackled the kitchen and had most of it done by the time Bob appeared in the doorway wearing his bathrobe and an expression of astonished delight. I explained that I didn't want our time *together* in Binningen to be *entirely* taken up with my cleaning!

Prior to my trip, I encouraged Bob to take advantage of my presence at his home to invite one or more of his acquaintances who'd kindly been inviting him to their place for meals. I felt fully capable of putting together a pleasant meal to enable him to return the favor as the host. So he invited a French couple, former colleagues at Roche who lived across the border in France and commuted daily. His name was Jean-Claude and hers was Roswitha. They were a few years older than me, but a bit closer to my age than to Bob's. They both spoke English fluently, but while Roswitha spoke with very little accent, Jean-Claude spoke much like Inspector Clouseau.[5]

---

5   As played by Peter Sellers in *The Pink Panther* movies

While I was in the kitchen preparing the meal, Bob was entertaining his guests in the living room with sherry and nibbles. After 10-15 minutes, I came out to see whether anyone needed a refill. I found myself involuntarily mimicking Jean-Claude, "*Vood yuu lahk...*" (in my strongest French accent), then catching myself and turning off the Clouseau before I got to the end of the sentence, "*... some more sherry?*" I felt deeply embarrassed, but nobody appeared to notice, or at least didn't comment.

Two days after my return to Malmö, Jenny, Lena and I were off to Brantevik on the Baltic coast of Skåne, to visit Øivind and Gunilla, who were staying there with her aunt. We stayed for two days, came home for two days, then took off up the west coast to Grebbestad to visit another of Lena's old friends (none of whom ever yelled at me or told me I was ugly, horrible or disgusting). From Grebbestad we continued on to Oslo to visit Jan, Grete and the boys. Their big new home was nearing completion and Jan was obsessed with it; it was an obsession I fully understood. We stayed for six days.

Then we were at home for two weeks before leaving for Öland for a week with Dave and Christina. The unusual topography of the island appealed to me greatly – 137 km long and a maximum of 16 km wide, windswept, mostly treeless and rugged, with large rauks (vertical stone formations) just off the northwestern coast, and a huge alvar (a 15-by-37 km barren limestone terrace) in the southern half of the island. It felt like another world, or might have, had the world not been too much with us.

Dave and Christina had two children: a girl who was a couple of years older than Jenny, and a boy who was around nine months younger than Jenny. The cottage was rather newly built, to a very high standard, with minimalist furnishings. It had one bedroom at each end of a large, open-plan living-room/kitchen/dining area. But it wasn't exactly soundproof, and their little boy had difficulty sleeping. In their efforts to get him to sleep, they drove him in his buggy back and forth over a threshold for several long periods during the night.

We (particularly Lena, as I recall) didn't get along terribly well with them. I don't remember exactly whether there was anything specific, although lack of sleep may have contributed. They were strict vegetarians and frowned on our non-vegetarian ways (albeit without condemning them overtly), but I don't recall anything that might have made that a relevant issue. Perhaps it was just a question of bad chemistry.

Dave seemed to be mostly interested in running (and in Lena?). Jenny was too young to bond with their daughter and too old for their 10-month-old son. Lena was growing more and more exasperated; the rainy, overcast, non-sunbathing weather might have contributed to that. But at least I wasn't the obvious target for a whole week.

[*One of the interesting insights I get as I write* Hindsights *is that whenever Lena found a target other than me to vent her irritation and rage upon, she fought less with me; and when she didn't instigate a fight with me, we didn't fight. One can wonder – I wonder – why I didn't take arms against this sea of troubles? There were several reasons. First, I was still hopelessly in love with her (I jokingly speculated that 20 psychologists could give me 30 theories about why); second, I remained an incorrigible optimist – things could only get better, Lena's ferocity towards me was a temporary aberration – and someday she would truly love me; and third, who in their right mind wishes to subject their children to the potentially traumatic experience of a broken home?*]

A few days after we got back from Öland, Bo and Peter got their loom back. It wasn't that they were eager to get it back, but I had to do some rebuilding upstairs before the arrival of Jenny's sibling. Lena and I would have the smaller room at the top of the stairs, while Jenny (and Junior II) would have our bedroom (the long, narrow room next to it). Since our new bedroom had no closet space, I had to build an extra closet at the far end of my former studio. I didn't mind; I loved to have a project, something to do with my hands. Besides, I'd never be painting again.

The following Sunday, we drove to Björn's pizzeria in Limhamn for a late-afternoon lunch, when there were few other customers. We were having a pleasant enough time, chatting, talking with Björn – who hung out at our table whenever he had a break –watching Jenny's cute antics, and enjoying Björn's delicious pizzas. I was on one side of the table, opposite Lena and Jenny (Jenny was kneeling on a chair opposite me). While Lena was chatting with Björn, Jenny slid down from her chair, snuck around behind Lena, and was about to grab Lena's saw-toothed knife. Had I lunged across the table to stop her, I'd have knocked over our Coke bottles. "*Watch out – what Jenny's doing!!*" I exclaimed in alarm, and Lena quickly pulled the knife out of her reach and continued speaking with Björn as if nothing had happened. Then she started smoldering. I had no clue why.

In the car on the way home (me driving, Jenny next to me in her special car seat facing backwards, and Lena in the back seat), it was time for another fight (and another comic strip that evening.)

Lena (sternly): *I couldn't help getting irritated with you back there at the pizzeria.*
Stan (mixed feelings): *What for?* [But thinking: What have I done now?]
Lena (angry): *You thought I wasn't doing what I should and I'm so sick and tired of your remarks and criticism!!*
Stan: *I wasn't criticizing you! I was just letting you know what was going on!*
Lena (triumphantly): *I couldn't even <u>see</u> her, so you didn't need to tell me!*
Stan (puzzled and exasperated at her logic): *But that's <u>exactly</u> why I <u>did</u> tell you!!*
Lena (fiercely): *Don't interrupt me!! You <u>meant</u> criticism and besides, you could have taken the knife from Jenny <u>yourself</u>, since I was having a conversation!*
Stan (irritated): *Can you <u>please</u> stop telling me what I meant!? You don't judge me for things I've said, but first you add stuff, then judge me for what you've added, and then it always ends up like this!*
Lena (in a rage): *Now you're interrupting me again! I can't imagine where this is going to end! You know very well that you could have taken the knife!!*
Stan (defensively): *No! I <u>don't</u> know that! I didn't have time to think, and the bottles were blocking the way. I just wanted you let you know, which had the desired effect, but unfortunately a lot of side-effects.*
Lena (accusing): *You just destroy, and besides, this discussion is <u>over</u>!! At least I didn't have your nagging to deal with for a whole week this summer when you were in Basel...*
[Stan (thoughts only): *Nagging?! I said, "Watch out!", then you began making your interpretations.*]
Lena (smoldering): *...because <u>you've</u> done <u>nothing</u> else all day!*

Perhaps she was right; perhaps I *hadn't* done anything else all day – apart from getting up at 2 AM for Jenny and getting her back to sleep, taking Jenny up at 6 AM, changing her diapers, making breakfast for the three of us, doing the laundry, washing the dishes, taking Jenny out for two hours in the morning so Lena could get some rest, making lunch for Jenny, feeding her, changing her, rocking her to sleep for her after-lunch nap, rushing out to continue building the sandbox as per Lena's orders, taking Jenny out in the early afternoon so Lena could relax on the terrace, doing the shopping, changing Jenny again, and feeding Jenny before driving us all to the pizzeria at 3:30 PM.

I considered a few things she *might* have said to me at the end of the day: "*Thank you so much for all your help today, darling,*" or "*I'm sorry for being so mean to you!*" I was pretty certain that she would say nothing until the next morning, and then she would smile and say, "*Let's just forget about yesterday,*

OK?" And that was exactly what she did, except for the smile. "Sorry" was indeed the hardest word (good one, Elton).

The apparent inability to apologize was far from unique to Lena; her brother Lars was the same. Although it wasn't *typical* of Swedish behavior in my experience, it was by no means unusual either. There's a Swedish expression for ignoring or moving on from an embarrassing or impolite misdeed without comment or apology: *Pretend it's raining* (Swedish: *"Låtsas som det regnar"*).

Many people have claimed that one person's memory is as valid as any other's; how you remember an event is valid for you, how I remember it is equally valid for me; it's all good, there *is* no correct version. To that I say: *Bullshit! Fried flaming bullshit!!* If you remember a Shakespeare sonnet in one way and I another, we can in fact go back to Shakespeare and check whose memory is right (not "right" for you or me, but *right*), or at least closer to the truth. Until we check our versions against Shakespeare's text, we can argue about our own versions all we want, but it won't change a damn thing; in this case the accuracy level is *measureable* and *verifiable*.

Suppose you and I witness a traffic accident. There are so many facets of an accident that happen so quickly (even simultaneously) that it is unlikely that our versions of the accident will be identical. If there are 100 witnesses, probably no two versions will be identical. Perhaps not one version will be *completely* accurate. Does that mean that all versions are <u>*equally*</u> inaccurate? Suppose it comes to light that there are video recordings of the accident from multiple angles. Then we have the means to assess the validity of those eye-witness versions objectively. It will almost certainly emerge that some versions that have been submitted are much more accurate than others. But without the videos, our versions are neither *measureable* nor *verifiable*.

This doesn't mean that the relative accuracy of the more-accurate versions only comes into existence once they have been compared to the videos. The superior accuracy of one or more versions *existed all along*. There does, however, seem to me to be cause for sufficient humility about one's own perceptions and memory capabilities to withhold *categorical* claims of accuracy until they have been tested against more objective and impartial references than oneself.

Lena's second ultrasound showed that all was well with Junior II. It also revealed that Junior II was a girl, so we intensified our search for a name as soon as possible.

We wanted Jenny to "get to know" her little sister a bit before she arrived, to minimize the risk of sibling rivalry. We decided on "Sally" for no particular reason other than that it was somewhat unusual (in Sweden), it worked in both languages, and it went well with "Jenny". [*A few years later I discovered that "Sally" is a derivative of "Sarah", the name of both my grandmothers, and that by interjecting a few letters alternately, "Sally" more or less includes my name, but these associations were coincidental, after the fact, and played no role in our choice.*] From the moment Jenny knew that the bulge in Lena's belly was "Sally", she seemed to find her big-sisterhood perfectly natural.

The major improvements in my lung function that seemed closely tied to my regular badminton sessions (with Ole, with many of my pupils, and with anyone else with whom I could coordinate my schedule) were tangible now. I could play for an entire hour, sometimes two, without any symptoms or need for extra doses from my inhalators. I'd also been able to reduce my asthma medication from three different pills and three different inhalators several times daily to just one pill and one inhalator twice daily. If only they worked on my head as well.

Lena's increasing tirades against me had now convinced me that Lena would rather see me dead. That could have been because she kept telling me how much she detested me. The void was once again my frequent companion, never far away. Every time Jenny looked at me, the void receded instantly. Then the fear of having to live without Jenny brought back my worthlessness. I fought surging feelings of depression actively, daily, but I wasn't convinced it was a battle I could win.

I didn't know how to prepare myself for Lena's attacks. She could start a fight over a triviality. She could spin angrily out of control like flipping the switch on a buzz saw by claiming I "meant" things I never said, but which she attributed to me. A particularly low blow came on October 7th:

You're the worst of all the relationships I've ever had. You're a real piece of shit[6]*. That's it – you're a piece of shit. I'm going to divorce you. The way you are, <u>I can understand why your wife did what she did</u>. Because you must have done something. Get out of here! Vanish! I'll be much better off without you!*

---

6   Lena actually said "djävul", which literally means "devil". But in English, "devil" doesn't render the emotional punch of "djävul", so to achieve the equivalent punch, I've substituted "piece of shit".

I felt like I'd been kicked in the face and the groin simultaneously. That she could and would say a thing like that (it wasn't the first time!) at last convinced me that she truly despised me, that her hatred wasn't the temporary aberration in her otherwise warm feelings for me, but vice versa: it was the warm feelings that were the rarely seen aberrations. It had gradually dawned on me – yes, even me! – that Lena would probably *never* come to love me.

Then my role as her defense attorney kicked in: She couldn't be faulted for failing to love me, painful as it was for me. She'd simply been listening to her biological clock and needed to "settle down" with someone who adored her, as long as he could learn not to criticize her; someone who would tell her she was right even when he was unable to believe it; an adoring (albeit not adorable) sperm donor. Yet even if I managed to construe excuses for her, her comment about Jeanette was patently cruel. She *had* to *know* how much it hurt. It was inexcusable. Did she ever apologize for that? Three guesses.

At about this time I had a new pupil from Perstorp for the day. She was by no means a beginner, but she wasn't particularly fluent either. Her heavy makeup and somewhat gaudy clothing suggested someone whose guiding lights came from gossip magazines and a *what-will-people-think* outlook on life. By early afternoon, our conversation had become sluggish, almost dental, so I pulled out the latest issue of Time and asked her to find an article that interested her, and underline words she didn't understand. I left her for about 20 minutes. When I returned, she'd underlined about 25 words, which I explained and helped her to use in examples of her own. One of the words was *kitsch*, which surprised me (that particular German word is used in both English and Swedish). So I asked her, "You know how some people have big porcelain leopards and dogs in their homes...?" "*Yes,*" she replied, "*I've got some of those....*" I gulped, squirmed and struggled to get out of that one by giving more far-fetched examples, then quickly told her that the word wasn't that important for her to learn anyway, so we could just move on (as my writing will now).

My 40th birthday came and went with little ado. But Lena did give me a 12-string guitar. I would have greatly preferred a hug and some kind words, but those I didn't get. Jan and Eva and their kids came by the next day (Saturday) and Lena was, as usual, more civilized towards me in the presence of others, even more civilized than a porcelain leopard. My painting *Despair* pretty much portrayed the way I felt.

CHAPTER 7

Joyful desperation

Because Lena had had such a rough time delivering Jenny, she prudently insisted on a C-section for having Sally. It was scheduled for Friday, November 8th, more than a week before the estimated due date. Lena and I were told to report to the hospital at 11 AM. Eva and Emil came to Korngatan to look after Jenny while I was away. Jenny knew that she'd soon be meeting Sally.

Lena was nervous and needed me to lean on; I was determined to be the most supportive husband and father ever. This time, I kept out of the way and out of the conversation when not called upon, and kept close by while she was being prepared for surgery and got her epidural. I also scrubbed down and put on a green sterile hospital gown, because we both wanted me to be present throughout the operation.

A nurse wheeled Lena into a bright, stainless-steel-and-green-cloth operating room where what seemed like a dozen or so members of the team were whizzing around. I remained at her side. Once her surgical bed was in place with her in it, I sat on a chair next to it, level with her shoulders. They set up a screen over Lena's midriff so we wouldn't get to (or have to) see the ongoing operating procedure itself, although I could crane my neck around to get glimpses behind the screen if I was up for it (or if Lena asked me to). I held her hand whenever she allowed me to. A mild sedative took the edge off her nerves. I felt her feelings, spoke words of encouragement, and reminded her of Jenny's anticipation at home.

The team had a lot to prepare, and gave every impression of knowing what they were doing. The minutes felt long that afternoon, but the time finally arrived. I scrutinized the faces of the staff to see if I could read in them what was happening. When the surgeon began making the big, silent incision, I looked away, at Lena. Shortly thereafter, he told us to prepare for a little noise. When he punctured the placenta, it sounded like the burst of fizz when you open a can of soda after having shaken it. A flurry of activity followed for several seconds (could it have been minutes?) and suddenly, at about 5 PM, the doctor lifted Sally into the air and a nurse folded a soft towel around her. I turned to Lena and gushed, "*We've got our little girl – our Sally!!*"

I was laughing and crying. They laid Sally on her mother's chest. Lena smiled a wan post-partum smile. She was a little groggy due to the sedative, but calm

Joyful desperation

and very happy. The pain wouldn't come barging in until the sedative wore off.

After a minute or two, they took Sally away to be cleaned up and Lena to be sewn up. They asked me to wait in a little room by myself, where there was a single bed. They would bring Sally to me as soon as she was ready. When a nurse came in with Sally in a transparent Plexiglas bassinet some minutes later, my first question was how Lena was doing. Everything was going well, the nurse assured me. I would get to see her soon. Then I lay down on the bed next to Sally's bassinet, just looking at that beautiful baby. I felt she was looking at me – *really* looking at me, as if we were bonding. (The experts seem to disagree about the age at which a newborn can make eye contact – most say 6-8 weeks – so I can't know for sure, but I'm certain that any parent capable of a little wishful thinking will know what I *felt*, what I wanted to think I saw.)

During those moments I grew yet another heart, and loved Sally with all of it. My joy was torrential. I desperately hoped that the familial harmony we had during much of 1984 would come back for good. We'd almost had it by the middle of 1979 and on into 1980, but we never quite got to solid ground. Would we make it now? Because of my "heroic" support of her during the operation? Because she would at last understand that my whole life revolved around trying to please her, to thrill her, to love her? Because we now had two children together? I wobbled and vacillated, rising and plunging between hope and despair, between bliss and the void. Then I focused on Sally again and all the joy she was in her own right.

Lena and Sally remained in the hospital for eight days. Lena was in considerable pain after the caesarean – it was major abdominal surgery, after all – and of course Sally needed to remain there with her to be fed. Jenny and I spent some time at the hospital every day. Jenny was wide-eyed to meet her little sister for as long as her two-year-old attention span lasted. As I recall, no other visitors were allowed until Lena was discharged on Saturday, November 16th, and the four of us could be at home together for the first time.

Right from the start, it was clear to me that Jenny and Sally had different personalities. Jenny might have been an energetic teacher, but Sally wasn't always interested in listening. I studied every aspect of Jenny's behavior with unquenchable curiosity and thrilled to every minute of it. Now I not only had Sally's behavior to study as well, I also found the interaction of the two little girls endlessly fascinating. And I knew it would only get exponentially more interesting as Sally grew and became able to communicate and interact.

For quite a few weeks, Sally didn't sleep well. We feared that she might have colic. I spent many a night holding her, rocking her in my arms, taking her downstairs so I could place her in the buggy and drive her back and forth from the kitchen to the living room (over two threshold bumps). I eventually got her to sleep. My second greatest concern was to enable Lena to get enough sleep as well, so as not to exacerbate her already borderline hostile mood towards me.

We gave Sally some drops of an anti-colic medication that was supposed to put an end to her colic, but it didn't help. Nothing helped. We eventually consulted the midwife, who suggested that Lena should try to eliminate certain things from her diet, one by one, in case something was presenting in her breast milk and upsetting Sally's stomach. One of the things on the list was coffee. When Lena tried skipping coffee (on January 2nd), Sally stopped crying – just like that, like switching off a light. I stopped drinking coffee too, out of solidarity.

Leif came by a couple of times in the first half of December. He seemed to have taken a great personal interest in my family, although I sometimes wondered whether his growing dependence on my writing ability might have played a role.

Bob arrived on December 19th and stayed until January 2nd. Lena expressed no objections to his presence in our home. In fact, she'd used her sewing machine to make life a little easier for him. On one of my visits to Binningen, I'd noticed the enormous difficulty Bob had in changing the duvet covers on his bed, so of course I did it for him. But then I thought that if the duvet cover had snap fasteners along one short and one long side (instead of a single opening along one short side), Bob might more easily be able to change them himself when I wasn't around. Lena volunteered to make the alteration. Bob was both thrilled and relieved.

He was fascinated to see little Sally, and thoroughly charmed by Jenny's markedly increased ability to express herself verbally – and bilingually, no less. The demands that two small children were making on my attention and my time were quite noticeable, particularly when Bob wanted to pursue the type of philosophical discussions we'd been having for years, only to be interrupted when Jenny entered the living room to show us something or listen in on the conversation or make sure she was getting all the attention she wanted – and that both Bob and I felt she richly deserved.

As Lena tended to retire shortly after Jenny and Sally went to bed, Bob and I prepared to relaunch our old topics. Unfortunately, I was so tired myself that I found it hard to concentrate. I struggled to keep my eyes open, and had to excuse myself an hour or two later. Bob understood – that was clear – but I could see he was a little disappointed. I had a vague memory that I'd reacted similarly to the early evening drowsiness of some of our acquaintances after they became parents.

Bob still had no suspicion of anything amiss between Lena and me – he was preoccupied with Jenny's development. His discordant discourse with my mom led him to reflect on the indoctrination to which he and I were subjected in our own childhoods, noting with alarm every indication of my mom's designs on Jenny. *"What a pity that children have to learn about complex things in black-and-white terms, and much worse, generally remain fixated at that stage of thinking! [...] Ah, little Jenny and Sally, if only you could know how lucky you are!"*

I got a phone call from Al in the early days of January 1986, telling me that Mom had suffered a stroke while on her annual pilgrimage to visit her sister Maxine in Florida. (Mom was not yet 73 years old.) According to Al's early report, the stroke caused severe tunnel vision and some dizziness. The visit Mom was to have made to Sweden in the spring (accompanied by John's daughter Janet) had already been cancelled.

About a month later, Mom wrote that she had advanced a theory to her doctor that the stroke could have resulted from excessive straining and pushing with her sluggish bowels, which frequently caused her to see stars. The doctor agreed with her, she wrote, *"... so my help must be sought in that direction."* I noted, in a letter to Bob (not to Mom!) that for once she was not seeking help from above, unless she stood on her head.

Bob and I frequently discussed ethics, ethical systems, the foundations for ethical systems, and whether those foundations were defensible or not. People like my mom had no need to worry about such things; "defensible" had no other meaning for her than conformity to the Bible. But the Bible condemns homosexuals in one verse (which my parents followed), and says they must be put to death in another (which my parents didn't follow). Nor did they follow commands to stone their children to death for insolence, and they ignored hundreds of other grounds for execution, such as the capital sin of being a rape victim!! Their confused moral starting point was the result of worshipping one of the most bloodthirsty gods that man has ever invented.

"Ethics" itself is one of those terms few people define in the same way; and people are always especially in danger of talking past each other when they use the same word to mean different things. Some claim ethics concerns all behavior, some claim it only concerns interactions with others. Some claim that "others" is limited to other people, some claim it also covers animals and the environment. My parents took the maximum-sin approach; *"the plowing of the wicked is sin"* (Proverbs 21:4) was a favorite quote. Matthew 5:28 (*"whosoever looketh on a woman to lust after her hath committed adultery with her already in his heart"*) was another. Everybody is guilty. The thought police are coming to get you, you damned worm of the dust!

Our discussions centered on social ethics – interactions within a society. Although the majority of Europeans seemed to have escaped the full force of America's paradoxical greed-is-good, me-first-and-last, Bible-thumping, Reagan-driven 1980s, there were clear signs of a rightward drift throughout Europe as well. Bob and I felt that some form of socialism would inevitably be needed for the sake of justice and the common good. But the term "socialism" is also emotionally charged and means so many different and incompatible things to different and incompatible people (Stalin and Bertrand Russell, to mention a couple of polar opposites). Our starting point was to try to find principles that support individual freedom while preventing exploitation of others; that stimulate individuals to achieve while assuring that the greed of a few will not be to the detriment of the many; that encourage taxpayers to see taxes as rightful and necessary contributions to a just society and not penalties; that healthcare and education must be seen as universal rights and not the sole privileges of the already privileged.

The only societies we found that embraced such ideals were those in Western countries (apart from the US) that identified themselves as democratic socialists or social democrats. We also recognized the disparity between ideals and certain realistic factors: (1) that people are different, have different capabilities, different desires and needs, and different priorities; (2) that people are born into different circumstances, including family status and wealth, different intellectual potential and aptitudes, different talents, different appearances (other things being equal, a physically attractive person will always have an advantage); (3) that people are by nature selfish to some extent, a factor which affects greed, empathy, narcissism and kindness – and thus a factor that must be balanced.

A fair and just political system, it seemed to us, would have to adopt measures to level the playing field – not to make it flat, but to assure that no level differences would be insurmountable to any individual. (We were highly *individualistic* socialists!) Is it OK to be wealthy? Perhaps! – provided that *nobody* needs to be destitute as a result. If identical levels of healthcare and education for *every* member of society are the only levels available, it becomes imperative for the wealthy to assure that those levels will be high, but if people are given the "choice" of public or private medical care or schools, and only the wealthy can afford the better choice, it means the disadvantaged have no choice at all, no fairness, no path forward.

How many conservatives rail against government spending and the burgeoning public sector, and while at the same time clamoring for even more government spending and government employees – provided that the spending in question comes under the headings of "military" and "law and order"?

As far as Bob and I were concerned, the fundamental principle of socialism – *"from each according to his ability, to each according to his need"* – was as beautiful and defensible a moral proposition as the Golden Rule: *"do to others as you would have others do to you."* (Various formulations of The Golden Rule are found in numerous ancient societies and religions. It is not, however, a religious rule, but an appeal to empathy.) In both cases we focused on the principles, not their sources. The socialist principle came from Karl Marx, whose other teachings made me highly skeptical, particularly concerning his presumption that the oppressed and exploited working class (and they were clearly oppressed and exploited pretty much everywhere in Marx's day!) were somehow endowed with an inner altruistic nobility. The hardhats who helped elect Richard Nixon certainly seemed to squelch that theory!

I'd met many top-level executives in my teaching work who sneered (and snarled) at Sweden's Social Democratic Prime Minister Olof Palme, and called him a "caviar socialist" or a "stone-house socialist" because he espoused socialist principles, yet he was born (no choice of his own!) into a wealthy family. A poor person espousing socialism could always be accused of acting solely in self-interest. A rich person espousing anti-socialist principles may also be acting out of self-interest. What about a poor person supporting anti-socialist principles? It seemed clear to me that such a person would have to be duped, ignorant or morally repugnant. The only one indisputably acting out of altruistic motives would have to be the wealthy person supporting socialist principles – someone like Olof Palme. They'd have to be altruistic right out of the gate! Why wasn't this obvious? And admirable?

The treatment of Olof Palme in Sweden's Conservative press was merciless.

He was reviled for stripping the wealthy of their right to opulence, for no other reason than to make life decent for those worst off. He was castigated and caricatured for speaking out against the gross injustice of apartheid in South Africa by people who wanted to do business there despite the horrific treatment of Blacks. Some expressed the view that since Sweden wasn't perfect, then Sweden had no right to express criticism of other countries or regimes for their wrongdoing. I wondered how you'd ever get someone to referee a boxing match if the referee had to be a better boxer than those he was refereeing?! Just because I can't play the piano, I can still hear when a great pianist plays a wrong note!! In any case, the list of Palme's "crimes" against the moral insensitivities of the cream of society was long and growing, and the political rhetoric was increasingly caustic and merciless.

On Saturday, March 1st, 1986, our clock radio went off at the 6 AM news broadcast. I was going to play badminton with Ole at 7 AM, as usual. The news reader sounded unusually agitated. He said something about Olof Palme having been *shot*! He'd been taken to the hospital with what appeared to be mortal wounds. I was almost too bleary-eyed and fuzzy to take in anything of such monumental magnitude. A reporter was out and about at Stockholm's nightclubs, which were closing down for the night that morning. The reporter approached one of the patrons and said, "Olof Palme has been shot, what's your reaction to that?" The half-drunk guy replied "Cool!" (Swedish: "*Schysst*"!) It sickened me.

Ole's reaction was similar to mine. This wasn't real; it *couldn't* be real. We started warming up in the badminton hall, but soon found ourselves sitting on the floor, trying to come to terms with the awfulness of what had happened, trying to hold back or at least control our tears. This was Sweden, one of the world's greatest democracies. Things like that didn't happen, couldn't happen, in Sweden. We cried. We were angry, furious. The disgusting comment of that drunk rang in my ears.

When I got home, Lena was also extremely upset. We cried together. We were sad, outraged, confused, alarmed, distraught, *together*. That afternoon we were scheduled to visit Gunilla and Øivind in Vä. We had mixed feelings about going, knowing that they were (at least at that time) staunchly Conservative – adherents of the phalange of the Swedish political spectrum that fueled the fires of hatred towards Olof Palme. On the car radio, we listened to the flood of news bulletins about the assassination, and we remained teary most of the way to Vä.

When we arrived at our destination, our hosts looked at us and asked what the matter was. "*Haven't you heard the news?!*" we exclaimed. "Oh, that," was all they said, making it pretty clear that we came from different planets. They suggested that we play a game called "Trivial Pursuit" – which in the wake of one of the greatest tragedies in my life became for me a suitably named metaphor for disengagement and superficiality. Perhaps they were also in shock and weren't thinking clearly, but they displayed no grief.

Bob grieved. I grieved. When my brother John wrote to inquire about my response to Palme's death, I replied on March 18th that

> *...for the 3rd time in my life I feel truly personally grieved by the death of another individual [first my dad, then Jeanette]. Apart from the principle of abhorrence of violence in general, or from the ramifications for democracy when an elected leader is assassinated, Olof Palme was a person whose life was devoted to active efforts for peace internationally and for social justice and equality at home. [He was...] in most ways the person who was saying what I would have wanted to say and doing it better than I could have done. Now "my" spokesman on such issues has been silenced. [He was...] a gadfly to the superpowers, an upholder of the rights of smaller nations against the incredible arrogance of the USSR and the USA.*

The longer I lived outside the US (and the less I was under the influence of its self-aggrandizing rhetoric), the more I came to see its multi-level hypocrisy. Claiming to support global "democracy", America ignored the rape and pillage of Cuba by the right-wing dictatorship of Fulgencio Battista for nearly a decade, then slapped a strangling embargo on the country as soon as Castro's left-wing revolution toppled him. The US interfered with and overthrew elected governments all over the world if they were deemed left-wing, but actively supported brutal, anti-democratic tyrannies like Saudi Arabia as long as they were *bona fide* anti-Communists.

During my childhood, the born-again Plymouth Brethren probably fit most Americans' definitions of the lunatic fringe. But by the late 1960s, when I left the country, the fringe was already starting to become mainstream – or the mainstream was moving out towards what had once been the fringe. Although many local gatherings of PBs were reportedly liberalizing slightly (more and more openly owned TVs – how shockingly progressive!), other currents in the US were at work. The 1970s saw soaring popularity for Billy Graham's evangelism, as well as the rise of the Jesus People movement. By the 1980s, some 40% of Americans openly identified themselves as "born again", and the Religious Right was born. More and more Americans claimed to derive their values from the Bible in general and the teachings of Jesus in particular. But unlike the trend in nearly all other Western democracies, the US remained staunchly opposed to universal healthcare and rejected an assured, decent level of care for the elderly – the very issues that Jesus nagged about.

And yet I remained a US citizen, for three main reasons. First, Sweden didn't permit dual citizenship at that time, except for children who by virtue of their parents' respective citizenships were born to it, like Jenny and Sally. (Sweden began allowing acquired dual citizenship in 2001. When George W. Bush invaded Iraq on false pretexts in 2003, I finally acquired Swedish citizenship so that I could at least be proud of one of my citizenships....) Second, there were no clear benefits to changing; my only limitation in Sweden was that I couldn't vote in national elections (but I could and did vote in county and municipal elections). Third, because I'd retained US citizenship, Jenny and Sally had it too, automatically, which gave them a few options they wouldn't otherwise have had. [*Sally lived and worked in New York for five years (2009-2014) and needed no green card or work permit to do so.*]

The two brightest spots in my world were my two little girls – and my quixotic, undying hope for a good and loving relationship with Lena. Jenny became extremely verbose and liked to explain anything and everything. Sally babbled on and on in her most charming way, trying to follow her big sister's lead. With Lena at home on maternity leave, however, the linguistic balance tipped in favor of Swedish, so nearly all Jenny's verbal communication soon switched to her mother's tongue. It was the line of least resistance for her; if she spoke English, many wouldn't understand her, particularly her playmates like Sara and Anna. But if she spoke Swedish, everyone in her daily life understood her, including me. Her comprehension of English, however, remained good.

Having a child shrinks the family car. Our little Daihatsu was pre-shrunk, and every outing with Jenny shrank it further; we now also had a buggy and/or a stroller, a bag of diapers, changes of clothes, and toys. If we spent a night away from home, we usually had to bring a travel crib or bed as well. But somehow we managed to squeeze them all in. The arrival of Sally intensified our need for space without providing a single cubic centimeter more. Somewhere, a couple of years before, I'd seen a few cars with nearly cubicle roof boxes that seemed capable of swallowing a great deal of stuff. Most roof boxes we'd seen were long and sleek, primarily designed for transporting skis, not a baby buggy. Furthermore, such boxes were nearly as long as our Daihatsu and would have been an aerodynamic nightmare.

So I began phoning car-accessory dealers listed in the Yellow Pages, and described the cubicle kind of box I was looking for. Nobody had such a thing. I thought perhaps my description was unclear, so I began visiting them. Some were modest enough to simply say they'd neither seen nor heard of any box that would meet my needs. One particularly arrogant dealer claimed that boxes matching my description didn't exist, despite the fact I'd seen them.

Weeks went by. I began looking into ways to construct something myself, to build a box that could be supported by our roof rack. Then one day I saw a parked car with just the kind of fiberglass box I'd been looking for. I hung around a while for the driver to return, then approached him and asked where he'd found it. He gave me the name of the company he'd bought it from, in Blekinge (the province to the northeast of Skåne). I phoned them. They sent me a leaflet. I bought the box and fit it on our roof rack. Then I drove to the car-accessory dealer who'd most adamantly insisted that the box I'd described absolutely did not exist. I asked him to step to the door where I'd parked. I'm sometimes a persistent jerk like that.

Shortly after my mom's visit to see Jenny in early 1984, my crazy aunt Marion wrote me a long evangelical rant with almost no other content. When I told Bob about it, it brought back to him further details of his mother Edna's illness. She was suffering from severe diabetes in about 1941 or early 1942 and went to stay with Marion in Glendale while undergoing "treatment" at Dr Dreier's homeopathic clinic (where Marion worked and believed in it) for six months. The treatment consisted of a diet of grapefruit, combined with multiple "high colonics" (aggressive laxatives) that would allegedly cure her diabetes. Marion kept Harold, Bob's father, in the dark for six months before sending him a telegram saying that Edna's situation had become desperate. Edna was practically reduced to a skeleton and was nearly comatose.

For once in his life, Harold turned to his 13-year-old son for advice – the only time he ever did so, according to Bob. Being precociously well-read, particularly in matters relating to his mother's health, Bob gave advice that was swift and unambiguous: send a telegram and see that she gets *immediate* insulin treatment;

take the next plane to LA, get her some *real* medical care; then bring her home. Harold did so. Bob met his parents at the Detroit Central Railway Station. His mom weighed about 27 kilos and was unable to stand without support. (Bob loved homeopaths almost as much as he loved astrologers, Bible-thumpers and wife-beaters.) Since his father elected to praise a fictitious Lord rather than his real son for the life-saving advice – and immediately resumed browbeating said son – Bob's furious feud with his father resumed for good. And when I in April 1986 passed along to Bob the news from my mom that Marion had been diagnosed with intestinal cancer (she died in early November that same year), Bob was underwhelmed with grief.

The rest of the spring passed with relatively little domestic conflict. Jenny and Sally were growing and thriving. And I'd learned to live with a baseline of griping from Lena so well that I no longer felt compelled to defend myself against every nasty comment, nor did I take them all to heart. Besides, almost as soon as school was out, we'd be travelling to Sweden's largest island, Gotland, for two weeks, June 14th -28th. Gotland is situated farther out in the Baltic Sea than Öland, and a bit farther north. I was chiefly interested in visiting the small, medieval walled city of Visby (population around 25,000), as well as the rugged island of Fårö, the summer residence of Ingmar Bergman just north of the main island. Bergman used Fårö, known for its rauks, as a shooting location for several of his films.

Fårö was also the site of some of Sweden's secret military bases. Since I lacked Swedish citizenship, I had to apply for special permission to visit Fårö. Together with my permit, they sent me a map on which all of the few places I was *not* allowed to visit were clearly marked. Guess where the "secret" bases were located?

We rented a cottage near the sunbathers' beach in Tofta (the Höllviken of Gotland?) on the west coast of the island. It was not the spot I would have chosen, particularly since the water in the Baltic in the early summer was dauntingly cold, but I had to keep Lena happy, so I hid every trace of objection. We were joined by Charlotte and Kent (Charlotte was also a teacher) who, after a drawn-out process, had adopted a little girl from Columbia. We were also joined for parts of the trip by Ole and Birgitta and their kids, but they were staying in another part of the island, so we didn't see much of them. For this trip we put our new roof-box to its first real test, and it worked well.

When we were at the beach one day, we saw two families arriving, each with a child or two, as well as strollers, wagons, beach toys, picnic hampers, beach towels and robes. The adults were probably in their late 20s or early 30s. They were struggling through the dunes and loose sand towards a level spot where they could put up their parasols. More precisely, the *wives* were struggling to carry and pull *everything*. Their burden-free, musclebound husbands (who were obviously bodybuilders) presumably didn't want to risk any muscular asymmetry that might result from lending a helping hand!

I was greatly impressed with Fårö. I found the long, craggy shorelines serenely beautiful. Perhaps the cragginess was too hostile for most tourists (the rocky shoreline certainly didn't lend itself to sunbathing), and we seemed to be the only ones around. Visby, on the other hand, was full of tourists, but looked to have the capacity to handle them. I was charmed by its narrow, winding, cobblestone streets lined with houses and cottages much older than ours on Korngatan. Every little cottage seemed to be adorned with roses and hollyhocks. We had perfect weather the whole time. Most importantly, the kids had a great time. And Lena had few harsh words for me.

A week after we got home from Gotland, Bob arrived to spend two weeks with us. I happened to have Frigoscandia's video camera on hand to record snippets of Bob as well. The camera had a sound track, but Bob's unexpected shyness in front of a film camera rendered the sound track superfluous, apart from my constant cajoling to get him to speak. Although I tried everything, I could barely elicit a smile, but Jenny had somewhat greater success. He did drop his guard ever so slightly, however, when I asked him to tell me his opinion of Reagan: "*In all respects, very low. He represents one of the worst retrogressive tendencies in the US since Prohibition.*" After that solemn pronouncement, he went silent.

Lena was nearly always all light and smiles – in front of the camera. It frustrated me that it took a camera to make her smile in my direction. Once I even made an on-camera comment: "*You're very photogenic – no one would ever know.*" Only a couple of times did her on-camera irritation with me seep out. She had no interest in including me in the film, so I parked the camera on a table and let it run for a few seconds while I played the clown.

Jenny was a natural actress. Happy as a puppy, she demonstrated her ability to work the cassette player in order to play the audio tape Bob had brought, with American classics like *Jimmy Crack Corn*. Sally babbled away joyfully and tried to crawl, oblivious to the camera. Those were moments to treasure.

Despite our two weeks on Gotland, with plenty of beach visits, Lena said that two weeks with Bob at our place made her feel "imprisoned" in Malmö, and besides, being in town was no place for children in the summer, so why the hell couldn't we have a place in the country too? Although I agreed that it would be "loverly", I pointed out that we simply couldn't afford it. That was not an answer she wanted to hear.

A couple of weeks later we drove up to Barkåkra to visit Marie-Louise. Barkåkra was apparently an acceptable summer venue by Lena's standards (a five-minute drive to the sea), so I began ruminating. Marie-Louise lived there alone. The house was far bigger than she needed it to be, and was quite a burden for her to maintain. But she definitely didn't want to move. She was devoted to her fairly large and beautiful garden, and spent a great deal of her time tending it, from early spring and well into the darkening autumn.

There was an outbuilding with an extra room or two (where Lena and I celibated [*sic*] our wedding night). In my estimation, the whole outbuilding could be insulated rather easily, and inexpensively transformed into a tiny but decent apartment. I was eager to use the skills I'd acquired. I figured out how I could expand Marie-Louise's tiny kitchen, and how I could replace the extremely steep stairway up to her bedroom (or make her a downstairs bedroom!), and make other changes to assure Marie-Louise a comfortable and practical home for the future. She was considerably overweight, which took a severe toll on her knees and other joints. Negotiating that stairway was painful for her, painful to observe, and possibly dangerous. I made a simple, affordable plan that I was certain would thrill Marie-Louise *and* give us a modest separate annex to use as a summer place – a countryside retreat – without encroaching on Marie-Louise's living quarters or privacy. I only got as far as mentioning the possibility to Lena; I had no chance to outline or explain it. She looked at me as if I were crazy, and snapped angrily at me *"Don't be ridiculous!!"* She quashed the idea without considering it. [*Decades later I told Eva of this idea. She said she was shocked that Lena had never mentioned it.*]

Back in Basel, Bob was upgrading his audio-video equipment (with the costly help of his trusted supplier, Hägen). He added a second video player to be able to make copies and edit out commercials and other unwanted material. His collection of videos was growing faster than his vast collection of books, although the books had a head start of several decades. One consequence was a rapidly approaching shortage of available shelf space – *again*. Consequently, I volunteered to spend a week with him in mid-December and build more shelves.

I'd been cooking more and more Chinese-inspired stir-fries using the electric wok Bob sent. More recently, I discovered several authentic Asian food stores near Möllevångstorget in Malmö, where I could find fresh Asian vegetables, peanut oil, Chinese spices and noodles, and many other ingredients I'd long since given up on finding in Sweden. Everyone seemed to enjoy the food and the freshness of vegetables prepared in that way, even though Lena continued to grumble at me for my failure to prepare boiled potatoes.

In the beginning of September, Lena and I replaced our Daihatsu with a later, nearly identical, but slightly more powerful model. The extra power would enable us to make the not-terribly-austere hill at Glumslöv without slowing down on the entire upgrade despite squashing the gas pedal to the floor. We picked it up on September 5th. Jenny was now old and tall enough to sit in the back seat on a special elevated cushion, while Sally took over Jenny's old backward-facing infant seat in the front (airbags were rare in Sweden then).

Sally and sleep were seldom on good terms with each other. She simply didn't need as much sleep as Jenny or most other children. She often remained awake till midnight, then slept for about four hours before obliging us to face a new day. I tried to take care of her at both ends as often as possible, to enable Lena to get enough sleep. Although I was chronically sleepy, Sally was a fantastic kid, full of piss and vinegar, cuter than most things anyone was likely to see in a lifetime.

Jenny loved to sit in the swing in the corridor between the kitchen and the back door, where we could see each other while I prepared our next meal. To entertain us both, I sometimes made up songs, which she learned quickly and sang lustily, for example *"Jenny knows where Jenny's nose is / Where's Jenny's nose? Jenny knows!"* With minimal interruption to my cooking, I could keep her swinging as high and for as long as she liked.

In addition to my load of translations and copyediting (with a little copywriting occasionally thrown in), I was teaching five days a week to make up for all the time I'd taken off during the summer and the free time I wanted to have in the fall and beyond, when Lena would return to work in January. Mom arrived on September 23rd for a 10-day visit, the first since her stroke (less than two years earlier). After much persuasion, she agreed to let herself be assisted by the airline staff all the way from the Seattle airport (Al picked her up at her home and brought her there) to the hovercraft terminal in Malmö. I met her there and conducted her safely to our home. I was saddened by her near-blindness, but if she wasn't going to let it get her down, I certainly wouldn't either.

Bob couldn't grasp how Mom and I could enjoy each other's company so much. My brothers also seemed baffled. So was I. A prerequisite for that enjoyment, I believe, was my refusal to cave whenever she attempted to exert psychological blackmail: her ostentatious and histrionic displays of distress when my behavior crossed her narrowly defined boundaries. (She clearly feigned the exaggerated aspects of her displays.) Since her boundaries were so narrowly defined and mine were not, she would have had to display distress nearly all the time – far too arduous a task even for her. Perhaps it came as a relief to her, when it quickly became obvious that her manipulative distress was not going to be legal tender in our relationship. She realized that she *could* let it go, focus on her *other*, fun-loving self, and enjoy the show that Jenny and Sally put on every waking minute. I sometimes wondered whether she didn't use her stroke-related blindness to achieve "selective vision", to see only what she wanted to see and nothing else. (This "selective perception" would soon apply to her hearing as well....)

Although Sally immediately warmed to her American grandma, at just over 10 months old, Sally was of course still pre-lingual. Jenny ran into a brick wall of incomprehension when she realized that Grandma didn't understand a word of Swedish. But halfway through Mom's visit, Jenny temporarily regained her bilingualism.

On the second day of Mom's visit, Jenny put on *Jimmy Crack Corn* – now one of her favorite new audio tapes (from Bob). Mom and I sat on the sofa while Jenny gleefully danced around the living-room floor and Sally bounced up and down to the music, grinning broadly. (Sally wouldn't take her first steps until a few days before her first birthday.) Mom seemed vaguely familiar with most of the songs on the tape, but both she and I had forgotten the lyrics. When the song came to the line *"the devil take the bluetail fly!"*, Mom shot up from her seat, almost in panic, eyes blazing, and *ordered* Jenny to put on something else, but Jenny wasn't having it. Since I clearly had no problem with the lyrics, Mom left the room hurriedly, ostensibly to visit the bathroom. She didn't return for a while. But she didn't react overtly the next time Jenny played that tape. (Was audio selectivity already setting in?)

On a couple of occasions during her stay, Mom and I found ourselves alone together for as much as half an hour. I think we were both eager to make use of those occasions for serious conversation, though not necessarily on the same topics or for the same reasons. On one such occasion, she began sighing and fixing her bun, always a telltale sign of strong disapproval. My brothers and I knew it well from early childhood. So, presumably, did Dad.

I knowingly took the bait; I confronted her. I asked her point-blank to tell me what was bothering her. She feigned innocence, but I persisted. She admitted that her disapproval stemmed from concerns about my kids' "spiritual welfare". My facial expression seemed to tell her that this was not a path she would want to pursue. She changed the subject, as was her wont in such circumstances, so abruptly that you'd wonder whether there were some minutes missing in the tape. She told me that this or that Meeting person (whose name I vaguely recognized and whom I might have met briefly when I was a small boy) told her to be sure to send me their "love".

"*Do these people love you, Mom?*" I asked her. She was certain of it, she replied firmly, defiantly, yet with a note of hesitation, as well as some confusion about how on earth I could even ask such a question. I continued: "*And would they still love you if you told them you'd become a Jehovah's Witness or a Mormon or a Muslim?*" After thinking for a brief moment, she reluctantly replied that they probably would not. I pursued the matter further: "*Isn't it more likely that they wouldn't even speak to you again and certainly never visit you or have you over again?*" She didn't need to reflect more than a second before admitting that that would be the case. I put a hypothesis before her: "*And isn't that because they don't love you – they only need to surround themselves with people who believe the same things?!*" She nodded, stunned, almost shamefully. Then I let her have my conclusion as to how this applied to our relationship: "*Well, I love you for who you are, not what you believe, and I wish you'd do the same for me!*" She started, stung by the truth of what I'd said. Then we had a long and heartfelt hug.

I asked her to describe her stroke-altered vision in detail. It seemed to have left her with only small *patches* of vision, no contiguous *field*, which made her insecure about walking. She'd been a surprisingly vigorous and energetic walker; most people half her age might have had difficulty keeping her pace once she turned on the turbocharger. But now, unable to look both forward and downward simultaneously, she risked tripping over something or running into something or both. But when I gave her my arm, she quickly learned to trust my guidance, and she could still take off.

It seemed important to her to have made the trip, not only to visit us, but also to prove to herself (and others!) that a mere stroke wasn't going to stop her. Seeing us (and Sally for the first time) was part of it. But she also needed to feel and demonstrate that she wasn't ready to be confined to quarters just yet. Her "good side" had a knight in shining armor of its own! We had lots of laughs, and we told lots of anecdotes about my kids, about me and my brothers as kids, and about her own childhood. (If she noticed that the wind-up music box in the stuffed lamb she brought when Jenny was an infant didn't work, she didn't ask why.) I cannot claim to *know* that there was a causal relationship between my confrontation with her early in her stay and the very loving and harmonious ambiance we enjoyed for the duration of her stay after that confrontation. Could it really be no more than a coincidence?

The week after Mom returned to the US, Perstorp at last supplied me a precursor to a PC, an old word processor called Bitsy (Stig Troell had just acquired a full-blown PC for himself). On Friday, October 10th, an instructor came to Korngatan to show me how to use it. I could type about two full pages before having to change floppy discs. Using a long series of commands, I could remove a text from one place and insert it in another place (provided it was on the same disc!), add words, remove words, copy words and adjust margins. I could also remove the disc for one unfinished document in order to work on another, then go back to the first one. Each such step required numerous not-terribly-intuitive commands, but it still saved time.

My favorable impression of Bitsy was undoubtedly enhanced by my instructor, an exceptionally lovely, down-to-earth young lady with the less-than-lovely-sounding name of Bodil. I managed to channel all her charm into an incentive to learn (and impress her by learning) rather than charming her back. It wasn't easy, especially since her pleasantness towards me was so refreshing compared to the absence of pleasantness I was struggling to get used to from the woman I loved on my domestic scene. On October 15th, I wrote my first-ever letter on Bitsy, to Bob.

On December 14th I flew to Basel (via Zürich) and spent a day helping him reestablish order in his apartment. Then I spent the rest of the week building him yet another set of shelves to house acquisitions since my last visit: a few hundred more books, an equal number of videos, and a new photocopier. I got rid of the stacks of mostly unread newspapers and advertisements, sorted out the mail that needed his attention (including a few unpaid bills) and discarded the rest, cleaned his kitchen and bathroom, and gave the whole place a thorough vacuuming. He was delighted; it picked up his spirits noticeably.

It had occurred to me that each time I got his home in order and built him more shelf space, I was also giving him an incentive to buy more books. While that might have been true, or at least demonstrably had that result, Bob was never one who acquired books for the sake of acquisition; he read them all. He simply had time to read so many more now that he was retired. He put aside those that disappointed him, or those from which he felt he'd gleaned all that was of value or interest to him. Those he particularly enjoyed he devoured, several times.

He told me of a few recent episodes when his legs failed him and he nearly fell. It was a new phenomenon for him to realize that his legs simply might not obey the commands his brain was trying to send to them. I asked him if he felt safe driving. He wasn't yet prepared to hear such a question. He dismissed it, saying he felt safe enough. I said I wasn't thinking only of *his* safety. He started, his jaw dropped slightly, and he said he would take the matter up with his neurologist at his next appointment. I was aware of the enormity of the symbolic milestone of no longer being able to drive: the loss of the *feeling* of independence. But I was also aware how devastated he would be if his right foot couldn't make the transfer from the gas pedal to the brake in time to stop in front of a child dashing across the street in front of him.

As planned, Bob and I returned to Malmö together, one of many such journeys we made. My ability to find our way at airports in seconds saved him many long and stressful minutes. I carried easily whatever cabin bags we needed, freeing both of his hands for balance. And we had each other's company to exchange observations or explore theories about the universe or the layout of concourses, the bargains on single malts and other liquor, or the bane of religion.

As soon as we entered the front door and the kids spotted him, they ran gushing to see him. A warm and loving sense of belonging enveloped him. His brow unwrinkled. His eyes twinkled. A broad, natural smile that would not be denied covered his face as he settled into his favorite corner of the living room sofa, with Jenny and Sally scurrying to curl up in his lap.

He expressed his gratitude for my help with his apartment by buying us a video cassette player/recorder. He also had designs on supplying us with a collection of pre-recorded video cassettes – especially targeting Jenny and Sally. On returning to Binningen after the two weeks, Bob wrote:

> *The development of your charming girls is a thing that would soften the heart of anyone capable of the experience. To think that they are being raised to be themselves and not somebody's notion of what they should be provides me with a deep sense of satisfaction.*

CHAPTER 8

Delamination

Our lives slipped into a new phase when Lena returned to work on January 7th, 1987, the day Bob returned to Binningen. It was three days before Jenny's third birthday. Lena had a new and somewhat better-paying job at a new school (Heleneholmskolan), located on the same street where she and Larry once lived as neighbors with Björn and Isobel, as well as with Dave and Christina. She was still teaching special-needs children, now with somewhat older pupils. She also had new colleagues, of course....

To limit our need for a sitter to half a day per week, I again reduced my working hours to 50% (20 hours a week) and had a maximum of two pupils a week, plus text work. I spent the rest of the time with Jenny and Sally (just 14 months, but walking and running like a champ). We played games and read stories. I made them lunch and took them for walks and drives. We turned grocery shopping in Burlöv into a delightful adventure, and went swimming at the nearby municipal indoor pool, which also had a warm, shallow children's pool. Jenny was already learning to swim and Sally was eager to keep up with her big sister. A couple of times a week I took them to an "open pre-school", more to appease Lena than to please the kids. I had dinner nearly ready when Lena got home.

Whenever the kids were occupied with their own play projects (or when they took a nap), I worked with texts – translating, editing or copywriting. When Lena and I went to bed, I dealt with my now-customary rejection by getting up after she'd gone to sleep and working for a few more hours in my office downstairs in the little house. Thanks to our intercom, I could stay alert in case Sally woke up and needed attention. In such cases, I hurried across to see to her, usually before Lena was awakened. Sally was now allowing us a full night's sleep about two nights out of three. I was very efficient at my work; my most limiting factor was that I typed slowly [*and still do*].

I continued to play badminton, usually three or four 1-hour sessions a week, two of which (one in Malmö, the other in Staffanstorp) were on weekday evenings after I'd helped put the kids to bed. The other one or two sessions were with my pupils. (I didn't *refuse* pupils who didn't want to play badminton, but....) The results were fantastic. My lung function was now *above 90%* of the norm (having been below 40% just three years before)! I'd been able to reduce my need for medication to a single puff from a single inhalator every morning and every evening – and no pills at all. Physically, I felt great.

I don't recall exactly how or when I met Hans and Ove, two badminton-playing friends of Jan and Eva (they were also Jan's golf partners). It must have been at a party. They were tall and slender, and both played badminton with a group of others every Wednesday at 8 PM at a hall in Staffanstorp, a 15-minute drive from Kirseberg. They invited me to join them, and I readily accepted. (My Saturday morning badminton with Ole had pretty much come to an end by this time, as his interest waned.) I enjoyed the sport tremendously, and Lena seemed to welcome having me out of the house once the kids' needs had been seen to.

Ove was a math teacher at Pauliskolan, a high school in Malmö. He was from Göteborg, Sweden's second largest city, known in Sweden as the place where even Swedish people enjoy hearing and creating puns. (What would life have been like if Jeanette and I had settled there instead?) He was seven years older than me and wiry, with sad, kind eyes. Hans was a pleasant person, a city planner from northern Sweden, now working in Lund, who frequently looked astonished (whether he was or not). He worked in Lund and had two small girls close to Jenny's and Sally's ages. He was plodding and methodical, like the nature of his work. I wondered whether that was why he'd chosen to become a city planner. He didn't tell many jokes, but greatly appreciated hearing them.

Bob's platonic relationship with Carmen finally hit the rocks. One of the triggers was a huge fire at Schweizerhalle, the main Basel warehouse belonging to Sandoz, a Swiss pharmaceutical giant just upstream from Roche. The fire led to an enormous spillage of chemicals into the Rhine, one of Europe's major fluvial arteries. Most of the eels and other fish for a long stretch downstream were killed. The incident grabbed headlines and fueled environmental debates everywhere. It took place on November 1st, 1986 and had become a hot topic for Bob and Carmen by early December. Bob was disgusted by the company's efforts to evade responsibility; Carmen defended it, and seemed to feel that her late husband (a colleague of Bob's, and former executive at Roche – a Sandoz competitor) was thereby also under indirect attack from Bob.

According to Bob, Carmen felt entitled to be "hurt" by his attack on Sandoz. She wrote him a letter to that effect. Bob replied that he in no way intended to hurt her, but if their continued relationship was to be characterized by his not being allowed to express his views, while she was free to express hers (*now where had I experienced that before?!*), then it would be best for them to take an indefinite hiatus in their meetings and correspondence.

Then Carmen began writing to *me* about the situation – long, handwritten (and difficult-to-decipher) letters – and I found myself thrust into the unwelcome and ill-suited role of diplomat. I did my best to encourage Bob to let reason temper his emotions, and not to draw hasty conclusions about Carmen's motives or put words into her mouth. I tried to convince Carmen that a little cooling off or cooling down might benefit them both, but little rationality was in evidence on either side. I think Bob was simply weary of playing a role he neither enjoyed nor was good at. As he put it, "What kind of friendship is it which breaks when one party speaks his mind?" I had no trouble understanding exactly what he meant.

Despite having called for a hiatus, Bob soon wrote her again and they continued to cross postal sabers for months. And I continued writing to them both. (Bob sent me copies of his letters to her and hers to him; I sent him copies of hers to me and mine to her. Phew!) To Carmen, I wrote as little as possible about Bob; instead, I focused on general friendliness, and promised to continue our correspondence for as long as she wished, and to regard her as a friend. They both seemed to miss each other's company for reasons none of us quite understood.

Now that we had a video player, Bob ordered some videos he thought the kids might already be old enough to enjoy, even though Sally was just over a year and her linguistic development was literally in its infancy. The first two videos were a highly entertaining cartoon version of *Wind in the Willows* and a recording of the operetta *H.M.S. Pinafore* by Gilbert and Sullivan, performed by Bob's beloved British D'Oyly Carte Opera Company. Jenny found them *both* delightful (her enjoyment of the operetta surprised me). Sally, eagerly following her big sister's lead, watched them raptly, long before she had a clue what they were about.

Bob was pleased (and also surprised about their response to Gilbert & Sullivan – who'd been among his favorites since high school). He promised to send more. I was happy that the kids were being exposed to – and clearly enjoying! – classic stories as well as the music. I was doubly glad for the expansion of their interface with the English language beyond myself. I felt certain that exposure to multiple voices (and accents) would enhance their comprehension, vocabulary, and the value of eventually being able to express themselves easily and well in two languages.

At this point (before Sally had learned to say "b"), as soon as she saw Bob in a photo she'd squeal "*Op!!*" I'd been teaching her to recognize and make various animal noises – cows, dogs, sheep, horses, lions, elephants, chimps, crows, and many others – which she did with great pleasure. Then we came to fish. What the hell do fish say? They don't say *anything*, they live underwater! So I made something up, a kind of lapping, gargling noise. Then, when I asked her what a fish said, she gleefully burst out, "pladdle, laddle laddle" and squealed heartily with delight. I nearly collapsed with laughter every time.

Jenny could count to 10 in Swedish and to 12 in English. One day I heard a thump from the next room and called out to see what had happened. She came running to me and said, in English, "*I fell off the stool and hit my buns!*" We both roared. Her vocabulary was growing daily, and her enunciation was clear and endearing.

Bob also sent me highlights from college football games he'd recorded on video cassettes for my benefit (he now had access to Sky Channel as well). American football was one of the few things I missed since moving to Sweden, and now I had a reintroduction. I hardly noticed that I was only seeing the highlights. Many years later, during a trip to the US, I watched a full game at my brother's home while they were at some sort of church function. I couldn't believe how boring unabridged American football felt to me. It seemed like constant commercials and huddles, with an occasional burst of action lasting no more than a few seconds.

From the time Lena moved in with me at Korngatan in 1979, she'd co-signed my letters to Bob, and all of his were addressed to both of us ("Dear Stanley and Lena"). Only rarely did Lena add a note, but nearly all of those came in the first three years ('79-'81). At the end of his letter to me/us of February 28th, 1987, Bob wrote, "*And to you Ms L, thanks for the co-signature; please send me a dissent from time to time if you think it indicated!*" I have no memory that Lena and I ever spoke of that comment, but she immediately stopped co-signing my letters to him. [*I discovered this remarkable fact only on reviewing my correspondence with Bob while writing this book!*] Was that merely a coincidence or did she interpret Bob's comment as criticism instead of a request or an invitation? Nevertheless he continued addressing his letters to both of us even after she bowed out.

Lena said she enjoyed her new job. She seemed obsessed with getting her pre-pregnancy figure back and took various food replacement concoctions to speed up the process. She also started taking greater care with her make-up and grooming prior to leaving for work. I was relieved that she was starting fewer fights, although she showed me no affection either, and was more scornful. Those factors seemed strangely at odds with each other somehow, but I tended it. She was always pissed off with me for analyzing too much anyway. I tried not to dwell on it, but it was getting to me, bringing me down, making me veer towards depression. The intense joy of Jenny and Sally was my shield, or antidote, or analgesic.

Sally was becoming more and more verbal every day, and even though she nearly always spoke Swedish with me, I persisted in speaking only English to her and got her to repeat new English words after me. Once, when we were driving to Lund, I pointed out the same windmill I'd pointed out to Jenny a couple of years earlier (which Jenny called "veem-low" even though she could say both "wind" and "mill" separately). "*Can you say 'windmill', Sally?*" She grinned back at me cheerfully and said "*oh-noy*"! At first, I thought she might have been trying to say "*Oh, no!*", so I repeated it, with the same result. Then I asked her to say *wind*, which she did effortlessly. Then *mill*. No problem. Then *windmill*? "*Oh-noy!*" It gave me a hearty laugh every time.

When Jenny and Sally outgrew the young toddler swing in the kitchen corridor, I put up a new swing upstairs in my former studio, where they could swing to their hearts' content. My heart wasn't always content, however; they could be pretty fearless – especially Sally – standing, swinging upside-down with her legs wrapped around the ropes, or swinging so high that she almost hit her head on the ceiling.

School let out on June 5th and we went to Gotland again – to the same cottage near the beach in Tofta – for two weeks, with Charlotte and Kent and their little girl Clara. We didn't go to Fårö this time. I was the only eager one last time, so I didn't bother to apply for the permit that only I needed.

A few days after our arrival, Jenny and Sally developed chicken pox. The damn pox were all over their poor little bodies: front and back, top and bottom, close to their eyes and ears, and they itched like hell. We covered them with lotion and felt awful for them, but they remained surprisingly good-natured.

Lena told me that one of her new colleagues, a guy named Johannes, was also spending his vacation on Gotland during our time there. She kept phoning him to persuade him to come to see us (her) in Tofta. He was visiting his two aunts who owned a cottage somewhere in the middle of the island, in the middle of nowhere. It was clearly important to Lena that they should meet up, so during our second week, when he still couldn't come to Tofta, we *had* to look him up. I was puzzled about the urgency; the kids were still battling their chicken pox, even though they were receding. The excursion took (wasted) the better part of a day. It was extremely boring for everyone else. But Lena insisted on seeing him. And I had to drive, because Lena couldn't find the way on her own, which meant that Jenny and Sally had to tag along.

I found the way. We entered a charming little old traditional cottage with two little old traditional ladies and a little man in his mid-forties, a few years older than me. We sat there in a formal parlor filled with lace and brocade and fussy china. They served coffee (juice for the kids) and an assortment of seven cakes and cookies as dictated by Swedish tradition. Johannes sat there staring at Lena the whole time. She was glowing with charm. I was invisible to everyone but Jenny and Sally. The aunts tried to make some ado about the kids, who were restless and wondering – like me – what the hell we were doing there. I don't remember how long we stayed. To me and the kids it felt like hours. To Lena, perhaps a few minutes. And then we left. Nothing further was said about that bizarre excursion.

I don't remember much else about our trip to Gotland that year. I associated it with suffering – perhaps from more than the kids' chicken pox. Charlotte and Kent seemed strangely embarrassed (for my sake?) and avoided conversation beyond the mundane. I longed to get back home, to be somewhere else and to feel something real, such as love. Lena was there in the same cottage, but it didn't feel like she was there *with me*.

We got home from Gotland on June 28th. Bob arrived at our place on July 7th for a 12-day stay. I was, as always, delighted to see him. But everything felt surreal, as if I weren't present, as if I were seeing myself, my aspirations, my years of longing, my frustration and desperation rising up against me like a tidal wave I'd discovered far too late to escape. I felt panic and paralysis, rage and apathy, inadequacy and fear and depression, all at the same time. I'd been given a bad cocktail to drink, one that consisted of the most incompatible and unpalatable ingredients imaginable. I couldn't deal with it. I didn't even want to try, didn't dare to try. I was under water, struggling to hold my breath long enough for all the bad to go away.

And yet I kept my mask in place for Bob's visit – a visit that gave him three days with John and Marj at the tail end. In a typical gesture of his unbounded generosity, in the early part of his time with us, Bob took me on a shopping trip to buy us a video camera with which to *"keep me supplied with the nearly unbelievable developments of these two remarkable little girls."* How like him to disguise his selfless generosity as selfish motives!

John and Marj arrived on July 16th, their first trip to Europe since 1977, ten years earlier. How different my life had become in one decade – almost unrecognizable in many ways, yet far too recognizable in some! Then I was in deep despair and grief, and alone; now I was on the edge of despair in my marriage, yet paradoxically overjoyed with my darling kids. I was a walking contradiction, teetering on a crumbling rock on the edge of a monstrous waterfall, trying desperately to enjoy the view.

My big brother and his wife stayed for two weeks (including a side trip they made to Stockholm for a few days). After Bob's departure, we took a day-trip to Barkåkra and Båstad. I recall several other incidents and events with crystal clarity (largely thanks to having documented them at the time in letters to Bob and in my own notes). They'd never met Lena before (nor Jenny and Sally, of course), so they responded to her façade, having nothing to compare it with. John wanted to take a couple of family pictures. In one of them he asked the kids, Lena, and me to wear the identical (except for size), bright blue T-shirts they'd brought for us, with our respective names printed on them. I realized that the staging of those photos gave me the only two hugs I got from Lena all year. Who could have known that her staging would go that far?

After Bob's departure, John and Marj wanted to look around the center of Malmö one day. Lena wanted me to take the kids along – there wouldn't be room in the little Daihatsu for all of us, and she needed to take care of some things.... It was a warm, sunny day. During the five-minute drive to the center of Malmö, both Jenny and Sally fell asleep in the back seat with Marj. When we got to Gustav Adolf's Torg, I aimed for a small parking lot opposite the new Burger King restaurant in the southeast corner of the square. [*That parking lot no longer exists.*] There were around 10 parking spaces on either side of the lot, which had a single entrance/exit. I was very fortunate to get the one remaining free space. Since Jenny and Sally were already asleep, I suggested that John and Marj might like to wander off on their own, and I got out of the car to point them in the direction of Södergatan, which would lead them past lots of shops and a few beautiful old buildings along the two blocks towards Stortorget.

I waited by the car with the kids. I rolled down the windows for fresh air and stood outside, leaning against the car, enjoying the warm sunshine. I was glad I brought my sunglasses. After some minutes, a car drove up to the parking lot entrance/exit and stopped. The woman behind the wheel looked at me and gestured to ask whether I was about to leave. I shook my head. She turned off her engine and sat there waiting.

A few minutes later, a man and woman approached the parking lot on foot from the opposite direction. They got into one of the parked cars and started the engine. The patient lady in her car at the entrance started hers. As the couple backed out from their space, the lady inched forward. Just as she was about to pull into the freshly vacated space, another car swooped past her, taking the space instead, and two defiant-looking young men jumped out grinning. The lady protested valiantly that she'd been waiting for that space. They laughed scornfully at her and said that she'd have to be quicker next time. Then they began walking off.

The extremely rude behavior of those two guys made my blood boil. I quickly ascertained that they didn't know which car, if any, was mine. Before they could turn away, I took a couple of steps out to the middle of the parking lot, glaring at them. "*She was waiting for that space!*" I projected my voice just below a yell. "*We don't give a damn,*" they sneered, "*we got there first!*" I stiffened, threw out my chest and glared menacingly, then started sauntering slowly over in their direction, seething. I was absolutely furious. They were sizing me up. My adrenalin was pumping. "*Do you really think,*" I snarled with as much intimidation as I could muster from behind my sunglasses, "*that you'll have any windshield wipers or rearview mirrors left when you get back?!*"

It wasn't a bit like me to behave like that. But the two punks froze, turned pale, jumped back into their car and tore off without a word. The lady got her parking space and thanked me profusely. It felt so goddamn good!! [*Years later, I saw a movie called* Fried Green Tomatoes *in which a similar parking-lot confrontation takes place. Even though my confrontation lacked the movie's destructive elements, I knew the feeling exactly!*]

Since Bob's overlap with John and Marj came at the end of his visit, and since John and Marj were initially pretty jet-lagged, Bob and I had time to discuss in the late evening what we had discussed with them during the day. Bob was fascinated with John's buffet-style criteria for selecting a religious denomination ("eternal security" was the deal-breaker). I pointed out that it was the most natural thing in the world to seek a religious affiliation that met one's personal emotional needs. Bob carried the metaphor further: "*Since multiple gods offer themselves to my worship, I'll take the one who offers me the best terms. In the phrases of an auto salesman: no down payment, no interest on the loan, free accessories like a perfume distributor in the cooling, etc.*" I added that before signing up, John might perhaps have checked to be sure the church of his choice included a heaven with the best wine cellar!

On returning to Binningen from his whirlwind tour of Malmö (every trip to Korngatan was now a whirlwind of perceptions since the arrival of Jenny and Sally), Bob had time to think about his own deteriorating condition. He wrote, on July 24th, that he was painfully conscious of the growing difficulty he had to project his voice. He was acutely aware of rapidly increasing absent-mindedness, forgetfulness, and loss of cognition. He also recognized that his Parkinson's made him less able to control his emotions. Empathy often led to uncontrollable weeping – not a bad reason, but Bob felt it was socially awkward. I asked him to specify why he cared about impressing people he didn't care about. He stared at me for a moment, then grinned and shook his head. He thought maybe the time had come to cease resistance to taking the next and more powerful level of drugs – "the hard stuff" (Madopar) – to deal with the symptoms of Parkinson's.

Many people of retirement age or beyond complain of memory loss – and seem to make themselves the worse for it – a self-fulfilling prophecy. I had a theory about age-related memory loss that perhaps applied to Parkinson's as well, which I outlined in a letter to him of August 3rd:

When I read your accounts of forgetfulness, I could have been reading about myself. Qualitatively, there's not much difference. I can go up to the local supermarket for the sole purpose of buying a loaf of bread and return home with several items – but no bread. Maybe you do that kind of thing more often than I do, but then the difference is quantitative. While Parkinson's may well aggravate some of these things, from your perspective you may have a tendency to render unto Parkinson's that which could also be explained by:

- *being over 40*
- *no longer living under the discipline and structure of a full-time job*
- *being human.*

Of course Parkinson's was making him feel down. I was trying to get him not to make it worse by attributing more to it than it "deserved".

I also gave Bob an account of the only "serious" discussion John and I had during the latter part of their visit. Since I knew of John's aversion to discussing religion with me, I avoided all controversy in our conversations, with the result that our discourse, although friendly, remained largely superficial. One evening, however, after everyone else had gone to bed and I'd poured a small whisky for us, John asked if there was anything at all I felt we ought to talk about. I said I couldn't understand why for years he sent me books by Francis Schaeffer, C.S. Lewis, and other Christian apologists for me to comment on, then ignored my responses – my detailed criticism of the works I read at his behest.

He replied that he felt unable to match me intellectually and therefore felt disqualified from debating me on such subjects. But he was curious about my views on a few things. How could I *not* believe in a life after death when I had two such darling little girls? In reply, I pointed out the *non sequitur* of his question ("Do you walk to school or carry your lunch?"). He took this with a shy, muffled giggle. I said I tried to avoid believing things without a reason for doing so – and that I couldn't see that wishful thinking constitutes a *valid* reason. And since I could see *no* valid reason for believing in life after death, I considered it a human invention to resolve several insoluble or uncomfortable issues:

1. Nobody wants to believe that someone as fabulous as him- or herself "just disappears" upon death. Since it's impossible to prove that there is <u>no</u> life after death (most negatives can't be proven), many are comfortable believing there is.

2. The egocentricity of this belief shows up in the extensions from the self, whether in relationship or time. "Reuniting" with loved ones? Very attractive. With friends and acquaintances? Very nice. With distant relatives? Possibly interesting. With total strangers? Uh.... And what about pets? Nasty snakes, spiders, pathogenic bacteria, each with a life after death!?

3. We have a hard time accepting injustice, especially if things are not put right "in the end". We need to think that villains who torment others while enjoying a life of prosperity will be punished in the end, and that good people who've suffered unrelentingly all their lives will be rewarded.

4. *As humans, we continually ask questions we cannot answer, but we find it unacceptable that there might not be answers (at least not in our lifetimes). A "god" who has those answers solves the problem for some people, even if that same god chooses not to tell us what the answers are (or we don't like His answers).*

Yes, I admitted, those can be seen as reasons for believing in life after death, but they're not *good* reasons – they're based on wishful thinking, not evidence. John seemed unsettled by this, and wanted to change the subject; I suggested that we could agree to disagree.

Within an hour of John and Marj's departure on July 30th, Lena, I and the kids packed ourselves into the car and drove to Oslo to spend a few days with Jan and Grete and their boys. Then we had a week at home before spending a week at a rented cottage in Torekov, together with Øivind and Gunilla and their kids. I wouldn't have minded being at home for a change, but Lena frequently pointed out that "home" for her was *never* going to be Korngatan; it would always be the vicarage in Barkåkra where she grew up, next door to where Marie-Louise now lived.

She claimed that our home on Korngatan wasn't "ours" because it was part of *my* history, not hers. But the vicarage had never been hers either, nor her father's. As soon as he retired, he and Marie-Louise were obliged to leave it. And what about people who live in ancestral homes, manors, etc? What was the difference? There were steps in her logic I just couldn't see.

When others were present during our week in Torekov, Lena wore a friendly mask even in my presence, such that I felt the underlying chill to my marrow whenever we were alone. It was pure anguish for me. I focused on the kids, desperately crafting a mask of my own.

I think Lena's mask of pleasantness towards me might have slipped enough for Øivind and Gunilla to notice it that week. Moreover, my sexual frustration was becoming unbearable. Øivind hinted at similar marital problems himself. The surroundings in Torekov were pleasant and picturesque. We all visited beautiful gardens in Norrviken, and the kids were thrilled by a large flock of flamingos ("fingos" is what Sally called them). The four kids had great fun together. But nothing seemed to matter; Lena was somewhere else. The only warmth (apart from the kids) was meteorological.

The day after we got home from Torekov (August 17th), Lena's fall term began. She seemed enthusiastic about getting back to work, to my unreflective surprise. But her attitude towards me immediately became gruffer, harsher and more hostile than ever. As usual, I excused her by attributing this to the stress and strain of starting a new semester and frustration about the end of summer. And yet, in light of her obvious eagerness to resume work, I couldn't fully convince myself at all this time. I was trying desperately to squelch my imagination. My biggest problem was that every direction I tried to take to move forward seemed to lead to the abyss.

Bob was experiencing severe adverse reactions to Madopar. His legs turned to lead. Akinesia set in. When he was with us that summer, he could no longer tilt his neck and head back far enough to finish a glass of wine or orange juice. (I offered him a straw, which he accepted for the juice but declined for the wine.) He seemed confused and not a little frightened. After consulting his neurologist in Switzerland, he stopped taking Madopar and reverted to his former medication instead. Relief was almost instantaneous.

Once Lena's fall term began, I cared for the kids on my own except when Lena was off work, and for the few hours a week when they were with Barbro, their sitter. I got back into my routines – a couple of pupils a week, and badminton about three hours a week – at the same time.

Throughout my childhood, Al coached me to be highly competitive. Nearly everything we did instantly became a contest or a race. American society also encouraged a win-or-die attitude (cf. "Show me a good loser and I'll show you a loser," attributed to Vince Lombardi, coach of the Green Bay Packers, and a favorite quote of Nixon's). As I grew older, I frequently observed another side of win-or-die: cheating and ruthlessness, athletes using everything from banned drugs to brutality in order to be first, to get the gold. I felt that competitiveness threatened to turn me into a person even I wouldn't like. Although the vigorous exercise I got from badminton improved my lung capacity greatly, and although I always played to win and liked doing so, I had to work hard to learn not to be disappointed about losing, provided I played *my* best, or at least as well as my health permitted (many of the guys I played with were considerably better than me). Playing well came first, winning was the occasional bonus for doing so.

I have similar feelings about debates; they *should* be worthwhile efforts to find out what's true, not pointless contests to win. Being right is *un*important, but trying to find out what's right, what's factual, *is* important. After all, most knowledge gains come through mistakes. [*A relative of mine once told me he'd gladly take any side of any issue and argue it to win. Such a view disgusts me. I see it as devoid of sincerity and integrity. When it occurs in courts of law it makes me sick, for example when a prosecutor's only concern is winning the case, not in finding the real culprit. When it occurs in politics, I want to puke, for example when politicians lie viciously only to pad their power; this practice has by no means ended as I write!*]

Many people equate criticism of an ideology or belief with criticism of the person or persons holding it. For example, many scream "anti-Semitism!" in response to harsh criticism of Israel for its outright theft of Palestinian territory and inhumane treatment of Palestinians – and instead blame Palestinians for fighting back (?!). In the same way, many Muslims equate criticism of Islam with criticism of Muslim people, and scream "Islamophobic!" or even "Racist!" One thing should be perfectly clear: a religion (or any other ideology) is *not a race*! Your race is in your genes, religions and ideologies are not. (Another detail in this particular feud that some people seem to enjoy forgetting: the word "semite" refers to *both* Jewish *and* Arab peoples!!)

Calling an *argument* "idiotic" (completely OK in my book, as long as you can show valid reasons why) is not the same thing as calling the *presenter* of that argument an idiot (not OK in my book, and hopefully I haven't done so in *Hindsights*). Fuzzy thinking poses a serious threat to freedom of expression.

On around September 1st, Lena *informed* me that on Friday evening, September 4th, the teaching staff at her school were having a party (at the school) as a delayed kick-off of the new term, and that she would be going, and that I would have to take care of the kids that evening and put them to bed, because she might not be home until quite late, as late as midnight. Taking care of the kids was what I enjoyed most of all. And I didn't begrudge Lena having a bit of fun on her own with her colleagues. I thought it might even do her – and our crippled relationship – good. [*!!*]

She spent longer than usual getting dolled up. She looked gorgeous, I thought, but when I told her so, she just sneered and gave me a withering look. I hate having words put in my mouth by anyone (as Lena did to me at the start of nearly every fight we had), but I found it hard not to interpret her withering look as if she were saying "*You don't think I'm doing this for you, do you, asshole?*" That's how withering her look felt to me. [*Wasn't the alarm bell loud enough for you, Stan, I ask myself rhetorically?!*]

She was off with lovely words for the kids and icy barbs for me. I brushed them aside. I let the kids stay up a bit longer than usual, thinking that if they stayed up later, Lena might get some extra sleep in the morning in case she came home late. When they could no longer stay awake, I put them to bed. I didn't wonder whether I could stay awake until Lena got home; I wondered if I could fall asleep.

I couldn't. I lay in our bed and read. Then I lay in our bed in the dark. Well past midnight, I lay in bed and wondered if she'd been in an accident, if she was injured somewhere, if she'd been abducted. I banished all other possible explanations from my mind. I tossed and turned in the dark, listening to every sound, hoping she was safe. I had no idea how to reach her. [*We had no mobile phones in those days.*] I tried to squelch the most horrific fantasies by thinking of the kids, their needs, their delightfulness, anything but disaster.

Shortly after two in the morning, I heard from our bed upstairs the sound of a key unlocking the front door. I froze. *She's safe!* I waited and waited, listening, making sure that none of the sounds she was making downstairs indicated that anything might be amiss. I heard the fridge open and close. I heard her entering the downstairs bathroom and, after one of the night's many eternities, leaving it, then making her way up the stairs as silently as she could. I heard every sound. She entered our bedroom, and I, pretending to have partially awoken from a deep sleep, propped myself up on one elbow. "*Hi!*" I whispered, "*Everything OK?*" "*Yes!*" she shot back with a whisper that was more like a hiss, "Go back to sleep!" "*What time is it?*" I said, sleepily, looking at my watch. "*Oh, it's after two!*" She glared at me, reacting to the inferred accusation I hadn't implied. She hissed again, "A person only lives once!! I need some sleep!!" And she slid into bed with her back to me. She reeked of smoke. *It must have been the others.*

The regular sounds of her breathing convinced me that she'd fallen asleep almost immediately. It took me a long and trying time to fall asleep myself. Why would she say that about only living once? What had she done?! My horrific fantasies continued, but now they felt real and were expanding and morphing in agonizing directions, as if they were pushing and shoving my left side while I was walking along with my right side on the edge of the void. I was trying desperately *not* to hear any alarm bells. I had to banish every such thought; it was now a matter of survival.

The next morning we were awakened by two wonderful kids. Lena turned her attention, her love, her devotion to them, giving her an escape route from my possible questions about the night. I focused on the kids too, partly because I *always* focused on the kids and their magical, infectious power to turn the darkest night into the brightest day. Lena avoided eye contact with me. When I made it impossible to avoid, all I met was defensive aggression and thinly veiled hostility. *There was a sea change* in her mood towards me since yesterday, from mere overt disdain to unrelenting, outright hatred. After 4th gear, her turbocharger had kicked in.

Perhaps she didn't look me in the eye because she couldn't stand the sight of me. That interpretation was my best option! It was also what she'd be telling me repeatedly during the coming days, weeks and months, as the last layers of security in my life were delaminating. My 42nd birthday, nine days after her party, was a sham. Yet she managed to hide from the kids how much she detested me.

About a week later, I noticed in *Sydsvenskan* that one of the two Swedish public service television channels would be broadcasting Ingmar Bergman's brilliant version of Mozart's opera *The Magic Flute*. I had an empty video cassette on hand to record it. I figured the kids might possibly enjoy it some day; it would certainly be worth the effort. There was nothing to lose.

At some point in the autumn (might have been that same month, September), Lena joined a choir. She had a lovely soprano voice, and I was glad for her sake that she wanted to use it. Besides, I loved looking after the kids as many extra evenings as she might need for choir practice.

CHAPTER 9

Derailment

During the summer of 1987, I thought my relationship with Lena could get no worse. In the autumn she proved me wrong. She *hated* the sight of me and frequently told me so (mercifully not in front of the kids). Fortunately, they showed no signs of suspecting that anything was amiss between us. But they did seem to notice that I was down, no matter how hard I tried to conceal it. Yet I was and am convinced that my behavior that autumn gave them no reason to think that there might be any connection between my low spirits and my relationship with their mother – at least not yet.

Sometime between September '87 and April '88, there was an incident that suggested that the turmoil was reaching their consciousness. I remember the location and the words but not the date. I was standing in the front doorway. Lena was at the car, which was parked on Källargatan, in full view of our front door. She was yelling ugly things back at me. Jenny ran across the street to her and began beating her stomach, pleading, "*Stop yelling at Daddy!! Can't you see he's sad?!*" Lena told Jenny with a forced smile that she wasn't yelling at me, but Jenny clearly knew what yelling was and who the target was. Lena tried to blame me somehow, for playing for Jenny's sympathy, against her. It was sickening.

On September 25th, Mom arrived for a 10-day visit. For the first time I could remember, she wore no bun, but sported a relatively fashionable, curly hairdo. Her new look gave me high hopes for a new outlook and behavioral changes as well. (Unfortunately, a lifetime of fixing her bun to express strong disapproval seemed to have become a conditioned reflex; during her stay she would spontaneously continue reaching for a bun that was no longer there.) But on her first day at Korngatan, she made it clear that the change was cosmetic only. When she and I were alone for a couple of hours, she held quite a little sermon for me: how *her* views constitute the "true" comprehension of reality, while those of others (like me, although she didn't say so directly) were skewed and screwed up by bitterness, bravado and bullshit (not her exact words). She informed me that she'd been "deeply hurt" by "certain things" during her '84 visit (she'd had time to rewrite history), to the point where she'd been up until 3 AM writing a letter to God, which she now pulled out of her handbag (she'd presumably been unable to find His ZIP code) and read it to me – in Elizabethan English, of course. Her reading ended with a not-so-veiled command that I was not to confront her with whomever I was; I was not to be me. She was here to see her grandchildren and I was not to spoil it by being myself. I avoided leaving the kids alone with her.

Lena was all sweetness and light, as usual, but she came home late most days "due to work commitments". Mom retired at 7 PM, when we put the kids to bed, so she and Lena saw relatively little of each other most days. Mom never suspected how derailed our marriage had become. After Mom retired for the evening, Lena would have nothing to do with me. Her hour or two with Mom were a show, a charade, a sham. If Mom noticed anything weighing on me, she apparently attributed it to the weight of responsibility I felt for the kids. Why would she think otherwise? Why would she search for an explanation she would have found unbearable? And why would I?

Fortunately, she didn't sermonize again after that first day, but the atmosphere between us had been poisoned. My outrage at this soon turned to pity, however, as I began to realize how frightened and unhappy she was. She was not only proud of being humble, she also proclaimed possession of "true happiness" – while showing a face that would have made a depressed basset hound look like a guffawing jester. Her arcane interpretation of life seemed designed to shield her from life itself. Since she already "knew" that her views were *right* and everyone else's were *wrong*, she was impervious to questioning. In this mode, Bob became Robert – the name by which she referred to him when expressing disdain for his beliefs or lack of them.

Shortly after her return to Kirkland, Mom phoned, effusive with affection and charm. I suspected she was now aware of having been way out of line on her first day in Malmö, and that she was as jumpy as a cat about it. But since I (not the kids) was on the receiving end, I was long over it. John wrote me that he wasn't surprised I'd been so frustrated with her; when he spoke with her after her visit to us, she'd told him that I "sweetly" gave her permission to read her letter to God to me (she told John it was a poem!!), but that I didn't say a word in response. John asked her what kind of response she expected. She answered, in her best Eeyore mode, "*Oh, I didn't expect anything. I don't expect anything from anybody!*" John just sighed – both when she told him and when he told me.

The unfolding of the kids' abilities and personalities was a constant source of joy to me: Sally the soon-to-be-two-year-old little bundle of fire and energy, Jenny the soon-to-be-four-year-old protective and instructive big sister. But I resisted turning to the kids for support. I should be the one providing the support and encouragement to them, not vice-versa. Apart from a few daily, withering, insulting, hateful comments, Lena said almost nothing to me and asked me less. She might have shown a cesspool more affection, as far as I could tell (I was getting pretty much like Eeyore myself). And still I couldn't bring myself to discuss my situation with Bob, despite our openness in all other areas. I clung desperately to the hope that Lena would realize how badly she was abusing my love for her, and I was afraid – now more than ever after seeing Bob's rejection of Carmen – that a way back for Lena and me would be jeopardized if Bob rejected her too.

Yet I *needed* a gadfly, someone who could poke holes in my assumptions if they were false: "a way back?" – but how can one go back to where one has never been? Treating me badly (and getting away with it) only seemed to spur her to treat me even worse. Could we be running off the rails if we'd never been securely on them? I felt trapped, paralyzed. I could see no solution, no escape, no exit, the hell behind our closed doors. Thoughts of suicide flew unbidden into my brain multiple times daily. It took tremendous energy and concentration on the kids to ward off such thoughts.

Bob thought I might be interested in a sample of the twisted logic of an American writer named Martin Gardner, who claimed that belief in God is necessary to assure that we will have an afterlife. Bob didn't know whether to laugh or cry about that one. I replied that Gardner's claim might enable a revision of the Cartesian syllogism: I don't think, therefore I will be.

The derailed friendship between Bob and Carmen was proving difficult for both of them to shake off. They weren't speaking or writing to each other, but continued to make me their go-between. I urged them each to take a break and simply accept their no-fault incompatibility. It was easy to make progress on someone else's behalf.

On October 19th, four years and five days after the most recent move of Lena's piano, she felt it was time again. The piano had now stood downstairs in the big house, downstairs in the little house, upstairs in the little house, and would now stand upstairs in the big house, completing the cycle. This was the only "easy" move; it took the movers no more than 20 minutes to carry it from the library and across the garage-roof terrace to the recreation room (my former studio). [*It has recently, in 2021, come to my attention that in Lena's view it was I who wanted to move the piano so many times. I must concede that she might not have <u>ordered</u> it,* *but only said where it would have to be if she were to play, and that I, having learned that taking "your wish is my command" as the path to greatest familial harmony, acted accordingly.*]

As in the past, Lena still didn't or wouldn't play. Although I didn't know how, I didn't let that stop *me*. While the kids and I were playing together or they were swinging, we often sang children's songs (a few of which I'd made up for them). I tried, with some success, to tap out the melody with one finger. As long as I stuck to the key of C major, I was soon able to pick out most of the tunes in our repertoire by ear. Then I began to add a couple more fingers. Soon I had a whole list of songs I could pick out by ear, well enough for the three of us to sing lustily when we were alone together. I did, after all, want the kids to realize that the piano was more than an oversized black shelf for plants. They might even come to be interested in trying it out for themselves someday.

Their interest in music was growing, and I sought to encourage it – not by forcing them into anything, but by tempting them with the kinds of things I noticed that they responded to favorably. They loved to watch and sometimes to sing along with the film video of *The Sound of Music*, *My Fair Lady*, the cartoon video of *Wind in the Willows*, and the operetta *HMS Pinafore*. (All of these gave them the added benefit of hearing other English voices and accents than my own.) One day in mid-autumn, I thought I'd test their responses to the video I'd recorded of Ingmar Bergman production of Mozart's opera, *The Magic Flute*.

Throughout the overture in the Bergman version, live close-ups of faces in the audience – men and women, elderly and children, of different races – cascade in time with the overture that prefaces the drama to come. The overture is followed by a more-comical-than-fearsome dragon pursuing the protagonist Tamino, and the silly plot begins to unfold. Jenny and Sally were spellbound – for about 20 minutes – then wished to do something else, which we did. I figured it was an experiment worth trying, but perhaps it was premature.

The next day, however, they asked if we couldn't please watch "that dragon thing" again. It took a second or two for me to realize they were referring to *The Magic Flute*, and I agreed without hesitation but with puzzled astonishment. This time they watched (from the beginning again) nearly half of the two-hour production before telling me they wanted to do something else. I sat with them the whole time, sometimes answering their questions about who this or that character was or what something meant, but mostly they were absorbed by it, and were absorbing it.

On the fourth consecutive day of exposure, they watched the whole opera. In the days and weeks that followed, they kept coming back to – requesting and even demanding – *The Magic Flute*, to my continued astonishment and delight. I told Bob, who was dumbfounded and immediately prepared to open another door. He'd recorded several ballets from various TV broadcasts: the Alvin Ailey Dance Company of New York (a Black troupe with brilliant performances of spirituals and modern dance music) and Balanchine's New York City Ballet performing Gershwin. The kids loved those too. They referred to the Ailey tape as "Rock-a My Soul" (Sally said "*woka myso*"), the title of one of the spirituals. I kept my descriptions of the kids' reactions to all this music pretty low-key in my reports to Bob, however; I wanted him to see for himself when he came to visit us at Christmas.

Lena resumed smoking that fall, but didn't smoke at home or in front of the kids. I don't know exactly when she began (at that teachers' party in September?); I picked up the smell again one day (she seldom allowed me within smelling range nowadays), and I asked her in great surprise whether she'd started smoking again. "Yes!" she snarled back. I was astonished that anyone who'd escaped that addiction for over a year would voluntarily stick their head back in the noose. I hadn't planned to comment, but I couldn't squelch a spontaneous "*But <u>why</u>?!*" She shot back, "Because the teachers in the smoking room are nicer." I froze. *Don't think. Don't analyze. Don't. Nothing. Move on.*

That autumn she frequently said that she had to get out of the house in the evening and see a movie or something, that she was becoming claustrophobic. She didn't ask about my willingness to look after the kids on my own, nor did she express any appreciation. I was so deeply in denial that it didn't occur to me that she never suggested that *we* should get a sitter and go out *together*! Her regular screaming sorties on me continued, and yet she dismissed my every plea for us to get marital counseling. I was battling depression and thoughts of suicide every goddamn day (and night). *Don't think. Don't analyze. Don't. Nothing. Move on.*

In mid-November, my boss (who'd been using a PC for nearly a year) finally agreed to upgrade me from my Bitsy word processor. It took me about five minutes with a PC to realize just how primitive the Bitsy was. I expected Perstorp to give me another cast-off, but what I got was a brand-new model. Now I could write and store a multitude of documents without printing them out. It felt like a cage door opening.

Early one morning, Lena and I were awakened by the sound of Jenny approaching our open bedroom door from down the corridor. She was singing something familiar. I grabbed my camera in time to catch her just before she crossed the threshold to our bedroom, wearing a gold-crown party hat. She'd swept some black lacy cloth around her and was singing, full-throated and solemnly, one of the arias of the Queen of the Night from *The Magic Flute*. She was having the time of her life (and of mine).

On November 18th, I participated in a badminton tournament in Staffanstorp and won a frozen goose. Whatever expectations I might have had about bringing it home to Lena like a cat bringing home its catch of a mouse to its master, I quickly realized that nothing I did would elicit more than a sneer. Her sneers sickened me. I had no place to go.

I thought of the time she sneered at me for being an "idiot" for bringing home a pine instead of a spruce as our Christmas tree, or for suggesting a Christmas turkey once in a while instead of ham every year. (I'd wondered why we couldn't just take turns.) Now I told her – didn't ask – that we were going to have a pine that year, and we could have a spruce again the following year. (I left the ham alone.) For once, she kept her low opinion of me to herself.

Why didn't I just leave her or kick her out? Strange (and sick) as it may sound, my misplaced loyalty knew no bounds. I hung on to the now-ridiculous hope that she'd have a major change of heart, that she'd also love me, at last. With hindsight, I'd like to believe that protecting the kids was my only true motivation for staying or letting her stay. But that wouldn't be true. At that time, I could only see suicide as my escape from the torture of her hatred. And that was another reason I didn't dare to take up my problem with Bob. His poor health was more than enough for him to deal with.

In late November 1987, I believe, I received a phone call from someone out of the past: Elsa Braun! She was my and Jeanette's Swedish teacher from September 1969 and onwards. It was Elsa who helped us (also using influence from her judge/husband Sven) to obtain our residence and work permits, and to find a place to live when we were evicted from our sublet in early 1970. It is no exaggeration to say that Elsa enabled Jeanette and me to remain in Sweden.

A few years later, Elsa and her husband moved from Malmö and out of our lives when Sven's position as a judge took them to Ystad. Now they'd returned to Malmö, back to their house on Norra Klockspelsvägen (they'd been renting it out all this time). I was thrilled at the prospect of a reunion. Lena seemed only mildly inconvenienced.

On November 26th, Leif invited me to visit Frigoscandia in Helsingborg for the first time openly, despite my having worked closely with the company's promotional material for nine years. I was still Leif's ghost writer, and remained a well-guarded secret from Frigoscandia's ad agency, but by now five or six of his colleagues had heard of me. I would eventually chat with a few of them, but only Leif would ever know the full extent of our collaboration.

Al visited us over the weekend of December 12th-13th in connection with a business trip to Europe. It was pleasant but uneventful. Jenny and Sally hijacked his attention and I was grateful for that.

Bob arrived on December 18th, the day that Lena's school term came to an end. I was almost numb with pain, panic and depression. I remember how amazed he was to see how fond Jenny and Sally were of the ballets and the Gilbert and Sullivan he'd sent to us, and most of all, of *The Magic Flute*. Bob was himself taken by the Bergman production, but since it was in Swedish, some of it was lost in translation. He'd been speculating on whether the kids reacted primarily to Mozart's music or Bergman's wizardry. He therefore brought with him several other recordings of the opera, taken from French, German, Swiss and Italian television channels. At first, the kids rejected all the new versions, but before long they began watching every one of them.

One thing Bob wanted to get us for Christmas, mostly as thanks for my latest efforts to make his apartment a pleasant home, was a new pair of loudspeakers to match the capabilities of our stereo. We visited a number of stereo stores together. Most of the speakers that had the desired technical capabilities would take far too much space in our living room. At last, we found a stereo store that had what we were looking for. While we were studying the technical information about the speakers we were interested in, a salesman approached us and began chatting incessantly about the sound these little babies could deliver. The system was currently playing some kind of brassy pop music that was the furthest thing imaginable from our taste, so we asked if we could hear what the speakers could do with classical music. (The music he'd been playing reminded me of a description in Joseph Conrad's *Victory*: "*The Zangiacomo band was not making music; it was simply murdering silence with a vulgar, ferocious energy.*")

The salesman disappeared for a minute, came back and asked whether "some dude named Brahms" would be OK. We said yes. As the beautiful tones of a

Brahms piano concerto began to fill the room, the salesman was standing there, half bent-over, viciously chewing on his gum, wildly snapping his fingers to a beat Brahms never imagined, madly grinning at us, and muttering *yeah, yeah*, as if agreeing with himself for our benefit. In spite of his performance, we left the shop with the speakers – and then burst out laughing.

Every time Bob and I went shopping for speakers, I would pop into nearby stores to buy extra little Christmas presents for Lena, things I thought she'd like, things I thought might impress her and show my love for her, to try to pull our marriage back onto rails it had never really been on. I suffered real *angst* that I wasn't doing enough to please her. Then she would go out Christmas shopping on her own, leaving the kids with me and Bob (not that we minded), returning hours later with little to show for it. I might have found it strange, the way she got all dolled up to go on long and largely fruitless shopping tours by herself, but I didn't. I had my new mantra: *Don't think. Don't analyze. Don't. Nothing. Move on.*

Christmas Eve came. I'd purchased something like a dozen presents for Lena. From her I got a record album (*Good Old Boys*, by Randy Newman). It was music that neither of us was crazy about. She didn't even seem to appreciate my attempts to fake liking it. Lena often complained that I always dressed in dark, gloomy colors. Although I could easily have proved that untrue (e.g. the colorful Pendletons I frequently wore), what did surprise me was her only other Christmas present to me: a charcoal-gray striped shirt.

By New Year's Eve, Lena's expressions of outright hatred for me were so flagrant that I found it almost inconceivable that Bob saw none of it. Maybe he'd become inured to not seeing? It was striking how prophetic my painting *But Maybe I Don't Want to See* (#72) felt at such times. In desperation, during one conversation in which Bob was lamenting the difficulty of keeping his house in order (in the housekeeping sense), despite now having a good cleaning woman, I suggested that I might come down and spend the second week of February with him. Bob, suspecting nothing, readily agreed. There was only so much mental abuse I could bear.

On New Year's Day, Lena was off "to the gym" again. She told me she liked spending time at the gym so she didn't have to see me. (Yes, she actually said that!) It felt strange keeping all this from Bob, but I refused to let go of the naïve and ridiculous hope that one day soon things between Lena and me would change for the better and then what would have been the point of upsetting Bob? I knew there was a risk that if it all derailed, Bob might interpret my silence as having been a vote of no confidence in him and would be grievously disappointed. A friend of mine used to tell me whenever we spoke that everything was fine and great. One day he said that a change in his duties at work meant that he could only come home for weekends, and thus had to live close to his place of work for several months. When I later found out that he'd been arrested for drunk driving and had to spend his weeknights at an open correctional facility in another town, I felt a bit hurt that he hadn't felt he could tell me about it. Wasn't that what friends are supposed to do? Wasn't that what I was *not* doing with Bob? I saw no clear answer, except this: *Don't be too quick to judge!*

Bob returned to Binningen on January 5th, 1988. Before Lena, the kids and I left to go to dinner at Ole and Birgitta's that same evening, Lena told me, completely out of the blue (at least in terms of what was on *my* mind!), "*You ought to find yourself another woman.*" (!!)

Two days later, we were invited to visit Elsa and Sven at 2 PM (out of consideration for the kids' bedtime). Not surprisingly, Lena charmed them both at this first meeting. Since they'd never met her before, one might say they'd never seen her so charming. I hadn't seen them in years, and although I'm sure they must have understood how happy I was to see them, a lot had been wreaking havoc on my grounds for happiness; there were new grounds, different grounds, complex grounds, and ultimately grounds for withholding judgment as to my current level of happiness.

Around 10 kids came to our house for Jenny's 4th birthday celebration that Sunday, January 10th, 1988, the day before school resumed. Lena played the gracious hostess, but glared at me when nobody was looking. I was an open, invisible wound, which made concentration difficult and smiling harder. Rubbing salt into my wounds, Lena got angry with me for looking sad.

After what seemed like more than a dozen sessions with each of the new *Magic Flute* versions Bob brought with him, Jenny and Sally seemed to know the opera by heart, as well as by which version. (And they had thus clearly answered Bob's question about whether the main appeal was Bergman or Mozart.) One day in mid-January, while the three of us were watching the opera for the *nth* day running, a client of mine came to the house to enlist my help in revising a short text. We stepped into the kitchen and sat at the table to start discussing it. But before we got going, he expressed great surprise that kids as young as four and two could enjoy opera! I explained how taken they were with *The Magic Flute*, how they listened to it almost daily, and knew it almost by heart. "It wouldn't surprise me," I said, "if Jenny even knew who wrote the libretto!"

"*Emanuel Schikaneder*," Jenny announced, loud and clear, and in a distinct *French* accent, as she strode into the kitchen! My hair stood on end. My jaw dropped. Jenny had overheard her name being mentioned and wandered into the kitchen just as I was making the claim about her ability to identify the librettist. I'd never told her, never mentioned it. It took me weeks to figure out that she'd picked it up from one of the tapes Bob brought, a recording from French TV, in which the French narrator's introduction to the opera included the statement that *"l'opéra est composé par Mozart sur un livret d'Emanuel Schikaneder."* Even though I was aware that children's minds often absorb things like blotters, I've never to this day understood how Jenny's comprehension of that was possible.

On Friday evening, January 22nd, Elsa and Sven came for dinner. They were extremely taken by the kids, taken by the house, and again taken (*in*) by Lena's charm. I was grateful for the distractions. Elsa seemed convinced that all these things symbolized how well I'd managed to do for myself from my humble situation in a cold-water apartment on Vårgatan back in 1970. On paper, I should have been the happiest guy in the world. I *could* have been, I felt, if only.... But I did share Elsa's pleasure that she and I had reestablished contact with each other – a contact that would continue. Two days later, Lena told me I was *such a pain* to live with.

During the first week in February, she told me she had to work on Monday and Thursday evenings, and she was hours late getting home on the Tuesday as well. This was apart from her evening of choir practice, which at least posed no threat, I told myself. I asked no questions. I didn't challenge her, didn't try to find out what she'd "really" been up to. *Don't think. Don't analyze. Don't. Nothing. Move on.*

On Sunday, February 7th, I flew to Basel. Bob paid for my ticket. He said it was the least he could do, since I was coming to put his apartment in order again. I worked quickly and efficiently. I buried myself in the task at hand: making things more convenient for him. I phoned home every evening. Lena answered, but quickly handed the phone to Jenny and Sally, who, unlike their mother, were both eager to speak with me. I finished nearly all the work on Bob's apartment by Tuesday evening.

One evening over a post-prandial cognac, Bob told me that he'd heard from a former colleague at Roche about another colleague (let's call him Urs; I've forgotten his name) whom Bob knew only slightly. Urs was impeccably punctual, introverted and reserved, pleasant, dutiful, dependable, somewhat boring, and was thus Swiss down to his toes and out to his fingertips. One day several months earlier, Urs didn't show up for work. His colleagues figured he was ill. They didn't react much at first, but thought it unlike him not to have phoned in.

He didn't show up the next day either, or the next. After another few days, one of the colleagues phoned Urs's home. His wife was astonished to hear that her husband colleagues knew nothing of his whereabouts. She'd assumed he was on a business trip. But then she found his passport at home. The police were notified and began making inquiries and a search. They found no traces; no money was missing from his bank account; no personal items had been removed from his home. Urs had just *disappeared*. Nobody knew where he'd gone or why. Nobody could explain it. I asked Bob if he knew anything about Urs's marriage. Bob, clearly startled by my question, shot a strange and inquisitive look at me. But then our conversation drifted on to another topic.

The week after my return to Korngatan, I had just one pupil. I was glad to have extra time to spend with the kids; I'd missed them so much while in Binningen. And they were delighted to have me home again; Lena greeted me and treated me with sarcasm, harsh words and screaming. The following week was Sweden's winter sport vacation week. Lena, Eva and Marie-Louise flew to Lanzarote (one of the Canary Islands) to soak up sun, and I had the kids all to myself.

Lena got in touch once or twice, but would only speak with and about the kids. She spoke to me as if I'd been an employee in a freight office that had failed to make a prompt delivery or had lost the merchandise. I only saw Eva briefly when she and Jan dropped Lena off at Korngatan on their return on February 28th, exactly two years after Olof Palme was murdered. Eva looked strange – she looked at *me* strangely: pensive, alarmed and angry – but not with me. I was very puzzled. After Eva had gone I asked Lena what was up with her sister, but she brushed off my question with a highly irritated "*How should I know?!*"

The next day, a Monday, a Leap Year Day, it felt clear to me that the worn fabric of our frayed marriage was so threadbare that the slightest added pressure would leave it in tatters. To my weary surprise, Lena acquiesced to my desperate desire for emergency stitching. What I didn't know was that it would be our last time. But it just felt strange and mechanical to me because I was almost certain that she was just "letting me", like a bank clerk who grudgingly permits an acquaintance to make an after-hours deposit.

I agonized through that week, struggling to focus on the kids, struggling to ignore the barbs, too worn out to defend myself any longer, fighting off the irrepressible thoughts of suicide that were now wreaking their worst in my mind most of the time. Then came a shipment from a bookseller in London, a gift from Bob, in two burlap sacks from the Royal Mail. I was a big question mark; in my raging chaos, I'd totally forgotten that Bob told me he was sending me a complete, 32-volume, leather-bound set of the venerable 1911 edition of the *Encyclopedia Britannica* as thanks for all my help. My sorrow was temporarily blown away by Bob's irrepressible generosity and by the prospect of exploring such a treasure, just as the Compton's encyclopedia was for me in my childhood home in Oak Park. In my excitement, I exclaimed to Lena how wonderful it was to seek answers rather than suppress questions. "*Ha! Like you need that! Like we need more of that around here!*" she sneered and left the room snarling. I watched her go, wondering how her mind worked.

On Tuesday, March 8th, I had a pupil from Perstorp. Her name was Karin. Under normal circumstances, I would have seen a sweet, smart and humorous girl, but *my* circumstances were far from normal. I was living in a painful daze, battling irrepressible and harrowing thoughts of self-destruction. I wasn't sleeping. Lena was getting dolled up for *somebody*. All the walks on her own, the gym visits, going "alone" to movies she never talked about afterwards, the hatred and contempt. *If this be madness....*

There were too many indicators, too many clues pointing in a direction I couldn't bear to see. I kept trying to think and not to think. My brain was in chaos. My thoughts were discombobulated fragments. My mantra broke down. I'd been someplace different but nearly equally chaotic and terrifying ten and eleven years before, under other circumstances. I'd tried to get away from it then and it nearly killed me. I knew that this time I had to deal with it, to confront it, to confront *her*.

On Wednesday evening, after we'd put the kids to bed, I told her I *knew* there was something going on, and that she *had* to tell me what is was. She turned pale. She could probably see from my expression that I was deadly serious. She didn't deny that something was going on. She just said, "*not tonight – tomorrow night.*" I'm not sure why she wanted the extra 24 hours. Perhaps to figure out how to sugar-coat hemlock?

CHAPTER 10

Destruction

On Thursday, March 10th – 10 years to the day since I sat down in an alcoholic fog to write my suicidal treatise, *The Unparallel Lines* – I tried to behave naturally all day. [*I'm sure Lena was struggling too, but I can only speculate about what was going on in her head, and thus I can only write truthfully about what was going on in mine.*] Jenny and Sally didn't appear to notice anything abnormal, even during supper, with the showdown rapidly approaching. Horrible as it sounds, the total lack of affection from Lena towards me was something quite normal to the kids. Supper felt interminable.

    What sort of bomb was Lena about to drop on me, on my life, on the lives and future of our kids? After dinner, the kids were their usual playful selves. They needed considerable coaxing to get into their pajamas. My tension made me afraid I would vomit when I took them to bed and began reading them their bedtime stories. If my tension affected my voice, that too would have been normal; they were used to my giving different, often exaggerated voices to each character in the bedtime stories I read. The roles had become a hiding place; I felt disembodied. I was soon to be disemboweled.

    Once they'd fallen asleep, I lingered with them. When I entered the dimly lit living room sometime later, at around 8 PM, Lena was sitting on the sofa. It was darker than usual. She hadn't turned on any lights. The cheerless streets outside were wet from a light rain. The wet asphalt absorbed and dissipated the light from the neighbors' houses up towards the square. The only thing that could have made the staging more dramatic would have been a rumbling soundtrack of foreboding Hollywood-type music. Lena appeared to be sitting on broken glass. I felt like I'd wandered halfway across a frozen lake and was hearing loud cracking noises beneath my feet. I waited for her to speak.

    She spoke at last, in a soft, slow, sweet, trembling voice. It was her intention to move out because she no longer had any feelings for me at all. I listened. I had no idea what was happening to my pulse. "*You're moving out…?*" My words – a string of unrelated sounds relating what she'd just said – came slowly, like I was pushing dead birds out of my mouth with my burning tongue. I heard myself saying them. The room began rotating. She nodded. The room began to spin. "*You've met someone else…,*" I said, not asking. She stared at me. "*…Haven't* *you?"* She continued to stare, trembling. Can blood pressure plunge and soar simultaneously? I felt ready to faint and roar out my agony at the same time. I began to shake.

Then it came, like ripping off a bandage over a poorly healed wound. Yes, she'd met someone else. *Who?!* A colleague – she was in love with him and he was in love with her. My eyes shot involuntarily upwards, beyond the ceiling, up to where the kids were sleeping. She saw my panic and began crying, not necessarily for that reason. She reassured me that we would leave all our routines regarding the kids intact, that she would be moving on her own to a furnished apartment for a month while she came to a decision about whether she felt more for me than for her colleague. My mind began to race. *This is no spur-of-the-moment impulse! This has been* planned*!! Does she really think that whatever decision* she *makes is what I – or the other guy – will simply accept or submit to? Why is* she *crying?! She's the one* doing *this! If she doesn't think it's good, she could just* not *do it*!

"You must have seen this coming," she said, "that we couldn't go on. I mean, we've been at each other for such a long time now." I most emphatically did *not* realize that we'd been at *each other*, but I was *fully* aware that *she'd* been at *me*. And if she felt that way, then *why* had she rejected all my pleas for us to get counseling?! She ignored my question; "*I can't go on in a loveless relationship,*" she whimpered. And here I thought I was the only one not being loved! Then she begged, "*I just want to know, please tell me it'll be OK if I come back from time to time to see the kids?!*"

I was unprepared for such a question. Did that mean she would *not* be taking the kids from me? I could see no other interpretation. It calmed me, just a little, just for a moment, until the next wave of fear and doubt hit me. I felt I would vomit or faint – or both. I was about to rush out of the house in desperation, into the cold dark rain, but Lena pleaded with me to stay. She said she needed me to understand her. I asked her for his name. She refused to tell me that or anything more about him. There'd been "nothing physical" between them, she insisted, they'd just met and gone to the cinema a few times.

I *knew* she was lying. Memories and questions were popping up in my mind like cinematic popcorn, things I'd been suppressing began falling into place. Her sudden major, tangible increase in hostility had begun when school started in the fall. *This goes back a long time, more than eight months at least!* I continued to probe and penetrate. She stared at me, turning pale. Then she became furious and frightened. "*Stop asking questions! Now you're burning your bridges!!*" How on earth did she figure that *I* was the one burning *my* bridges?!

Waves were crashing around me, over me, washing me away, turning everything black. Horrific pictures of Jenny and Sally waving goodbye to me began swirling before my eyes: the kids, my darling kids, being ripped from my arms. A new "daddy"? *No, this can't be true, it can't be real, this isn't right, it's a nightmare.* I couldn't feel the floor. I was in free fall, but there was nothing free about it.

My mind continued to whirl as I hurried out to the kitchen and poured myself a huge whisky. I chugged it down and poured another. The pain just kept growing. That light, chilling rain multiplied the darkness of the early March night, absorbing headlights, streetlights, shop lights, house lights, light itself. I hurried out to the garage, opened the door, threw myself onto my bike and raced furiously and drunkenly off into the black, rainy night, trying to outpace the pain that was sucking at my throat like a lamprey.

I had no goal, no destination, no direction. I pedaled furiously as I grew colder and wetter in the abominable night. My sole outer garment was a thin jacket. Only once before in my life had I experienced such intensity of pain and chaos. I couldn't escape it. I couldn't think a thought through, nothing close to a complete sentence. Before I could get from subject to predicate in one thought, a new subject would blindside the first, and another would blindside the second, on and on like that. I had to do something.

I cycled back home (*"Home"? I no longer had more than a house!*). I slowly passed our front windows along Korngatan. Lena was on the phone. *Probably to him!* Silently, I entered the garage and went directly into the little house to listen in on an extension in my office. As soon as I heard it was Eva, I carefully and quietly hung up. I collapsed on the bed in the guest room, my head reeling from alcohol, from her hatred of me, and from the destruction of my life.

I got up and grabbed some paper and a pen. Without turning on any other lights, I returned to the guestroom. The door was half open. The dim light from my office was enough for me to see by. I struggled to compose a short farewell letter to Lena: I was only ever going to be a wreck, unable to provide what my beloved kids needed. It was best for everyone if I just ended it. From the medicine cabinet in the guestroom bathroom I took one of the elastic bandages I occasionally used for knee support when playing badminton. While sitting on the bed, I wound it tightly around my neck until I passed out.

I have no idea how long I lay there unconscious – perhaps several hours [*calculating backwards, I must have been unconscious for around five hours*] – but I clearly remember hearing Lena enter the room. She turned on the light but didn't touch me. *And she did not remove the bandage from around my neck.* For all she could know, I was dying and she did nothing to remove the bandage from around my neck.

She found my farewell letter and read or skimmed it enough to get the gist. Then she left the room, just walked away from me as I was. The next thing I recall was Eva entering the room. She immediately removed the bandage, shook me gently, and spoke to me, tried to rouse and revive me. It was around 4 AM. [*During the writing of this book in 2018, Eva confirmed my recollection of her role in the events that transpired that evening.*] Eva was highly agitated. Lena, standing in the doorway to the guestroom, looked nervous, defensive and defiant. Had I ruined her plans for a quick and easy getaway by not agreeing with them? Was she furious with me for my implied criticism?

I don't remember many details from the rest of that night and morning. I do remember that Eva spoke very sternly to Lena, that Eva checked on me from time to time, and that before the kids woke up that morning, Lena promised me – in Eva's presence – that she wouldn't leave me. I was numb. My head was whirring. It felt like a beehive.

Lena had previously arranged to take the kids to Barkåkra that next day, Friday. Leif was coming to Korngatan that day to go through some texts. When Lena and the kids left, she said she was still uncertain as to whether she would mention anything to her mother. Eva, it turned out, already knew about Lena's intentions and was appalled. Lena had told her on the plane to or from Lanzarote, but they kept Marie-Louise in the dark. I just wanted to disappear, get a heart attack or cancer – anything that would make me vanish forever.

Numbness prevented me from cancelling Leif's visit (by the time I recalled the appointment, he was already *en route*, and this was before the era of mobile phones). About two seconds after he arrived he saw that something catastrophic had taken place. To his great credit, he let me talk, pour out my heart and my despair. I will always be grateful to him for that. Even if he might have realized that he wouldn't be getting any useful work out of me that day, he stayed to listen and be there for me, which was what I sorely needed.

Perhaps Lena did tell Marie-Louise that day, or perhaps Eva did. I don't know. What I do know was that they were both furious with Lena and issued her an ultimatum to have no further contact with her mystery man apart from the professional contact she might be required to have with him as her colleague. If not, they let her know that she would no longer be welcome in their homes.

When she and the kids got home from Barkåkra, she was surprised that I supported this demand (but not nearly as surprised as I was that this surprised her!). She reluctantly agreed, but on condition that she could tell him in person. She said she needed to go for a walk. I said she could phone him from home. She hesitated, baffled that I had seen through her instantly. At last I realized the purpose of her many "walks" in recent months. She called him, and they agreed to meet that evening.

I phoned Bob and told him the whole sorry tale. He immediately feared for my mental stability. And he said he instantly and retroactively understood my enigmatic question about the marital status of his colleague Urs who'd gone missing. Our conversation was short; that kind of "meal" was too heavy to digest on the spot.

Eva was singing with her choir that evening in Malmö, and Jan came to be with me while Eva was at the concert – and while Lena was breaking the news to her colleague. Lena's concern for him and his feelings contrasted markedly with her failure to rescue me from my bandage the night before. Eva spoke a bit with Lena when they both returned to Korngatan from their respective errands. Jan said nothing to Lena, just glared at her. Something Eva said, I believe it was about Lena's disregard for my welfare, reopened the floodgates of Lena's "deep inner hatred" (her words) towards me. Rather than let me face another round of that, Jan and Eva took me back to Lund with them for the night. At around midnight I fell into a deep cognac coma, fully dressed.

I awoke, terrified, at around 4 AM. Everyone else in the house was asleep. My thoughts were convulsing. The pain was insufferable. I couldn't stop crying. I felt as if I were losing my skin, more like being flayed than molting. Thoughts of *Why can't I just die?* alternated with *She said she'd stay! Let's just forget it ever happened!* I forgave her even though she neither asked for forgiveness nor uttered that strangely impossible word "sorry". *Everything will be all right, as long as she understands how much I love and always have loved her*! My self-delusion, with years of practice behind it, refused to give up.

In my mind I was turning over every word she said. I told her I knew she'd been sleeping with him. She continued to deny it, but added: "*Now you're burning your bridges!*" when I suggested that she was lying. Why would she say that unless my accusation was true? I realized that Lena wanted to stray *and* stay, test the water, but retain the possibility – the "right" – to return if *he* turned out not to be better! Eva said that Lena wanted butter on both sides of her bread.

How did it get to be this way?! I realized that ever since our first couple of months together, she'd always found it so very hard – impossible – to love me, but had finally given in to my constant pressure. Maybe for her, the time had just seemed ripe – it was time for her to settle down – time to settle for someone who clearly adored her as much as I did, someone in whose spotlight she could be all alone. My life and my feelings existed solely for her benefit, to be used at her discretion whenever it suited her. Yes, there was a period, around the time of our engagement and marriage, when she was probably *infatuated* with me, but that infatuation never turned to love. Instead, when the kids came, she was no longer *alone* in my spotlight. Never mind that she too was in my spotlight. She had to share it! *Unacceptable* if you don't love that someone! And then the unacceptability degenerates into contempt and hatred.

My thoughts continued to grind and spiral that night in Lund. I couldn't sit or lie still. I left Jan and Eva's house on Mångatan before anyone else was up, at around 7 AM, after writing a note that I was going to see Ole. I took a long walk to a bus stop and found myself at the same bus stop I'd used when going home from Lena's apartment back in early 1979, almost exactly nine years earlier, when I *almost* got away.

While I was at Ole's, Lena phoned to check. She expressed no concern. I supposed she was simply monitoring my movements. I went home. I felt cold, lonely, full of fear and anxiety, yet drained. *Full and drained. Fully drained. Like a full drain.* Lena looked tired and sad. I wanted to think it was the sadness of regret, but not a word she said suggested it. More like the sadness of having to put longed-for plans on ice. The kids looked bewildered. Something they couldn't begin to understand was happening in their lives, to their lives. Something that could no longer be hidden from them. Eva came by and took them to the park.

When Eva and the kids returned, she spent the rest of the day with us (she would be singing in Malmö again that evening). She told me (aside) that when she explained to Lina and Emil what was going on, Emil had frowned and shook his little head for a long time, saying *"Bad, bad, bad!"* Eva advised me to try to appear cheerful, not to subject Lena [*How weird is that?!*] to the pressure of my mournful expressions. She thought we should try to do things together that had no direct connection to what was going on. Although I was no good at pretending to feel things I wasn't feeling or vice-versa, and disinclined by nature to follow orders that made no sense to me, I suggested to Lena that we all go out to the beechwoods. I had to persuade her, to convince her that it was for the kids' sake! Following Eva's advice, I did my best to put on a happy face, which made me feel sick. I was now totally convinced that Lena had slept with the guy, which did nothing to diminish my burgeoning jealousy. But I played my cheerful role that whole afternoon, as well as I could, trying to find something – anything – that might offer realistic grounds for hope. There was nothing. The only way back would have been if Lena sincerely wanted it, sincerely wanted to love me, sincerely wanted something and someone she'd never wanted before. As I reflected on it, my cheer turned to anger. And my mind kept digging, churning, analyzing.

Had our roles been reversed, I reflected, was there even the slightest shadow of a doubt that she'd have screamed at me full blast, terminated our marriage on the spot, and kicked me out? Hardly. No doubt whatsoever. Yet here I was, begging her not to leave, begging *her* to forgive *me* for whatever might have caused her to feel wronged, since in her view I had forced her to hate me and treat me like shit year after year and finally forced her to go find someone else! Wasn't it something like that?! Hold on, why wasn't *she* begging *me* for forgiveness? Because she regretted nothing! Because her only reason for being upset was that she and lover-boy had to put their plans on hold for a while in order to avoid inevitable guilt feelings and the disapproval of others? I *should* kick her out! She hated me (or so she said countless times), she'd lied to me, betrayed me, cheated on me, and here I was trying to comfort *her*, trying to win *her* back! How insane was that?! What a lame fool I was!!

I related all this to Eva when I picked her up after the concert. She said she understood, but urged me to take it easy. Eva aired these thoughts to Lena when the three of us were having a cup of tea (!!) at Korngatan before Eva drove home to Lund. Lena seemed to be a *bit* more understanding – briefly.

My subconscious was apparently working ceaselessly on situation analysis, retracing steps, stages, phases, actions. Suddenly, as soon as Eva left, it hit me like a bulldozer. *That* was the guy – the little colleague of hers we just *had* to visit on Gotland! I *knew* it! So I asked her pointblank. Her face showed me I'd hit the nail (or perhaps the screw) on the head. She was unable to deny it. I felt dizzy. *So I'd <u>met</u> the bastard!* I dissolved in despair. For some strange reason, being caught out led her to a moment of something resembling compassion. I slept in our bed that night, me shaking with tension and angst. She said in the darkness, "*I do like you, but so much has happened between us, to me, so I feel no desire for you right now.*" I managed to fall asleep thanks solely to my inexplicable and unwarranted emphasis on her words "*right now*".

I awoke an hour or two later, anxious, desperate, chaotic. I got up, pulled on my robe, went across the yard and into my office in the little house, turned on my computer, and got to work. Writing *The Unparallel Lines* saved my life almost exactly 10 years earlier. The unintentional catharsis I'd experienced had come from imposing a grammatical structure on my chaotic thoughts, imposing order where there had been none.

 I wrote and wrote, first reconstructing the events and conversations of the past few days as faithfully and in as much detail as I could, while the memories were still all too fresh and painful. Writing helped me to connect the dots, to face the pain, to record all the details and dialogues before memory could begin distorting or whitewashing them. By writing down exactly what was said each day, including the context, I brought more objectivity to my chaos and could deal with it better. And I had two very special reasons for needing to achieve balance within myself *without delay*: Jenny and Sally. There was no time for me to "indulge myself" in a year of depression, or to waste a year hiding in a bottle. Their lives were also plunging perilously towards chaos through no fault of their own; I could only help them by somehow achieving my own stability quickly and thoroughly.

 I could do nothing about what Lena said or did; I couldn't make her love me (I was *finally* beginning to accept that!!), nor could I even make her apologize. But I could be a fixed point, a point of stability and order *for my little girls*, and hopefully it would render the chaos around them less frightening. I imagined being in a totally dark room with nothing to hold onto, no sense of space, a complete and terrifying unknown; you don't even know whether the next step you take will send you plunging off a rocky precipice. But if there were a solid pole to hold onto somewhere in that room, the darkness would be far less terrifying. I resolved to be that pole for Jenny and Sally – without even going to Warsaw or Świnoujście.

 As I sat there at my computer writing down all that had been said and done, I came to think of my old diaries, the ones from 1978 and onwards in which I'd made notes of the difficulties I was having with Lena, the harrowing rollercoaster ride, right from the start. I dug them out of a box in a storage cabinet I'd built beneath the fax in my office. As I began reading them, a feeling of profound bitterness engulfed me. I discovered the many times I'd recorded pleading with Lena for us to get some counseling, or to talk to Eva, and being flatly rejected every single time. I slept no more that night. By morning I saw no trace of compassion in Lena; all I saw was outright rejection, hostility and loathing.

That evening, we went back to Lund for another concert with Eva's choir at the cathedral. The music turned all my thoughts black. I felt like a lost little boy who couldn't find his way home. For some reason, Lena responded to this and assured me that I didn't have to worry about further contact she might have with her colleague at school. (But no "*sorry*"!) She was inscrutably *almost* tender towards me. I once again cast aside my faculties of critical thinking, and hope came rushing back within me, knocking me down.

That night, nightmares woke me up several times. In the morning, however, hope had returned to me – I was holding Lena's hand when Jenny entered our bedroom. She observed us slowly, carefully, then grinned, jumped up into our bed and burst out, "*I've got my mommy and daddy!*" After we dropped Lena off at school, I took the kids up to Barkåkra. Although Lena warned me that Marie-Louise might be a bit "reserved" towards me, that wasn't *at all* the case – on the contrary. She was warm, considerate and anxious. She was also angry, but not with me. When the kids were safely out of earshot, Marie-Louise and I talked frankly and openly about everything.

It was becoming increasingly clear to me that Lena *had* been sleeping with her colleague, despite adamantly denying it. But Marie-Louise found it highly unlikely that Lena would jump into bed with somebody "just like that". (I didn't tell her about my first "date" with Lena in December 1977 and tried unsuccessfully not to recall it myself.) Yet for some reason, Lena's aggressive reply to me that night in September when she'd come home in the middle of the night from the staff party popped into my brain: "*You only live once!*" I realized I'd forgotten the name of the colleague Lena insisted on meeting on Gotland. Marie-Louise, to whom Lena clearly confided much more than to me, seemed to think he had a German surname.

I tried to look it up as soon as we got home. I found Lena's copy of her school's teachers' registry and scrutinized it for German surnames. I stopped when I got to the first German-sounding name I came to. It rang a bell at once. (No wonder; it also happened to be Jan's surname....) Thinking I knew the guy's name relaxed me, for some strange reason. When the kids and I picked Lena up after school, she was hostile again, throwing me back towards the abyss. When we got home and the kids ran off to play, I asked what they'd been talking about that day. "*You mean me and the schoolchildren?*" I told her I was pretty sure she knew whom I meant, and that I was referring to whether they'd talked about us. She responded in fury. "*Of course we have, and we'll continue to do so! You don't think this can be fixed in a day, do you?!*" I felt dizzy. I phoned Marie-Louise, because she'd urged me to keep her in the picture.

When Lena found out that I'd phoned her mother, her rage increased because. I told her I now knew the name of her colleague. She stopped short, stared at me. I told her the name I'd found. She hesitated a second or two, then burst out in a short jeering laugh. I could see that she was relieved – and that I'd gotten the wrong name. But I was determined to find the right one. I felt ill, phoned my next day's pupil, and cancelled the lessons. When the kids were bedded down for the night, I tried to find the teachers' register again, but Lena had hidden it. I'd caught a glimpse of it in her bathrobe and said so. She denied it, pretending not to know what I was talking about. I went to bed but didn't sleep. I heard her messing about in her closet at the far end of the playroom.

In the middle of the night, while she was sleeping soundly, I got up quietly and went to the closet where I'd built shelves for Lena's many sweaters, just inside the closet door. I tried to think where she might try to hide a slender catalogue. A good place to start looking might be tucked in somewhere among a hundred or so stacked sweaters. Maybe at around eye level – *her* eye level. I found it within a few seconds. I took it into the bathroom and began hurriedly thumbing through the list, *beyond* the *K*s. I soon found another German name, farther down: "Schad, Johannes". I didn't recognize the Schad part, but instantly remembered Lena mentioning "Johannes" many times on Gotland. *Schad. Schade.* At once, my penchant for punning made me associate Schad with *Schade*, the German word for damage, injury, misery, as in *Schadenfreude*, the term used in psychology to denote taking pleasure in the misery of others. It was all coming together. I found his address – Davidshallsgatan – not far from a number of Malmö's cinemas. *Aha! How convenient – almost tragicomic.*

When I presented my discovery to Lena in the morning, including my ever-so-appropriate *Schade* variant, she first displayed surprise, then guilt, then scorn. *OK, I'd figured it out. It didn't change anything.* I told her I now knew exactly when her affair began: at the teachers' party in early September. She didn't try to defend herself now; she just sneered. I wondered to myself why hadn't she already left? Was she *hoping* I'd kick her out so she could tell everyone that I *forced* her to leave?

At four years of age, Jenny now appeared to sense that something was horribly wrong, even though she couldn't quite verbalize it. Sally, at two, was even less able. At the breakfast table, several mornings in a row, our little four-year-old kept trying to get us to hold hands around the table. Lena told her gruffly not to be so dramatic.

On Wednesday, March 16th, Lena bitched throughout breakfast about what an awful, unpleasant place our home was. It was too dark. The floors were too cold. The neighborhood had no class. I tried to come up with feasible ideas to address these new complaints, but nothing helped. At lunch that day, Jenny suddenly began sobbing for no apparent reason. I asked her what the matter was, and she cried, "*I don't know!!*" I took her into my arms and asked her cautiously whether it had something to do with Mommy and Daddy. She didn't answer in words but began sobbing twice as hard. *So tragic! So unnecessary!* I told her that all would be well one day soon, but I convinced neither her nor myself.

I began to understand the deeper problem. It wasn't just about Lena's *infidelity*; that in itself was more of a symptom of a much greater, deeper problem that I was trying hard to grasp. I was convinced that I could forgive her for the infidelity itself, if not immediately, then eventually. Neither was it about her inability to love me; I'd accepted on some level that I could never *make* her love me, and that I in the meantime had provided all the love in our relationship, and still harbored the hope (at least in my wildly optimistic world) that she could change some day. No, it was about her *active hatred* of me. She'd told me those very words, countless times. She told me she loathed me, abhorred me, despised me. And at last, after all these years, I was starting to get the message.

When the kids and I drove to pick Lena up after work that day, my thoughts returned to the egocentricity of her actions. All consideration had to be for her, and no demands were allowed to be placed on her. She offered no apologies, showed no regrets, no remorse. After a day's work with Schade, she was even colder towards me than before. But not towards the kids. She put on a real show of affection towards them, a demonstration. *To what end?*

I decided not to ask any probing questions about her day. I would wait and see what she might have to say for herself. But she told me nothing. She hardly addressed me; there wasn't even a modicum of ordinary Swedish civility. I was nothing more than the chauffeur, the butler who must know his place and keep silent, the servant who would take all manner of abuse without reacting or responding.

I was feeling so poorly at the dinner table that she told me to go lie down. Later, when I returned to her and the kids to play a game at the table, she glared daggers at me. Her looks made me so ill I *had* to leave again and head for the bedroom. When Jenny followed me, Lena called after her to stay and play, but Jenny said defiantly, "Daddy's not feeling well!" Lena rushed into our bedroom where I was lying down, glared hatefully at me and hissed, "*Is this your strategy – to turn the kids away from me?!*"

Jenny noticed Lena's rage and began turning to me. Then Sally began doing the same. I tried to get them to go to Lena too, and they probably wanted to, but they seemed to sense her vitriolic hatred and wanted to steer clear of it. Did Lena think that kids don't notice things like that, even things they can't verbalize?

Once the kids were asleep that evening, I tried to give Lena space. I retreated to my office in the little house to catch up on my writing in detail about the day's drama that was still unfolding. After several hours I went back into the kitchen to get a drink. I was agitated by what I was writing, since I was only seeing the storyline with clarity through the writing of it; the experience of it was far too distressing for me to comprehend in the moment.

Lena asked me what I was doing over there in my office and I told her. I said that what was going on wasn't good for the kids, and that *she* would have to shape up and start to take *her* share of the responsibility. "*I'm not going to repent for anything!*" she shot back defiantly. She displayed no traces of anything that gave me hope. Just hatred. When she raised her voice at me, Sally woke up and called for me. I let Lena go upstairs to her so as not to give Lena more fuel for her argument that I was trying to take the kids from her. But Sally continued calling for *me*. I went upstairs to comfort her and prevent her from waking Jenny as well. Lena hissed furiously at me, "*Typical!!*"

When Sally fell back to sleep, I came downstairs and told Lena that she shouldn't start turning our love of the kids into a competition. I was in no way trying to take them from her. And besides, it was Lena who wanted to leave; I wanted us all to be together. But Lena wasn't receptive to *anything* coming from me. I said that we needed to talk with each other. "*What about?*" she sneered, "*the Bible?*" I had no idea why she made such an out-of-the-blue, nonsequitous reference. I was completely baffled. And angry. I thought to myself that if that was what she wanted, I could have provided some pithy biblical retorts. But I refrained and returned to my office to write. As I recorded this latest exchange, I felt my rage swinging back to grief of the kind I'd felt after Jeanette's death.

On Thursday morning, Lena was cold and hostile. She snapped at me for everything. This led to the following exchange:

Jenny: Stop being nasty, Mommy!
Lena (in her silky voice): What do you mean, Jenny?
Jenny: Stop being angry with Daddy! He doesn't feel well!
Lena (shooting murderous daggers at me): Did Daddy tell you to say that?!
Me (angry at last): Stop this, Lena! I know, and Jenny knows, that I've told her no such thing! You're just doing yourself a disservice saying such silly things.

Then Lena drove off with the kids, to leave them with the sitter before going to work. She didn't want them to be with me; they were spending too much of their time with me. I didn't know what to do, so I wrote.

Then I suddenly remembered that my trove of old calendars and notebooks from as far back as 1978. As I started going through them it almost made my hair stand on end. All the times I'd proposed something or expressed a thought, to which Lena's only response was to call it idiotic or ridiculous – all right there in fine print in those old notebooks. All the times I'd tried to use reason to defend (!) myself, when she became hysterical and screamed uncontrollably – even back then. Defend myself! How dare I!! Of course she would become hysterical – I'd disagreed with her, and disagreeing means criticism and criticism *of her* is intolerable!!

The disaster that was transpiring now was so clearly foreshadowed in our early relationship. Clear patterns in my original notes were emerging, shoving into my face the connections I'd previously refused to see.

I had a long talk with Marie-Louise about these things. To my surprise, she told me that Lena, her daughter, was "completely mad" (her exact words in Swedish: "*fullständigt galen*"). Spontaneously I sought to defend her. I asked her whether Lena might be a restless soul who was feeling too "settled" as a wife and mother. Marie-Louise found it plausible; perhaps Lena was rebelling, I suggested, trying to free herself from responsibility, guilt, criticism and insight. Marie-Louise found all that plausible too – without withdrawing her original assessment.

There was little to suggest that Marie-Louise was wrong. Lena repeatedly made it clear that she continued to believe, as she first told me back in 1979, that she was "*above all criticism!*" Yet now she was facing a veritable *wall* of criticism for her actions, and thus she turned to the one person who presumably didn't criticize her at all: *Schade*! Perhaps she realized that I would never again let her be in my spotlight alone – that she would always have to have to share it with Jenny and Sally. But now she'd found someone she thought would give her his spotlight all to herself.

She was, as far as I could tell, in the process of creating something I felt would eventually catch up with her: a "lifelong lie". (The Swedish for this is *livslögn*. The German equivalent, *lebenslügen*, is sometimes used in English in the field of psychiatry to describe a permanent self-deception, a false premise one is unwilling to examine or question, whereby living a lie is more comfortable, more crucial, than finding out what's true.) Ibsen wrote (in *Vildanden, The Wild Duck*) about the total dependency of some people on this *livslögn* – like a respirator. I knew quite a few people who seemed be dependent like that! To my surprise, it made me feel sorry for her.

Lena fed me a few selected details about Johannes. He was two and a half years my elder. He was a clergyman's child (*like me, in a way, and Lena!*). He sang in a choir (*aha, that's why she joined!*). He was proud of his "spiritual" side (*Could this have been the reason for her sarcastic biblical reference the day before?*). Lena seemed to think these revelations would somehow impress me. She was now, for the first time, presenting spirituality as a quality she shared with him, one she now claimed that I'd repressed in her, despite her previous indications to the contrary! "*I suppose he's so holy he follows the 10 Commandments?*" I asked, unable to repress my own sarcasm. "*I hope he doesn't follow the other 603 and stone you to death for sleeping with him!*" I knew it was a cheap shot, but in the context of having Schad's nauseating "spirituality" rubbed in my face, I just couldn't resist.

I told Marie-Louise about the "Birgitta incident" in 1983, knowing that Lena would probably try to use that as a trump card against me sooner or later. That evening I told Lena that when I told her mother about it, she'd more or less dismissed it with a shrug. Lena was noticeably disappointed.

My writing was proving to have tremendous therapeutic value for me, far beyond what I'd expected, similar to the effect of writing *The Unparallel Lines*. It helped me to give structure to my thoughts and feelings, to regain control of them, to gain insights, and to set new priorities. I was getting more sleep. There were now moments when I didn't need to fake a happy face. I could give the kids joy and fun and love; they certainly needed and deserved it. Eva phoned that evening; we had a long talk. She asked me frank and probing questions and I gave her frank and forthright answers. She was disappointed to learn that Lena wasn't keeping her promise to confine her contact with Schad to work-related matters. She wanted Lena to change jobs at once, and to work at a different school.

During our conversation, Lena entered the room and demanded to know with whom I was speaking. I told her and surrendered the phone to her. She also had a long talk with her sister, a talk that left her (Lena) visibly shaken. Eva later told me she'd warned Lena that she might lose the kids, which made Lena so upset that she expressed no further hatred towards me for the rest of the evening. And again I felt a bit sorry for her. I decided to sleep in our bed that night – at least until I got up for a couple of hours after Lena was asleep to write about our day.

Early the next morning, Sally, who lay between us close to Lena half the night, turned towards me when Jenny joined us. Jenny also wanted to lie next to me. Lena jumped out of bed and hissed bitterly, "*I might as well leave!*" And she stormed out of the room. This caused Sally to start crying and run after her. I got extremely irritated and said to Lena, "*How can you be so childish?! Don't you see what you're doing to the kids?*" She glared at me and shot back sarcastically, "*Is that going to be your tune today?!*" Could she have thought over what I said for a moment before dismissing it outright? Well, yes. But she didn't.

Lena went swimming alone – at least she said so (her credibility was zero) – while I went to the park with the kids. When we were all back at Korngatan, I said we'd soon have to make up our minds about the planned trip to Gotland that summer. "*Obviously we're going!*" Lena exclaimed. I wondered (to myself) how the hell that could possibly be obvious! Were we to spend another few months in Malmö with Lena's unapologetic infidelity and unbridled hatred towards me, and then take a trip together besides? How was that even *conceivable*?!

I told Lena that the ball was in her court. Her anger was rising by the second. She said it wasn't at all up to her, it was my "unnatural" working conditions that had to change. (This was a new tack!! It was the first time she'd *ever* expressed any objection to my working from home, with all the advantages it gave us – and her.) Suddenly it wasn't even negotiable, she claimed. Quite simply, she said, she couldn't stand the sight of me.

The topic of repentance came up. "*What do you want me to do – fall on my knees?*" she said sarcastically. "That might not be a bad idea," I replied acidly, and her temper boiled over. We spent the rest of the day keeping our distance. That evening I went to a neighbor with the present we'd gotten for his 40th birthday party the following evening. I told him we'd be unable to attend.

Saturday was the 9th anniversary of the first time Lena succumbed to my unrelenting pressure and told me she loved me. We began the day with a discussion about how to move forward. She now said that she wouldn't leave alone – she'd take the kids and have them half the time: shared custody. What changed her mind about her intentions as stated on March 10th, when she said she'd move to a furnished apartment for a month, leave the kids at Korngatan, and come back to see them during the daytime, if I would permit that? Now she denied ever having said any such thing. Then she admitted she did say it, but had changed her mind. She gave no reason. In her world, truth seemed to be a greased eel.

The next morning I again pleaded with her to help us see if we could find a way back to each other. But now everything about me made her tremble with fury. How was this possible? According to Lena, when something wasn't good, it had *never* been good and never *could* be – all or nothing, always or never, two counterpoles, nothing in between. Once her mood passed, she brushed aside the horrible things she'd screamed at me and couldn't understand why they still caused me pain ("*What? Are you still moping?!*").

We'd now entered a darkness that had no end. Lena was rewriting history. She had no more feelings for me. Moreover, this had been the case for an awfully long time. "Then why did you want to have kids with me?" I asked. "*Because I felt that I needed a child!*" she replied. I wondered (to myself) whether this involved anything like responsibility or honesty. And if she was being honest? Then she was expressing a level of cynicism that made me want to puke.

At one point she claimed she *had* to have an affair *because she knew she was treating me "like shit"*!! What?!?! She claimed I'd never even tried to understand her. I protested vigorously, that I'd been trying to do that ever since we met. She said that at least I'd never succeeded. That evening when I was writing about what was said and done during the day, I made a list:

- Until very recently, Lena always presented a mask to others and did it so well that what she presented to me might have been the mask instead, or another mask.

- Lena must have been just as aware as Eva, at least at times, of what Jan called "the Johannisson temper". If she's not in the right mood, she'll fly off the handle in a flash, and for no real reason. This makes understanding her quite a bit more difficult.
- This exacerbates Lena's innate rejection of criticism ("I'm above it"), which in turn is connected to her strong aversion to using the healing word "sorry".
- Lena has lied and denied everything the whole time relating to Schade – until she's confronted with factual evidence.
- The warnings she now claims to have been giving me for years were, until a couple of months ago (since when everything has seemed surreal), issued in a state of extreme agitation and were without exception simply glossed over once her mood has passed.
- Every single one of my attempts to arrange talks or consultations with an outsider, whether a family member or a professional family counsellor, has been flatly rejected.

Against these odds, is it any wonder I didn't succeed in understanding her? Does she understand herself?? I showed her my list, hoping it might lead to better understanding, but she haughtily rejected all of it. I returned to my office to write down my thoughts:

> Her course was staked out: emphasize to family and friends how unhappy she's been; blame everything on me for not understanding; admit no major role in it; downplay (for the moment) the role of Schade; say how sorry she was for me (it sounds so magnanimous); arrange for the kids' lives to be split between a devastated daddy and a happy family with mommy; gloss over the rest; and never look back.
>
> I felt like I'd never really had an honest chance. I'd always been madly in love with her, so she never needed to lift a finger to reciprocate, and she didn't. Inertia took over. The more I gave, the more she expected. A warm, loving contact (yes, it had really been there for a while!) slowly morphed into dissatisfaction, then contempt, and finally hatred. We were now on the brink of ruin.

I could feel the writing process helping me to achieve some kind of equilibrium again, to get the venom out, to stand up again, to be a rock for my kids in the tough times to come. But both my common sense and my intuition told me that the aftershocks hadn't even begun yet.

Eva (and Jan) and Marie-Louise were exasperated with Lena's antics and repeatedly broken avowals to cut off contact with Schade. They made it clear to her that she was no longer welcome to see them in Lund and Barkåkra, respectively, until she honored her word – and agreed to seek professional marital counseling. My words carried no weight with her, but theirs did – although not enough for Lena to lift a finger to *find* such counseling, nor to display anything but prejudicial pessimism about it.

It thus fell upon me to find a counselor, a task I undertook still hoping to rescue our marriage and home and family. I consulted the Yellow Pages (no internet back then!) and began calling the counselors who identified themselves as marriage or relationship specialists. Some were fully booked for the coming months. I asked if they could recommend another, and called that one. Within a few hours I eventually found what looked to be an ideal solution: a husband-and-wife team of psychotherapists who preferred to meet as couple-to-couple, to avoid the imbalance of two men versus one woman or vice-versa. It seemed like a sound and fair-minded approach. Unfortunately, they couldn't see us immediately; we had to wait until March 30th for the first of the four sessions I booked with them.

Once again, I was full of hope and enthusiasm when I told Lena that I'd found some help. She scowled and sighed. I was looking for a miracle; she seemed only to be looking for a way out. Eva and Marie-Louise crossed their fingers. (Or would have if they hadn't been Swedish. Since they were Swedish, they held their thumbs instead.)

Throughout this ordeal, and despite my former refusal to involve him in anything that led up to it, Bob was my rock – again. When I phoned him on March 11th to let him know that the destructive forces had been unleashed, he was understandably taken by surprise. After all, Lena had worn her mask well, as I had by helping her to keep hers intact. On March 14th, Bob wrote:

> There's no point in saying: if Lena only knew how well off she is, how many nice women would change places with her without hesitating etc, all the routine locutions of the jilted. The fact seems to be, the real-life Lena thinks otherwise, and it is she who has the worm in her throat and has become active. And she is the only one who can get rid of that worm, even if the operation causes as much pain and disruption as it seems will be the case. [...] What does Lena really want, and does she know it?;

what does her swain really want, and does he know it?; are their notions primarily romantic or do they include alternatives which consider the welfare of others most directly involved, specifically her daughters and husband?

When I told Bob that one of Lena's biggest, bitterest, and most repeated complaints about me was that I "analyze everything to death," I thought he'd hit the ceiling. "*Shades* [sic] *of my father!*" he raged, recalling the fury and violence his father displayed towards his young son whenever Bob asked questions, trying to understand what he was supposed to believe instead of swallowing without question what he'd been commanded to take on faith. "*How could wanting to understand the world, one's life, one's surroundings be a fault and not a feat, a vice and not a virtue?!*" Bob wrote. He told me that plenty of acquaintances had told him he was too analytical, and to him it "*became a matter of instant death for such a friendship after the first experience of it.*"

Bob never suggested I shouldn't fight for my marriage, nor did he suggest that I bend over backwards to save what she seemed hell-bent on destroying. He provided a rational (analytical!) sounding board for me, a haven of sense in a sea of roiling, mindless emotion. At one point he even offered to make a trip to "neutral ground" (he thought of Copenhagen) to meet us and mediate, but as I revealed the depths of Lena's hatred of me, layer by layer, he began thinking in different terms.

I phoned Rob and Chris in London one evening to pour out my heart to them as well. Rob answered, and I tried to tell him what was afoot. He seemed both surprised and ill at ease, as if he were embarrassed to speak about matters of the heart. It – *he* – disappointed me, but I'd always found it easier to talk with Chris anyway, so I wasn't awfully surprised. Chris responded sympathetically and allowed me to talk. She listened, which was all I needed.

My phone call to Mom on her birthday (March 28th, also the anniversary of Jeanette's death) was pretty disastrous. I'd sent her a letter a week earlier, saying that the recent infrequency of my writing was due to "marital problems that we are working to solve". She was fully capable of sensing that the situation might be dire, and that understanding was needed, but instead she launched into a torrent of garbage: I must "come back to the Lord", she insisted, He this and Him that. I finally cut her off, after several unsuccessful diplomatic attempts to either ignore her or change the subject. "Look Mom," I said, "I *really* don't need this!" and she finally shut up. It left a bad taste.

I'd been keeping a careful record of conversations (mostly fights) and events, as well as my thoughts and feelings for years. I had collections of notes since 1977, and I wanted to compile them in some useful way. On March 30th I wrote to Bob:

> *I'm really starting to take the idea of a book seriously. Correction: I'm starting to take the writing of a book seriously, and I'm already underway. This is something I've been wanting to do for several years now, more or less since I ceased painting. A year ago I would have said that I would wait to launch into it until Sally had started school (i.e. for the time it would consume every day), but that was a year ago. Now it will have the added therapeutic benefits I so well need, in addition to a few extra chapters to take up a few extra twists and turns in my strange life. As a matter of fact, a break-up would likely relieve me of a few inhibitions as well. [...] I see this as a project of at least two years, depending on how many practical problems arise in the meantime. It's every bit as hard work as painting!* ["At least two years"?! This has taken me 33 years!!]

This was the Easter vacation week, so Lena was off work, giving Lena and me extra time together, which she hated. My hopes, feeble as they'd become, were now pinned on meeting with the psychotherapists on Wednesday, March 30th, at 3 PM. I drove us to their office. Lena snarled and grumbled the whole way there. She made it *perfectly* clear that she *really* didn't want to do this. I guessed that she was just going through the motions to be able to tell her mother and sister she'd complied with their demands.

But to my astonishment, all her hostility seemed to fall away as we walked through the door, like a superfluous silk robe gliding off her shoulders, or as if invisible soft brushes surrounding the door opening brushed her clean as she stepped into the room. Her soft, silky tone – the one I'd loved instantly more than a decade before, the one I had lately come to doubt and mistrust even as I still longed for it – prevailed. *Was she out to fool them, too?*

They asked us to sit at a table, next to each other. The psychotherapists – Harry and Jocelyne Korman – sat opposite us. They began by explaining how they worked, couple-to-couple. If possible, we would find each other again and they would help. If not possible, they would offer advice towards attaining results that would individually give us the stability we needed in our separate lives. They sounded professional, yet caring.

First they asked Lena to relate what things about me she found hard to accept. She found it easy to find her words, but seemed to find it difficult to maintain her soft, silky voice while listing her complaints. Traces of rage slipped in between subjects and predicates, articles and nouns, before and after prepositions. Before she'd finished telling them how deeply she disliked the fact that I was always helping out with the kids, the cleaning, the dishes, the laundry, the cooking, etc, her face was contorted with anger; she was almost seething. They interrupted her. "*Lena,*" Jocelyne said, "*I don't really understand. Most people consider the things you've mentioned to be <u>positive</u> qualities in a partner! We've never before encountered anyone who's <u>complained</u> about that kind of thing! Perhaps you are <u>searching</u> for things to fight about?*"

Lena immediately backtracked, catapulted, backpedaled, did an instant about-face pirouette. Her expression flipped from hostility to extreme tenderness in a split-second, her silky voice returned as she blurted out, "Yes, yes, I <u>know</u>. They <u>are</u> positive things, but, well, it's just that he's always <u>there</u>, and I need more space!" They looked at her, at each other, at me, back at her, still somewhat puzzled. She was struggling to retain her silky voice. My impression was that they'd seen right through her too, but I can't be expected to be objective about that.

Then they turned to me and asked what it was about Lena that I was unhappy with. I said I was unhappy that she didn't love me, that she wanted to leave me, that she'd met somebody else, that I didn't know how I could be expected to be away from home since I worked from home, and that most of our childcare depended on my being at home, that I feared for the welfare of our two little girls if we were to separate, and that I was afraid she'd only reluctantly joined me for this meeting because her mother and sister had pretty much forced her to. The more I talked, the harder I found it to hold back my tears and keep from trembling. They asked me if I wanted her to stay, and I said <u>yes</u>. I'm not sure they understood why. [*I'm not sure <u>I</u> understood why.*]

I said that Lena promised her mother and sister not to have further contact with her lover. They concurred that it was a good idea, and probably necessary if we were to have any chance at all of saving our marriage. The more they talked, the more Lena seemed to listen and truly understand what they were saying. She was, after all, nodding thoughtfully and gazing earnestly, as if hanging on their every word. After some time, she told them – in her silky voice – how she in fact really had strong feelings for me, and that I really was a wonderful person, and that she was really up for really doing her best to bring this whole thing to a really happy conclusion.

At the end of our first session, the psychotherapist couple gave us a little assignment: *"We'd like you to go out and get each other a little present tomorrow. Nothing big – just a token, a symbol: a candy bar, a pencil, an eraser, whatever – and give it to the other without a word. Just hand it over and say nothing. Will you do that?"* We both agreed. Then we stood up, slowly put on our coats and headed for the door. I was convinced that a miracle had already happened.

As their office door closed behind us and we started walking down the corridor, I felt such joy that I went to put my arm around Lena. She recoiled sharply. *"What do you think you're doing!?!"* she hissed sharply. My face fell. So did my heart. *It had all been an act!!* I knew deep down that I should have known that, but I still resisted the inevitable. Desperation welled up inside me, and I fought back tears. *"But I thought you said…"* was all I could get out of me. She glared at me, with that look of pure hatred I'd come to recognize. Then she sneered, *"You don't think this problem can be solved just like that?!"*

The walk to the car and the 10-minute drive home took place in silence and seemed to take hours. I was numb. Lena growled at me to get it together before we got home to the kids (I forget who was staying with them that afternoon, probably a neighbor), and I did my best. Shortly after we got home, I hurried up to the store at the square to buy a candy bar to give her the next day, as agreed.

After we were on our own again for a moment, Lena told me that she assumed I'd be playing badminton in Staffanstorp that evening – it was Wednesday, after all. I said I couldn't possibly play, I had no ability to concentrate, I was a complete mess. She snarled angrily, *"But you said you understood that I need some space!!"* I admitted having said that. I agreed to leave for Staffanstorp at the usual time, around 7.30 PM, which meant soon after the kids were asleep.

When I arrived at the badminton hall, I could hardly move. Ove and Hans were in the locker room getting changed, along with the others in our group. I hadn't played for the last few weeks, and their initial jovial welcome was instantly quashed when they saw my state. They asked what the matter was, and I began pouring out my story. There was no point whatsoever in my changing clothes. Ove stayed in the locker room with me, to listen. His kindness was incredible – and unexpected.

Since Ove was also off work for the Easter vacation week, he was spending a lot of time working on their new country house in Beddinge, on the south coast of Skåne. He told me he could use some help the next day if I had the time. His proposal was sincere; it would take me years to realize that his sincerity stemmed from a nobly humane desire to help *me*. In any case, I agreed. He said he'd pick me up the next morning at seven, on the corner of Vattenverksvägen and Källargatan, if that was all right. The kids were usually up at around six, so it wouldn't disrupt them – I'd be able to spend some time with them before I left – and this would be an ideal way for me to give Lena more space.

When I got home from Staffanstorp at around ten that Wednesday evening, Lena was about to go to bed. She'd taken to going to bed with her hair in curlers; I knew that her desire to look pretty the next day wasn't for my benefit. I told Lena that I'd be helping Ove all day tomorrow, and that he'd be picking me up on the street corner in the morning. She grumbled about my leaving her with everything, and I reminded her that she said she wanted space. If looks could kill....

When I'd returned from Staffanstorp that evening, it was immediately apparent that Lena's hostility level had soared during my absence. I couldn't figure it out; the space I'd given her was supposed to have done her good. Why was she even more hateful towards me than before? "Have you spoken with Johannes this evening?" I asked cautiously. "*No!*" she snapped fiercely. "Are you sure?" I asked (even I was surprised by her vehemence). "*I told you 'no'!!*" she lashed out again. "Then what's happened to you this evening? Why are you extra angry??" At first she glared at me, then she softened and said in her silky voice, "*I just want somebody to love, somebody who loves me!*" I was taken aback and exclaimed, "But Lena, you've got me!!" and held out my arms. Instantly, her face clouded over, she sneered and hissed, "*Well, it's certainly not you!!!*" Then she charged off to bed.

I stood there in the middle of the kitchen floor, stunned and heartbroken. (Why wasn't I used to it yet?) My day had been eventful, confusing and dire. I had a lot to write about that night, a lot to try to make sense of. I'd loved her, deeply, right from the start. But I'd also had certain irrepressible and very chilling suspicions: *Might I have subconsciously "chosen" to love someone whom I felt certain would treat me badly??!* Was it because I subconsciously wanted to punish myself, since I could never *prove* to myself that I hadn't in some way contributed to Jeanette's mental anguish, as Lena kindly pointed out to me on at least two occasions. As my head began spinning faster and faster, I went to my office to write.

I sat there untangling, unravelling the day's exceptionally confusing events on my computer. One might think I was just wallowing in it, exacerbating my own pain. But I already knew how beneficial to my equilibrium and insight it was to recount verbatim as much of the day's dialog as I could. Well after 1 AM, when I had painstakingly recounted everything, I'd become convinced that Lena *had* spoken with Schade while I was gone during the evening, and that she'd thus broken her promise again. Part of me was always ready to defend her, however, to search for other explanations. Maybe she hadn't lied; maybe she'd only *tried* to phone him and he wasn't there. And there was no way I could check whether he'd phoned her, except that he couldn't have known I'd be out? So perhaps she *had* tried?

We tended to use the wall phone in our front hall when making or receiving a late-evening call, so as not to disturb the kids' sleep. It suddenly occurred to me that that particular phone had a button for redialing the latest number dialed. (It was the only phone in the house at that time that had such a function.) So it came to pass, that at 2 AM, I picked up the receiver and pushed that button. The phone rang five or six times before a sleepy voice mumbled "*Johannes*". I quickly hung up. She *had* lied.

Without warning, my years of intense sexual longing for Lena simply and abruptly *vanished*. Just like that. It came (or left!) as a total surprise to me.

Now I knew that writing to clear my head and structure my thoughts was my only path to stability – and I needed all the stability I could get for the sake of the kids. It was the kids I had to focus on, completely. There would be no more crying myself to sleep, no more waking with a tear-soaked pillow. I slept in the guest room and arose at about 6 AM, well before the alarm. I dressed quickly, had a bite of breakfast and went upstairs quietly to see the kids before I left to meet Ove at the street corner. I said I'd miss them that day, but was sure they'd have a wonderful time with Mommy. At about 6:30, I entered the bedroom that was formerly ours. Lena was just waking up. The kids were playing together in the next room.

"I'm off soon," I said softly. She just scowled. Then I added: "I have to ask you again – are you sure you didn't phone Johannes last night?" Her body stiffened and her face flushed. She hissed, "*No!! I told you I didn't and I didn't!!*" I remained very calm, and asked again, "Well, did you try to phone him?" She struggled to suppress her rage. "*What is this, some kind of cross-examination?!?*" She didn't seem to realize that such an answer already pretty much confirmed her lie. Still very calm, I asked again, looking her squarely in the eye, "Do you swear that you didn't call him – or try to call him – last night?" She saw that she was trapped in her lie. "*All right, I did call him, if you must know!*" she replied defiantly. I shook my head and asked, "So why did you lie about it?" Her face became even more defiant. "*I didn't lie! I just told you that I phoned him!*"

    I *honestly* didn't know whether to burst into tears or burst out laughing when I heard those words. I had never before heard of logic being stretched so far into oblivion, not even in the most satirical comedies or farces. She was diluting the truth as if it were a homeopathic "medicine". At last I understood that she had no intention or desire *whatsoever* to continue our marriage, that nothing would stop her from her one goal: her *schadenfreude*. (Sometimes circumstances practically thrust a pun in one's face, like a big cream pie!) It was time – high time – for me to get some new priorities. At last I understood the hopelessness of the situation. *I was at last ready to give up on Lena* – but *not* to stop looking for answers, *not* to stop caring for my kids, and *not* to stop living and loving life.

CHAPTER 11

Damage control

I didn't say much in the car on the way to Beddinge. Ove didn't seem to mind. He'd looked at me long and carefully, with kind eyes, when I got in the car. Being somewhat taciturn by nature, he had no problem waiting for me to speak. Perhaps he also had a good sense of when to leave me to my thoughts, of which I had plenty. I reflected on the brief and bizarre conversation I'd just had with Lena, and what it told me about her grasp of the concept of truth, and what impact that had on the possibility – or the *im*possibility – of trust. Was this the turning point? It wasn't that I had various courses of action to choose from; it seemed that I would have to live with Lena's decision. But one minute I was hoping to find a way for our marriage to go on, the next I had almost convinced myself that it was over.

I didn't know from one minute to the next, because I had no previous experience of falling *out* of love. Now I had to find out or invent *how*. Actually, I don't think I *fell* out of love; I was pushed. I'd probably been prepared to forgive her infidelity, but not her hatred and contempt. That left no way back.

My productivity that day was limited to helping Ove move a few unwieldy sheets of plasterboard and trying to cut a few of them cleanly without letting my thoughts (and my knife) stray too much. Ove listened whenever I needed to talk, even though he might well have preferred not to. I bless him for his kindness and humanity. The day passed. At times I felt an inner calm, the kind that comes with resignation – not surrender, but the realization that there are situations in life where acceptance is better than beating one's head against a concrete wall. And yet.

When I got home in the late afternoon (I felt certain that Ove abbreviated his working day for my sake – what a remarkable human being he was!), one of the first things I did was to present that little gift to Lena. She looked at me and at it suspiciously, totally baffled. "*What's this for?!*" she asked, and seemed genuinely puzzled. "*Don't you remember? The therapists asked us to give each other a small, symbolic gift today.*" She wrinkled her nose, growled something about having forgotten about it, and walked away.

I had to try one last trick. A couple of months earlier, Rob sent me a video recording from British TV of the highlights of the 1987 NFL conference finals, and I remembered something from the closing scenes after Cleveland's heartbreaking loss to Denver: Whitney Houston's recording of *Didn't We Almost Have It All?* [q.v.]. I put it on and fast-forwarded the tape to the song when I knew Lena would hear it. She did. She came into the living room looking agitated. "*Yes, I guess we did!*" she burst out, in English. Then she turned hostile again and added emphatically "*But it's too late now!*"

Later that day I discovered among her papers a couple of poems Shade wrote to her. One was about how one day soon they'd be walking in the sun together, hand in hand, and that she should regard the new Leonard Cohen song *I'm Your Man* as coming from him (Schade) to her. It made me nauseous, but I said nothing. I devoted my attention to the kids, ignored Lena, gained control of my outrage over her dismissal of the gift, that little attempt at some kind of reconciliation. *It wasn't going to happen. It was <u>over</u>!*

Once the kids were asleep, I went to have a word with Lena. She glared at me, ready for a battle I wasn't going to give her. I looked her in the eye and told her I'd given up. In terms of saving our marriage, the psychotherapy sessions were a joke, I said. Therapy can't work if the parties involved aren't seriously interested in the outcome, which she clearly wasn't. She didn't deny it. She looked relieved, perhaps because she would be off the hook if she could tell her mother and Eva that I was the one who wouldn't continue. I knew they'd see through it. Eva was already counseling me to move on. She reiterated her view that Lena wanted "butter on both sides of her bread" and that there'd always been something missing: Lena *couldn't* love me. But Eva seemed to love me, in a kind and sisterly way. And Marie-Louise loved me – also mutual – and made me understand that she would never turn her back on me [*and she never did*].

So how did Lena end up marrying me? Did I just happen to be there when she felt it was time to settle down, and I so obviously *adored* her and could therefore be relied on to take shit whatever she dished out? I was OK. I would do. And I not only adored her, I was so persistent, and I waited on her hand and foot. That, for a time, might have been enough.

I theorized that Lena had a strong need (possibly unconscious) to be in the limelight, to be adored no matter what she did or said, right or wrong. That would explain why she couldn't tolerate criticism, even the constructive kind. She'd never loved me; she never needed to. My love for her was enough for both of us, because it was always about what *she* needed. She was always in my limelight. But sharing the limelight with anyone else was out of the question.

It was unacceptable when people came to our house and admired the house I'd built, the paintings I'd painted, the food I'd cooked (sometimes she preferred to cook when we had guests, but she often left it to me).

But when the kids arrived, even though she remained in my limelight, she was no longer there *alone*. Thus she needed to find someone else, someone in whose limelight she could be all by herself, without sharing, someone who criticized nothing she did or said. *Enter Schade*. I was unable to find anything to contradict that theory, even though I kept looking for faults in it. Bob had another theory. Lena was trying to shake me to my very foundations in order to gain even more power and/or control over me in our marriage. He speculated that she would leave me in despair, wait a month or two, then offer to come back *on her terms*, which I would accept gratefully, without reservation. (He didn't speculate what terms those might be.) I dismissed his theory outright, and he dropped the subject.

Ever since Lena's repeated lies that morning about having spoken with Schade, then admitting she'd spoken with him, but still claiming she hadn't lied, my whole focus switched to damage control. I told Lena that I wanted to keep our three remaining appointments with the therapists anyway. She looked confused; I'd just called the sessions a joke. "*Why?*" I asked rhetorically. "*Because they're family therapists, and I want to get their professional advice on how we can limit the damage to Jenny's and Sally's lives. You don't have to come if you don't want to, but I'm going.*"

Lena looked startled. I'd displayed a kind of determination towards her that she might never have seen before. Was it because I wasn't the push-over she thought I was? Was there something to Bob's theory after all?

I had little doubt that Jenny's and Sally's lives would be impacted in a big way by our split-up. (Lena just sneered at my fears every time I mentioned them.) I couldn't see how they could not be: suddenly two homes, one in a new neighborhood somewhere, many uncertainties about routines that previously gave them security. I'd heard and read many times how a good divorce is better for children than a bad marriage. Fair enough, but she didn't seem willing or able to lift a finger to achieve a *good* marriage. *Why?* Why had she flatly rejected suggestions for getting help before it was too late? And why all the hate? Those questions kept bugging me, like a sharp stone in my shoe.

When I informed Bob about the latest developments, he told me that on March 5th, 1979, he'd drawn up a new will making me his sole beneficiary. Although this was touching and surprising news, it was not exactly *good* news – I was doing everything I could to help him live longer! His reason for telling me at this time, however, was something he now found urgent. He wanted to make certain that nobody else could get a share of his estate. He wanted to know the name of my lawyer. I had to tell him I'd never had one. He urged me to "rectify that shortcoming forthwith", but it would take more than his urging to get me to act.

Mom's written response to the news of the breakup was worse than useless to me. Although it may have been useful to her to write it, she might have done me the favor of not inflicting it on me. Naturally, it was all about the Lord, i.e. her spontaneous, knee-jerk response to anything beyond her ken. She went on and on about how *He* knew the heart, and *He* knew what was best, *He* was in control. She also told me I had to forgive. I didn't have the strength to tell her I'd already concluded that I could forgive Lena's infidelity; it was Lena's *hatred* of me that I couldn't deal with. There are always two sides, Mom wrote, meaning well, I'm sure. But never having seen the side of Lena that hated me so much, how was Mom to know?

Why do so many people assume that the very existence of two sides of a story automatically implies two equally legitimate sides? (*Is it equally plausible that a murder victim might have impaled his chest on the knife – 16 times?!*) I didn't write that to Mom. Instead, knowing that she would never argue with Scripture, I quoted her a Bible verse, Proverbs 21:9: "*It is better to dwell in a corner of the housetop, than with a brawling woman in a wide house.*" That changed her tune!

Both Lena and I had long ago installed a child's seat on the backs of our respective bikes, originally to give each of us the possibility of taking Jenny places other than by car. After Sally was born, we could theoretically have taken both Jenny and Sally on our respective bikes for a family outing once Sally was old enough to ride safely that way. We planned to wait till she was at least two. That remained a theory. Well before Sally turned two, Johannes happened, end of family outings, end of family.

During the Easter vacation week when Lena was off work, I found a kind of bicycle seat for mounting on the front of my bike in addition to the one I had on the back, so I could take both kids on outings on days when Lena needed the car. I was strong then, and there would be no problem for me to have them both, but

Sally initially felt a bit insecure riding there, so we left it for the time being. She was otherwise bold and brave; she would learn in her own good time – which turned out to be about a month.

I have no clear recollection of how or where we passed that Easter weekend. I'm certain that it involved informing Eva and Marie-Louise of the latest development: that I was convinced that further attempts at reconciliation would be futile. I also informed Bob by letter. In any case, on Easter Monday, April 4th, Lena announced that she was going to launch her search for an apartment without further delay. That didn't surprise me at all. What did surprise me was that she intended to limit her search to Slottstaden and Gamla Väster (the Old Town), two of the priciest areas for apartments in the Malmö region. And both were far from Kirseberg (our part of town).

I pointed this out to her. She sneered and said they were *nicer* and had the best schools. I said that I'd hoped she'd look for something in Kirseberg. She grimaced and said it was an awful place, unthinkable. [*She'd lived with me in Kirseberg for close to nine years without expressing anything negative about it, and she returned to Kirseberg less than five years after our divorce, and remains there as of the publication of this book.*] I mentioned the convenience that Kirseberg would offer the kids *and* us: the ease of going back and forth between two homes, not ending up with two sets of friends, and the great disadvantage to one of us of if they were attending a school in the other's neighborhood. She remained unwilling to discuss the matter.

The next day I received a reply from Bob to a letter I'd written several days before. His ruminations regarding his will led him to fear that my ownership of the house might be in danger, a thought that had never occurred to me. After all, I figured, it was the house that Jeanette and I bought and restored; Lena waltzed in on a *fait accompli*, and was able to save a considerable amount of money during her years living there, thanks to the low living cost the house afforded. She had, however, always explicitly refused to consider it her *home*, despite my reminders that it was, even if it wasn't her *house*. Nevertheless, Bob's fear triggered my own, and I felt my heart in my throat.

I now had another reason to talk to a lawyer. Knowing that the Brauns knew quite a few lawyers, I phoned Elsa. She was appalled to hear of our breakup (although perhaps not as surprised as I might have expected). But her very first reaction was, "*Oh no! You'll lose the house!*" I had to sit down and catch my breath. I was incredulous, dizzy. *That can't be!! That's so horribly unfair!!* Elsa then asked me if we'd signed up a prenuptial agreement. I told her we hadn't. She said she was sorry, she agreed that it was awful, but as far as she knew, nothing could be done about it. I moaned audibly. Then she said that I might have nothing to lose by talking to Ulf Strandmark, a lawyer friend of hers who was a partner in a highly respectable law firm with offices at Stortorget.

I phoned him immediately, identified myself as a friend of Elsa's, and outlined the situation. He suggested I come to his office to discuss it. I made an appointment for the next day, when the kids would be with their sitter. He was in his early 50s, balding, and dignified in ways I would never be nor strive to be. But he was also straightforward and rational. After hearing my story in detail, he drew the same conclusion as Elsa: legally speaking, the house was community property and its value in a divorce would be divided between us.

I was stunned again, and sickened. It meant that I would have to buy out Lena's share with money I didn't have and would probably never have. Or *she* could buy *me* out; maybe she *and* Schade – perish the thought. Either way, I'd lose it and the kids would be torn from their childhood home. I hoped that somehow, deep down inside, Lena wouldn't want that to happen to the kids. Might she already be feeling guilty enough to forgo taking their home from them?

What I now had to do – assuming Lena didn't have a change of heart – was to seek the *least bad* ways of minimizing my losses by salvaging enough from the rubble around me with which to start anew. I had to do this intellectually, financially and emotionally – in that ascending order of difficulty, and probably in that sequence.

I asked the lawyer if it were legally possible to make a prenuptial agreement *ex post facto*. He looked confused, flabbergasted. He thought for a minute and said that it was theoretically possible and legal, "*but do you think she'd sign it?!?*" I said it was my only hope. I asked him to draft one, because I had nothing to lose (except his fee) if she signed it, but *my home* to lose – and possibly half my paintings – if she didn't. Then I asked him to make the draft as favorable as possible to Lena in every *other* way: the car would be hers alone and I would sign over to her *all* child allowances for *both* kids, half of which I was legally entitled to.

That evening, Lena decided to accompany me to the psychotherapists for our second meeting. They could see at a glance that a fundamental change had taken place. I was now hobbling, no longer crawling (figuratively speaking). I told them at the outset that we were no longer there to fix our marriage, but only to hear their thoughts on how we might to the greatest possible extent prevent and avoid damage to the kids. Lena's eyes were averted during this. Jocelyne asked (parenthetically) if we'd gone through with the exchange of the little gifts. I said that I had, but that Lena "forgot".

This was clearly an unexpected development for them: sudden, profound and presumably irreversible. They asked a few questions to confirm that they'd grasped the new situation correctly. Then they began responding to my request. The most important thing, they said, was to shield the kids from acrimony. They proposed five rules:

- Avoid arguing or using harsh words in their presence;
- Don't blame or badmouth each other to the kids;
- Don't coach or bribe them to gain an advantage over the other parent;
- Answer their questions about the relationship only to the extent they are able to understand;
- And above all, don't ever put them in a position where they can feel that they are in any way at fault.

It was sound advice, obvious to me the moment they said it. But I realized with some wistfulness that it would be impossible to keep the promise I'd made when Jenny was born: *never to lie to the kids*. Why impossible? What if Lena had just said something to me that hurt me deeply and Jenny saw me looking down and asked me why. If I told her the truth, I'd be breaking the second rule, and I found those rules more important than my self-imposed one (which had also included "white" lies).

We'd booked two more sessions, and I told the Kormans that I wanted to keep those appointments too, because I supposed they had further advice to offer, and I was sure that further questions would arise over the coming weeks. I made it plain that I would be there even if I came alone, but Lena added that she'd also come.

Our poor kids! Jenny was old enough to be struggling valiantly to understand the chaos around her that couldn't always be hidden. Sally clearly felt the chaos, but could articulate few of her feelings, and when it got to be too much she would cry. Leaning on the therapists' advice, I kept reminding the kids how much Daddy *and* Mommy loved them – and always would, no matter what happened. But it was hard to make them understand a situation I barely understood myself.

Two days later, on April 8th, I picked up the prenuptial agreement at Strandmark's office. That evening I told Lena that we needed to discuss where to go from here, and how best to manage the impending separation. I told her that as things stood legally, the house would have to be sold, and Jenny and Sally would find themselves in two new homes, in neither of which were they likely to feel as much at home as they did at Korngatan now. Lena hadn't considered that possibility, nor had she been aware that Swedish law and practice prioritized leaving kids in an "unruffled nest" (Swedish "*orubbat bo*") after a divorce. I said that we had a choice: we could strive together to make things as easy as possible for the kids if she would sign a prenuptial agreement and keep that nest unruffled (which would allow me to keep my house and paintings), or we could turn it into a legal battleground. She read the agreement and signed it without hesitation. (We had called in two neighbors to duly witness the signing.) As far as I could tell, Lena was hell-bent on moving forward with Johannes, and would do whatever it took to make that happen. As for me, I thanked Elsa from the deepest depths of my heart.

[*After Sven Braun died a year or so later, I invited Elsa to come to Korngatan and spend some time with me and the kids. Since we'd discovered that we all enjoyed swimming and had a great time together, we began making weekly visits to the swimming hall in Burlöv, called* Burlövsbadet. *Then we'd all have ice cream at the pool or back at Elsa's place, where I'd help her with practical chores. This continued for well over a decade; until her death, Elsa was like a bonus grandma to Jenny and Sally.*]

I took the signed agreement back to Strandmark the next morning. He was almost shocked that I'd succeeded. He did, however, feel it was the *morally* right thing to do, even if the law didn't require it. As I saw it, I'd made a horrible mistake when I married Lena without bothering to get a prenuptial agreement; now that mistake had been put right.

Strandmark said it would take a couple of weeks for the agreement to be officially registered at the courthouse. I asked him about obtaining a divorce. Although Lena had been threatening me with divorce for years, I knew nothing about the procedures. He said he could draw up the document (which would also have to be registered at the courthouse after signing), but because we had children together, there would be a mandatory waiting period of six months, provided neither party contested it. I wasn't about to contest. Neither was Lena, as far as I could tell; she only wanted her *Schadenfreude*.

In addition, we would eventually (once the divorce became final) have to draft another agreement regarding the division of property, which would cover personal effects. He said it could be done as a complicated document, or we could keep it simple by agreeing on some basic principles. (With few exceptions, alimony was not among the terms of a Swedish divorce. Besides, Lena's income was greater than mine; I was working part-time.)

Strandmark also mentioned that we could sign a binding agreement regarding the custody of and costs relating to the kids. I'd always loathed formalities of almost every kind, but for once I could see the necessity of having a few things written in stone, so as to prevent Lena's whims and moods from moving the goalposts when and where I least expected it.

Even though I had basically given up, there was still a small part of me that wasn't quite finished trying; I still entertained a glimmer of hope. What if I could make her jealous? I tried contacting by phone a few young women I used to know, so that Lena would see me having an enjoyable conversation as she looked from the kitchen across the yard and into my office. I figured that if it failed to arouse her curiosity and jealousy, I might at least end up with a contact or two for later reference. I first tried phoning Majlis, with whom I hadn't spoken in nearly 10 years. She remembered me all right, and said she'd like to meet – but not on the terms of our former, purely erotic relationship. It would have to be with a view to having a "completely serious" relationship. Feeling nowhere close to being ready for anything like that at this point, I told her so, sorry, and that was that. If Lena had bothered to ask me with whom I'd been speaking, I would smile knowingly and say *"Wouldn't you like to know!"* As it turned out, she never did.

Lena's apartment-hunting hit a wall. She'd apparently expected doors to open wherever and whenever she wanted them to, but available apartments were scarce. Affordable apartments in her targeted areas didn't exist. Her new search areas were broader and cheaper – and closer to Kirseberg.

At my suggestion, we started spending our evenings (after the kids were asleep) by going through all our things – our furniture (although there was relatively little that I hadn't built in place!), the contents of our cupboards, bric-a-brac, carpets, lamps, portable appliances, the kids' toys, etc. We went systematically from room to room, floor to ceiling. I told her she could take pretty much whatever she wanted and stash it in the garage until her moving day came, but that I did *not* want her to keep coming back and taking more once she'd left. I had to be able to feel that I was living in *my* home, not her storage depot! She said she'd do that. During the sorting process in one of the cupboards, I came across the chef's hat ("Kiss the Cook") that Carmen brought for me two years earlier. I made a mental note of where it was, thinking it might come in handy some day.

The first problem with the division of property was about the piano, Lena's famous old piano that she never played (but that I now did). It was currently in its fourth location in our home and couldn't be moved back out the way it came in. The only way to remove it would be to hire a crane to lift it off the terrace roof (after hiring movers to move it out there). The total cost of moving it to her new place would be significantly greater than the value of the piano or the cost of buying another good second-hand one for Lena. I offered to pay her for the latter, and she agreed. I gave her 6000 kronor for it (considerably more than its market value). I didn't want there to be any need for further negotiations on it in the future.

Otherwise, the material side of things went smoothly. She'd had her own set of kitchen utensils and dishes, towels, sheets, blankets, lamps etc, when she moved in, and now she'd be taking them with her, leaving behind the corresponding sets that Jeanette and I had. To my considerable surprise, she wanted to keep *Priming the Pump*, the painting I gave her for Christmas in 1978. I agreed, but I told her to return my mom's wedding ring. When she balked, I pointed out that Mom specifically gave it "to Stan's loving wife".... She took it off and handed it to me without comment. I did, however, sense a strongly symbolic note of finality in that act, a feeling I suspect she shared. I no longer knew how often she was talking to Johannes, nor did I particularly care – or at least I tried not to dwell on it.

We made our third visit to the Kormans on April 13th; our fourth and final visit came six days later. Those visits might have been superfluous – there wasn't a great deal more ground to cover that we hadn't already covered with them or discovered on our own, but it still felt worthwhile to me (and I was the only one paying for the sessions).

On April 15th, Lena said *yes* to the contract on an apartment she'd found on Ivögatan, a block or two from Möllevångstorget, the square with Malmö's biggest produce market. I often went shopping at that market and at the surrounding small shops for Chinese and other Asian ingredients. The neighborhood was interesting, vibrant and working-class. Although it was closer to Kirseberg (compared to Slottstaden and the Old Town), it was by no means within walking distance for the kids. But it was entirely her decision. *Pick your battles, Stan.*

In keeping with the Kormans' advice, we told the kids, together, that Mommy would be moving to a nice new apartment where Jenny and Sally would have their own beautiful new room. It would mean that they'd have *two* homes and *two* beautiful rooms and wouldn't that be *exciting*? (Perhaps this wasn't a lie, or perhaps it wouldn't always be a lie, but it certainly felt like a lie to me *then*.) We told them that sometimes a person can have a wonderful cat and a wonderful dog, but sometimes the cat and the dog can't get along, can't be together, so it's happier for everyone if they're not. Does a message sink in if you keep repeating it? What I really wanted to know was: *Does it become true?*

Lena said she'd be taking the kids to Gotland on her own for nine days in June, as we had previously planned together. I decided to visit Bob during that time, and he would then accompany me back to Korngatan for three weeks. I didn't know whether she'd be meeting Johannes on Gotland. I was trying hard to convince myself that I didn't care (*"Frankly my dear, I don't give a damn!"*) and was largely succeeding. In any case it was something I chose not to ask about. But I knew it was going to be torture being away from the kids, so the distraction of being abroad (in man's clothing) would be merciful.

I had a long chat on the phone with Eva on April 17th. I told her of my resolve to pursue life, the future, to meet someone else if possible. *"I cannot dangle and squirm on her hook while she makes up her mind whether she 'really' wants me or not."* Then I told Eva of the note I'd found to Lena from Schade the week before: a newspaper clipping of a movie review of *The Unbearable Lightness of Being*, where he'd marked the point he wanted her to grasp: jealousy is tough, but no one can promise to spend a lifetime loving another person. [*Did he really think this wouldn't apply to him someday?!*] At the top of this clipping, he'd written, "Beloved Lena, will you see this film with me?" Eva went silent. She felt, as I did, how incredibly shoddy [*Yes, that <u>was</u> a pun!*] this affair was.

Whenever I caught Lena in a bald-faced lie, instead of admitting it, she would frequently counter-attack. In one of these she screamed, *"You'd better watch what you say, or I'll take the kids! Just remember that!!"* It took me years to lose my fear of being at her mercy regarding custody of the kids. I'd envisaged becoming a stranger to Jenny and Sally. But before despair could overwhelm me, my rational side remembered that Swedish courts would never allow Lena to take the kids from me – or vice-versa! – as long as I didn't become an addict or violent or something of that nature (and becoming an addict or violent were not at *all* my nature!).

After Lena had reached an agreement on her new apartment, she had to wait a full month before she could move in, as the existing tenant had a month's notice. Three days after Lena signed up for her new dwelling, I felt I needed another symbolic act to deal with the uprooting of my life: I went to the sign-maker on Stora Nygatan, the one who'd made the brass signs for our front door (first for me and Jeanette in 1975, then for me and Lena in 1979, then new signs to mark the arrivals of Jenny and Sally in 1984 and 85, respectively). This time I ordered one with just three names: the only three who would still be residing at Korngatan 12 after May 15th, Lena's official moving day.

In late April, Lena announced that she'd decided to enroll the kids in a nursery school starting in mid-August. I wondered why – we'd been able to manage well on our own since Jenny was born, with only a half day's outside help from babysitters. Her reply: *"Because then you'd have them more than I would, which wouldn't be fair!"* I asked whether she meant fair to the *kids*, and whether it *mattered* to her if they wanted to be with me rather than with strangers. She dismissed my objection as "sick" and "idiotic"; we were back to that low level. *"So in order to be fair, the kids don't get to be with either of us?!"* I asked, thinking of a quote perhaps mistakenly attributed to a US military officer in Vietnam in 1968: "It became necessary to destroy the town in order to save it." And now *I* was the one being idiotic?

[*Some years later, I would see a film called* Mrs Doubtfire *(with Robin Williams) about a divorced dad whose ex-wife won't allow him to be with his beloved children, so he dresses up as an older woman and gets a job as his own children's nanny. I never got the disguise, but I certainly knew the feeling!!*]

Nearly all Swedish children began some form of nursery school, day-care, or pre-school as soon as the generous year of paid parental leave of absence was over. And nearly all households were double-income. Housewives were pretty much a thing of the past in Sweden by the 1970s. My generation was the transition – or perhaps the Experiment. Not many in my generation attended nursery school before the age of five; among Lena's and my parents' generation, it was almost unheard-of.

Sweden had, as far as I could judge, a good system of nursery schools where children could (at least theoretically) develop important social skills through supervised interaction with other children. I could easily see that the nursery school system filled an important need. But was it *automatically preferable* to parental care? There are so many factors involved: the individual parent-child or staff-child relationships, the educational capabilities of each staff member, the time allotted for individual attention and affection, the needs of the child in question, the care environment, etc. It is hardly "idiotic" to want to ask questions, to wonder, to express doubts! It is, in my view, healthy to question this and *any* other norm.

    But as I saw no benefit to distressing the kids by arguing over them, I acquiesced (how unlike me!). Not only did I go along with it, I even agreed to share the cost of the nursery school – to *pay* someone else to have my kids even on *my* 50%, when I knew that my kids would have preferred to be with *me*, and I was therefore against it. But I was too battle-worn (and probably too cowardly) to put my foot down and refuse (at the very least to pay). And so it began.

In early May, with our prenuptial agreement duly registered, I told Lena that I was filing for divorce in a matter of days. She reacted with astonishment, which astonished me utterly. I asked her why on earth that should come as a surprise to her. She'd been insisting on leaving me, she'd just signed the papers for a new apartment, she was sleeping with someone else, and for years she'd been threatening to divorce me, and telling me how much she hated me. Why *wouldn't* I want a divorce?! She thought I was being hasty. "<u>Me?!</u> You've been at me for <u>years</u>!" She shrugged in resignation to the *fait* she'd *accompli*ed.

    I phoned Strandmark and made an appointment for the late afternoon of May 9th. He wanted both of us to be there, for the sake of impartiality. He went through everything carefully with us until we were in agreement, then said he'd need a day or two (the Thursday was a holiday) to have the papers ready for signing. Lena seemed to find it a mere nuisance, perhaps because she was now excited about moving and getting on with her new relationship. After all, she'd made up her mind. And yet. There was *still* a part of me that was dreading it, in spite of everything.

    Lena booked a small van (small enough not to require a license for driving trucks) for moving her things on Sunday, May 15th. She'd been filling the garage with her selections, and I kept reminding her to take what she wanted *now*, and then forever after hold her peace. From time to time I needed to remind the kids that some things that had disappeared from view in our home were in the garage and would be found at Mommy's new apartment – their new *second* home. I did my utmost not to make my clarifications emotional so as not to color their perceptions negatively.

We discussed Lena's moving day rationally. Eva and I were going to help her. In the morning, I would take Jenny and Sally to spend the day with Sara and Nina (and thus Ole and Birgitta), to reduce the risk of trauma. Our kids would stay with me that first night.

The next couple of days went by slowly, slowly, despite the flurry of activity and my rebounding, resurging mental chaos. The morning's mail delivery on Friday the 13th [sic] brought the divorce papers from Strandmark. I'm fully aware that Friday the 13th sounds like a literary contrivance, but that was when it happened. Besides, I'm "*sub*stitious" (my antonym to *super*stitious). To avoid wasting time unnecessarily, we signed the divorce papers as soon as we could summon in two neighbors as witnesses. Then I cycled off at full speed to Stortorget with the papers so they could be sent off to the courthouse that same day. The six-month mandatory waiting period would begin on Monday.

That afternoon, Lena received a call from the landlord of her new apartment; the previous tenant had just cleared out, the apartment had been cleaned, and she could pick up the keys that same afternoon if she wanted to, which of course she did, as soon as I got home from Strandmark. The moment the kids were asleep that evening, she began filling the Daihatsu – *her* car now – with plants and bags of small or fragile items. The moment she took off, I put up the new door sign on the front door of the house.

When she returned to Korngatan after her first trip and entered by the front door, she immediately noticed the new door sign and was furious. "*Are you trying to wipe out my memory here?*" she hissed at me. I said I thought it was customary for a door sign to state only the names of the residents, not the former residents. And by the way, was she planning to have a sign on her apartment door that included my name? She seethed, but said nothing further about it. [*And yet, several decades later, she still claimed to be "offended" by my action!*]

I don't remember how many trips she made that evening. Her last one took quite a long time. I didn't know how to switch off my imagination. When she finally returned home (I should say "to Korngatan"), I asked sarcastically whether she and Johannes had "christened" the new place. She just sneered – at last a sneer I deserved.

On Saturday I felt liked a caged animal, dazed and waiting to be released into a different world, a different life. Lena was keeping busy with the last of her sorting and selecting and packing. I was trying to downplay the high drama that was unfolding so the kids wouldn't become alarmed. There was little *open* hostility between Lena and me. She also spent a lot of time on the phone – it was about to be a new life for her as well, and she had a lot to rearrange.

My feelings were all over the place: profound sadness dominated, followed closely by disappointment, anger, anxiety, despair, anticipation, relief, frustration, confusion, jealousy, and incomprehension. At one point, Lena suddenly announced, "*You never know, I might decide to come back some day!*" – as if it were solely *her* decision to make, as if I'd be waiting in lonely sorrow for her to come to her senses, change her mind back to something it had never been, as if the whole world had been created just for her, and was breathlessly awaiting her next whim! I replied, "*You're welcome to stay, to make a fresh start – <u>now</u>. But once you leave, it's <u>not at all</u> certain you can come back. I'm not putting my life on hold. Be very clear about that!*" She shrugged and walked away.

We'd planned the next day – moving day – carefully. At 9 AM, I'd take the kids in the Daihatsu to Ole and Birgitta's place, where they'd spend the whole day playing with Sara and Nina. Eva would pick Lena up while I was gone, to take her to the van rental place and leave her car there. Then the three of us would meet back at Korngatan and load the van. I'd load my bike on the van so I could cycle home when we were finished. Eva would go with Lena in the van and I'd follow in *her* Daihatsu for the last time.

On Sunday morning, May 15th – moving day – the air was full of tension and apprehension. Lena seemed to be struggling; I wondered whether her resolve might be crumbling. "*You know that you don't have to go through with this,*" I told her aside. That comment immediately restored her contempt for me, and her resolve appeared to return. Our last breakfast as a family was unreal, a smokescreen to hide what was really unfolding, creating distractions for the kids and talking about how much fun they'd be having with their friends that day. We answered Jenny's direct questions ("*Yes, Mommy is moving today, to <u>your</u> new second home...*"), but also parried them ("*... and have you packed what you want to bring along to Ole and Birgitta's?*"), all the while wearing forced smiles. When the kids and I said goodbye to Lena, got in the car and were just driving off, I saw that the enormity of her decision had come over her and she couldn't entirely hold back her tears.

The kids seemed to be holding up surprisingly well. Sarah and Nina were eagerly awaiting their arrival, and the four of them were already playing happily long before I drove off. Ole and Birgitta were well aware of what a milestone this day was, and told me not to feel stressed about picking the kids up at any certain time, that everything was under control.

I hoped they were right. I thought they were, at least where the kids were concerned. When I got back home, prepared to start loading the van, Eva was running a bit late and had just arrived; she and Lena were about to leave to pick up the van. Lena pointed out a few more bags of things that I could load into the back of *her* car while they were gone. The high drama of the moment was crushing. I saw an old Elvis album and decided I'd have it ready to play one track, *There Goes My Everything*, when the moment was right – a silly, histrionic move on my part. I had considerable reason to doubt my ability to control my emotions, and I was uncertain that I could express how truly distraught I felt, even though I had no intention of remaining distraught after she was gone. I'd told her so.

While we were loading up the van, I put on the Elvis song. Lena stopped in her tracks, turned and looked at me with a sneering grin, and said, "*Oh, so now you've become religious?!*" It took me a few seconds to figure out the absurdity of her comment, until I recalled that a Swedish writer of religious songs had turned that Elvis song into a hymn, and that's what she thought I was playing! For me, at least, high drama instantly became low farce.

I asked for her house keys (four keys: front door, back doors and garage). She looked shocked, and began to protest. I asked her whether she planned to give me a spare key to her apartment. She shook her head and handed me her set of keys to Korngatan 12.

The three of us worked hard and fast to empty the garage and fill the van. All of Lena's things fit snugly. Just as I was lifting my bike (to ride home on) into the van and was closing the door, Eva apparently made a comment (out of my earshot) that Lena took as criticism. (I might have said "unwarranted criticism", but in Lena's view that would have been a tautology.) Lena flew into a rage and took off in the van alone. Eva and I scrambled to follow to Ivögatan in the Daihatsu. [*I have no idea what Eva's comment might have been; perhaps she made none.*]

By the time we reached our destination, Lena had calmed down somewhat, and we began unloading her things, starting with the pink striped sofas and the bed from the guest room, some tables and chairs, then boxes and bags of books, clothing and bric-a-brac. I had my first-ever look at Lena's apartment. It was attractive, spacious and light, with high ceilings and full of the character common among late 19th- and early 20th-century buildings (which I presumed it was). My first thought was how ideal such an apartment would have been for

Jeanette and me once upon a time, provided the rent had been affordable, which it wouldn't have been. But I freely admitted that it had potential to be a pleasant second home for Jenny and Sally.

Friction between Eva and Lena was palpable during the work, at least while I was still present. Then Lena began targeting me as well. As I saw it, she was feeling guilty, which made her hypersensitive to criticism, real or imagined, implied or inferred. Her typical response to criticism was to turn it around, take the offensive, and launch wave after wave of attack. I felt I'd already experienced enough of her attacks to last me a lifetime, so, as soon as the van was empty and my help was no longer needed to move heavy boxes or furniture, I said goodbye to Eva, and to Lena, then walked slowly down the stairs, trying not to lose my balance or my way. *This was really it.*

I left the building, went over to my bike, with its two child-seats, unlocked it, and stood there for a minute before daring to negotiate the streets of Möllevången. It was still early, possibly around 1 PM. Before I picked up the kids, I had plenty of time to cycle home and make sure that it didn't look any stranger or more torn apart than absolutely necessary, and to make sure that it would look as inviting as ever to the kids – that it would still look to them like *their* home.

While cycling home, I had strange new feelings I couldn't identify or put my finger on. Another new chapter in my life was about to begin, although it felt more like the first chapter in a new life and not a new chapter in my old life. When I reached Korngatan, I put my bike in the now-empty garage. I wanted to make sure that none of her stuff had been left behind. As I opened the garage door on Källargatan, I couldn't help thinking of another time I'd done that, another time more than 11 years earlier, a time that also marked a change from one of my lives to another.

I compared my life to a crab, molting its shell from time to time, except that I was molting lives. For the first five or so years of my childhood, we lived in Glendale, California, until my dad was transferred to Chicago, and we moved to Oak Park. For the next seven or eight years, my pre-pubertal childhood life was reasonably stable and harmonious (I had no clue that I was being indoctrinated in fundamentalist Christianity). My "third life" comprised five or so years of roiling adolescence and rebellion, until Norm and I fled to San Francisco in June 1964.

During "life number four" (another five-year period, my inner tumult and rebellion continued, I met and married Jeanette, I managed to complete my college education, I could easily have ended up in prison, and I forsook the Vietnam War and my domicile in my native land by moving to Canada. Time for "life number five", the move to Sweden, the struggle to settle and learn a new language, painting full-time, restoring a 19th-century house. After nearly eight years, my fifth life ended with the unspeakable horror of Jeanette's suicide. My sixth life, which lasted just one year but felt like 10, was spent in deep and suicidal depression.

I began my seventh life, the one that had now just ended, with a year of libidinous pleasure and joyful rebirth of my will to live and love. In my stubborn naiveté, I failed to realize that loving fervently in no way implies being loved in return at all. Years of trying, the abandonment of my painting, the birth of two lovely children, couldn't impede the inexorable destruction.

How many of those seven lives had I chosen, or how much of each of them? Nothing in my early childhood; I didn't choose where I was born, my race, my ethnicity, where we lived, my parents' religion or determination to begin my indoctrination. The move to Oak Park for my later childhood was basically more of the same; the little things I could choose – but only from among the few choices others allowed me.

How about life number three, my rebellious adolescence? My first impression is *YES*, absolutely, this was when I began making my own choices! But would I have become a rebel, started to become a free-thinker, if I'd had a "normal" childhood, without all the brainwashing? It seems unlikely to me, at least not in the same way, but I can never know.

In my 4th life, full of life-changing, redirecting, good and bad decisions, it's hard to attribute *all* of them to the influences of others, but it's impossible to dismiss the role of those influences – from family, my peers, American society, 20th century trends, books I'd read, my income (or lack of it), and my first true love, Jeanette. I don't believe, for example, that the notion of moving from the country of my birth would have *ever* entered my mind had the US not pursued its senseless War in Vietnam.

Everything in my 5th life seems to stem from Jeanette's wish for us to live in Europe. Where *her* wish came from, I will never know. Was our impetus about moving *to* Europe or *from* North America? Or was it simply to try something *completely* new and different? My desire to paint feels like it came only from within me, deep within me. And certainly my desire grew and thrived with Jeanette's support and encouragement, and Bob's. Bob was also a great influence on finally ridding myself of my religious indoctrination, repairing the damage. But that was a two-way street, or so Bob claimed. But I'd been an amateur in human relations, totally unable to impede the destructive development of Jeanette's mental illness that led to her suicide and the abrupt end of my 5th life in an abyss of anguish.

If I had any choices at all in that year-long 6th life, a self-destructive life of grief and whiskey and cigarettes, I certainly couldn't see them or didn't want to see them or refused to see them. But perhaps I did have the choice to write about everything that had gone before, although my purpose in writing was precisely the opposite of the result: my catharsis.

And then, my 7th life. My lust for life came roaring back as a result of the catharsis. I didn't choose the type of job I was offered, nor how incredibly timely the offer was made, but I did choose to take it. For quite a while, I was just accepting offers. Remember: Lena was initially the one who came on to *me*, at least until she had me on the hook. Did I choose to be hooked? Was my pursuit of Lena just my subconscious attempt to punish myself for having been blind to Jeanette's mental illness? Why didn't I, couldn't I, let Lena go when she so clearly didn't love me?

Did I choose to have children? I had chosen not to (or perhaps more correctly, I chose to follow Jeanette's choice), and to have a vasectomy to seal that deal. But when Lena insisted that *she* wanted children, I chose (?) the vasectomy reversal operations that enabled our pregnancies. And did I choose to love our little girls? One look at them and they gave me no choice at all! And still Lena didn't wouldn't/couldn't love me and she chose (?) her affair, her bilious hatred for me, and her departure.

And now, ready or not, my life number eight was about to begin.

CHAPTER 12

Deliverance

I entered the big house by the back door (from the garage) with a feeling of great weariness that, contradictorily, paradoxically, was also a great surge of excitement. I glanced at the kitchen countertops. No clutter. I sat down at the table. An enormous wave of relief came sweeping over me: *I'm no longer living under the same roof with someone who despises me, someone who dishes out the harshest, cruelest rantings, which I was supposed to accept without defending myself, yet never, ever to criticize her for anything!!*

I swore to myself that I would, to the very best of my ability, never stand for anything like that again, that I would never again give all my heart to someone, anyone, who did not love me in return – *NEVER AGAIN!*

As I sat there all alone at my kitchen table, I was completely unprepared for the powerful, unambiguously pleasant feeling of relief that washed over me, the big wave that an avid surfer has been waiting for all summer. I thought I might feel relief someday, but didn't expect it *now*. I was practically euphoric. I could have *thanked* Johannes. (Well, maybe not quite....) He'd been the catalyst; I'd loved her too much to leave her, even though it was making me suicidal. I *couldn't* leave her. He and Lena *made* it happen. I sat there for at least half an hour, enjoying the feeling, relishing it, exuberating in it, before pulling myself together so I could make a round of the house to be sure that everything looked as "normal" as possible for the arrival of Jenny and Sally. It would be a new "normal". So much would be new in so many ways, unforeseeable ways. A new life. Jenny and Sally were certain to sense their own internal chaos as well as mine, to a certain degree; there was no need to exacerbate the *external* chaos. Hence the need for an inspection round.

Just 24 hours earlier, I'd thought I might need to pull myself together due to sadness. I never thought I'd need to get my exuberant sense of *relief* under control! I didn't think it would be appropriate under the circumstances for the kids to see that reaction either. Falling in love at first sight is the stuff of books and films, and sometimes even in real life. But falling *out* of love at *last* sight?! I'd never heard of such a thing, and yet I was experiencing it.

I went from room to room, looking carefully for anything that might elicit a feeling of uprootedness for the kids. I knew it would feel strange anyway. I knew it would never feel the same. But even if it never felt the same again, it wouldn't always feel strange. It might even come to feel better. After all, there were so many ways in which it couldn't feel worse.

I tried to analyze my feelings – *hey, that's what I do!* – about Lena, to summarize a decade of futile, one-sided love. I was surprised that the infidelity itself mattered so little to me; it was merely the trigger. Nor could I *blame* her for never having loved me. Intellectually, I'd agonized for years over the realization that nobody can make another person love them (Sonja pointed that out to me quite clearly!). But love isn't intellectual. And yet I'd wanted Lena so badly, so single-mindedly. And now I *was* single!

What was hard for me to take was her outright hatred of me. Even harder was her begrudging me the care of my own children – that she insisted on sending them to nursery school when I was perfectly capable of taking care of them, and the kids would have preferred it. I knew I would *mourn* their absence. It tore me up inside. I felt that her begrudging me was *only* due to her pig-headedness and mean-spiritedness. I asked myself if I would have done the same if our career roles had been reversed, if I'd had a nine-to-five job in an office and Lena worked from home? Would I have insisted on sending the kids to nursery school so that Lena wouldn't get more time with them? I found it inconceivable.

I thought of the near certainty that I'd never get another shot at having a core wife-and-children-full-time family of my own, and how Lena fucked that chance up for me forever, both literally and figuratively. I could hear Bob shouting "*Danger! Self-pity!*" He was right. I stopped that train of thought in its tracks. I tried not to blame her, to understand that while making me happy was never her purpose, neither was fucking up my life. Her purpose in life had nothing whatever to do with me, only with herself. But the memories of all her hateful words made it difficult to think otherwise. No matter how strong my love had been for Lena, I was never good enough for her. Love shouldn't have to be like that. Love *doesn't* have to be like that! And where I'm concerned, I told myself, *love never will be like that again*!

I could do nothing about my new situation but learn to live with it. I remembered the old song lyrics, "*pick yourself up, dust yourself off, and start all over again.*" OK. Easier said than done. But would any other recipe be easier? New circumstances had been thrust upon me. To prevent them from dragging me down, I would have to compartmentalize my life: devote myself to the kids whenever they were with me, and focus on the new and unknown life before me (whatever it might entail) whenever the kids were not with me. If I tried to focus on the kids when they were with Lena, I would go stark-raving mad.

When I arrived on my bike to pick them up, Jenny and Sally were having great fun at Ole and Birgitta's. *Wonderful to see!* And they were thrilled to see me. *Wonderful again!* By now Sally felt secure in her new seat on the front of my bike. It was even a bit thrilling for her. When we got home, the kids peered around somewhat cautiously, but it looked pretty much the same as always. The paintings probably contributed a lot to that feeling. I made one of their favorite dishes for supper (it might have been tortellini with my well-seasoned cheese sauce). Then they picked one of their favorite music videos, and we watched it together, even though my head was swirling. I read them several stories. They asked a few questions about where Mommy was. (I had to remind myself that Sally was just two-and-a-half, and Jenny was less than two years older than Sally.) I reminded them that mommy was in *their* new apartment, getting some things ready for when she came to pick them up the next afternoon, after she got off work. I wondered how *I* was supposed to get ready for that.

Once the kids were asleep, I spent a long time on the phone with Bob. As usual, he was highly supportive of everything he felt would contribute to my stability, both immediate and long-term. And he was highly critical of anything that smacked of self-pity. When I told him of my first reactions at the kitchen table that afternoon, he was delighted. So far, I only knew what I didn't want, but little about what I did want, apart from knowing that I wanted whatever seemed to be best for Jenny and Sally.

On Monday, the kids and I had a good, fun day together, but I found it hard not to keep an eye on the clock, *time's wingèd chariot*. I dreaded having to say goodbye to them that afternoon, knowing they wouldn't be in my care again till Sunday. I did my utmost not to let it show. If I showed sadness, they might somehow feel responsible, and then guilty. I had to prevent that at all costs. I'd be having pupils on Tuesday, Thursday and Friday, which was certain to help me keep my mind on other things.

When Lena came to pick Jenny and Sally up at around 4:30 PM, we both did our best to act friendly towards each other. She told me she'd already managed to buy a couple of beds for them at IKEA. She thought it might be a good idea if they saw me assembling them, so they could feel that I was participating in their lives in the new quarters. That made sense to me, so as soon as they drove off, I came cycling after and got straight to work. I brought along a set of tools for Lena to keep on hand, so she could do future jobs like that herself (or get "someone else" to help her). I had no desire to spend a lot of time at her new place. I couldn't help feeling I was in the enemy camp; I'm only human.

I was pleased to see that Jenny and Sally, after cautiously looking around their new "second home", slowly began to settle in and begin playing together. When I say "slowly", I mean within five minutes. Small children can be so adaptable, and since Jenny and Sally were obliged to adapt, I was delighted to see that they could and did. Another worry off my list.

Lena had apparently wasted no time in getting everything she felt she needed to make her new place splendid – and it all had to be done NOW. It was clear to me that she was spending her savings at an alarming rate. In my astonishment, I couldn't refrain from mumbling whether she could afford everything all at once. She brushed it off; they were *nice* things. I suddenly remembered all the times when she was about to buy something (for herself) that was way beyond our budget, and I asked cautiously whether we could afford it. The answer she usually fired back was that it was *nice*. That was apparently all that mattered to her. I shuddered to think what would happen when the money ran out. But Jenny and Sally seemed to be fine, and that was what mattered to me.

My pupil on Tuesday, May 17th, was a lovely young woman, 37 years of age, named Karin. She worked at Perstorp Pharma, the subsidiary that dealt with pharmaceuticals. I vaguely recognized her name when I saw it in my calendar the evening before. As I paged backwards, I saw that she'd already been my pupil once, on March 8th, two days before Lena's announcement that she was leaving. *Why couldn't I remember what she looked like?* Then I realized that the trauma I'd been going through at the time must have blocked out much more than I realized.

It was an absolutely gorgeous day when Karin arrived, as pretty as a day in May can be. It was pleasantly warm, the sun was shining, trees and bushes were greening, the wisteria had just decided to bloom. I opened the door to greet her. She did look familiar, but much prettier than I'd been in any condition to see back in March. She had warm, highly alert greenish eyes. After greeting her and inviting her in, I told her that she might find it a bit different around my house compared to last time, since I was now happily separated. Then I smiled and added that she might want to watch out for me. She laughed, her eyes flashed, and she said coyly, "*I'm a big girl – I think I can take care of myself!*"

We went directly up to the library "classroom", talking all the way (she was already well along the road to fluency in English). I found her voice exceptionally pleasant, without a trace of affectation – the kind of voice that if I'd never seen her but only heard her, I'd *want* to see her. (*Hey there, get a grip on yourself!*)

We continued talking once we sat down on opposite sides of the table, as was customary. We talked about everything, freely and openly. No minefields. No tip-toeing. We *both* joked a lot (an unusual experience for me). We talked about serious matters as well. I spoke of my pending divorce, and of my two darling girls. She also had two kids, a girl of 13 and a boy of 10, whom she loved dearly. Her marriage wasn't turbulent, she told me, but had "kind of run out of gas". She said it with a sigh and a shrug.

She had a lovely figure. She was of medium height, had half-length dark-blonde hair, and a sharp, acrobatic mind. She seemed to understand fully and immediately every point of grammar I explained, as well as every new word, and every idea. She also seemed to want to understand *me*. It was incredibly refreshing to be able to speak so openly with her the whole morning, spontaneously. And she was equally open with me. Nobody was looking for ways to misunderstand the other, to take offense or to gain an advantage. She never told me what my opinions were, but asked me instead. She never insisted that I *really* meant something I'd never said. She knew the difference between inference and implication.

When it got to be lunchtime, she accompanied me to the kitchen so we could continue talking while I prepared our meal. That was standard procedure for all my pupils. (I could actually talk and cook, both simultaneously *and* at the same time.) Before I began the food preparation, I dug out the chef's hat I got from Carmen and put it on. Karin seemed amused. I measured out the water for the rice. (I was, as far as I remember, going to make something Asian, as was my wont.)

I turned on the stove to heat the water for the rice. Then I turned to face her. She was leaning back against the counter opposite the stove, less than two meters away, watching me and casually conversing with me. I smiled, pointed to the words on my chef's hat – KISS THE COOK – and said matter-of-factly, "*Y'know, you're <u>supposed</u> to <u>do</u> this.*" She looked at the words, and again at me. She smiled. She hesitated for half a second. Then she took two boldly cautious steps across the kitchen floor and followed the instructions.

I'd harbored some wild unfounded hope that she *might* do something like that, but I *never* expected that she *would*. Our kiss went on and on. The temperature was rising rapidly. Without breaking away, I reached behind me and turned off the stove; a whole new appetite was upon us. There would be time for lunch later; we had the whole afternoon ahead of us.[7]

That afternoon was unlike anything I'd ever experienced, pulsating warmth and joy and uninhibited affection. Karin had to leave just after five, to drive home to Klippan. We both hated that – and we were both ecstatic. I couldn't remember ever having felt more euphoric. I phoned Bob that evening. The prudent, practical, cautious me was telling me that no matter how thrilled I was at that moment, it was nothing more than that: *at that moment*. But I also felt that moments like that are such *extremely* rare occurrences, even in the most fortunate of fortunate lifetimes, so there was no reason *not* to bask in it for as long as possible, to live those feelings, even if they were never to return – even if *she* were never to return. It was difficult for me to stop smiling, particularly since I could see no reason to stop.

When I'd emerged from my deep depression thanks to a catharsis a year after Jeanette's death, the euphoria I felt and the recovery I experienced had been greatly amplified by my libidinous experiences. This, now, my unbelievable day with Karin, May 17th, was something *very* different. I couldn't yet explain it. I was still too stunned.

That evening when I phoned Bob, he was thrilled on my behalf, in a general sort of way, wishing me many more experiences of that kind in the months and years to come. After the kind of break-up I'd just had (two *days* earlier!!), he could be forgiven for fearing a new commitment on my part, for hoping that I'd be stand-offish and reserved, and for being suspicious that I risked being prey to that tiresome phenomenon of being on the rebound. One small part of me was echoing his appeal for restraint. *Hold on a minute! This wasn't about love! Get real! This was about pure pleasure! Surely you get that?!*

And yet….

---

7 The author (me) deems the details of this and other encounters with Karin to be of a sufficiently personal nature for invoking the right to keep readers in the dark. This isn't that kind of book. ☺

I was floating, soaring all evening and into the night. When I went to bed I discovered that Karin had placed a sprig of forget-me-nots on my pillow. She must have picked them in my yard while I was momentarily otherwise occupied in the late afternoon. *Forget me not* – how *could* I forget?! The memory of her smell and her warmth engulfed me through the night.

I'm sure I woke up the next morning with a smile. Lena came by because we had to take Jenny to the children's clinic for a routine hearing test. Lena glared at me suspiciously, then asked sharply, "*What's the matter?!*" I told her that *nothing* was the matter. "*Then why are you smiling?!*" she hissed. We'd had similarly bizarre exchanges before. Now I just found it amusing.

Something else happened at home that day. I was doing a translation, trying to concentrate. At 1:43 PM, I heard the fax machine start up. I thought more work was inbound. Quite the contrary – it was a message from Karin. In a large flowing hand, she'd written, "*Was I dreaming? I'm still feeling fine – are you? Love, Karin*". A powerful rush of pure joy nearly made me lose my balance – another unique experience. I could hardly grasp that this was happening to *me*! *Now! Already now*! Lena had been pulverizing and trampling on my self-esteem for years. She gave me almost daily reminders of my utter worthlessness, my nauseating ugliness, my disgust-inducing being. The torture of being hated by the one I loved so much had made me long for nothing so much as my own demise.

And now? I had to respond to Karin's fax, but not via fax – someone else at her office might see it and start asking questions. (Perstorp could be a proper gossip mill.) I phoned her direct line. The sound of her voice brought incredible, detailed memories rushing back from the day before, carrying me like a rubber raft in a rushing stream, exhilarating and free. Her voice was sweet music to my ears, as her touch had been balm to my soul.

She clearly took great pleasure in hearing my voice as well. But on her end of things, the situation was far more complicated and frightening. After all, Lena and I were already separated (even if only by three days). Karin's kids were older, pubertal or almost; they would certainly understand more but might be willing to accept less, or less readily. I knew little about her world, but it was clear that she faced far more daunting unknowns. Yet something extraordinary had happened to *both* of us. (My memory flashed to Forster's *Room with a View*.) She was *very* emphatic about that. Her finding it so was *another* new experience for me.

We began phoning each other daily. Within a week we were writing long, passionate letters to each other, several times a week (in addition to the phone calls). Neither of us knew where this was going. Both of us knew where we wanted it to go. We also suspected that despite the unexpected (and possibly ill-timed) and intense suddenness, this could be *IT* – the kind of thing that many search for all their lives, the kind of thing that inspires poets and that many never find. We had to be careful not to allow the highly unusual and improbable timing to allow us to dismiss it as merely a passionate fling, a deceptive rebound or a moment's infatuation.

For now, we agreed that May 17th felt like we'd been washed up together on a remote desert island, like Robinson Crusoe. She began calling me *Robinson*, and I countered with *Friday*, our first terms of endearment. We wanted to learn as much as possible about each other, but we only had time for relatively short phone calls. We couldn't foresee when we'd get a chance to meet again. Yet we were mature enough to realize that a forced waiting period could be beneficial. It would certainly enable (and oblige) us to take one step at a time with open eyes before daring to think about a possible future together.

I asked Karin when her birthday was. I can be embarrassingly terrible about remembering them, so I thought I'd need a head start to learn it, to memorize it. She told me it was February 14th. That's *Valentine's Day*, I thought. Then I thought, *When else?* [*I suspect, as I write this, that some future readers may be inclined to dismiss this birthdate as another literary contrivance. Be assured, I'm not making it up.*]

On May 26th, Karin wrote that she was unable to get me out of her thoughts but didn't want to make a mess of things for either of us. She wanted to be certain she wasn't being pushy, that she was giving me enough space and enough time, and that if I wanted her to stay "out of the way", I shouldn't be afraid to say so. She said she wanted nothing more than to phone me, write me, fax me, and a few other things with me, and that it filled her with joy when I also did, but she was afraid of being "too much". My jaw dropped. She'd just transferred *my* thoughts about *her* to her stationery, word for word, feeling for feeling.

I'd had plenty of experience feeling *lust*, but only two experiences of real, deep, lasting *love*. In both cases, I'd been the one to fall in love first. (In the latest of those, I was the *only* one to fall in love.) Now Karin was telling me she was falling in love with me before I even knew what was happening. How could this be?

The more we talked and wrote, the closer we felt to each other. We also discovered more and more things in common, not so much in our backgrounds as in our temperaments, interests, values, feelings, goals, desires and needs. In a way, it was like discovering a pair of long-forgotten favorite shoes at the back of the closet – the most comfortable shoes you've ever worn. You slip your feet into them. The only way shoes *ought* to feel! A smile spreads from ear to ear. You sigh with intense pleasure: *this is so right!*

There was no need for me to put on a happy face for Jenny and Sally. My happiness, exuberance and composure came from within and seemed to rub off on them and make them calmer. They did, of course, experience some disorientation about going back and forth between two places, one of them new, but my repeated promise – that they would *always* have a home at Korngatan 12 – reassured them. About the only thing that upset them when they were with me were Lena's early evening phone calls. Many of those calls happened to coincide with our time for reading bedtime stories. Lena told them how badly she missed them (which I'm sure she did), but the calls seemed to make the kids feel guilty and often left them feeling that they were supposed to *do* something to make Mommy feel better. It irritated me, because I felt that acting in the kids' best interests was about making *them* feel harmonious, not about making Mommy or Daddy feel better. I told Lena so, but she thought I was just pushing her out of the family constellation – the same constellation she'd insisted on leaving.

I could, however, easily understand her *temptation* to behave that way. I missed the kids terribly whenever they were with Lena, and would have liked to phone them every evening. But I didn't think it was worth the risk of making the kids feel guilty, so I gritted my teeth and told myself that Lena loved them and would give them all the care they needed until they returned to me. It would certainly have felt better if she'd allowed them to be with me when she had to be at work anyway. But that part was beyond my control, and the kids wouldn't benefit from my banging my head against that or any other wall. *Change what you can, accept what you can't.*

If Lena and I had had no children, our break-up would almost certainly have been a question of *żegnaj* – the Polish word I'd learned on the *Stefan Batóry*, meaning *goodbye forever*. But we *did* have kids, two small, adorable kids, and our lives would be intertwined to some extent throughout their childhoods, perhaps for as long as we lived.

I tried to think ahead, to the future. I thought about the role of a parent – my role as their father. Surely my main goal, my duty, my mission must be to teach my children to stand on their own two feet, while giving them the security and self-confidence to do so; to think independently, open-mindedly, and critically, *not* to accept blindly whatever they are told by whomever has assigned him- or herself the authority to order people about; to acquire certain basic values – *not* creeds! – that are based on compassion, generosity, kindness, curiosity, and a thirst for learning, *not* on selfishness and greed, not on prejudice, superstition or haughtiness.

I realized I wouldn't be unable to talk about any of this with Lena; past experience told me she'd just accuse me of ordering her around. Or she'd call me a goddamn idiot. Or both. Instead, I would simply have to be grateful for the extent, whatever it was, to which her values and mine coincided where the kids were concerned. *And then I had to learn to let go.* I couldn't do a damned thing about what happened on her time.

Moreover, I had to accept that if I succeeded in teaching the kids to be independent, I shouldn't be disappointed if they *were* – in their *own* ways! I should never try to bind them to me, but hope instead that they would freely desire my company once they left the nest. But having to say goodbye to them twice a week at *this* age of great dependency was never going to be easy.

When I wrote to Bob about my unfolding passion for Karin, I tried to limit myself to measured doses. I'd already put him through the ordeal of piloting me through my deep depression in 1977-78, only to put him through another ordeal in 1978-79 as my love for Lena grew out of control and he could only watch with mounting apprehension from afar. And even though Karin more than reciprocated my every feeling for her, neither of us could be *sure* – or at least had no way of *knowing* that we could be sure – that this was more than a powerful infatuation. Except for that one glorious day, this was still no more than a romance by phone, fax and letter!

In Karin's letter to me of May 31st, she wrote: "*One advantage of you over others is that you are lovely.*" Sometimes she wrote short, sweet messages like that. And then there were long, thoughtful, passionate, compelling letters. I reciprocated. It was a slow, intimate dance in words. Nothing at all felt incompatible between us. But sometimes the practical, rational, cautious side of me pointed out to my passionate side that the statistical base was still too small to draw any reliable conclusions about the future. We both had kids to consider, and consider carefully. For their sakes, we had to be *damn* sure.

In late May, I was invited to visit Maj and Lars at their tiny seaside summer cottage in Strandhem, along the coast just south of Malmö. I don't think I'd seen or spoken with them since the break-up began in March. It was odd seeing them on my own. They were curious about what I was up to, and the conversation kept entering gray areas between curiosity, concern and gossip. Since I'd never met Johannes (except for that weird visit to Gotland, of which I retained only a vague and totally unreliable memory of what he looked like) but they *had* met him, recently, I couldn't resist asking about their impressions. Maj did and didn't want to tell me. (I did and didn't want to know.) She would only say, coyly, and with a creepy laugh, "*He's nothing like you!*" Something in the way she said it made me take it as a compliment. When I spoke with Øivind sometime later, he said that his mother, who had met Johannes, referred to him as "*den lille pjosken*" (the little wimp). I know it was petty of me, but I chuckled. Øivind's brother Jan repeated the phrase numerous times and laughed out loud each time.

Karin and I were struggling to understand what was going on between and inside us and trying to maintain a modicum of level-headedness, yet not wanting to miss a minute of the giddy, soaring bliss we both felt deeply. I wrote to her in early June that "*it could turn out that you and I are what every poet has ever meant about people being 'made' for each other. We just don't know.*" I apologized for feeling hesitant, having been burnt so badly so recently. I felt it essential to be as honest as possible with her. "*If my responses should ever confuse you, please ask me to explain instead of making your own private interpretations. I will try to do the same.*" Karin understood completely and felt likewise. How wonderful it was to be able to *breathe*!

Based on my recent years of experience, I felt I needed to forewarn her about my constant questioning and challenging of everyone's ideas, and hoped it wouldn't put her off. She shrugged, smiled and said that if she didn't agree with me she'd say so, that we were entitled to have our own opinions even if they were sometimes different. It was, in other words, no problem at all. I was nearly dumbfounded. She made it sound so natural, so commonsensical, so obvious. We both felt we'd at last found a perfect fit. Neither of us had dared to hope for anything this good. It was exhilarating and terrifying at the same time.

On Saturday, June 4th, Al arrived for two days, in connection with a business trip to Europe. I had the kids that weekend, and we all cycled out to the Kronotorp windmill (the one that Jenny and Sally used to call "veem-low" and "oh-noy", respectively). Al and I only discussed my break-up from Lena and redemption with Karin when the kids were asleep. Al was concerned, interested and supportive, despite my fears that he would react differently. He was still one of my two most beloved brothers, and it relieved me to know that he *could* be there for me in a crisis.

When the first post-Lena bills started rolling in – for the home insurance, the mortgage, electricity, water, trash collection – I realized that I would have to stick very closely to a tight budget. Jeanette and I had long experience of that, and I'd never been financially frivolous. My total disinterest in status symbols came in handy. So did my boss's permission to let me increase my working hours to 75% again as from July 1st. I still had enough comp time to be off for much of the summer, including the entire time the kids were in my care. And since Lena still refused to let me have the kids even when she was unable to care for them herself, I decided I might as well work some extra hours during my "free time".

Mom sent me a generous and timely check to help cover some of the additional expenses she knew I'd have even before I'd figured them out for myself. Unfortunately, she seemed to feel that a gift entitled her to preach at me again, as she'd done in her misguided responses to the news of the break-up. I ignored her sermonizing but thanked her profusely for the financial support. I also indicated, somewhat cryptically, that I'd "met someone".

Soon after, a letter arrived from John, indicating that he'd heard about a "someone". He said he was glad I was moving on but was concerned that I might be on the rebound. Who could blame him? On paper it looked *exactly* like that! But Karin and I were convinced that this was nothing about paper – apart from the sheets and sheets of it we'd been using for our correspondence.

My partial relief from financial emergency, in combination with the explosive joy that Karin's calls and letters were bringing me daily, must have shown in my face when Lena dropped off the kids for a day on June 10th, the day before they took off for Gotland. When she again saw my happy, smiling, contented expression, she scowled suspiciously. I just tried hard not to think about the fact that I wouldn't be seeing the kids again until July 4th. Bob would be spending July 1st-20th with me in Malmo. He made no comment on the fact that "extra time" was now available to him at Korngatan.

I still didn't know when or if I'd *ever* get to see Karin again, even though we were communicating hungrily almost every day. But it felt like it might take forever until I could see her and be with her again. Her situation at home was in upheaval.

Bob once again urged me to let him pay my plane fare to come to see him for five days, and then return with me to Malmö. I figured that he could use additional help with his apartment, and would welcome my assistance on his trip to Sweden, and I knew he wouldn't permit me to decline. So I took him up on his offer.

At around this time I got a call from Chris in London. She was extremely upset, devastated, in tears. Rob had "done a Lena" – he'd announced out of the blue that he'd met someone else and was leaving Chris. She was in despair, her self-esteem shattered, her life in chaos. I found myself in the totally unexpected position of offering *her* comfort and support. And to my surprise, I felt *able* to do so. It was a measure of how far I'd come and how quickly I'd healed. Chris and I spent a lot of time on the phone that summer. I tried to contact Rob as well, to hear his side of things, but he wouldn't respond. [*I've never heard a word from him since.*] In retrospect, I understood his awkwardness in talking to me about my crisis when I phoned to tell them about it in March!

On June 11th, Karin wrote: "*Talking with you on the phone always has the same effect – it makes me happy, excited, joyous. All the 'right' feelings are there and if only my common sense would shut up, my joy would be complete. Stanley Erisman, I'm so terribly in love with you! And I'm going to miss your calls while you're in Switzerland.*"

The impact her words had on me was profound and thrilling. She was so refreshingly straightforward and genuine and open. There wasn't a trace of ulterior motives, selfishness or deceit. She was eager to understand me fully, and equally eager to be understood. A few days later, she wrote that she and her soon-to-be-ex had long been growing in different directions and that she was tired of having to be the one to hold things together.

"*I've never thought so much about my life as I have this spring. Now I look forward to living on my own. Perhaps it's because of you, I don't know. I really love you, Robinson! It will be a thrill to see what becomes of us. Will we live happily ever after or fight like cats and dogs? Please don't lose your wonderful sense of humour! I love your laughter and your word games, they really make me happy, as do you! A silly question: When I drive to you next time, will I be a screwdriver?"*

She told me about a place called Glimminge Plantering – her "paradise" – and the cottage her father built there when she was 10, and where she'd spent nearly every summer ever since.[8] She said she hoped I'd like it too. The name rang a distant bell. Once upon a time I drove to that very little community with Lena and Marie-Louise, to look up a one-armed German pastor friend of Lena's parents. I could hardly remember it. Now Karin was spending the weekend there with her son Peder, and longed for an opportunity to show me around. She hoped I'd meet her kids someday, and that they'd be able to accept me.

That weekend she found affordable accommodations to rent on the outskirts of Klippan: an attractive duplex almost literally a stone's throw from the same centuries-old paper mill that Jeanette and I visited with our Swedish class a few lifetimes ago, in early December 1969. She said she'd be moving there in the beginning of August. She and her husband had now officially filed for divorce. They'd settled reasonably amicably, with few recriminations or demands on either side.

They let their kids choose whom they wanted to live with. Her daughter Moa chose to live with Karin, her son Peder with his dad. Like me, she'd have both kids on alternate weekends and no kids on the weekends in between. The conclusion was hard to avoid: since our childless alternate weekends coincided, we'd soon be able to spend those entire weekends together while getting to know each other better and better, taking plenty of time to be damn sure of our feelings for each other before involving our kids in any way. Her kids, like mine, would be together every weekend. It seemed to be the fairest possible arrangement under the circumstances.

On June 20th, three days before my trip to Switzerland, she sent me a short letter in a large envelope: *"My dear wonderful Robinson, I definitely think a relationship can be as easy as ours. Then it will only grow if we allow it to. I have learned a lesson of which you speak in your letter: 'Don't ever pretend there are no disagreements! Discuss them, talk about them, but never ignore them.' I haven't felt so special, so loved, so 'important' for years!"* She signed it "KEW" – her initials. Like the Kew Gardens in London, I thought. I shortened them to the single

---

8 Refer to the Afterword for further information about Glimminge.

letter Q. Also inside the large envelope was another large envelope containing a number of small envelopes, one for each day I'd be away in Switzerland! I was reeling with flabbergastification.[9]

The only difficulty I had was getting her to send me a photo of herself. She didn't have any! – probably a measure of her total absence of vanity (or of not being appreciated. I took countless photos of Lena but there were relatively few of myself.) For the time being, I was thus unable to show Bob or anyone else what Karin looked like.

More than a month had now passed since that incredible Norwegian national holiday, May 17th. I hadn't seen Karin since then. Nevertheless my trip to Basel on Thursday evening, June 23rd, was buoyed by her voice and her letters. Even the incessant and painful echoes of Lena's hateful tirades were rapidly fading from my inner ears. As soon as Bob saw me in the arrival hall at the Basel-Mulhouse Airport, it didn't take more than a second for him to confirm the transformation in me. He shook his head in delighted disbelief. All the legitimate fears he'd had for my well-being evaporated. And when I showed him the envelope-filled envelope from Karin, I clearly no longer needed to explain to him the reason for my soaring hopes about a bright future with a most exceptional young woman. All this seemed to have the effect of a powerful anti-Parkinson's medication on him. His spirits soared. He was jubilant. Most of his tremors subsided. Even his walking seemed to improve. He exuded happiness – which made me even happier, etc – an upward spiral.

Although I'd tried to fill Bob in on my break-up with Lena since March 10th, there were years of details he'd never heard anything about, things I'd consciously kept from him. It turned out that most things he'd feared or puzzled over – especially in the beginning of my relationship with Lena, before it became *fait accompli* and he diplomatically withheld judgment – now made more sense to him. Those fears he'd had turned out to have been well-founded. Some might have gloated or jeered (*Told you so!*), but that wasn't Bob's way.

In many ways Bob and I understood each other better than we understood ourselves. Knowing my "somewhat" impulsive, intense and passionate nature, Bob felt obliged to advise me to exercise a great deal of caution about my budding

---

9   I again refer readers (as I did in Book 3 of *Hindsights*) to my neologism license number CX2433190-B.

relationship with Karin. It was, after all, early days. At the same time, he was nearly as enthusiastic as I was – and *he* hadn't even met her! His advice had nothing to do with a "rebound" case, which he could see that it clearly was not. Rather, it was based on the simple fact that we didn't know each other terribly well *yet*. But there was no denying that everything was clicking. So far, Karin and I were ticking *all* the right boxes.

I sailed through the tidying of his apartment and our review of his accumulated paperwork, finishing most of it before lunch the day after my arrival. He didn't need much help from me this time. We talked constantly, freely and cheerfully; we were making up for years of drought. I realized how much our conversation in recent years had been inhibited by my watchfulness not to let slip any signs or hints of the constant, ongoing domestic trouble and strife in Malmö.

But my domestic skies were far from cloudless. I was awfully worried about Jenny and Sally and the huge and inexorable disruption Lena's departure from Korngatan would mean in their lives. They'd seen little of the approaching storm that had now broken all around them. But they showed few outward signs of anxiety or distress. Was it because they'd never known anything but a certain ever-present level of dysfunction and friction? Or was I missing any signals? When I expressed my concerns to Lena on a couple of occasions, she snapped back that divorce was *good* for kids. Did she *seriously* mean shit like that? Yes, when a divorce is reasonably amicable, it's likely to be much more harmonious than continuing a hostile environment "for the sake of the children". But that doesn't make the lesser evil *good*, does it?!

I was surprised by how well Bob looked, sounded, moved and expressed himself. I asked him if he was on some new medication. He looked straight at me, smiled knowingly as if to say *"What, don't you know?!"* – then broke into a grin and said I should look in the mirror. It hadn't dawned on me that my happiness could affect him *that* profoundly. I was greatly moved.

And the dawn continued to break. When I stopped to consider it carefully, weren't my most intense moments of happiness usually – if not *always* – the result of seeking and seeing the happiness of those I loved, and not the result of some self-indulgent ego trip? It seemed to me that the pursuit of one's own personal happiness is almost always doomed to be selfish, and as such is equally doomed to be short-lived and fruitless, whereas striving to make others happy will deliver true happiness to oneself as a by-product. It made sense to me, and it seemed to work with Bob, with Jenny and Sally, and with Karin so far. But it hadn't worked at all with Lena. That failure, however, didn't nullify the worthiness of that line of pursuit. It did underline the importance of focusing on those who are receptive, and especially on finding love that is a two-way street.

On Sunday, June 26th, Bob and I were invited to the home of his former colleagues, Jean-Claude and Roswitha, for Sunday afternoon dinner. They lived in Alsace, near Mulhouse, about 30-40 km northwest of Basel. While we were having the early dinner in their garden and enjoying the beautiful sunny day, we noticed a huge plume of black smoke rising from the horizon several miles away. When we heard multiple sirens in the distance, Jean-Claude turned on the radio. A new Airbus 320, flying at a nearby airshow, had reportedly crashed after flying too low near the airfield. The cause of the crash would remain controversial for several years.

Soon after Lena moved out, I was obliged to admit to myself that I sorely needed a car. I was determined to get a Daihatsu of my own as soon as Bob and I returned to Sweden. My current three-on-a-bike solution was only viable in optimal weather conditions, in daylight, and over short distances that didn't require transport of anything else. Once the dark, rainy, slushy winter was upon us, getting around with the kids that way would be far too difficult and risky to manage. I also hoped to start visiting Karin soon. Bob offered to *give* me his Renault! (He'd owned it for quite a few years, but hardly ever drove it; the car still hadn't had its 10,000 km service, since he hadn't yet driven *half* that distance!) But due to prohibitive import fees, a great deal of red tape, and several mandatory (and costly) modifications to the vehicle to comply with Swedish highway standards, I had to decline his extremely generous offer.

Bob returned with me to Malmö on Friday, July 1st. Jenny and Sally would be returning with Lena from Gotland the next day, but we wouldn't get to see them until Monday. Three letters awaited me from Karin, the first of which she'd begun writing four days after I left for Switzerland. Apparently she'd faced some criticism and disapproval from her family about her marriage breakup, which made her feel insecure. At the same time, she was clear about her feelings for me. "*I love you so much and I want you so badly. Stanley Erisman, you are the best thing that has ever happened to me.*"

She phoned me that evening. She was as happy to hear my voice as I was to hear hers, but she was also more serious than I'd previously heard her. She said she needed to feel that we didn't *belong* to each other, but just wanted to *be* with each other. I knew exactly what she meant – couldn't have put it better myself. Out of the blue, I asked her what she'd be doing on New Year's Eve 1999 – more than 11 years down the road. She understood the implications immediately and erupted with joy. Then she replied that she wanted to know if I'd like to go to London with her sometime, and Paris, and the world.

On our Great Day (May 17th), I had cautioned her not to mess up her life for my sake, and I now reminded her of that. She immediately corrected me. That day, she said, had given her more than the power to go on; it gave her the power to break up, not because of me but because of herself. She needed solitude from time to time, and she knew she could manage on her own. *"I haven't messed up my life, I've sorted it out. I want you to know all about me and I want to know all about you. I want to know about Jeanette, and your tragedy."* This was another milestone for me – freedom from the millstone of silence; Jeanette had virtually been a taboo subject during my time with Lena.

Karin and I were reciprocating each other's feelings each step of the way. Our respective new routines and schedules were about to begin. For both of us, they meant that we'd have to be without our kids every other weekend. That gloomy prospect was now dramatically changed to the joyous opportunity to devote those alternate weekends entirely to each other. Everything about our relationship so far was passionate and sublime, yet down-to-earth and practical. (And we'd still only really met each other, spent time in the same room together, *once* – albeit for a whole wonderful day!)

Bob and I visited the Daihatsu dealer that weekend. I ordered a bright-red little Daihatsu Charade, and talked them into including a couple of car-seats for the kids. It would be ready for pick-up two weeks later, on the 16th. I dipped far deeper into my savings than my budget allowed but felt certain I could manage all right. Daihatsu's new G100 third-generation model offered even more loading space than the previous ones. I'd have no problem taking Jenny and Sally around, even if they had a lot of stuff to bring along. I was pleased, even though the engine was still on the weak side.

When Jenny and Sally arrived on July 4th, we were overjoyed to see each other. Seeing Bob only added to their delight. Lena dropped them off, then made her excuses almost immediately. She seemed very nervous and awkward about meeting Bob again. I asked the kids about their trip to Gotland, but I didn't ask them much about Lena; I didn't want them – or her – to think I might be using them as little "informants". Besides, I genuinely didn't care what Lena was up to, so long as she didn't do anything to mess *them* up, and I felt that they would tell me themselves whatever they felt they needed to talk about. Moreover, I trusted Lena implicitly to take good care of the kids during "her time".

On Friday afternoon, July 5th, Øivind and family came to Korngatan in the afternoon. My kids and theirs were best friends, so the four of them ran off playing together almost immediately, while Bob and I chatted with their parents. Although they both spoke fairly good English, I could see they had difficulty following Bob's eclectic vocabulary and convoluted syntax. Øivind joked to me again about *"den lille pjosken"*, which was a bit hard to translate (I hadn't yet revived the word "wimp" from my dormant vocabulary), but Bob got the point and grinned.

On Thursday evening, July 14th, after I'd put the kids to bed and Bob and I were talking over a cognac in the living room, the phone rang. It was Lena. She was crying. She said she wanted to move back to Korngatan. I froze. A million warning lights were flashing in my head. I went silent. She said that she'd "terminated her relationship" with Schad, and "missed" me. "*Why?!*" I asked skeptically. "*Because you no longer like <u>him</u>?*" (I also wondered silently whether Bob's hypothesis had been correct after all.) She replied that there were "too many obstacles" in the way for her to build up a new relationship. Besides, she added, what if the kids blamed her for the breakup?

A million more warning lights began flashing. I realized that this was – *as usual* – only about her: her needs, her wishes. There was – *as usual* – no apology, no declaration of love for me, no desire to show me kindness or affection, no interest in what I might want or what would please me. It was the same old one-way street. When I said nothing, she added, in her old silky voice, "*I just don't care enough for him, and I still have feelings for you.*"

Thank you so much! I thought to myself bitterly. *But what do you mean,"still"?! Hate is a feeling! The last feelings you told me about were hatred and contempt!* Yet I said nothing. As soon as she moved out, I'd made a startling discovery: *She'd left me <u>nothing</u> to miss*! The *only* antagonism I'd experienced since she left was from her, over the phone. It felt *wonderful* not to be hated! I wasn't a masochist after all! This was beyond Humpty-Dumpty; one can't put pieces *back* together when they've never been properly together to start with. She was just trying to mess with my mind. And I now knew a lovely woman who could actually love me for who I was!

Then it occurred to me that since the kids had now been with me for several days, this outburst from Lena, this drama, might be about her missing *them*, and I was the simply the means to fix that longing, and to make *her* life easier and more practical. Back to the shithole for me? *No way! Not ever!* Overcoming my negative response, and wishing to let her down gently, I told her I'd need time to think about what she said, and added that she ought to take more time to think about it as well. In her view, it seemed to me, since I'd failed to leap at her offer, my response amounted to borderline criticism. Accordingly, her irritation immediately became palpable, and she began fuming and ended the call.

Bob was gobsmacked when I returned to the living room and told him about the conversation that had just taken place. He understood my twinges of ambivalence, and was greatly encouraged that I'd resisted the siren's song. I wondered to myself whether I'd have been taken in by her again if Karin's incredible declarations of love hadn't already begun delivering me to safety on a totally different shore. There was no way of knowing, no control group. Either way, I knew that I never wanted to return to Lena's hatred and verbal abuse. What I did want was to find out the direction in which Karin and I might take whatever had started with our improbable yet incredibly wonderful encounter.

Two days later, Bob and I and the kids took a bus to pick up the new Daihatsu and take it for a drive. The kids were so excited about Daddy's new *red* car! Eva and family came by for dinner on the 18th and to meet Bob. We had a pleasant evening, despite a few (expected) areas of awkwardness. (I didn't mention Karin.) I had to drop the kids off at Lena's the next day. They immediately blabbed about my new car, which caused Lena to glare daggers at me. (*Why?*) But my relief at being able to close the door on her ill will towards me was again my deliverance.

Although Bob had to return to Basel on the 20th, he did so happily reassured of my balance and stability, and full of delight to see that the kids appeared unscathed. His friendship and kindness were astounding.

I spoke with Karin that evening. She was spending most of her vacation time in Glimminge and wondered if I – now that I had a car – might be able to drive up and visit her the following evening!? We couldn't be together at her cottage until her kids were asleep, but since that might not be before midnight, and since I might prefer to arrive in daylight, she wondered if we could meet briefly earlier in the evening in the parking lot at the end of the small paved main road, Knaggarpsvägen, the only road leading into Glimminge. (Most of the roads in

Glimminge were gravel.) Once she helped me get my bearings, could I then look around on my own for a while? Would I be willing to do it that way? As far as I was concerned, I'd do just about anything to see her again, and told her so. She was delighted and gave me instructions on how to find the way, as well as where to park. We were both nearly breathless with excitement.

Leif came to Korngatan in the afternoon, bringing along some documents for me to rewrite. We hadn't met for a while, and he had no trouble seeing how transformed I was. (My 8th life now underway!) I told him we couldn't work past 6 PM; I was going to meet Karin for the second time that evening. I couldn't keep from smiling, almost struggling to catch my breath. Did I mention that I felt like a nervous teenager?

Leif and I left Korngatan at the same time, so he got to see my new Daihatsu before he climbed into his big BMW. I didn't envy him one iota. I was on clouds and he knew it. We were both heading north on the E6 freeway, he as far as Helsingborg (about 65 km) and I towards Ängelholm, another 25 km, and then 25 km more to Glimminge. I saw him ahead of me, and I passed him, waving and laughing. My foot may have been a bit heavier than usual that evening.

I was listening to one of my favorite cassette tapes with ELO or JJ Cale or Dire Straits (all courtesy of Jan in Norway), when suddenly I began to hear strange noises. I felt panic rising. *New car. Bugs in it. I'm not going to make it to Glimminge. Total fiasco!* I pulled over on the shoulder. Leif, who was still right behind me, pulled over too. He got out and came over to have a look. With very little delay, I discovered that the problem was not with the engine, but with the cassette tape – it had broken in some way that made broken-engine noises, presumably audible only to those who are excessively wound up. I hadn't been that nervous in years.

Leif turned off for Helsingborg shortly thereafter, probably wondering who that teenage copywriter was who looked a lot like me. I was still trembling, but I could laugh at myself. What else could go wrong? I had some difficulty finding the way. Perhaps Karin knew the way too well when she gave me the instructions. I faced far too many choices that weren't included in her simple guidelines. One might say I was kind of excited, and I began to fear that even if I found the way, I might be unable to recognize her. At last I saw a sign for Glimminge Plantering. I was almost on time. Just before arriving there, as I turned to head down Knaggarpsvägen, I had a beautiful view of the landscape sloping towards the sea (Skälderviken and Kattegatt), across some fields of crops, mostly potatoes.

A small wooded area (which turned out to be Glimminge Plantering) separated the fields from the sea. The water was deep blue. Beyond it, the left-hand side of the panorama revealed some low mountains, and to the right was the clear sharp line of the horizon, where sea and sky meet and hold their daily debates about what shades of blue they would wear that day.

The wooded area consisted of majestic, fully grown pines, interspersed with birches of varying heights. These sheltered a scattered collection of unpretentious cottages – the summer homes of some 250 Swedish families. *How will I find Karin?!*

I'd no sooner asked myself that question when I saw a young blonde woman some 50 meters ahead of me, strolling along the road, away from me, occasionally looking over her shoulder. She was wearing jeans and a white shirt. My heart leapt; I *knew* it was Karin. When she heard an approaching car (mine), she turned around, clearly recognizing me too, and stopped. I stopped. She quickly got in and told me a bit nervously to drive on at once but slowly, to the parking lot at the end of the road, the place where she'd suggested that we should meet. There were very few people around. It was around 7.30 PM, so everyone was probably back at their respective cottages having dinner.

We sat there in the nearly empty parking lot by the sea, looking at each other, not knowing what to say at first; it all seemed so unreal. Then we kissed, timidly at first, then the wonderful reality began flooding back. Every look, every word, every touch confirmed the flood of first impressions we'd experienced on May 17th. We *knew* instantly that it had been no anomaly, no one-off, no casual fling. We both *knew* – despite all the chaos in our lives and uncertainties about how to achieve a new life together that would be acceptable to our respective kids – that *this could very well be the real thing*!

As improbable as our circumstances might make it, as far as the timing of our situation might suggest, as far as the fumbling, bumbling, haphazard chaos of our lives and of the universe might reasonably allow, we both sensed to the point of knowing, felt to the point of flying, that this was a one-in-a-billion throw of the dice that came up a winner. You *don't* walk away from that!!

Karin suggested we leave the car and take a walk along the grassy meadow that separated the little wooded community from the sea. I was more than willing to be guided. The meadow itself was a nature preserve that formed a band about 100 m wide around most of the coastline that is called the Bjäre Peninsula, stretching from Ängelholm to Torekov to the north-northwest, then on to Båstad to the east.

[*Not that I gave a shit about geography or topography at that particular moment!*] Karin walked quickly; there was a great need for discretion at this point. After several hundred meters we reached a stone wall with a stile that put Glimminge Plantering behind us. The next part of the shoreline meadow nature preserve was much wider; it continued gently upwards from the sea, along the entire southern border of Glimminge Plantering. It was speckled with juniper bushes. Huge hares bounded around and took cover at the slightest threat. Walking up the gentle slope, away from the sea, we soon came to some taller junipers, ones that might aspire to become trees some day. We were suddenly out of sight of everyone on earth. We stopped, turned to each other, fell into each other's arms and didn't let go, couldn't let go. I hadn't been hugged that hard, that lovingly, in more than 11 years.

We talked intensely whenever we needed to verbalize feelings or exchange facts or breathe. And whenever we could take our eyes off each other for a moment, we gazed wordlessly across a tranquil meadow at the sea – the Bay of Skälderviken – and the hills of Kullaberg beyond. (Not being oriented yet, I thought at first that I might be looking at Denmark across the water.) After our all-too-brief early-evening meeting, we went back to my car, where I had to wait until nightfall – after 11 PM (remember, this is southern Sweden, just a month past the summer solstice). Karin came out again briefly in the dusk to show me the way to the family cottage, so I'd be able to find it in the *real* darkness (Glimminge had no streetlights.)

The cottage was set back from the road about 30 meters, shielded from the road by lots of two-meter-high birch bushes. At around 11 PM, I pulled into the driveway and turned off my lights. There were still quite a few lights on in the cottage. I waited in the car in the darkness, joyfully impatient, full of nervous confidence. Karin came out to get me as soon as the coast was clear. I stayed for a couple of hours.

Five evenings later, on July 26th, I was back for my second visit to Glimminge, our third rendezvous. This time I stayed until about 3 AM. I was so blissfully tired, floating on clouds as I drove home to Malmö that I had to turn my car radio up full blast to fight crippling drowsiness. I kept the windows down, and *screamed for joy* along with the music to stay awake and on the road when it felt more like I was flying.

There were green lights everywhere, no forbidding reds, no cautionary yellows, just green. The more we found out about each other the happier we became. And it was all mutual, a two-way street.

I told Karin about the effect that writing *The Unparallel Lines* had on me on a decade ago – my totally serendipitous catharsis. She said she'd like to read it if I was willing to let her. I hesitated, fearing it might put her off or overwhelm her. I hadn't completely forgotten the very negative effects my manuscript had had on others a decade earlier. But then I realized that Karin was Karin and nobody else. And if I couldn't feel I could be me with her, what was the point? It was vital to have an open and honest foundation if our relationship was to flourish. I sent her a copy on July 30th.

CHAPTER 13

At last

Far from putting Karin off, *The Unparallel Lines* seemed to deepen and intensify her feelings for me, even though she found it hard to grasp the suicidal state I was in at the time I wrote it. As if in response, in the early days of August, she sent me a cassette tape with love songs and other music she loved and thought I'd love – songs that she said echoed her feelings for me. I was blown away. I listened to her tape over and over, nearly every time I was driving. And she said emphatically that she meant the words for me! (I'd never heard many of those songs before: *When Tomorrow Comes* and *The Miracle of Love*, both by Eurythmics; and *Once in a Lifetime* and *You're the Inspiration*, both by Chicago [*Listen to them!*].) This vicarious expression of her love was another new experience for me. The list was growing.

Jenny and Sally also liked the tape immediately and were soon demanding to hear it whenever we were out in the car. For the time being, I refrained from divulging its origin. Karin and I both felt it would be wise to delay introductions to each other's kids for at least half a year – until we felt *certain* about our future life together.

Karin's positive reactions to my story, *The Unparallel Lines*, relieved me greatly. I told her so in my next letter. In the same letter, I wrote "*I'm seriously planning to write a book about everything, including my most recent crisis, and I need to feel that you will 'let' me, i.e. that you can deal with someone who is a tireless seeker of truth.*" I also told her I would go on loving and wanting her until the year 2040. [*Dare I still think, beset by medical issues at the age of 76 as I write this, that I'll live beyond the age of 95?!*] Strange, weird, bizarre and wonderful though it was, Karin insisted that she wanted me to be happy. I hadn't heard anything like that in more than a decade.

She wrote that from time to time she sometimes had "down" periods for no reason or for any reason. Such a period never lasted long, she said, but might easily be misinterpreted as depression – which she insisted it was not.

In spite of having enough in my recent experience of being screamed at to last me several lifetimes, I *never* experienced it from her [*and still haven't as of 2021*]! It was *relaxing* to talk with her, in the sense that I could speak spontaneously, without inhibition, without having to weigh my words lest I give offense or sound critical. She listened to what I said and responded to that. She didn't insist I meant *B* when I'd said *A*, and then get furious with me about *B*. What a pleasure to speak freely!

Karin began moving into her new duplex during the first week of August, a month with few opportunities for us to see each other. Most Swedes (except teachers) went back to work in the early part of the month after long summer vacations. School resumed around the middle of the month for Karin's kids. At the end of the month, Jenny and Sally would start spending a portion of their "Lena-time" at a nursery school. Knowing that they *could* have been with me made the nursery school a chronic source of irritation for me, but I tried hard to look beyond myself. As long as the kids were happy.

But it would soon come to annoy me even more. Although Lena and I had officially and legally agreed to share custody (50-50), whenever the kids were with me she seemed to spend her time looking for loopholes. She phoned one evening to tell me that our arrangement was unfair to her. On working days, she claimed, she'd only get to see the kids from around 4 PM until their bedtime, and then briefly in the morning. But when they were with me, I got to see them during the daytime as well (never mind that I actually worked from home!). She said we had to rewrite the schedule on the basis of how many "waking hours" they spent with each of us!

Then, when I pointed out that I was always punctual when dropping them off at the agreed-upon times, whereas she was usually late, *she* accused *me* of "counting the hours"!! Was someone supposed to check that one of us wasn't keeping the kids awake longer in the evenings than the other?! Under her proposed new plan, only the nursery school would see more of the kids. And we would have to pay more *not* to have the kids with either of us. I vetoed the plan, but realized with a deep sigh that even though she was now thankfully out of my house, she would never be completely out of my life....

Back in May – just before Lena moved out, when we went through all our possessions room by room, drawer by drawer, shelf by shelf, cupboard by cupboard, we agreed on what she would take with her when she moved out. Our informal agreement was confirmed by a legal division of property, which left her with a few things that had once been mine before we met, and vice-versa. Yet less than a month later, she started coming back for more. If I said no, she became livid and screamed that I was being unfair. When the kids were present I tried to walk away so as give her nobody to scream at while they were present. Then she would sometimes cry instead. If I tried preemptively bringing her things that had once been hers even though she'd agreed I could have them, she accused me of trying to expunge her memory from the house where her children still lived. Damned if I do, damned if I don't – same old story, nothing new about that!

For quite a long time, I let her have her way to avoid upsetting the kids. But I put my foot down in the instance of the old dining table that I'd rescued from the barn in Eket in 1983 (the one that replaced the similar table I'd had before). I told her the table was going nowhere. "*Now see here*," she raged, "*it was mine!*" I reminded her that she had a few things that once were mine, so what? She quickly switched to her hurt, sentimentalist tone, "*But it was my father's!*" I reminded her that rescuing that table from Eket was *my* idea. Her father acquired many pieces of furniture at countryside auctions and threw them into the barn there, but she hadn't been bothered about leaving *them* behind. I wondered (to myself) why she didn't save his clothing, *et bloody cetera*.

Karin mercifully – and to my amazement – had no such exhausting quibbles with her ex. Although their breakup wasn't exactly a rose garden, and she knew that there are always reasons for a divorce, theirs was civilized. I couldn't help wondering what that might feel like.

My work with external (non-Perstorp) clients like Leif continued to grow. For a few of my assignments (excluding those for Leif), I had direct contact with advertising agencies, and occasionally got into discussions with their copywriters. I was shocked to discover that Perstorp was paying me *less than a quarter* of the going rate for the kind of work I was doing nowadays. Although I wasn't motivated by greed, this felt like outright exploitation – and on that I felt there ought to be limits!

Since I was now feeling the financial pinch of a single-income household, I talked to Stig (my boss) about it. He said he'd bring it up with the personnel manager. The outcome was a miniscule raise. Stig intimated that Perstorp seldom gave substantial raises to people over 40 – people who would be more inclined to hang onto their jobs than to voluntarily reenter the employment market. That sounded like a very cynical approach to me, especially in the face of management talk of "team-building" and "loyalty to one's employer". Stig also passed along the advice of the corporate human resources director: that if the small raise they were offering me wasn't enough, I should consider starting my own company. The very thought made me cringe. I *hated* administrative work, bookkeeping, red tape, tax calculations, everything I associated with having one's own company. As a result, I simply tightened my belt and trudged on.

I found it awkward to mention this to Karin at the time, despite our being able to share our doubts as well as our passion, fears and hopes. But we spoke openly of our fears for our kids and ourselves, and for the great unknowns of the future. It could be terrifying at times. We were two different people from vastly different backgrounds. And yet there was nothing (and no one) more exciting, more wonderful and more on my wavelength. As she wrote (it could have been me writing), she just had to think of me and she'd smile.

We knew there was a mysterious and inexplicable role of personal chemistry in a relationship, and how elusive it can be to discover what works for one person, let alone both. It could be pure chaos. What if one of us fell in love with the other, only to find much later that the personal chemistry didn't work out after all?

Somehow, that rang a bell.... I thought it likely in my case, but not in Lena's – because she'd never loved me. There was, however, no discernable mismatch between Karin and me. How we felt was much more important than what we thought. Love isn't about logic; nor are matters of taste, rapturous appreciation of natural or artistic beauty, or any other inherently subjective experiences. I couldn't give *reasons* why I'd loved Jeanette and Lena, nor *why* I felt that deep love was brewing between Karin and me. It was literally unreasonable to expect reasons.

Sometimes she'd send me a fax just to tell me again how much she loved me, or that she wanted to spend the next 50 years in my arms. I *adored* her for it. (And she frequently told me that she *adored* me!!) I'd heard of guys who didn't appreciate that kind of thing, and I pitied those who confuse manliness with macho.

Karin was worried that her kids would be bitter towards her and wondered whether they would ever be able to understand her and us. She wrote of her moments of darkest doubt and despair, and of being blindsided by her love for me. After all, who could have foreseen it? Neither of us, that's for sure!

I was overjoyed to have Jenny and Sally on my own for five days in the latter half of August and decided to see how they'd like a little road trip. On August 23rd we drove up to Mariefred to visit Christer and his wife Cecilia. He was a former pupil of mine who ran a big supermarket full of cheap imports. He generously gave Jenny and Sally lots of presents from his stock. Mariefred, the location of Gripsholm Castle, is close to Stockholm. It took us the better part of a day to drive there. The kids had a wonderful time.

We drove home by way of Barkåkra. Although I'd spoken with Marie-Louise many times over the last few months, and met her in Lund, I hadn't been to her home for ages. Yet our love for each other remained intact. She told me she'd long understood Lena's lack of feelings for me and found it painful and deplorable, but she also understood that I couldn't do anything about Lena's decision. Nor did she expect me to bring my own life to a halt.

When I dropped the kids off at Lena's that Friday evening, the kids and I were in high spirits. Our time together in the car – laughing and singing and joking, sightseeing and visiting their beloved grandma – was a great bonding experience for us. Lena didn't seem pleased that they were so happy and asked them with feigned chagrin whether they hadn't even missed her. I just said *"Lena...!"* in exasperation, hoping that she would understand the implied rebuke without flipping out.

I had an additional reason to be in high spirits. Karin was driving down to see me the next day – and would stay till late Sunday afternoon! It would be the first time we'd get to spend a whole night together, and we were determined to make the most of it. She'd written me two letters and a fax while I was away with the kids. Her parents had been to see her in her new apartment, and they'd had a very pleasant time, to Karin's relief. They were highly supportive now. They also said they noticed – as Karin had – that her daughter Moa was more relaxed than they'd seen her in a long time.

Our appetite for each other was insatiable – not just physically, but to learn more about each other. I wanted to hear more about her dad and mom, her three siblings and her kids. Her parents – Sven and Agda – sounded like terrific people. For years they'd owned and run a small glassware and china shop in Klippan, before turning it over to Karin and her husband. Sven had major health problems and had nearly died some years earlier. They'd recently moved from their home in Klippan to a split-level apartment in Ängelholm, just a 10-minute drive from Marie-Louise in Barkåkra, along the way to Glimminge. Sometimes the world *does* seem small!

Reading *The Unparallel Lines* seemed only to whet Karin's appetite for learning more about me and my life. We looked through all the photos I could find. I told her I also had a lot of slides, and she immediately asked me to set up the projector. (I couldn't help observing to myself that Lena had *always* refused my offers to show my slides and photos to her, and thus she never saw them once!) But getting to know another person deeply is of course more than learning biographical bullet points. Karin realized that the most important person in my life (apart from Jenny, Sally and her) was Bob, and she wanted to know more about him too.

Back in Klippan the next day, Monday, August 29th, Karin felt frustrated and wrote me how right and wonderful and romantic everything felt with me, but that out of consideration for everyone else – our kids, our families, our exes, our colleagues – we had to live in secrecy. "*The world is watching a beautiful love story and we must keep it to ourselves. It's not fair!!!*" [Until now!!]

Entirely on her own initiative, Karin wrote a charming birthday greeting to Bob, who turned 60 on August 30th. On September 1st, just a few days after our last encounter, Karin and I met again, when she spent the day with me in Malmö – as my "pupil"! We had a good laugh about both of us getting paid for our pleasure, although everything we did verbally that day involved the English language, so we saw no harm in that.

One of our discussions was on the subject of religion – our beliefs and non-beliefs. She told me that like most Swedes, she'd always followed the crowd in terms of the Swedish brand of quasi-religion, i.e. vaguely believing in "something", and observing certain traditions like christening and confirmation, which were inflicted as a matter of course on the next generation. It had all come about more or less automatically, as though it had never occurred to her that she might have a choice. But to her it wasn't about Truth; they were *just* traditions.

This turned into a discussion of my paintings, particularly *The Midian Children*, and soon her head was spinning. She said she was excited (and somewhat astonished) to realize that one could, in fact, choose *not* to believe. I suggested that she try reading *A Free Man's Worship* by Bertrand Russell. She asked to borrow my copy. Her first reaction, she told me, was that she'd never read anything so fascinating in her life.

On Saturday, Bob wrote a short reply to Karin:

Thank you so much for your birthday greeting. I feel already indebted to you because of the happiness you have brought to Stanley, who is my all-time favorite person. [... He]... hasn't got a suitable return on the warmth he spontaneously radiates, as I see it, until rather recently. And since that change is associated with you, I am prejudiced in your favor even though we haven't yet met each other.

On Sunday, September 4th, which happened to be the first anniversary of the beginning of her affair with Johannes (my presumption), Lena phoned in the late evening (the kids were with me, of course), at about 10:30, to tell me she'd broken off with Johannes in order to free herself from guilt feelings and feel better when our divorce became final. I said nothing about her astounding logic, but merely asked why she was telling me this. She said it was because she missed me and wanted to come back. *Here we go again,* I thought. As before, everything was about what *she* wanted. It certainly felt to me that she was just trying to mess with my mind again. *Two can play that game,* I thought!

I told her that despite many uncertainties on the road ahead, I would never again live under the same roof with someone who didn't love me. As soon as I'd said it, I realized I'd set myself up for her to claim fervently that she *did* love me, and could I forgive her? But she made no such claim. She asked nothing about what *she* could do to make *me* happy. It was, as usual, only about her.

Finding it extremely egocentric that she kept making these insincere requests every time she booted Schad out, I thought *Game on*! So I added that as long as she was still seeing him, there was no point in even talking with me about it. She protested, *"But I'm not seeing him anymore!"* I said I *knew* she was still seeing him. *"How can you know that?"* she asked in astonishment, again not realizing that the way she formulated her question confirmed what I'd just claimed. I told her it was because I knew someone who lived in her building. *"You've got spies?!"* she hissed, her rage rising instantly, further confirming my claim. I refused to answer her question. Then I heard in the background that someone was knocking on her door at that late hour. She put the phone down to get it. Not surprisingly, it was Johannes (I could easily hear their conversation in the background). She'd apparently kicked him out (again) moments before phoning me, and he'd been sitting out on the stairs crying until she let him back in. I was beginning to feel sorry for the guy. After that, Lena left me alone for a while. (By the way, it wasn't a lie; I *did* know someone in her building: I knew *her!*)

I had a different pupil every day during the following week. Fortunately, Karin was able to come down again to be with me again from Saturday morning till Sunday morning, leaving just before Lena brought Jenny and Sally home. Karin and I enjoyed an ecstatic 24 hours together, and I finally managed to take some photos of her, since she'd still been unable to provide me any portrait shots. Our more frequent meetings were bringing us closer and closer together – a fact that neither of us in any way took for granted, but that we both savored. It felt natural, right, astounding. [*Am I repeating myself, dear reader? Deal with it!*]

That same day, Bob wrote me that he marveled at my "*basic lack of bitterness in a matter in which you've been treated shabbily for utterly frivolous reasons by someone who simply was inadequate to judge the extent of the favor fortune had done her in letting her cross your path at a time of maximum vulnerability on your part.*" I knew better than to attempt to get him to dial down the flattery, but I did need to disabuse him of one notion: I could not deny a fair amount of bitterness – not for being jilted, but for the mean-spiritedness and begrudging me the time I could have and wanted to spend with the kids.

Karin and I had begun our new "normal" schedule of spending every other weekend together, usually from Friday evening to late Sunday afternoon, two and a half consecutive days and two nights every other week. Sometimes she'd drive down to Malmö, sometimes I'd drive up to Klippan. With few exceptions, we were only able to meet every other weekend throughout the autumn of 1988. But the forced 11-day physical separations played several important roles in our blossoming and thriving love. We had numerous and/or long phone conversations every weekday, and long late-evening ones on the intervening weekends when we had our respective kids with us.

Through phone calls and letters, we were building a metaphorical "home" – getting to know each other more and more, liking everything we saw and heard and felt. We covered just about every topic we could think of, found ourselves in agreement on a huge majority of them and were easily able to resolve, compromise and/or respect the few differences of opinion that arose. We also got to learn more and more about each other: preferences, habits, families, childhoods, experiences, problems, fears and hopes. And the more we got to know each other, the more our love grew. Perhaps if we'd been able to meet every day it might have taken us much longer to get to know each other so deeply; the dynamics of our mutual attraction might well have postponed everything else.

But the fact that it had all happened so suddenly, so unexpectedly, so *serendipitously*, gave our love a sense of incredulity that made it difficult simply to accept such a wonderful fact as real. Time would prove us right.

Having always had a propensity to plan far ahead (consider the thousand-day countdown Norm and I had prior to our departure from Chicago back in 1964!), at some point in the early autumn I began to sketch (literally and mentally) how I might undertake to rebuild my house to accommodate Karin and Moa if they were ever to move in with me and the kids. I agreed with Karin that it would be unfair to Moa to move from Klippan before she graduated from grade school (and would have to change schools anyway), which meant no move prior to June 1991 at the earliest.

It *sounded* so far off, so agonizingly far off. Even the prospect of being able to visit each other *every* weekend (once we'd met each other's kids in the beginning of 1989) was far from a sure thing. It was still only a wish. What if for some reason our kids reacted negatively to accompanying one of us to Klippan or Malmö on weekends? There were no guarantees. Karin hoped that Moa, after completing grade school in 1991, would welcome or accept or consider a move to Malmö for high school. No guarantees. And Karin would have to change jobs, as the Malmö-Perstorp commute was daunting. Could she find a suitable job to match her skills in the Malmö region? Again, no guarantees. But what if Moa *were* OK with the move and Karin *did* find a good new job locally? It would be many times more disruptive to launch a two-year rebuilding project if I waited till *then* to start. I'd have to begin planning at once!

Although the house at Korngatan was spacious, there were too few bedrooms, and the layout didn't lend itself to creating more bedrooms without making radical changes. The most important change – one that would enable all other changes, as I saw it – would be to connect the big house and the little house into a single U-shaped building. This would mean constructing an extension across the western half of the tiny yard. It would thus also mean sacrificing most of the yard, which was largely engulfed in shade anyway; after all, we were already spending most of our outdoor time on the roof terrace above the garage.

I made sketch after sketch. Each time I completed a series of drawings, I was convinced that this was the perfect solution. Then (usually during some semi-conscious moment in the middle of the night) another idea would occur to me, and I would sketch that. Another idea *did* occur to me: that I was following some primordial avian instinct to re-feather my nest, the way people often refurbish even a brand-new residence, no matter how ship-shape it was when they moved in.

I shared my ideas with Karin, who was moved by how prepared and enthusiastic I was to undertake a project of that magnitude "just" to please her and Moa. I told her that it would benefit everyone. Jenny and Sally could get rooms of their own; Moa would continue to have a room of her own; Karin and I would get a larger bedroom that gave us greater privacy when needed; and Karin would get a room of her own. And I would keep my home office. Bob was stunned by the scope of my plans but understood my need for long-range planning.

Lena's and my "normal" schedule for the kids didn't begin until September 12th. Lena had already managed to accumulate five extra days with the kids since she moved out, and called me a nit-picking idiot for pointing it out, of course. I considered that preferable to howls of "*Unfair!!*" directed at me if the deficit had been hers. In either case, she wouldn't hear of compensating me for her extra days. [*!!*]

She signed the kids up for violin lessons (Suzuki method). This made great sense, considering that we each already owned a piano. But I was in favor of continuing to promote the kids' musical interests in every way possible. She also signed them up for ballet lessons, most of which were on my time with them. It was strange, even to me, that while some people perceived me as being confrontationalist in debates and discussions (particularly when I poked holes in their logic), I repeatedly (but not always!) bent over backwards to accommodate Lena and *avoid* confronting her even on her most flagrant abuses of reason.

Eva and family came to Korngatan for my 43rd birthday. Bob was delighted to hear it. He recalled how much it meant to him to be accepted by his ex-wife's family after their break-up. When Jeanette's family went incommunicado on me after I'd told them I'd found someone new (even though they'd encouraged me to do so!), it felt like they'd never seen me as a person, but only as Jeanette's appendage. That hurt. And it added to my appreciation of the lack of rejection by Eva and Marie-Louise. (Lena's brother Jan and I always remained on friendly terms, even though our paths seldom crossed. Lena's brother Lars and I wanted nothing to do with each other, which was just as well; I'd lost all respect for him.)

Week after week, I continued to revise the building plans for the house. The best solution, I felt, would be to join the big and little houses on *both* levels, using the existing two-storey wall that divided our yard from Bo and Peter's house as the western long-side of the extension, and the walls of the big and little houses as the two short-sides. I would thus only need to build the eastern long-side wall and a roof, and could thereby save lots of time, materials and expense. The room on the downstairs level would serve as a dining room, and above it would be a light, airy room (using the big windows from my former studio). That room would be Karin's. Jenny's and Sally's long room would eventually be divided into two (when the day came when Jenny and Sally decided they'd each prefer a room of their own), with built-in beds and desks, as well as a "fort" in each in the high-peaked ceiling of each room. Moa would take over my former bedroom at the top of the stairs, with its view over the neighborhood.

The library in the little house would have to be divided into two again (it had been two rooms when Jeanette and I bought the house), with the western half consisting of a new bedroom and closets for Karin and me. The eastern half would remain the library. I'd use the boards from the bookshelves in the western half to extend the eastern bookshelves up to the ceiling.

This meant that I'd have to open up the contiguous kitchen countertop to make an open doorway with a couple of steps down into the dining room. I'd wall up the window to the yard from opposite the laundry room, and put in a window to the new, smaller yard on an angle above the sink. All this in itself might have been daunting enough, but the fact that the property was on a slight downward slope from south to north meant that the little and big houses were on slightly different levels; I'd have to put in a few steps here and there. But I did have quite a lot of experience now, and my expectations regarding costs and time were far more reasonable. But there'd also be the small matter of getting a building permit. And Henry was now retired and living in Smygehamn, on the south coast of Sweden, and we'd lost touch....

On October 5th, a month after Lena's latest impulsive call to ask to move back, it was time for another round. (Her call, for the record, once again came while the kids were at my place, the evening after she'd dropped them off.) She "confessed" to me that she'd been in contact with Schad "by phone and at work" despite having broken up with him, but that she was living alone. I found it bizarre that she was telling me this, and I couldn't help wondering whether such monthly phone calls were related to hormone cycles, but I didn't mention that. Instead, I just asked her why or how she thought it was any business of mine? She evaded my question and said – again – how hard things were for *her* on her own.

As before, it was *all* about her, her needs, her problems. I hated these calls. Her attempts to reel me back in, now that the spell was broken, came across as pathetic. I no longer became angry or defensive. The law of diminishing returns was in force: I reacted less and less each time. But I did want her to stop. Enough was enough. So I reminded her that I knew someone who lived in her building, then upped the ante by telling her I knew someone who worked at her school too. She went silent, which to me confirmed her lies. Lest she draw mistaken conclusions, I told her I was happy in my new life and my new relationship.

[*Now I must digress a bit into the future, beyond the main narrative of this book, to 1990. For the sake of continuity, I place it here rather than in the Afterword. There was one "final" call to reel me back in, after at least half a year's moratorium on the evening come-back calls, in the late summer or early autumn, more than two years after we'd parted ways.*

Lena began roughly the usual way: Was I absolutely certain I wouldn't have her back? I sighed wearily and said that we'd been over that so many times already, and that the answer was and would remain the same. Then she said that in that case, she had some "big news" for me, and that I'd better sit down. I said I was fine, I could remain standing, whatever her news. Then she dropped her "news": she and Johannes were going to buy a house together. Without hesitation, I asked, "Oh that's nice, where is it?" She sounded gobsmacked and exclaimed, "Aren't you surprised?!" I said no, not at all. They'd been together for nearly three years already, so it seemed to me like the natural thing to do.

They moved into their new house, in Rostorp, in December 1990. The house was no farther to Jenny's and Sally's future school than from Korngatan. It seemed to me like a reasonable solution. I had no idea what they paid for it nor whether they could afford it; it wasn't any of my business. She didn't say and I didn't ask.

After Lena moved out, I not only maintained good relations with Marie-Louise, but also with Eva and Jan in Lund. Karin and I were dinner guests at their place, they were dinner guests at ours. Amicability all around. In June or July of 1991 (incidentally or coincidentally at around the time Karin and her daughter Moa moved to Korngatan), Lena suddenly terminated her relationship with Johannes ("He's perverse!" she claimed to me on the phone, but she never explained why, nor did I ask.)

Lena pulled up roots and moved from the house in Rostorp to a large condo in an old, attractive building in Kirseberg, in a block called Östergård, down the hill, just 4-5 blocks from Korngatan. (I helped her with the move!) "More convenient for the kids" was my first thought. Then I remembered how she'd sneered at my suggestion that she look for something in Kirseberg for the kids' sake. My next thought was that the condo was very large, and I wondered (to myself only) whether she could afford it. But it was, again, none of my business.

Nearly a year passed by. Then one evening I got a call from Jan (Eva's Jan). He was furious, livid, with me! Apparently he'd just discovered that Eva had co-signed the loan that Lena had taken to cover her half of the mortgage that she and Johannes had taken to buy the house in Rostorp, and that instead of reducing her mortgage in connection with buying her condo, Lena had transferred the entire amount (or nearly). Again I thought it was none of my business. But Jan was adamant; I should have co-signed Lena's loan, he claimed. I was incredulous! "Do you really think I should have co-signed a loan for Lena to buy a house with the guy she was cheating on me with?!!" Jan had no answer to that, nor any interest in answering or discussing it. I should have done it, he insisted, end of story!

Jan refused to speak to me. He refused to take my calls or answer my letters and questions. And his position had the effect of making it impossible for Karin and me to continue our friendly relationship with Eva – the real casualty of Jan's close-mindedness. I continued to send him birthday and Christmas greetings and presents for a couple of years. He never thanked me. Years passed. We happened to meet in some context many years later. He behaved as though nothing had happened. [Pretend it's raining! Don't apologize, whatever you do, Jan!]

Now back to the timeline.

On a visit to Maj and Lars that fall (1988), Maj told me that in the spring of '83, she, Gunilla and Charlotte (Lena's three closest friends) had been astonished to hear that Lena and I were going to have a baby (our first, Jenny). Lena had apparently been telling her friends how disgusting she found me *that long ago*. And when they heard that we were going to have a *second* child, they could hardly believe their ears. I wasn't really surprised by what Maj said; it confirmed the conclusions I'd been fearing all along.

On October 9th, Karin wrote a letter to Bob, in response to his letter thanking her for her birthday note.

> You have no reason at all to feel indebted to me because of the happiness I have brought to Stan – he has brought at least as much happiness into my life. [...] I once told Stan that I believe in God and that was like throwing a piece of red cloth to a bull. He is so eager to discuss it and so bloody well-informed on the

subject that I'm afraid the arguments I have so far are not enough. I agree with most of his arguments (which I have no intention to admit, of course!) but I have to find a way of meeting them, if only to "spice" the discussion....

To me, Bob only wrote that he'd received a charming letter from Karin in which "she says you have doubts about her God, and I'm lusting to add to them."

Autumn continued with the delightful maturing of my wonderful relationship with Karin, and the joy of watching my kids grow and learn (despite my painfully limited time with them). I was slowly and very reluctantly learning to live with frequent separations. I had to remind myself that no matter how much I abhorred being away from them, they seemed to be happy and content with the part of their lives from which I was absent, even though separation from a parent doesn't usually happen at the ages of four and two (soon five and three). *Learn to let go, Stan!*

On November 16th, eight days after Sally's third birthday, my mail delivery brought notice that the six-month mandatory waiting period was over: *our divorce was now officially final*. I refrained from calling Lena to congratulate her (the thought occurred to me), but Bob congratulated me heartily when I told him. It didn't really feel like news to me; it felt like my new life had already begun on May 17th.

The next time the kids and I were out for a drive and they wanted to listen to their favorite tape, I felt the time had come for me to tell them it was "Karin's tape". They wondered who Karin was. I told them that she was my new friend, and that she was good to me. I said I hoped they'd get to meet each other someday, and they liked the idea. That was it. After that, they began referring to "Karin's tape". They also asked if they could bring it in, instead of having it only in the car. I said it would be fine. I never expected that "bring the tape in" might include taking it in with them to Lena's....

Sometime later, Lena phoned me, furious. What the hell did I mean with this "Karin's tape" business, she screamed, "*and this 'I wanna be with you when tomorrow comes'?! What the hell are you trying to do?! Take the kids away from me? Replace me?! Turn them against me?!*" It wasn't easy to calm her down. Even after her outburst, I feared she'd be plotting revenge, perhaps demonizing Karin to the kids or something. I feared it would come in one form or another, sooner or later, and I'd be unable to stop it.

Many have remarked on the amazing adaptability of children to just about any new situation. In every way that I could discern, Jenny and Sally bore that out. Although I had no way of knowing how they behaved when they were with Lena, they seemed remarkably happy when they were with me. They showed no signs of longing for Mommy when they were with Daddy, so I presumed the corresponding situation prevailed when they were with Lena. They had no nightmares, no tantrums, no crying for no apparent reason. I continued to speak English with them, and of course Lena spoke Swedish with them. They had two somewhat *different* lives, but they didn't seem to mind, and they didn't seem to rank them. That was a great relief to me!

Marie-Louise's 70th birthday was on December 1st, a Thursday. She decided to have her party on Saturday the 3rd instead. She rented the inn in Vejbystrand for the occasion – a catered afternoon dinner celebration with lots of family and friends. She phoned to let me know how important I would always be to her, and that she really hoped I could attend her reception. I promised I would; she was important to me too.

The kids would be with Lena that weekend, which meant that Karin and I would be together. I told Karin that I not only felt I should go, but that I wanted to go, because Marie-Louise meant a great deal to me. Karin understood perfectly (her ex-parents-in-law meant a great deal to her too). She made a suggestion: Why not spend that weekend with her in Klippan? I could come up on late Friday afternoon, and when it was time for me to drive to Vejbystrand on Saturday afternoon, I could drop her off at her parents' place in Ängelholm (about half an hour's drive from Klippan), which was on the way. Then I could pick her up again after the birthday event and we'd return to Klippan. That sounded like an excellent idea.

It also sounded great to Karin's parents. I still hadn't met Sven and Agda, but I liked everything Karin told me about them. Karin indicated that such feelings seemed to be mutual. Then they upped the ante: they told Karin they'd love to invite both of us to dinner at their place that same evening, after the birthday reception in Vejbystrand, so they could meet me at last.

After a wonderful Friday evening, night, and Saturday morning together with Karin, we made the half-hour drive from Klippan to Ängelholm. I dropped Karin off just outside the low-rise row house where her parents lived. I wasn't able to say exactly when I'd be back, but she said it was no problem, they'd be waiting. Then I drove off to find the inn in Vejbystrand, only a 10-minute drive away (it would probably have been a bit shorter if I'd known beforehand how to get there).

The moment I pulled into the parking lot, just after one o'clock, Lena hurried out to intercept me. Her face was disfigured by her foul mood. Her first words were to hiss furiously at me, "*You're not going to tell people we're divorced, are you?!!*" I looked at her in surprise, puzzled by the aggressive question that seemed so weird, so out of place and so incongruous with reality. After a moment's pause, I replied, trying to stay calm, that I was *not* planning to make a speech about it, but since we were now in fact divorced, I saw no reason to lie about it if anybody asked me a direct question. Her lip curled in a sneer, she did an about-faced, spitting out "*You bastard!!*" ["*Din jävel!!*"]. Then she disappeared back into the inn. After a welcome like that, things could only get better.

They did. As soon as I entered, Jenny and Sally came running up to me with big hugs. Eva and her family were all smiles and hugs. Lena had her mask back on in front of the others, but I focused on Marie-Louise. She gave me a huge welcoming hug and told me how happy she was that I could make it. I called her my "*svormor*". She looked at me in puzzlement. After I'd explained how I came up with that word, she laughed and hugged me again.

This is a bit tricky to explain. The Swedish word for mother-in-law is *svärmor*, from *svära* (*swear*, in this case as in an oath), and *mor* (*mother*). Like the English verb "to swear" (swear, swore, sworn), the Swedish verb is irregular: *svära, svor, svurit*. Since the past tense is *svor*, and since the divorce meant that our son-in-law-mother-in-law relationship was now officially in the past tense, I used the past tense in my neologism: *svormor*. I'll never apologize for my love of wordplay.

Lena's "greeting" on my arrival left an aftertaste of being a fifth wheel that afternoon. The feeling was hard to erase. I had to keep reminding myself that I was there for Marie-Louise's sake. Lars and I didn't cross paths or swords or words. Lena's brother Jan was friendly but subdued by his own problems. Most of the others – distant family members, Marie-Louise's neighbors and friends – were elderly people I'd hardly ever met or knew. I tried to speak a lot with Marie-Louise, Eva and my kids, but it was difficult in a gathering of perhaps 40-50 people. As the time approached four o'clock, I felt it would not be perceived as rude if I took my leave. I said goodbye to Marie-Louise, hugged her and thanked her for inviting me. She told me I'd always be welcome where she was concerned. Then I said goodbye to Eva and my kids and left the party speechless – without calling attention to myself or to the fact that Lena and I were now divorced, whether in a speech or in conversation.

As I drove back to Ängelholm, I tried to put the awkwardness of the experience behind me and figure out what to expect when I met Sven and Agda for the first time. I rang their doorbell. A light went on in the hallway, and I heard footsteps on a stairway. Sven opened the door, with Agda right behind him. They both held their arms wide open towards me, and they wore big smiles of somewhat shy but effusively friendly anticipation. Karin was just behind them on the stairs, grinning with pleasure. The vestibule was not quite big enough for all four of us. I hadn't been expecting such big warm hugs on my first meeting with them, and I was much moved when I got them.

Karin's dad looked a bit frail, yet energetic. He impressed me immediately as someone unafraid to show his feelings – or perhaps he was simply resigned to the fact that he was unable to hide them (kind of like me). The same applied to Karin's diminutive mom, who couldn't stop smiling from ear to ear. They both exclaimed that they'd heard so much about me and just *had* to meet me. Since I was there anyway to pick Karin up, they explained, they weren't about to let an opportunity like that pass. Then they led the way up the stairs to their living quarters. The smell of something incredibly delicious began having fun with my nose – not caring that I wasn't at all hungry, but determined to make me hungry again.

Sven and Agda were of the older generation, a fact borne out in their old-fashioned but tasteful furnishings. They'd been in the glass and china business for decades, which the numerous fine glass and tasteful china pieces – vases, bowls, figurines – in their home also reflected. The table was set as if for royalty, with fine china and cut crystal glassware. The warmth of their hospitality was unmistakable.

After some warm and pleasant chit-chat, laughter and drinks in their living room, it was soon time for dinner. The smells had by now won the battle to restore my hunger. Karin's mom had prepared a divine dish: filet of sole in a dreamlike sauce of wine and butter, surrounded by *pommes duchesse*. I couldn't remember ever having tasted anything quite that good. Karin knew the dish from rare special family occasions before, and was well aware of the trouble and expense to which her mom had gone to make this meal truly memorable.

We sat down around a somewhat oval (or rounded-off-rectangular) table. Karin and I were seated along the two long sides, opposite each other, Agda was to my left at one end, and Sven was to my right at the other. The initial hesitation we all felt on meeting for the first time hadn't lasted more than a few minutes after my arrival, and we were now all speaking freely and cheerfully, on a wide variety of getting-to-know-you topics, full of rapport.

At some point in the middle of that delightful meal, as if he could restrain himself no longer, Sven abruptly put down his knife and fork. I thought he was going to propose a toast, so I put down mine. Instead he turned to face me, reached over and grasped my right hand in his left. He looked at me with intensity, as tears began welling up in his eyes. In a trembling voice he said, "*Stan, we don't know what it is you're doing with Karin, but whatever it is, please continue – we've never seen her so happy!!*"

What an introduction!! What a contrast to the fifth-wheel feeling I'd just come from! Nobody had ever said anything like that to me before. And there wasn't the slightest doubt about its sincerity. Karin was glowing. Agda was glowing. Hell, all four of us were glowing!

Bob arrived for his Christmas visit on Thursday, December 15th, and would stay till January 4th. I picked up the kids and brought them to Korngatan the same evening that Bob arrived. Unfortunately, I had to take them to a Christmas party at their nursery school the next afternoon; that couldn't be helped. What was extra exciting was that Karin would be coming down for the weekend and would meet Jenny *and* Sally *and* Bob, all for the first time.

Karin was wonderful with the kids; they took to her immediately, like a good friend. I'd explained to them that this was *the* Karin, Daddy's very kind friend, the one who'd made the tape they liked so much. They accepted her warmly, matter-of-factly, as if they'd always known her. They hugged her as if it were the most natural thing in the world. Bob looked *mighty* pleased to meet Karin. His initial awkwardness, which I'd pretty much expected, soon dissolved by Karin's genuine congeniality.

During that weekend, however, Bob, Jenny, Sally and Karin all had time get better acquainted and relaxed together. Karin and Bob quickly launched what would soon be a permanent friendship. After Karin had to leave on Sunday afternoon, Bob turned to me with a warm, twinkling, earnest smile.

"*At last*," he said, "*two givers meet!*"

END OF BOOK SIX

AFTERWORD

Do you see the story? Do you see anything? It seems to me I am trying to tell you a dream – making a vain attempt, because no relation of a dream can convey the dream-sensation, that commingling of absurdity, surprise, and bewilderment in a tremor of struggling revolt, that notion of being captured by the incredible which is the very essence of dreams....

No, it is impossible; it is impossible to convey the life-sensation of any given epoch of one's existence – that which makes its truth, its meaning – its subtle and penetrating essence. It is impossible. We live, as we dream – alone....

– from Joseph Conrad's *Heart of Darkness*

I'm guessing that nearly everybody has a story to tell. Some are far more tragic, traumatic, exciting, funny, edifying or interesting than what you've just read. I've written my story because I felt I had to try to figure out (and to explain to my progeny and anyone else interested) how it came about that I found my way from Dallas to Glimminge, through upheaval and tragedy and more upheaval, at last to peace, love and a better understanding of my life and its sometimes crazy circumstances and relationships.

I decided to end my narrative at the end of 1988 when I was just 43 and relative tranquility began to inundate my life. I'm 76 now, as I finish writing *Hindsights*. If I should happen to live another 10 years, I'll only have covered the first *half* of my life. So why did I choose to stop *here*?

The primary reason was to avoid stepping too hard on too many too-sensitive toes. A secondary reason was that it wasn't until this point that I at last felt I was on the right track. Naturally, a great deal has happened to me since 1988 as well – both awesome and awful – but I'm not prepared to abandon my criterion for writing as honestly as I possibly can, and there are probably too many toes in the way.

But I do have a few story lines to summarize, as well as a potpourri of thoughts and anecdotes to follow up and round off, and a tangle of some loose ends to unravel.

* * * * *

My mom lived to be 101 years (and five days short of one month) old. She died on April 23rd, 2014, after having been a widow for nearly 41 years. During the last several decades of her long life, we had a very loving relationship. Preceding that, it took a series of tough confrontations to level the playing field. A few lines were eventually drawn. The grounds for mutual respect – tolerably *level* grounds – were laid. Love transcended.

Until the last week or so of her life, she retained a fabulous memory and was an outstanding source of information with whom I could confirm numerous dates and events from my childhood and family history in the writing of *Hindsights*. But her most important gift to me was that she *forced me* to understand the need to exercise my freedom of expression. She didn't *teach* me that; she made it *necessary*.

As I grew up, I came to understand that Mom's non-religious side was amazingly kind, warm, and fun-loving. I'm sure that Dad must have been aware of the polarity of Mom's nature, although I doubt that he recognized the role religion played in it. It was no easy task to tackle her religious side without causing her to feel that I was attacking her!

Dad lived a mere 61 years, 8 months and 28 days. It was through writing about him that I came to know him far, far better than ever before. He totally lacked Mom's overbearing zeal. Now that I've reached my mid-70s, I often find myself wondering what might have happened if Dad could have mustered the courage to say to Mom, whenever she mounted her religious high horse: "*Now Fran, why don't you just back off!?!*" Then again, why did *I not* say that kind of thing (not the "Fran" part, of course!) until I was in my late 30s?! Maybe I inherited that passive trait from Dad?? *What if??*

I have at last understood that Mom was the Chief Engineer and Enforcer of nearly all the prohibitions in our household. Dad simply concurred without question. I suppose Dad followed the line of least resistance. Mom clearly wore the figurative pants.

Not until after Dad was gone, after Jeanette was gone, after I couldn't hold my tongue any more, did I begin to confront Mom with reasons why I didn't share her beliefs, for the sole purpose of compelling her to lead with her kind side. That approach enabled us to achieve a *modus vivendi* based on mutual kindness. I loved her deeply. Karin loved her. Jenny and Sally adored her.

Bear in mind that when I was a child, if I happened to utter something as "naughty" as *darn!*, Mom would either march me to the bathroom and jam a bar of soap into my mouth (to "clean out the filth") or beat me with a hickory yardstick – or both.

A great example of Mom's incredible "softening" comes from Jenny's and Sally's first-ever trip to the US in early 1990 (my first trip to the US since 1978). The kids had been far too excited to sleep a wink on the plane – until 20 minutes before we landed. Al met us at the Seattle airport and drove us straight to Mom's apartment in Kirkland, where Mom, Nancy, Andrew, Judy and Amy were waiting for us. So were three different pizzas, all family size, that Mom had ordered for our lunch (it was still breakfast-time for us jet-lagged travelers). Jenny and Sally seemed a bit bewildered now and then, suddenly finding themselves for the first time in an environment where nobody spoke Swedish. But they adapted quickly. I was a bit bewildered to find myself in the US for the first time in 12 years, and even more to find myself in Mom's new environment (her apartment in Kirkland), still furnished with framed Bible verses on every wall.

Mom was seated at one end of the table, with me on her left. Nancy was on my left and Al on her left. Jenny and Sally were at the other end, opposite Mom. Al's kids Andrew, Judy and Amy were on the long side opposite me. Mom asked Al to "give thanks", and everyone but my kids and I closed their eyes and bowed their heads (although Andrew and Judy peeked a lot!) while Al intoned gratitude to his god for having delivered us safely. (I might have added a few words about the role of the pilot, the airline and possibly Al himself [as a Boeing executive and our airport limo chauffeur], but I held my peace.) During this prayer (which was Jenny's and Sally's first experience of anything like it, except vicariously in *Sound of Music*), my kids looked at me in quizzical confusion; I smiled at them, held a finger to my lips, and indicated that they needn't do anything but wait.

Then we all tucked into the pizzas. Jenny soon found a clear preference for one kind. It was a bit beyond her reach, so she politely asked for someone to pass it to her. Nobody responded. She repeated her request. Still no response. Then she hauled out a line from *My Fair Lady*, and loudly commanded, "*Move your bloomin' arse!!*" There was an immediate stunned silence. Mom shot a glare at me, as if to tell me "*there's a bar of soap in the bathroom!*" I, however, had already burst out laughing; Jenny was so goddamn cute! Al, Nancy and Amy all looked downwards with the utmost piety and disapproving solemnity; Andrew and Judy had to struggle to muffle their own laughter. And then it all just faded, and everyone resumed eating. It was that simple, that undramatic.

Jenny, Sally and I stayed with Mom and went shopping with her at malls for several days, before moving over to Al's, then flying down to John's in Santa Rosa. At Mom's place, there was little for the kids to do except work on Mom's many jigsaw puzzles. When a piece wouldn't fit, Jenny and Sally sometimes burst out "*Shit!*" or "*For Chrissake!*" or "*Damn it!*" And what did my dear Mom do, when she saw that I was just sitting there at the piano, smiling? I'm almost certain that she simply decided she hadn't heard it! She just moved on! *Bless her heart*!

In chapter five of this book I mentioned confronting Mom on her abuse of the Swedish language concerning the Swedish word *runka* (masturbate). It was pretty funny the first time, in 1984, when Mom was 71 (five years younger than I am now). Jenny was of course too young to understand anything verbal. But it happened again (Mom had obviously forgotten my admonition and her own horror over the need for it) by our next visit, in 1993, in connection with Mom's 80th birthday celebration at Al's place in Bellevue. Jenny was now nine and Sally was seven. Once again, Mom felt compelled to show off her "Swedish" to the assembled family. She started by counting in Swedish, which she did remarkably well – but only Jenny, Sally and I could know that! Then she added a discombobulated Swedish tongue-twister. I suddenly recalled her "*runka*" nursery-rhyme masterpiece, but before I could throw the switch on her train of thought, she uninhibitedly blurted it out. Jenny and Sally both understood, not just what she *meant* but also what she *said*. It was fortunate that neither of my daughters had just taken a big gulp of soda pop; it would have come out their noses! But it didn't *matter*!! They loved their grandmother all the more for it. Did she love them all the more for all the times they said *damn* and *shit*? My guess: certainly not *because* of it, but probably *no less* in spite of it!

Throughout *Hindsights*, I've related numerous confrontations between Mom and me. One of the last, which I am about to relate, was actually *not* a confrontation – thanks to all the previous ones – but rather a rational conversation, one that I feel could only have happened thanks to all the previous confrontations. It took place during one of Mom's last visits to Sweden, in the late 1990s when she was in her mid-to-late 80s, and the two of us were on our own one day. Karin was at work; the kids were in school. To my *great* surprise, Mom asked me for the first time *ever* (and quite unrelated to whatever we'd been talking about earlier that day) to explain to her why I didn't believe in her Lord. I'd never told her (I'm actually not that confrontational!). And I never thought she'd ask. But she did.

As I outlined my reasons, she listened calmly. She didn't interrupt me. Although she shook her head very slightly a couple of times, she nodded far more times than she shook her head. She didn't become hysterical or histrionic, nor did she even display any agitation (for once, neither did I). When I finished, she said she thought she understood what I did and didn't believe – and why. Then we hugged. We never (*What?! Never?! Well, hardly ever!*) *needed* further challenges or confrontations after that. Yes, she'd mellowed with age. Yes, that *might* have happened without our confrontations, but there's no way of knowing. What I do know is that in the last decades of her life, my relationship with her was seldom anything but loving and caring. I have no regrets about taking the confrontational path we needed to achieve resolution, and I doubt that she did either.

When demagogues, dictators and snake-oil peddlers remain unopposed, they are empowered. They thrive on the silence of critics. Some feel it's respectful to remain passive and silent, thus allowing the tyranny of misinformation to reign. But bear in mind that freedom of expression is only yours when you exercise it. In my view, respect for a belief (idea, ideology) should only be given where respect is earned, not by claiming Truth where none can be proven, and by not simply demanding submission. It's crucial to distinguish clearly between respect for a fellow human being and respect for whatever beliefs he or she may hold, whether sound, helpful, loony or evil. It's possible and desirable to respect all *people*, but it's not necessary to respect loony or evil beliefs or actions.

For the atheist or skeptic, belief is little more than a working hypothesis, one which should be challenged repeatedly and doubted constantly. Religious belief is a brand of certainty that *admits no challenge*; it is the axiom on which all further reasoning or decisions is based. Non-religious belief is *not about certainty*, but merely an ongoing search for what is most likely to be supported by evidence. Because of that, it *requires constant challenges* to find all available evidence.

People aren't born with ideologies; religious faith isn't in anyone's genes. Sometimes it's learned, but all too often it's imposed, force-fed and coerced through peer pressure and/or brainwashing and indoctrination. This is done most effectively to children, when they're pressured into becoming emotionally dependent on a set of beliefs at an early age. Dogma generally works best when imposed on children before they know what hits them.

Some societies are overwhelmingly Christian, others are overwhelmingly Muslim (or Buddhist, or Hindu etc). No infant has ever chosen which society or religion to be born into, but few ever deviate significantly from the creed they are first taught (or force-fed). Oft-repeated bullshit – presented as fact and coming from people you implicitly trust – might *sound* like fact if you never doubt it. Creeds shape public opinion. They warp it and codify – and often make it compulsory. That's why, throughout history, people who at birth have no genetic predisposition to any faith have ended up fighting most of the world's wars to "defend" a particular faith (in a particular religion or any other "unquestionable" ideology like Nazism or Stalinism and quite a few other *–isms* that share with religions a dogmatic approach). Also bear in mind that *you don't have to know what's right to see what's wrong.*

* * * * *

Jeanette shared 12½ years of her life with me, all but two of those as my wife. The impact she made on my life – her personal legacy to me – is immeasurable. We were young when we met (she was 20, I was 19). Our lives and minds were still innocent and naïve, but also earnestly searching and highly inquisitive. I fell in love with her (or realized that I had fallen in love with her) within about six weeks of our first meeting; it took her somewhat longer. We were still just beginning our transition to adulthood, facing formidable challenges. But we soon found ourselves looking for and testing new paths together. She was my first true love. She was also my muse, the tender and caretaker of my brief artistic flame. I could no longer conceive of life without her. I overcame her initial hesitation to reciprocate my love for her – with a persistence that perhaps only succeeded because she was also who she was. We came to love each other deeply, with a love I will never forget.

Faced with my being sent to Vietnam, we didn't hesitate to move to Canada. We pulled ourselves up by our roots from our native soil as if we'd been ripe carrots. We stayed in Canada for just a year, but that year was a watershed in many ways. It was in Vancouver that we pretty much abandoned religion entirely and pretty much decided against having children. It was there I grew weary of academia and began to paint again. And it was there that we decided to take the next great step – the move to Sweden. The step to leave North America was in many ways even easier emotionally than the first step, despite challenges that were much greater in number and magnitude.

After a tumultuous first year of getting settled in Malmö, for years life remained simple and sweet. I thought our mutual love would be enough and would last forever; she seemed to think so too, and said as much. She became my muse without asking or being asked. She created the role for herself without knowing it. She ignited my creativity without my realizing it. I thought our lives were growing sweeter and simpler by the year; I failed and feared to see or understand the roiling complexity growing inside her troubled mind. She'd learned to swim in a pond, then plunged into a stormy ocean, not geographical but within.

Where did her mental imbalance come from? Was it from the uprootedness of our lives? She *never* complained of that; she had in fact been the driver of our move to Europe. Was it from something in her childhood? If so, she never gave any clue as to what it might be. Was it congenital? I have no way of ever knowing.

Perhaps she could have been a poet. The fragments and few short poems she left behind showed signs of considerable talent. Would there have been a way to encourage her to develop it? Did it reflect her inner demons, or was it driven by them? Again, I have no way of ever knowing.

I look back at our life together with a kind of melancholy, howling joy, a complex chaos of contradictory feelings. A core part of me will *always* miss her. We had some incredibly formative years of exceptional intensity, wonder and love, discovery and meaningfulness, yet encapsulated in naiveté beyond our recognition. Her death crippled me, tore me limb from limb and sent me on a nihilistic path to rock bottom.

The catharsis I experienced through writing about it (in *The Unparallel Lines*) made me understand the necessity of working actively, ceaselessly to avoid taking any good thing for granted. Jeanette's death thus forced me to understand the value of life, of *living* – a lesson I only learned after all I valued had vanished. I also realized that although there are things one can never get *over*, my love for her eventually made it possible to move *beyond* the pain without forgetting the joy.

In leaving life she took my former one with her. She also left me with an enigmatic and powerful injunction: "*teach art to the world to help us all.*" But how was I supposed to do that?! Without her, I found it all but impossible to continue painting, for reasons I've described in *A Sea of Troubles* (Book 5 of *Hindsights*). Eventually I realized that writing – also an art form (at least in some cases) – had not only brought me out of one very deep depression, it had prevented me from being enmired in a second. I hope that at least some readers of *Hindsights* will find in what I've written some help in dealing with their own hobgoblins and sorrows.

* * * * *

It seems to me that it has taken many years for Lena to forgive me for her having left me [*sic*]. Apart from a few brief periods of relative harmony, love between us always flowed in one direction, a one-way street. For that I cannot fault or blame her. Perhaps she never saw in me sufficient reason to take the steps beyond fascination and infatuation all the way to love. Whether or not that was the case, our relationship turned out to be impossible.

I've learned that there are people in this world who seriously believe that it is no big deal to scream "*I hate you!!*" at another person, and then, when *the screamer's* rage has subsided, find no need to apologize or make amends, but just move on, because *they* are not injured by their own screaming.

I'm also aware that many people are fond of saying "*It takes two to make a quarrel.*" In my view, this stupid adage is frequently (if not usually) misunderstood to mean that both parties in a quarrel bear equal responsibility for its fierceness. This seems to me as inaccurate as it is unfair, at least in my own experience.

After more than 33 years together, Karin and I have never screamed at each other. This is not to say we've never disagreed, but our disagreements have always been civilized. One might be justified in drawing the conclusion that I am not the quarrelsome type. But I've never been above or beyond being provoked.

As far as I could tell, Lena was a wonderful mother to Jenny and Sally throughout their childhoods. That counts for a lot. Bob said that he'd never observed a person so lacking in self-insight as Lena. I hope for the day when I can safely say that her days of screaming at me are all in the distant past, which is to say that I hope that Lena will someday forgive herself and find peace.

* * * * *

For months after Karin and I met on May 17th, 1988, we had no clue that she would transform my life and I hers. Our instant and all-consuming passion for each other seemed far too good to be true. But it certainly was good. And it certainly turned out to be true. For me, the change – from a deeply depressing, direly dysfunctional marriage (that had been grinding down my self-esteem to a suicidal level), to a relationship of mutual, exuberant, deep and lasting love – was and remains blissfully wonderful.

Now, after *more than a third of a century* together as I write this, we not only still love each other; we're still in love. We're able to disagree. And when we do, we work things out amicably. Compromise seems to come naturally to both of us, probably because the love is there.

However, adjusting and adapting to a new family constellation was not without what I suspect to be a "normal" share of problems, friction, blips and glitches. In view of the fact that Karin and I had two kids each and no kids in common (and our respective kids had another parent, of course), we decided that our cohabitation would be on the basis of separate economies: Karin would pay for everything her kids needed and I would pay for mine. Her kids would be her heirs, mine would be mine. And we would share our living expenses. As a result, we've never argued about money – either.

I undertook another major revamp of the house on Korngatan during 1989-91, just in time for Karin (and Moa) to move in. It meant transforming the parallel little and big houses into a single U-shaped house, accomplished on schedule.[10] Karin didn't have to look for a new job in or near Malmö after all; in early June of 1991, Perstorp Pharma (her employer) moved from Perstorp to Lund, giving Karin a free move, a short commute, and allowing Moa to start her high school studies at Latinskolan, the school where she'd said she wanted to go anyway.

During a New Years' Eve party we hosted at Korngatan, marking the new Millennium, Karin proposed to me, despite our having previously declared that we had no intention of remarrying. It was an impulse, and a very joyous one, the height of the party! The next day, New Year's Day, we told our four kids about it. Let's just say that 75% of them were not amused. So we called it off. (What was the point if it couldn't be grounds for celebration?) Instead, Karin and I got officially engaged on May 17th that year. We didn't ask.

Then in 2002, when Karin and I were 14 years into our relationship, our

---

10 See Appendix – house on Korngatan

kids got together and proposed to *us*! They planned the where and when of our wedding (in the yard at the old house in Glimminge) and told us about it about five months in advance. Our kids helped with the logistics and arrangements. Peder, by now a highly qualified cook, created a magnificent buffet. A number of our guests told us it was the most loving, genuine and romantic wedding they'd ever been to. I'd never argue with that.

Our love is still new and growing stronger than ever. The fact that we are still *in love* today seems to be a rare thing, but I wish it weren't. If everybody could experience the kind of mutual love Karin and I have – the caring, the passion, the fun – I'm guessing the world would be the better for it.

* * * * *

From the time I started my full-time university studies in the Bay Area in 1965, I never had single a year of full-time income until the early 1990s, when Karin helped me start my own company. I was certainly not lazy; I simply had unusual priorities. I worked part-time while I studied full-time, so I could afford a good education. Then I worked part-time while I painted full-time, so I could have complete artistic freedom and not be dependent on selling my art for my livelihood. Then I worked part-time while we rebuilt the house full-time, so we could afford the house of our dreams. Then I was out of the loop entirely for a year, consumed by grief. Then I worked part-time while caring for the kids full-time, so I could be as close as possible to the ones I loved the most. The problem with that approach was that in 1988, almost immediately after my divorce, the newly single Stan made two discoveries: that with two children to support, I could barely pay the bills on my own; and that my many years of having no more than a part-time salary were destined to leave me without a pension I could live on.

Perstorp then agreed to let me increase my working hours from 50% to 75%, but they were paying me only around a quarter of the going rate for the type of work I'd been doing in recent years, and they explicitly had no interest in bringing my salary up to speed.

Karin told me unequivocally and kept reminding me that she would gladly handle my bookkeeping and paperwork if I were to start my own company.

(Administrative work had always been my nemesis, my chief objection to running my own company.) And still I procrastinated. For years, my self-confidence had been pulverized on the domestic front. By the time I met Karin in 1988 and she moved to Korngatan in 1991, however, I finally realized I had to act – and thanks to her I dared to act. She not only gave me practical assistance and lots of love; she *believed* in me. Without her loving support, I strongly doubt I'd ever have dared to take make that leap into self-employment.

Initially, when I got going in 1991, my company served as a complement to my part-time employment at Perstorp, but within a few years those roles were reversed, and I returned to my former 20-hours-per-week role in Perstorp. Just a year or two after launching my company, my financial advisor thought I should incorporate it. It thus became S. Erisman AB. As much as I disliked *following* orders (at least when I was not allowed to question them!), I disliked *giving* anyone orders; I had no employees. And I had enough work in my own company to make the sum total more than full-time!

It was my great fortune that nearly all the work I did through my company was *creative* work. Not only that, the pay was so much better. And it was *fun*. Since I was already *almost* getting by financially before starting up, I only took out a minimal salary from my company, just a little more than what I needed to live on. The rest I began plowing into pension funds to start compensating for over two decades of shortfall. What on earth would I do with luxury goods I didn't want, status symbols I didn't care about, and the very latest whatever?! Much better to keep it simple!

Throughout the early 1990s, the Perstorp side of my work was more and more focused on just one company within the corporation: Formox, a small but world-leading unit of around 50 specialists in formaldehyde technology, with a global client base.[11] In 1995, Max, the Formox plant sales manager, asked me to create a customer newsletter as a sales support tool. The first issue of *informally speaking* (the name reflects my love of wordplay: *informal inform*ation about the *formal*dehyde industry) was published in the autumn of 1995. I wrote or edited all the texts, did the layout, took most of the photos, and even drew an occasional cartoon to lighten it up. We published two issues a year, the last being in the

---

11 In 2013, Perstorp sold Formox to Johnson-Matthey; Formox was quickly subsumed by London-based JM.

autumn of 2010. My work took me all over the world (mostly for Formox). I travelled on business to Denmark, Norway, Germany, Netherlands, Belgium, England, Wales, France, Switzerland, Italy, Spain, Portugal, Russia, Turkey, the USA, Canada, Venezuela, Brazil, Argentina, Chile, Ecuador, Singapore, Malaysia, Thailand, Indonesia and China.

In 1998, when Formox wanted the total share of my part-time work (20 hours per week), this created a bit of a problem for other Perstorp businesses that needed my help. Then Eibert, the Corporate HR Director, came up with a solution: my company (S. Erisman AB) would invoice the other Perstorp Group companies (excluding Formox), while I would continue as a part-time employee at Formox. All concerned parties were happy with that arrangement.

In my own company, I worked as a freelancer, mostly through advertising agencies. Their clients were constantly pushing me into new and challenging fields: Ericsson (telecom), Tetra Pak (food processing and packaging), Getinge AB (disinfection and sterilization systems for hospitals), Swep (heat exchangers), Trelleborg (rubber and tires), Axis (high-tech surveillance cameras), Heidelberg Cement (concrete), and numerous others. I was writing graphic identity manuals, brochures, trade press advertisements, technical data sheets, customer presentations, brand-building campaigns, promotional film manuscripts, websites and press releases.

The diversity of my clients was extraordinarily stimulating, educational, challenging and exciting. My first copywriting assignments for a client in a new field often meant that I had to start writing convincingly (to their customers) about technologies even before I'd had a chance to learn anything about them myself, while struggling to grasp all I could as quickly as possible. Many of the subjects and terminology I'd studied with only minor engagement in high school and undergraduate university suddenly became both useful and essential in my work.

This confirmed my growing conviction that _all learning is important_, even if for no other apparent purpose at all (at the time) than training the mind. People who pump iron at gyms seldom do so solely to be able to pump more iron at more gyms. Muscles – and brains – turn out to have usefulness in the real world too.

In 2004, Eibert, Perstorp's Corporate HR Director, was replaced by Martin. He informed me that I would no longer be allowed to remain a Formox employee

<u>and</u> have other Perstorp Group companies as clients – the very solution devised by his predecessor to the satisfaction of all parties! I, being me, asked *Why not?!* He told me that the Swedish tax authorities *prohibited* such arrangements, and that was all there was to it. When I continued to argue (his decision made no rational sense at all to me), he suggested that if I didn't believe him, I could contact the tax authorities myself and find out.

Guess what I did? I contacted the Swedish tax authorities and posed the question. *"No, it's not forbidden!"* they told me. *"It's a bit unusual, but as long as the employer agrees, it's all right with us."* I phoned Martin. He was clearly shocked that I'd done as he'd suggested. Then he asked me nervously and angrily, "You didn't say that this was about Perstorp, did you?!" I said I did. He harrumphed, then announced that the legal advisors at The Swedish Employers Federation (SAF) prohibited such arrangements anyway, and that Perstorp was obliged to abide by them. Guess what I did? After getting a similar reply from one of SAF's legal experts, I told Martin that SAF did *not prohibit* such arrangements, even though they might not *recommend* them. It was up to the employer, they said. Martin, seeing he didn't have a leg to stand on, at least if he wanted someone else to be responsible for his decision, became livid and blurted out, *"It doesn't matter!! I'm the boss here, and it's what <u>I</u> say that matters!!"*

After he'd calmed down a bit, he told me that when he'd been studying at the University of Lund, he'd been working during the summers with the immigration police, screening foreign arrivals. Then he added, with seething casualness, that if he'd been the one working in the Malmö harbor on the day I arrived, he'd have deported me directly!

I let the matter drop. Thereafter, whenever another Perstorp Group company wanted my help with a text, I had to tell them "Sorry, I'm not allowed to. Martin forbids it!" They moaned at the stupidity of having to turn to another source, because, several of them said, "It takes twice as long, costs twice as much, and is half as good. We'll *lose* money!"

A couple of months later, Martin got in touch with me by email. He offered me 40 thousand Swedish kronor as a "consolation". I assumed he was having problems with his conscience, and that was the price he was prepared to pay for a clear one. Initially, I knew I'd lost a fair amount of business by having to drop the other Perstorp companies from my client list – considerably more money than he was offering as a "consolation prize". I refused the offer. Within a few months, work for my other external clients more than made up the shortfall.

About a year or so before I reached the customary retirement age of 65, I consulted my financial advisor about what my pension would be like if I retired at that time. He told me that by plowing much of my company's revenues into pension funds instead of taking a bigger salary, I'd *almost* made up for the shortfall I'd had from working part-time all those years. Since I was enjoying my work so much, I decided I would continue to the age of 67 at least. I also intended to continue at Formox, as before, until I was 67.

But in January of 2010 (the year I was going to turn 65, in September), the Perstorp Corporation issued a proclamation to all employees: any and all accumulated extra working hours (comp time) above 150 hours at the end of 2010 would be summarily *nullified*! (*Isn't that <u>stealing</u>?!*) My agreement with Perstorp when I was employed in 1978 was that there would be no such limitation on my comp time. I'd never agreed to change it. At the time of the proclamation, I had something like 500 hours of comp time and was certain to accumulate even more before the spring issue of *informally speaking* was ready. They were already paying me far less than the going rate for my kind of work, and now they wanted me to have worked well over 350 hours for free?? With Martin still in Corporate management, I knew this was a fight I couldn't win – at least not in that way.

Soon after the Corporate proclamation, Marie, my latest boss at Formox, told me she needed to know whether I intended to work beyond the age of 65. I said *yes, until 67*. Although I hadn't yet figured out *how*, I said nothing more. Suddenly I saw a path to preventing the Corporation from once again "maneuvering" a great deal of money out of my hands.

I had two primary responsibilities at Formox: one was to design, coordinate and write the twice-annual publication of the customer newsletter, *informally speaking*. This meant two periods of very intense work: March-May and September-November. My other responsibility was to assist in arrangements for the annual customer conference hosted by Formox, including review and revision of all presentations to be made by Formox people, as well as the correct signage and numerous other brand-building tasks.

My plan, my counter-measure to the Corporate ploy, was to continue to work my ass off as usual during the spring to be able to deliver the spring-summer issue to the printer's by the end of May. I knew that this would add another big chunk to my already burgeoning "pot" of comp time! (I always called it my "pot".) But this time, instead of my usual procedure to complement my five weeks of vacation time that summer with extra weeks from my comp time, I would take *no* vacation time at all that summer, but *only* comp time, and would do only minimal work from late May all the way until my birthday in mid-September. I would also lie low on the preparatory work I usually began in August. By so doing, I calculated that I'd be able to use up all but the maximum 150 hours remaining in my pot.

What then? I contacted the union to confirm a rumor I'd heard. Normally, a white-collar employee had to give three months' notice of resignation, but in the year one turned 65 (2010 in my case) just *one* month's notice was required. I therefore submitted my letter of resignation a few days after my 65th birthday. Marie phoned me immediately. She was furious. "*You said you'd be working until you were 67 at least!!*" "Yes," I replied, "that remains my intention – but I won't be working as an employee. From now on I'll be working as a consultant, at the going market rate."

On such short notice, there was no chance of finding anyone else to fill my shoes as the editor of *informally speaking*. Given the value of the newsletter as a marketing tool, she was grudgingly obliged to accept my terms. I put together the autumn issue with the same diligence and professionalism as always, while she smoldered. (I had, in fact, no feud with *her* – it was the *Corporate* proclamation that made my plan necessary, but I could hardly have forewarned her about it!)

By mid-autumn 2010, preparations for the next formaldehyde conference, in San Francisco in March 2011, were in full swing. I would be writing the invitations and cover letters, preparing all the signs and name tags, arranging promotional giveaways and, most importantly, helping colleagues who were going to be holding presentations. I was willing to continue with my work unabated – as a consultant – but I knew they were planning to replace me. Of course I expected that.

Then in January 2011, Marie told me that the only ones from Formox who would be allowed to make the trip to San Francisco were those holding presentations. I replied that if I were not allowed to attend in person, I would immediately discontinue all my work on matters relating to the conference, including the presentations. Or would she prefer that I came along? I went to San Francisco. To her chagrin, I suppose, one of our biggest customers in attendance greeted me as "Mr Formox!" on the first day there. My association with Perstorp (and Marie) ended somewhat acrimoniously immediately after the conference in San Francisco in the early March of 2011. I didn't do the spring issue.

When Leif needed a new graphic identity manual for Frigoscandia, he turned to a different agency, Borstahusen, with whom for some reason it was OK with Leif for me to collaborate. My working with them led to a number of long-term working relationships jobs with all sorts of new companies, Tetra Pak being foremost among them. Tetra Pak remained my client to the end of my career. I would retire completely at the end of 2015, three months after I turned 70, in order to devote myself full-time to *Hindsights*.

* * * * *

I can never say enough about Bob, my mentor and best friend, and about his huge and vital influence on me, from our first meeting in September 1970 and until his death on April 1st, 1999. As my mutually loving relationship with Karin grew and thrived, and much of the turmoil disappeared from my life, Bob seemed to gain an inner peace and calm. He warmed to the affection Karin showed to me – and to him. If there were limits to his admiration for Karin, I never saw them. And since Karin and I nearly always spoke English when we were alone with each other, she was well accustomed to it, so there was no linguistic barrier to her joining our discussions.

For much of his life, Bob truly enjoyed *solitude*. Perhaps by doing so, he seldom experienced loneliness. For some reason, my gregariousness didn't put him off, but only amused him. (In this respect, more of him probably rubbed off on me than vice-versa!) He arrived at his opinions and positions slowly, methodically, yet he hardly ever held any he was unwilling to change if there were sound reasons for doing so. He had boundless compassion and tolerance – but none for cruelty, exploitation, belligerence and willful ignorance. He knew the difference between respecting a person and respecting a belief. He taught me that, as well as much of what I know about biology, music and history. He fed me all I could handle (and more) of cosmology and quantum physics, although I can't claim to understand much.

Had he and I remained in the US, we might have encountered a few others who, like us, had escaped not only from the indoctrination of a Meeting-style background, but also from superstition as a whole, as well as from a blinkered amerocentric outlook. Finding anyone else in Europe with a similar background was highly unlikely.

Most contemporary Europeans (including Swedes!) simply cannot grasp the implications of a Plymouth Brethren upbringing. Bob and I helped each other clean out the cobwebs – the last vestiges of that pernicious dogma – and dogma itself. Together we continued our endless exploration of philosophy and science: questions that may not have answers but are stimulating to ask.

For most of the time I knew him, Bob's physical health was in a state of slow but obvious deterioration. After he received his Parkinson's diagnosis, he of course read as much as he could get his hands on about the latest medical findings, but he realized that there was little that offered any realistic hope. He was acutely aware of the prognosis, the degenerative one-way downhill street he was on through no choice of his own. Yet he never succumbed to self-pity. He rejoiced in all that he *could* do, but showed little interest in mourning what he *couldn't*. I learned to accept that on his own he would never win the battle to keep his living quarters from descending into chaos between my visits. So I began visiting him more frequently. And to counteract his dark medical outlook, we increased the frequency of our visits to three or four a year (each visit lasting 1-3 weeks). He claimed that my visits to him helped him deal with his external chaos. He was already doing so well on the internal bit.

Bob's health declined noticeably and inexorably throughout the 1990s, but he continued to revel in music and reading; the activity level of his mind was enough to put most people with 10 times his health and half his age to shame. By 1996, immobility had become a real burden to him. For years, he'd frequently told me of a secret inner longing to revisit Detroit (his hometown) and Ann Arbor (where he attended the University of Michigan). But he felt that such a trip would be too arduous to undertake. I frequently offered to accompany him, to be the squire to his knight, as it were. But he always declined; it was hard for me to tell whether it was for his own sake or for mine.

When I found I'd be attending a conference for Formox in New Orleans in late October 1997, I contacted Bob's nephew Dan, who'd recently taken a position at Michigan State University in East Lansing. I said I might try to get Bob to join me on a flight to Detroit, and could he (Dan) help with the arrangements to satisfy Bob's longed-for sentimental journey? Dan assured me he could.

I'd arranged to fly to New Orleans via Amsterdam, meet Bob at Schiphol (the Amsterdam airport) before flying on to Detroit together. All he would have to do was book a round-trip flight from Basel to Amsterdam, and I – and Dan – would arrange the rest. Bob was stunned and delighted. He accepted immediately.

Bob and I rendezvoused as planned at Schiphol and flew out together. Dan met us at the Detroit airport and drove us to his home in East Lansing. The next afternoon, Dan drove us to Ann Arbor, where Bob was delighted to recognize several of the old haunts around his Alma Mater, the University of Michigan, even though many had disappeared.

The following day, Dan's father – Bob's semi-estranged brother Charles – arrived at Dan's home, a total surprise for Bob. Bob had a hard time concealing his shock. The first thing Charles said to his elder brother – his first spoken, face-to-face words in the 30-40 years since they'd last met – was: "*Well, Bud, I've got a bone to pick with you!*" He said it jocularly, but with teeth. Bob just looked back at him, like a poker player holding a royal straight flush, waiting, waiting for Charles to clarify the bone in question. So Charles continued: "*I heard you were in my neighborhood a few years back* [when Bob had gone to visit Kathy near Endicott, NY, in September 1979] *and you didn't even come to see me! What've you got to say for yourself?*" Without batting an eye, Bob replied, as assertively as I'd ever heard him speak: "I was pissed off with you because of the way you were treating your sons!" Charles did a double-take, laughed nervously, said something like "*Well, there's me told!*" while trying to chuckle it off. Then we all settled down, but Bob remained guarded.

Bob stayed with Dan and Charles in East Lansing while I went to on New Orleans two days later. On my way home, I picked Bob up for our flight back to Amsterdam. In my absence, Charles had taken Bob on a car tour of Detroit, to all the old familiar places Bob remembered (some with nostalgia, some with bitterness). The two brothers spent the whole day together. Bob was grateful to Charles for the tour, and gratified to have fulfilled his ambivalent desires to "see the old places once again".

But he was mentally exhausted. The trip had more than lived up to his expectations. But I got the impression that something within him had given up, died. Was that the result of fulfilling a decades-long dream and no longer having one there to entice him, to help keep him going?

Once safely back in Binningen, Bob was *weary* in a way I'd never seen. He wasn't depressed. He absolutely refused to succumb to the siren-song of self-pity, despite arguable and obvious grounds for embracing it. But music brought him a little less joy. His passionate interest in science and global politics abated noticeably. He simply seemed to feel "*Now it's enough*" (cf. the "*It is enough*" aria from Mendelssohn's *Elijah* – another of Bob's favorites). The stronger medication he was taking no longer gave full relief, but could only counteract some of the symptoms of the inexorable degradation of Parkinson's; it was never going to be able to stave off the destructive underlying progression of his disease. I sometimes felt that he was hanging on for my sake, because he understood I couldn't bear to let him go. He'd found contentment with his life, and with life itself; the anguish part about his life coming to an end was nearly all mine.

During 1998, the amount of medication he needed to maintain anything resembling mobility began to cause major – and scary – side-effects. Although he was occasionally elated by a boost in his walking ability, that summer he began experiencing hallucinations of increasing severity, with signs of psychosis. They usually took the form of menacing people in his apartment who were there to hurt him. His doctor prescribed clozapine, a powerful anti-psychotic, anti-schizophrenic drug – one with common side-effects that Bob claimed to know too much about to feel comfortable about taking. (I didn't really understand Bob's objections at the time. Hindsights often arrive late.)

There were moments when the delicate balance worked: when taken precisely as prescribed, the anti-Parkinson drugs gave him a fair degree of mobility and clozapine let him remain relatively free of disturbing hallucinations. Achieving this balance, however, required *strict* adherence to the right dose of the right medicine at the right time. But Bob was administering his medication himself. Unfortunately, his ability and will to adhere to prescriptions had a lot in common with his ability to keep his apartment in order.

Managing his medication became the dominant topic of our conversations. He was seldom up to writing, so our letter-writing pretty much ceased, and with it most of our stimulating discussions. I tried to make up for it by phoning him more often. By the late summer of 1998 I was phoning him almost daily. It took me a maximum of 20 seconds to ascertain whether he was sticking to his regime. Sometimes he couldn't talk to me at all because he had to "see to his guests". I asked him who they were. As soon as he told me it was Sigrid (his ex-wife) or Theiss (his ex-boss and Sigrid's ex-husband), his two most frequent and most menacing guests, I knew he'd skipped the clozapine. When I asked to speak to his guests, my request occasionally had the effect of bringing him closer to the real world for a moment or two.

He turned 70 on August 30th. He viewed it as a milestone he'd never expected to reach, and in his moments of clarity, it pleased him greatly to have reached it. There was still never a trace of self-pity regarding his limitations.

During the autumn of 1998 his condition shifted gears and began deteriorating more rapidly. The imaginary visitors were now increasingly frequent and their threats more terrifying. Sometimes his apartment was "full of people" about to attack him. He had to watch what he said. They *knew* everything. I assumed he'd *forgotten* to take the damn clozapine. But I was wrong; he was *refusing* to take it. He'd been reading (probably not while in a balanced state) about the possible side-effects, and they frightened him much more than the very real and severe adverse effects of *not* taking it. In his searches of the latest medical research, he'd come across a paper on clozapine-induced agranulocytosis, a very rare but life-threatening reduction in white blood cells. Even though the risk was low, it apparently spooked him much more than hallucinations.

During one phone call in mid-November, his "guests" were giving him a harder time than usual and Bob seemed terrified. He set the phone aside. I could hear his agitated and incoherent mumbling and distressed grunting in the background. I didn't know how to reach him, how to get him to pick up the receiver again. I screamed into it, but got no response. Then I heard crashing noises in the background. Had he smashed something or smashed into something? Had he fallen? Injured himself? I got no response. There was complete silence on Bob's end. I quickly hung up and phoned Meier, who dropped everything he was doing and hurried to Bob's apartment, 5-10 minutes away. Bob ended up in the hospital for more than a week. Only strict monitoring of his medication restored enough stability to enable his release on November 23rd.

He managed for about a week before he again stopped taking his clozapine, and the severe hallucinations returned. I decided to spend some time with him in Binningen in mid-December, and bring him back to Malmö to spend Christmas and New Year's with us, as he'd done so often in the past, hoping it could restore some stability. I also went to our local pharmacy and bought him a dosette box (for sorting a week's medications according to the day of the week and the time of day). I hope it would help assure that he'd take the right medicines at the right times. But it would only work if he used it.

When I arrived at his door on December 12th, he whispered a furtive warning, looking anxiously over his shoulder, that his apartment was "full of people from Roche", but he said that my presence kept them from attacking him. He saw mold growing everywhere and vermin crawling all over everything as he frantically attempted to brush them away. He couldn't or wouldn't eat because every potential bite appeared to him to be crawling with maggots. Inwardly, I was devastated by my inability to penetrate the nefarious barriers his disease had erected. Outwardly, I tried to persuade him to enquire about increasing his dose of clozapine. At the same time, I thought that increasing the *prescribed* dose wouldn't help one bit if he was refusing to take any at all. I showed him the dosette box and tried to show him how it worked, but he made a gesture of dismissal, waving it or me away with the back of his hand.

Two evenings after my arrival, his hallucinations were particularly wild. I couldn't reach him in any way. I was, needless to say, greatly alarmed. He hurried madly half naked from room to room, his eyes darting suspiciously into the unknown, to see what his "enemies" were plotting. He looked right through me; I wasn't there, but his enemies were. I felt that I had no choice but to intervene, at once. After he'd finally fallen asleep for a while, I carefully loaded up the dosette box, with the help of information about his dosages on the medicine bottles, packages and jars. The next morning, I began giving him his pills as prescribed. Then he told me he could take over and would henceforth use the dosette box. Within a day or two, the hallucinations subsided to a relatively manageable level. On the 17th – the day before our trip to Sweden – he visited his neurologist. I had good reason to be afraid that Bob wasn't providing the full picture. I offered to help Bob explain – I *urged* him to let me – but Bob refused to let me accompany him and speak with the doctor about what was going on. [*I should have insisted, should have pushed harder!*]

The trip to Malmö and the first four days there went relatively well, although he was constantly flicking away the tiny worms he saw everywhere – on his clothing and in his food. Seeing worms in his food of course destroyed his appetite. I suspected that he'd emptied his dosette box by now. He had, but hadn't refilled it. In his hallucinated condition, his assurances that he'd filled it and was using it properly were not to be trusted.

Communication was becoming increasingly sporadic and futile; he was mostly in his own world. In the evening on December 22nd, his hallucinations began getting noticeably worse – and included his unwelcome, frightening visitors. That night Karin and I heard roaring and crashing from the guestroom beneath us (our bedroom was in the upstairs of the little house). I rushed down the stairs and switched on the light, to find Bob out of bed, turning his room upside-down in complete darkness. His eyes were wild and terrified. I *made* him lie down again. Pills of every kind were scattered chaotically all over the floor, *everywhere*, like confetti after a parade. I found the empty dosette box under the bed. He'd been taking medications randomly and liberally, in the dark, with no apparent knowledge of how much or of what kind or at what intervals. When he occasionally drifted off to sleep for a few minutes, I gathered up all the pills and began sorting them. I knew I had to take control of administering them. I hated doing anything against his will, but I hated even more seeing him like this. I sat on the edge of his bed for the rest of the night to keep him calm. He tried to rush up many times. He had no idea who I was or where we were. I had no idea where *he* was or whom he was seeing or seeking.

Exhausted at last, he slept soundly from the early hours of the morning until past noon. I slept for two or three hours. When he woke up, he was quite a bit clearer than before, but his speech was extremely slurred, nearly incoherent. From his slurred speech I worked out that some days before, he'd apparently decided to replace the clozapine with testosterone (I had no idea he was taking that drug, nor why, nor what effect it might have). He'd also increased the doses of his anti-Parkinson medications to unknown levels. I wanted to cry. I figured it would take at least 24 hours of strictly administered dosages to enable him to regain some semblance of control. His hallucinations worsened during the afternoon. I sat with him again that night.

On Christmas Eve, Bob was in his own world, unreachable, but relatively calm. I was alarmed that he remained in limbo despite my control of his medication; it was a new situation. I tried to get some sleep in my own bed that night, but Karin and I were again awakened by loud crashing noises. I leaped from bed and plunged down the stairs. Bob's room was empty. I heard crashing noises from the kitchen, so I raced across the dining room to find the kitchen floor covered with broken dishes. He'd opened the kitchen cupboards and begun pulling and sweeping out dishes from the shelves before heading for the front door. When I arrived on the scene, Bob was already halfway out the door, unclothed, heading into the black and cold December night.

Karin swept up the broken china and I got him back into bed. I was too exhausted and too sad to sit on the edge of his bed for another night. After he'd fallen asleep, I crawled under his bed so that I could fasten two luggage straps around him (over his comforter) to prevent him from rushing wildly out of bed before I had time to intervene. Then I lay on a mattress on the floor in my office, just outside his room. I hoped to be able to respond quickly to any commotion and to prevent another delusional foray. He remained "awake" until about 4:30 AM and again slept till noon. We were able to have a little contact the next day (Christmas Day), when Jenny and Sally joined us after having spent Christmas with Lena, as usual. They were appalled and overwhelmed with sorrow to see what was left of their Bob. They were unable to reach him.

Then his wild hallucinations began returning. I didn't know what to do. I was giving him all his prescribed medications, at the prescribed dosages and frequencies, to no avail. (I could only guess that he might have a secret stash of one or more of them somewhere.) In a moment of partial clarity on the 26th, Bob said he'd like to have a look at the Bridge. I knew he meant the incredible, ongoing bridge-tunnel construction that would soon join Malmö with Copenhagen (i.e. Sweden with Denmark). It was about a 20-minute drive from our home to the viewpoint. Bob spent the entire trip there searching for snails crawling on the floor of the car, and for maggots on his trousers. When we reached our destination, Bob barely looked up; the snails had taken control. We remained in the car. After some minutes, with Bob totally absorbed in brushing the invisible snails away, I accepted the futility, sighed and started the engine.

On the freeway on our way home, at a speed of about 100 km/h, Bob suddenly tried to open the car door and get out. In a flash I threw myself over him and pulled the passenger door closed with all my might, while keeping him inside and keeping control of the car while pulling over to the shoulder until order was restored. He said he thought we'd "arrived at the restaurant". We got home safely. But that incident scared the hell out of me. I was shaking all over. And I knew that no matter how much I loved and cared for him, I could no longer deal with his condition on my own.

Karin immediately saw what states we were in and took charge of Bob, who was entirely in his own world. I phoned the airline and booked tickets for us on the first available flight: two days later, in the evening on the 28th. Then I phoned Werner Meier and asked him to make arrangements for getting Bob readmitted to the hospital the morning after our arrival. Bob wouldn't stay put that night (the 26th) in Malmö. I stayed by his bedside until he fell asleep, then went to my mattress just outside his bedroom door. Within 10 minutes I heard him getting up again. I had to go in and gently force him to lie down. This went on for hours. My nerves were completely raw. It was breaking my heart to see Bob's state. I was ultimately so exhausted and exasperated and sad that I was again obliged to use the straps to restrain him from leaping wildly out of bed before I could respond. I was afraid I'd become too tired to wake up in time and would find him gone.

I was somewhat relieved to find Bob in a relatively clear state of mind when he woke up on the day of our return flight to Basel that evening, but his legs were still very wobbly. At the airport, I asked for a wheelchair to get him to the gate. In the taxi on our way to Binningen, he told me that he should have brought his anti-anxiety drug (a benzodiazepine called Lexotanil) with him to Sweden. I had no idea he even had that drug, nor what it was. He'd never mentioned it. But we made it to Gorenmattstrasse. I let us in with the key Bob had given me years earlier. Bob was somewhere else, in his own world, a world not of his own making or desire. I was unspeakably downhearted.

The next morning, Werner came by to pick Bob up. We took him to the hospital, then returned to Gorenmattstrasse to have a chat. Werner insisted that Bob was no longer able to live on his own. Werner (approaching 80 himself) never complained, but I was reasonably certain that there was no way he could provide the kind of support Bob needed locally. And Bob would probably require even more care (perhaps full-time) in the very near future. I was thus unable to disagree with Werner on any rational grounds, but I was keenly aware of Bob's powerful aversion to nursing homes or similar institutions, regardless of how nice they were or whatever euphemisms are used. I told Werner that I would try to reason with Bob on the subject.

In 1997, when his mind was still sharp, Bob had joined Exit International, a newly formed organization that supported assisted suicide. He told me that he loved life dearly because of the endless fascination it held for him, and because existence itself was all we have (*"having only this"*[12]), yet he was vehemently opposed to being kept alive beyond his ability to enjoy life in any way ever again. He wanted me to promise to do whatever I could to prevent that from happening.

By the time Bob was released from the hospital in mid-January 1999, reality forced me to accept that he could no longer live on his own, and that I would somehow have to try to convince Bob of that. I continued to phone him daily. I phoned Werner several times a week. Werner was now visiting Bob weekly, trying to make certain that Bob was managing his medication within acceptable limits. I was looking hard for options that might provide the necessary minimum

---

12 Words he frequently quoted to me from one of his favorite books, *The Aristos*, by John Fowles

of care while assuring Bob a maximum of private space and personal integrity. At my request, Werner sent me some folders (I struggled through the German) from suitable homes, including dimensions of possible rooms. I then drew floor plans to scale. And I made drawings of how a room might look when furnished with Bob's favorite pieces of furniture: his mole-gray leather swivel chair that could easily be reclined (from Hedberg's in Vinslöv, Sweden); a handcrafted, custom-built octagonal mahogany coffee table from a local cabinet-maker; the teak sofa from La Boutique Danoise; the old gigantic roll-top desk; the bed Bob built himself in the US; enough bookshelves for more than a thousand books; and even a number of my paintings, which Bob loved passionately.

I flew down to spend the last week in January with him. He'd been having a couple of good days – a clear mind – and was able to converse rationally. He said he was impressed by the sense of home that my sketches conveyed, and he seemed at last to open up to the idea. For the first time, he also expressed awareness of the urgency of his situation; he was now aware (but didn't yet accept) that he could no longer manage on his own. I could see that it was heart-rending for him. (And not just for him.) He said he needed a little more time to think about it.

Several weeks after my return to Malmö, one of our daily phone conversations revealed that Bob had again lost control of his medications, and was in danger. I phoned Werner. Bob went back to the hospital for about a week. I flew down to Basel again on Wednesday, February 24th, to be there to receive him when he got home. Each stay in the hospital left him looking weaker and gaunter, but this time he seemed paradoxically energized. Since he was still seeing worms in every bite he tried to eat, however, it was a struggle to get him to eat anything. He was looking more and more emaciated.

The next day he surprised me. He announced, with obvious great clarity, that we'd take a taxi to his bank in central Basel, close to the Art Museum (*Kunstmuseum*). He'd terminated the life insurance policy he'd had since he lived in the States and wanted to withdraw the payout in cash (mostly in 1000-franc bills), with me acting as his security guard to bring it to his home in Binningen! I was mystified (and nervous), but he seemed content to have it that way. He said something about not wanting to have to sign over all that money to to an assisted-living home if he had to move to one.

He was still reluctant to surrender any more independence – the essence of his experience of the quality of his life that he'd so treasured – and accept assisted living, but during one of our conversations he suddenly seemed to drop his resistance. To my surprise (again), he told me he was willing to take a look at the place that Werner had suggested.

We made an appointment for a viewing a day or two later. It was spacious, light and surprisingly homey. The views from the windows were similar to those he was accustomed to (the building was just a two-minute drive from Gorenmattstrasse). I brought along my sketches and a measuring stick so I could point out where his furniture might be placed. We discovered that he'd even have room for an additional bookcase, which made him smile. I assured him I'd be on hand to supervise the placement of furniture and books and paintings. But he still wanted another month to think about it.

On the 27th he gave me the names and addresses of all his favorite charities (Amnesty, Doctors without Borders, Save the Children, UNICEF and several others). Then he asked me to make out envelopes to each one. He filled each with a large wad of cash, but wrote no explanation, no messages, no return addresses. After weighing them on his old-fashioned brass postal scale, he put plenty of postage stamps on the table and told me how much to use for each envelope. Then we went up to the corner post office together and mailed them. He was alert and seemed to be following a clear and rational plan. I assumed that he knew that this period of mental clarity wouldn't last; he was determined to make the most of it. We had dinner with the Meiers that evening. Werner was pleased and relieved that Bob spoke clearly and coherently, and that he gave every impression of no longer being opposed to moving.

When we were alone again in his apartment, Bob reminded me that in the event of his death he wished no funeral or grave, but to have his ashes scattered in Binningen, as close as possible to Gorenmattstrasse 41, where he'd spent the past 30 years. I immediately thought of the Birsig, the little brook that flowed past his apartment building. I asked him what he thought of that. Bob smiled and thought it was the perfect solution. I felt a bit ill at ease talking about it, but Bob wasn't being mawkish or morbid, just realistic.

On Sunday morning, February 28th, Bob and I spoke about the move itself. We agreed that I would come to Basel in mid-April to help the movers put things right. He looked peaceful, but weary. He was resigned. Then he gave me an envelope containing well over 10,000 Swiss francs "to cover expenses". He felt too weak to see me off at the Basel-Mulhouse Airport as he'd always insisted on doing in the past. I told him not even to think of it. It would be much simpler for both of us if I just took a taxi there on my own.

Afterword

When the doorbell rang, indicating the arrival of the taxi down at the building entrance, we hugged, a *big long hug*. I went to the elevator. Bob stood in his doorway a few meters away, while I waited for the elevator to arrive. He'd always looked sad whenever I left, no matter how happy our time together had been. When the elevator came, I turned to him and before getting on the elevator I said, "*I love you, Bob.*" He looked at me, tears welling up. He nodded. I would never look upon his like again.

I continued to phone him every day. He sounded so weary, so resigned. I told him that on April 1st Karin and I had tickets to see a performance of Mozart's *Requiem* – one of Bob's (and our) most treasured pieces of music – and he sounded happy for us. But he again fretted about what to do with all his things when he moved. I told him not to worry, I'd take care of everything. He said he accepted my reassurance.

One evening when I phoned him, about two weeks after my departure from Basel, I could tell unmistakably that the frightening hallucinations had returned, although not yet in full force. I contacted Werner to let him know. He promised to be extra watchful of Bob's medication, and began stopping by Bob's place more than once a week. A few days later, when the psychotic aspects began returning (people in his apartment who were there to *kill* him!), I phoned Werner again. Bob had to be taken to the hospital once more, I insisted, and Werner agreed with no persuasion needed. I tried phoning Bob at the hospital. I was told that Bob was currently in such a bad state that he was unable to speak with me. I asked to speak with his doctor. I ended up telling Bob's doctor in some great detail everything I knew about Bob's situation. He asked me to write it all down and fax it to him. Since I'd been keeping it as a journal. I faxed it to him a few minutes later.

On March 31st, Bob and I had our last conversation. He sounded weaker than ever. I told him that Karin and I would be going to the Mozart *Requiem* concert the next evening, April 1st, so I wouldn't be calling until the following evening, April 2nd. That would be fine, he said.

The *Requiem* on April 1st was sublime, transcendent. After it was over, Karin and I walked home. It was a clear, tranquil, almost balmy evening, in contrast with our inner emotional turmoil after such a moving concert in the shadow of Bob's critical state. The half-hour walk helped us to "land". I thought how all the wonderful music I'd come to enjoy and love so much was in a very real sense

Bob's gift to me – Bob, the giver of music. We got home at around 10.15 PM. A few minutes after our arrival, the phone rang. We were upstairs at the time, so I picked up the phone on the piano. The call was from the hospital – Bob's hospital. Bob had died just a few minutes earlier.

My head was fully prepared for such news. My heart hadn't even begun. My head said *How like him! April fool's day! Thumbing his nose at the world one last time!* My heart was shattered. Without Karin's loving support, I would most likely have fallen apart. I found (and find) it altogether plausible that Bob had somehow "willed" his end rather than face a few months of upheaval and "assisted living" before the inevitable. He was just 70 according to his birth certificate. For the last 10 years, his body had been more like 100, but in his mind he'd been whatever age he wanted to be at any given moment, including a young man.

I phoned Werner the next morning to tell him the news. He was saddened, but dealt with his sadness by immediately turning the conversation to "the practical arrangements". I could hardly bear to hear it right then and might have lashed out in my grief, but I also knew that Werner meant well, that he was one of so very many of my gender who hate to show their emotions. I also knew that Bob liked and respected him. I told Werner of Bob's wishes not to have a funeral, but to have his ashes scattered nearby, perhaps in the little Birsig River. Werner was absolutely *appalled* at the idea. He said it was *illegal*, and that he would arrange for the ashes to be placed in a "memorial grove" nearby. I was too blown away with grief to resist Werner's forceful command of the situation. I didn't even get to tell him that I thought I would be able to export the urn into Germany, quite legally from the Swiss viewpoint (his principal concern), then bring it back to Binningen and scatter the ashes on my own, without telling anyone.

But Werner had his way; a small gathering was arranged in the memorial grove – a place with no connection to Bob whatsoever. At least there would be no religion involved. I flew down to Basel and took a taxi to Bob's apartment. It felt unreal and heart-rending to enter Bob's apartment knowing he was gone. I phoned Werner to let him know where I was and discuss those "practical arrangements". He was again shocked to hear that I was phoning from Bob's apartment and told me I had to leave forthwith! I wasn't allowed to be there until Bob's estate had been cleared by Swiss probate, or whatever it's called. (I knew that Bob had left everything to me anyway, so it was a mere formality, but few formalities are *mere* in Switzerland.) Werner came to pick me up at once and told me I could stay at his home instead.

I'd already invited Bob's few friends to join Werner and me for the "funeral", and I'd made arrangements to invite everyone for lunch afterwards. In the grove, I read a short tribute to Bob's life (I had to read from my own script – I was in no condition to speak extemporaneously). These were my concluding remarks:

> For the last 10-15 years of his life, Bob was in constant pain. Did you ever hear him complain about it? I'm sure you didn't. Bob had learned that self-pity is destructive, no matter how good your reasons for it. He learned to tolerate people, to think of their needs and not their faults. "Don't ever exploit anyone" was his creed. Bob didn't believe that Life has a Meaning in itself, nor did he believe in a life after this one – but he strongly believed that each of us can make our lives meaningful *while* we are living – and he certainly helped bring meaning to mine.
>
> Bob would have been quick to point out that the ashes in that urn are not him. This place is not where we remember Bob. He is in my heart and my mind. Yours too, perhaps. He was a grandfather to my children, a dear friend to my wife, a life-saver and a mentor to me. I will always miss him. And he will always be with me.

Using the money Bob had given me, I paid the rent on his apartment until the end of July, to allow myself time to get it cleared out. (It would take until early June for Swiss probate to settle the estate and allow me access.) Karin and I set aside two weeks for the task, including the trip. We left Malmö on July 2nd in a small rental van, arriving in Binningen on the 4th. We filled the van with whatever we could possibly bring back with us to Sweden. Since I knew we couldn't find use for more than a fraction of Bob's furniture, books and other possessions, I invited his nephew Dan to come to Bob's apartment a couple of days after our arrival, to take whatever he wanted that we hadn't earmarked for ourselves. Being in Basel without seeing Bob felt like one or two of my major limbs had been amputated. Dan arrived on July 6th. For some reason, I gave him four of the paintings of mine (as well as several drawings) that had been Bob's.

My plan had been to go through Bob's books immediately on arrival on the 5th, and take whatever books I really wanted that we had space for (or that I could make space for). I think I took around 600 books. Then Dan would go through the remaining 3500 or so and take several hundred more. I phoned a couple of local libraries, the university library, and high schools to offer all the rest to them. *But nobody was interested!* I couldn't believe that Bob's eclectic collection of literary works in English was of *no* use to *any* of them!!

Before we started on our trip to Basel, I'd tried phoning the Swedish customs office to find out whether I needed to do anything about a customs declaration for all the stuff I might be bringing back to Sweden. The customs officer asked me what things. I said I didn't really know, it was an estate; probably a few pieces of furniture, perhaps some household items, and *lots* of books. *How many books?* I didn't know yet, but there were several thousand to go through. *What is their value?* I had no clue, I said. There were no rare books among them, but they meant a lot to me. So how much could I expect to pay? He said they would probably charge a flat rate *by the kilo*! (I immediately thought of selling paintings by the square meter!) I thought I'd heard wrong and asked him to repeat it. He said I could declare everything at the border, and they would go through everything there. I just sighed and thanked him. All I could think of was fucking red bloody tape.

Dan stayed on for a few days after Karin and I left. I arranged for Werner to pick up the keys to the apartment from Dan when he was ready to leave, and Werner would then turn them over to the lawyer. She and Werner would arrange for the final cleaning of the apartment, for a fee to be deducted from the estate.

Karin and I left Basel in the fully loaded van very early on Monday the 12th. Our aim was to drive all the way home that same day, and since summer nights in early July were very short, we expected to have daylight all the way. We decided on the short ferry crossing, from Helsingør (Denmark) to Helsingborg (Sweden). When we came to the Swedish customs – a bit apprehensive about a possible long delay due to our load – it was around 9:30 PM. The sun was still shining, but it was very low in the sky. The customs officer looked at us briefly and waved us on through without a word. Just like that.

Karin rejoiced with me after that little relief amid the big trauma churning inside me. We were at Korngatan about an hour later. It was still twilight, the long fade-out of a summer evening, long enough for us to empty the van (quickly), return it to the gas station we'd rented it from, and be back home by midnight. The trip was over; the ordeal was not. It would take years before I could experience a Sunday evening without wondering when I should phone Bob, when I'd once again hear his reassuring greeting on the other end of the line. Again, I don't know how I would have managed without Karin.

* * * * *

When Karin was a little girl living in Klippan, her dad thought it would be good for the family to have a place in the country, not far from the sea, where they could spend their summer vacations as well as a few weekends in the late spring and early fall. As a result, in 1960, he bought an 1800 m² lot in a large pine grove (a small woods) called Glimminge Plantering, a few hundred meters from the bay of Skälderviken on the Bjäre peninsula on the west coast of Skåne. (A couple of kilometers farther inland is a hamlet called Glimminge.) He had a small cottage built there, at Havsvägen 5, the following spring, when Karin was 10.

In view of the difficulty most Anglophones seem to have in pronouncing "*Glimm*inge", let me help you: say "gleaming embers" but leave off the "mbers". The stress is on the first syllable. In "Plant*er*ing", the stress is on the second syllable, which is pronounced something like "air", with a Scottish accent. Back in the late 1800s, the local farmers whose fields lay between the hamlet of Glimminge and the sea had grown tired of having their crops (especially potatoes) battered by the sand-bearing westerly winds off Skälderviken. So they got together to form an association to buy up an 80-hectare swath of land along the coast where they created a "plantation" (the "*plantering*" part of the name) of pine trees to form a wind-breaker to protect their crops. (I know nothing of the farmers' personal habits of breaking wind; their principal crop was potatoes, not beans.)

The farmers were said to have been keeping options open for leasing the land as a possible site for a tuberculosis sanatorium there someday, but instead, in 1903 the government opened a sanatorium among the older pines in Veybystrand, around 15 kilometers closer to Ängelholm. As a result, the farmers eventually began parceling off the land in Glimminge Plantering, selling lots, mostly for recreational homes, with the proviso that buyers would preserve the grove for wind protection.

Between Glimminge Plantering and the sea is another swath, up to a hundred meters wide: a beautiful rolling meadow – grass and wildflowers – that is protected by law as a nature preserve. There is also a public beach, for enjoying sea and sun. In Sweden, it's almost redundant to say "public beach", since the public has free access to *all* beaches, with very few exceptions, under the Right of Public Access (*Allemansrätt*).

Most days, the hills of the Kullaberg Peninsula are clearly visible across Skälderviken. At the outermost tip of Kullaberg there is a lighthouse, and then what appears to be open sea. (It's actually the waters of Kattegat; Denmark is beyond the horizon and not visible from Glimminge.) It's not, in my view, *spectacular* scenery, not like the Alps or huge waterfalls, but it is serenely beautiful in its low-key way.

At the time I met Karin in 1988, she'd spent nearly every summer in Glimminge since she was 10. Sven and Agda's four children generally had their summer vacations there with at least one of their parents. It was originally a tiny, three-bedroom cottage with a cramped kitchen and an outhouse. As the kids grew up and began having families of their own, Sven and Agda added a two-bedroom-and-TV-room annex, as well as an indoor flush toilet connected to the municipal sewage system. The shower remained outdoors.

By the 1980s, there were something like 250 homes in Glimminge Plantering, of which fewer than 30 were used for year-round living. A large variety of birds – blackbirds, four kinds of woodpeckers, crows, starlings, cuckoos, swallows, owls, finches and many other small songbirds – made the grove their home. Down by the sea there were gulls, terns, lots of swans and cormorants, eiders and mallards. Sometimes we'd see seals. In the woods, squirrels chased each other up and down the pines, and leaped from treetop to treetop, covering hundreds of meters without ever touching the ground. Large hares and smaller rabbits bounced and bounded everywhere. We'd occasionally see deer. With the exception of the one paved municipal road into the little community, nearly all roads were (and still are) unpaved gravel, but are well kept. There are no streetlights; the stars are glorious on a clear night. Glimminge Plantering has its own road maintenance association, its own water supply association (but municipal sewers), and a homeowners' association. Glimminge meant and means the world to Karin.

When I entered the family picture in 1989, Karin and her elder brother Jan (yes, another Jan!) had become the sole joint owners of the house. The two families spent most of their long summer vacations there, usually together, an arrangement that worked fairly well. Towards the end of the millennium, with Karin's and Jan's children grown up, Jan and his wife began talking about finding a place of their own upon retirement. Karin and I also talked about possibly retiring in Glimminge, but Karin was alarmed that she'd never be able to afford to buy out her brother's share, which meant that we'd almost certainly have to move out.

Just over a year after Bob's death, I was out for a short walk on Midsommarvägen, just around the corner from Havsvägen. I spotted a sign on a tree in a vacant lot partly adjacent to Karin's and Jan's property (between that property and the two tennis courts). The sign said "Lot for sale by owner." (He lived next door.) I stared at the sign for some minutes, my mind whirring.

Within a couple of days, I knocked on that neighbor's door. His name was Klas-Göran, but everybody called him *Kase* (two syllables). He and his wife had two grown children. Kase owned two properties – one was the empty lot that was for sale, the other was the site of his summer cottage – he'd been intending to bequeath one property each to his son and to his daughter. But his son had recently gone and married a girl who was also to inherit a property in Glimminge. That meant one property too many, so Kase put the empty lot up for sale instead.

Kase and I soon agreed on a price, and shook hands on the deal. At that time I had no plans, no idea at all about what I wanted to do with a vacant lot. But I knew that at the very least it could secure a future for Karin in Glimminge, whatever else might happen. And I was certain that the value of the lot wouldn't depreciate if we ended up making other arrangements. I went to my bank the following week and set the paperwork machinery in motion. The improved financial situation thanks to my company and Bob enabled me to afford it.

I knew the lot quite well, by sight at least, from having observed its sorry, overgrown state while I was raking the back yard at Havsvägen. I was eager to restore it to the special atmosphere of a pine forest. I began by having all the non-pines felled, with the exception of a single majestic weeping beech in one corner of the somewhat undulating lot. The tangled underbrush was daunting. Wild, non-flowering honeysuckle vines covered much of the ground like tripwires. Saplings and weeds were everywhere. I attacked the underbrush with a machete, shears, and a handsaw.

I built a fairly large woodshed to fill with firewood for a future wood-burner in a future house. I sorted out every twig that had kindling potential. Sitting still was never my thing, but I took my time and worked methodically; I had no schedule and thus no deadline. It was when I'd nearly finished transforming the jungle into a lot that Karin and I got married, in July 2002, under the pines in the front yard at Havsvägen 5.

While clearing the underbrush, I began to think of where a house might be placed, should it ever come to that. I first made a detailed sketch of the lot, and marked the location of each pine tree. I also made notes about the level differences. Then, in August 2001, I transferred my sketch to a PowerPoint file as a scale drawing. Next I made a layout of a house. I placed it on the lot in such a way as to avoid having to take down more than two or three of its century-old pines. I saved that first file as *Glimminge-A.ppt*.

All this time, I was warming to the idea of living in Glimminge someday, at least as a summer house. I was now in my late 50s, and retirement no longer belonged to the realm of science fiction. At the same time, Karin was warming to the idea of living in a *new* house next-door to the one where she'd grown up. She began to get involved in my numerous revisions of the house plans. Each new revision got a different file name: *Glimminge-B.ppt, Glimminge-C.ppt, Glimminge-D.ppt, Glimminge-E.ppt,* etc. (Later, the Municipality of Båstad would also have some "input".) The house we eventually built was *Glimminge-T.ppt*.

Ulf, an architect-builder neighbor of ours in Malmö, told us that many prefab house companies in Sweden were prepared to build in accordance with clients' own designs. They would then supply all materials. The outer walls, load-bearing walls and roof beams were all prefabricated in sections in sections, while indoors in their dry factory, for fast assembly at the customer's building site. Ulf recommended this approach, since it meant that the entire perimeter (as well as the load-bearing inner walls) would be delivered nice and dry, and would be under the protection of the roof within a few days.

A neighbor in Glimminge recommended Villa Nordic as the prefab supplier; that neighbor had good experience from their own new home, and Villa Nordic had a reputation for quality. We designed the house to be well insulated to enable year-round living with low energy consumption and thus lower environmental impact and lower fixed costs. Then we had to find a local builder, someone we felt we could trust. When we told Ulf that we'd chosen Harmarks, a small construction firm in Torekov, Ulf assured us we'd found the best. (Ulf knew of them rather well; he grew up in Torekov and knew nearly all the local builders.)

Karin's brother Jan had the house at Havsvägen assessed and bought out Karin's share for half the assessed value. I put in some additional money, and we got a mortgage for the rest. Karin's deal with Jan included our right to remain there until our own house was completed.

After some delays for municipal approval, work on the site began at last in October 2006, with the well-insulated (30 cm of polystyrene) concrete foundation and slab. In mid-November, when Jenny came home from London for a visit, she and Sally came up to Glimminge for a brief look at the new foundation on which the new house was soon to be built. We stopped in Barkåkra on the Sunday to spend a few hours with Marie-Louise on our way back to Malmö, little knowing that we'd never see her again; she died on Friday, November 18th. She left specific instructions that Karin and I were to be invited to her funeral; we loved each other to the end.

The entire, well-insulated structure (including triple-glazed windows) of our new house was delivered in sections on Thursday morning, December 14th, 2006. Karin and I spent the night before at Havsvägen 5 to be able to witness the big event early the next morning. At 7 AM sharp, large flood lights, temporarily mounted on strategically placed pines on our lot, suddenly illuminated the building site, making a bubble of light in the thick darkness. Long trucks loaded with building materials and the prefabricated outer walls, as well as the roof beams, slowly emerged into the floodlit site in the chilly, misty, early winter morning. The crew was on hand, patiently eager to get going.

Karin and I were as jittery as a couple of kids as we watched from our small bedroom window in the house on Havsvägen. When we weren't jittering, we were nearly paralyzed with excitement. Then we realized that if we weren't to miss the show, we'd better hurry up and get dressed. We pulled a couple of outdoor lounge chairs out onto the little hill on our (!) lot, overlooking the site. We brought blankets and a thermos of coffee to help keep us warm, and umbrellas in case the very light mist turned wetter. (It was unlikely to turn to snow; this was *southern* Sweden!)

The last of the wall sections was secured in place well before the mid-afternoon nightfall. The whole house was under a watertight roof two days later, December 16th, when we took time off to attend Marie-Louise's funeral. It felt both strange and natural to be there. To my great relief, no conflict of any kind arose at the funeral. She left a hollow spot.

Karin and I visited our future home every weekend throughout that winter and early spring. As the work progressed, we chose to do certain jobs ourselves – puttying, painting, installing the kitchen cabinets – in order to make the house feel more like our very own home. Thus we experienced, for the first time ever, what a dark, chilly, isolated winter would be like in Glimminge. And we loved it, we loved the solitude, the tranquility, the trees, the stars, the silence.

Our house was officially completed on May 17th, 2007. We moved in our things from Havsvägen that same afternoon – 19 years to the day after our first real meeting ever. During 2007 and 2008, we spent more time at our new home in Glimminge than at our old home in Malmö. When Karin's job transferred from Malmö to Helsingborg (halfway between Malmö and Glimminge) in the autumn of 2008, we made it full-time; Glimminge officially became our sole residence on December 1st, 2008.[13]

When Jeanette and I moved to Malmö in 1969, it was the smallest town we'd ever lived in, and it felt very small to us. We were in our mid-twenties; we were both used to metropolitan life. I'd never liked the idea of living in a small community, since I feared a gossiping, back-biting environment with more space and less privacy. But with age, countryside living became more and more appealing to me. Before Karin moved to Korngatan in 1991, she'd lived most of her life in Klippan (pop. ~ 16,000), and for her, Malmö was a *big* city. Although Klippan was twice the size of neighboring Perstorp, the idea of living in such small towns made me shudder.

But nearly 20 years of summers in Glimminge made me see the place more as country living than small-town living. The possibility of taking walks among the tall, old pines, or along the meadow – with its tranquility and soul-restoring views of the sea and the horizon – in complete solitude (except in July!) made the idea of permanent residence there more and more attractive to me.

Until we built our new house, neither Karin nor I had ever experienced year-round living in Glimminge. It didn't take long, however, to discover that the difference between loneliness and solitude is not to be found in the external world; it's in the mind. At last I understood the joy of solitude – what Bob had known all along.

For some people, a forest or grove is the ideal retreat. Others prefer the seaside. Much of the charm of Glimminge Plantering was that it offered both. Being on the meadow, by the sea, is often a very windy experience, but walking just 10 meters into the grove is like closing a door; nearly all the wind stops, or rather is deflected to the tops of the tallest trees. Only rarely (once or twice a decade, usually in the autumn or winter) does a storm reach hurricane force, making the tall old pines sway and groan – but most of them continue as they've always done: stopping most of the wind. In extremely rare cases, the wind is strong enough to uproot trees. For some people, however, this turns the long-term protection into a short-term threat.

As a result, instead of replacing the tall, century-old trees when they fell, and

---

13 See Appendix – floor plan of house in Glimminge

planting new ones to boost the protection, many trees have been intentionally and unnecessarily felled in recent years. Others have been mutilated to serve as bushes. Felling the grove to clear lots for sunshine (screw the squirrels and birds!) has also become popular, despite the huge meadow and beach just a short stroll away. *Why do people choose to live in a forest or grove if they don't like trees?!* Unfortunately, neither I nor anyone else can choose to live in a seaside grove if the neighbors choose to chop down their trees. *Nothing gold can stay.*

* * * * *

I've written in Books 1 and 2 of *Hindsights* about many steps in the saga of my first painting, *Guitar and Bottle* (1963), as well as in Book 4, in which I gave the painting to Jeanette's parents (in 1974). When I began compiling a catalogue of all 86 of my paintings in 2002, I discovered I had only a couple of low-resolution photos of my first. I knew from my mom, who'd heard from Marilyn (Jeanette's elder sister) some years before, that Rose (Jeanette's mom) had died and that Jeanette's twin brother Michael had moved from the house on Seville Street. Since Marilyn chose not to keep in touch with me, I had to start from scratch to try to locate her or anyone else in her family to ask for a high-resolution digital photo of that first painting.

I found no up-to-date address for any of them. But now I had the internet. After many fruitless searches, and many phone calls to the wrong people, I reached Marilyn, who happened to answer the phone when I dialed a number I hoped might be for her son. She seemed nervous to hear my voice out of the blue like that, but she didn't hang up. After asking lots of questions about the family, I asked her about the painting, and stated my request for a photo. She wasn't sure what had happened to it, said that it had been in the garage on Seville Street for many years, but that the old house had been sold, and my painting might have ended up in a dumpster. She said she'd ask around and get back to me. I managed to get her email address and gave her mine.

About a week later I got an email from her saying that she'd located the painting! Her nephew, Rosanne's son, had rescued it when the house on Seville Street was being emptied. He'd hung it on the wall in his college dorm room. *Where do you want us to send it?* Marilyn asked me in her next email. I replied that

I was *not* asking them to return the painting to me, just to get a photographer to take a high-resolution photo that they could email it to me. Instead, the painting itself arrived about a week later! I could see that it was damaged, presumably from having spent years in a damp garage. *Guitar & Bottle* is now hanging on our wall in Glimminge.

* * * * *

Prior to 1988, I experienced two huge losses: my dad's death in 1973 and Jeanette's death in 1977. There have been further losses since then. I've written about my mom, Bob, and Marie-Louise. I was very sorry to hear of the death (in 2008) of Lena's brother Jan, whom I regarded as a good friend. Two of my dearest and kindest friends and helpers – Elsa Braun and Henry Carlsson – died a few years later. Bo, my former neighbor and friend, died in 2017.

Since the narrative of *Hindsights* ends shortly after my first-ever meeting with Karin's wonderful parents, Sven and Agda, here's a bit more about what endeared them to me so much. From the first moment they met Jenny and Sally, they treated them as their own grandchildren, always with joyful affection. They were full of fun and humor; Sven's jokes were not always the latest, but he told them frequently and it was impossible not to laugh with him, every time. Sven and Agda were not at all prudish; there were only two kinds of jokes I couldn't tell them: (1) jokes in English (their linguistic accomplishments weren't up to it, but they often made up for their lack of language skills with highly creative body language!); and (2) jokes *they'd* already told *me* – jokes of every color (including "off"). Their fun-loving spirit often meant seemingly hastily (but actually carefully) organized family outings, picnics and games. And they were not ashamed to show their feelings, especially feelings of love. Sven died in 2002, and sadly missed our wedding. Agda died in 2008, when Karin and I were still in the gradual process of moving to Glimminge full-time.

One of the most painful losses to me in recent years was the death in 2013 of Preben (the eldest of the four sons of Grete and my former close friend Jan in Norway).[14] An exceptionally vibrant young father of four children, he was cut

---

14 I first met Preben in February 1981. See Book 5 (*A Sea of Troubles*), chapter 12.

down by virulent cancer at the age of 39. For some reason, his face pops up in my mind whenever anybody seeks to proclaim to me the goodness of their god.

Unfortunately, I have to count Preben's father as another loss. In 2012, he abruptly and inexplicably tore up his relationships with family (including Preben) and friends (including me), and refused all contact. I'd counted him as one of my few close friends for some 30 years. Grief isn't only brought on by death.

Fortunately, the close friendship I've always had with Preben's brothers (Carl-Victor, Jørgen and Rikard) and their mother Grete lives on. My friendship with Jan's brother Øivind (one of only five people to have read *Hindsights* in its entirety prior to publication) has grown in recent years. I've valued his comments and observations on *Hindsights*, although not nearly as much as I value his friendship.

Another particularly painful loss was the death of my dear friend Christer in 2019. His wife Eva was Karin's old "summer friend" from Glimminge, with whom she reconnected by chance in around 1990. The four of us soon became close friends. In around 2016, Christer required extensive surgery for his dangerously weakened abdominal aorta, a condition from which he never fully recovered.

Sometimes people ask me whether I think I'll meet departed friends and family again in some sort of "hereafter". My answer is *no*. So are they "just gone"? No! In one sense, they come alive in my mind every time I think of them. They live on in my (and others') memory. I've never seen or otherwise experienced any evidence of anything else.

In connection with moving from Korngatan to Glimminge, and knowing it was most unlikely I would ever make Korngatan my home again, there was something that required resolution. Jeanette and I had agreed that the sea was the place for our ashes.[15] We didn't want a funeral or a grave. If anyone needed a *place* of remembrance, the humungous, contiguous, globe-spanning sea provides nearly endless opportunities for people whose remembrance requires an physical place. Yet the sea doesn't give anyone the burden of tending or putting flowers on a grave – or visiting. Your nearest waterway will do.

Back in 1977, when I was an emotional trainwreck and totally incapable of following through on those wishes, I paneled Jeanette's urn inside the base of the sloping roof upstairs in the big house. It remained there for some 30 years. Once

---

15 See the last chapter of Book 4, *Slings and Arrows*.

Karin and I had moved to Glimminge full-time, another solution was required: closure. In the autumn of 2010, I told Sally (who'd returned to live at Korngatan after five years in New York) that I needed to undertake a small job there in the old house, and it would be good if I could have the house to myself for a couple of hours. I didn't specify my errand, but I think she understood.

I brought the urn home to Glimminge with me. And one lovely October day shortly thereafter, Karin accompanied me on a meditative and purposeful walk down across the meadow. Not another person was in sight. We proceeded down to the rocky shoreline, where I emptied the contents of the urn into the sea. Then we sat together on a bench overlooking the water and the horizon for a while. Karin held my hand and squeezed it from time to time. It was a beautiful late autumnal afternoon, not too chilly, perfectly still and peaceful. I told Karin *that* was what I wanted for *my* resting place as well. Karin has always understood what Jeanette meant and means to me. I love her for that too.

* * * * *

In the spring of 1993, while visiting my brother John and his wife Marj in Boise, where they were now living, I also met my nephew Brian. It was only the second time we'd met since 1978, when he was a teenager living in Santa Rosa, California. He was now 31. He told me, during our long, late-night discussions, of his serious and growing doubts concerning religion. He wanted to hear my views and the history of my liberation. Those face-to-face talks led to correspondence, first by letter, then email exchanges a few years later when I got the internet, and eventually Skype discussions of increasing length, frequency and depth. A deep and lasting friendship soon emerged.

In recent years, Brian (often accompanied by his wife Marla) has visited me and Karin many times, occasionally for the primary purpose of helping me undertake a few of the physical tasks that have become too difficult for me. I am truly grateful to him for that. Since the first time he saw them, Brian has shown exceptional interest in discussing my paintings as well, particularly those that relate to my outlook on life and religion. Brian is in fact one of only a handful of people I've known who have wished to discuss my paintings in depth with me. Brian's "eagle eye" in helping to proofread *Hindsights* (all six books) has proved to be of great value to me, but of even greater value has been his detailed feedback on the content – and his friendship.

I only saw Norm a dozen or so times since we split up in the fall of 1964 and through the remainder of the millennium. For many years – decades – neither of us even had each other's phone number or address. In 2009, Norm managed to obtain my email address, and we began corresponding. On a trip he was making to Norway with his Norwegian girlfriend May the following year, we at last met in person, at the old train station in Båstad. Right there on the platform we both knew instantly that the roots of our once-powerful friendship were still intact, still alive and well, and we were overwhelmed with the emotion of it.

So much had happened in the interim to change us and make us into very different people – two guys who had taken hugely different winding, twisting paths, but also two guys who had frequently been rudely shoved onto paths neither of us had chosen. When Norm related to me the story of his incredibly successful professional career, I was amazed. But both of us had had to deal with profound tragedies. And yet somewhere inside the years of added girth and accumulated layers of heartaches and joys, those two teenage rebels of the early '60s were still kicking, boats against the current, forever grateful to each other for the mutual, massive support that once made the Great Escape possible.

Norm has also kindly provided me a great deal of useful feedback on *Hindsights* (he too has read all six books, both the early drafts and much later revisions). His feedback – particularly on our Greater Chicago childhood and youth in *Natural Shocks* (Book 1), and the upheavals that starting a new life in San Francisco entailed – has been of great value to me.

I hadn't seen or heard from Lee Whitehead (my old English literature professor at UBC) more than two or three times since 1969 when I at last got the internet. At first I thought I'd be able to find anything or anyone. It took me many years longer than that. During one of my searches, in 2016, I was testing the image banks associated with the names I'd searched and was able to identify Lee from a photo in an obscure newspaper in the Okanagan, about 400 km due east of Vancouver. From that I quickly found his address and sent him an old-fashioned letter (in an envelope), along with my email address. We immediately began intense email correspondence. I spent a week with him at his ranch near Osoyoos in September 2017, and we decided to maintain contact via Skype. We've been spending around two hours on Skype together, nearly every Monday evening since then, discussing a broad and often deep range of topics – pretty much like I used to enjoy with Bob.

Lee, who has since moved to Victoria BC, has been extraordinarily supportive and encouraging in my efforts to complete and publish *Hindsights*, and has kindly bestowed on me his professional critical literary expertise; I needed it! In the process, or in another process that the first process launched, Lee has become my dear and trusted friend.

* * * * *

For me, the most difficult aspect of my separation from Lena following the final break-up of our marriage, was that I was forced to deal with the agony of separation from Jenny and Sally. I had to learn to disconnect, to let go of what I could not possibly change and only obliquely influence. And I had to trust that the one I trusted least (towards me) would at least see that the kids got proper love and care when they were with her. I managed, by embracing the love that Karin and I shared, by listening to Bob's voice of reason and by refusing to give in to self-pity. I had to be the best father I could be every time I was able to be a father at all.

Ending the narrative of *Hindsights* in December 1988 means that I have intentionally excluded nearly everything in and about the lives of our four kids: my Jenny and Sally, Karin's Moa and Peder. When I started writing this opus, we had no grandkids; we currently have seven. Jenny and John have Bella; Sally and Jonas have Allan and Selma; Peder and Lina have Mille, Emmett and Ivar; and Moa and Michael have Svante. We love them all to bits. Among those who follow, perhaps someone will someday read *Hindsights* and be inspired to pick up where I've left off. (*Hindsights II* or *Return to Hindsights*? No! Find your *own* title – and your own hindsights!)

I will, however, relate here one particularly precious annual activity from Jenny's and Sally's childhoods. It began in the summer of 1991, three years after the break-up and after two summers of frenetic building at Korngatan whenever the kids weren't with me, I drove to Switzerland with them for two weeks. Jenny was now 7, Sally was 5. We spent the first few days with Bob while I undertook the usual clean-up while he and the kids had fun together. Then I took the kids hiking in the Alps for a week (except for that first year), ending our trip with a few more days with Bob before driving home to Sweden.

 On our first-ever, very guarded, prudent hike, we took a cog-wheel train up to the Alpine meadow in Kleine Scheidegg, where we would spend the night at the foot of the sheer face of the Eiger and glacier-encrusted Jungfrau. In the crisp air, we heard the sounds of small rockslides from the steep mountainsides in the distance, and the clanking of cowbells reverberating up and down the deep valleys on several sides. We saw deer and antelope and marmots and hawks. After we'd been hiking for nearly an hour, at a very leisurely pace, upwards and onwards along fairly steep trail beneath the majestic Eiger, I thought it might be best for us to turn back so as not to wear out the kids' legs that first day, and to have time to rest up before dinner. The trail was narrow, but it ran through a gently sloping meadow, teeming with wildflowers, distant cowbells clanking. There were no risks involved. Jenny walked carefully a few meters in front of me as we headed back down the trail, and Sally was about the same distance behind me. Not one other person was in sight. After some minutes, the sound of Sally's footsteps ceased. I whirled around in alarm to see her sitting on a boulder next to the path. She was crying. I told Jenny to stop and I rushed to Sally's side. Was she in pain? Was she tired? Did her feet hurt? "*No*," she said, her voice trembling, "*but it's so beautiful!!*"

 As from the following year, the hiking part of our Swiss trips followed five-or-six-day pattern. We'd stop in a village along the way to one of the Alpine passes. There we'd buy what was needed for a backpack full of our picnic lunch: fresh rolls, slices of cheese and ham, a couple of tomatoes, a bag of paprika-flavored potato chips, bottled water and fresh fruit. Then we'd drive to one of the mountain passes (above the treeline).

 Every Swiss Alpine pass we visited had some form of accommodation, from a cheap hostel to a pricy lodge or hotel. We took what we could get, checked in during the late morning, and immediately took off on one randomly picked hiking trail that led upwards from the passes. We hiked across exquisitely beautiful meadows, the whole afternoon, always at a leisurely pace. We rested when we felt like it, ate when we were hungry, topped up our water supply from the brooks, marveled at the flowers and the views and the silence, and watched for wildlife, of which we saw plenty. The playful marmots were particularly entertaining.

The panoramas of the mountains and valleys were unceasingly staggering and majestic.

I timed our ascent to last no longer than I could be quite certain that darkness wouldn't arrive before our descent was complete. Back at the hotel, we'd have a good hot meal, then jump into bed laughing and talking about our day. I'd read numerous favorite bedtime stories, with the kids making sure I read them all using the "right" voices for each character. Then we'd sleep soundly.

Early the next morning, we'd have breakfast, check out, drive down from the pass to a village in the next valley, buy new provisions, and head for another mountain pass, where we'd check in. We repeated that procedure for five days, then returned to Binningen and told Bob all about our adventures. He loved hearing the kids' enthusiastic tales. We made those trips to Switzerland every summer until 1998, which turned out to be Bob's last summer. We didn't know it at the time, but I was certain there couldn't be many more. During those seven magical summers, Jenny, Sally and I probably spent a night in something like 40 of Switzerland's Alpine passes and hiked in the breathtaking Alpine meadows beneath the snow-covered peaks, creating a huge trove of happy memories and loving bonds. And we always had good luck with the weather.

I also feel compelled to follow up on the fate of my house on Korngatan. When Karin's and my move to Glimminge became permanent in 2008, I'd thought to sell the house in Malmö and let Jenny and Sally share the money. But to my surprise, they wouldn't hear of selling the house – even though they were living in London and New York (respectively) at the time.

In the early years following the divorce, when the kids were still small, the turbulence of divorce posed certain risks of adding stressful chaos to their lives. To abate that stress, I promised them that Korngatan 12 would always be their home. I couldn't exactly explain to four- and two-year-olds that I *meant* "for as long as they chose to live there, and that it would then be the *value* of the house that would be theirs."

I was unprepared for the power of the emotional ties they'd developed for the place as they grew up, and that they'd even remember my promise verbatim when they reached adulthood. But they did, and they made it clear that they weren't going to release me from it, even after they'd both moved out to start lives of their own. To avoid unnecessary conflict, we had to find a solution.

To make a long story short, my kids and I reached a three-way agreement:

Sally, who was already living in the house on Korngatan again (after Karin and I had moved to Glimminge), would receive the house as a gift from me, with the proviso that she would take out a mortgage equal to half the market value of the house, then give that amount to Jenny, who'd been living in London for more than 10 years. In fact, the three of us arrived at the same solution independently of each other! And thus it was done. Now, farther along the line in the summer of the second year of covid 2021, Sally and Jonas have sold the place (I have no problem with it) and are moving to the countryside near Ystad (two weeks from now as I write this). Jenny and John are planning to move to Sweden within a year or two, as close to Sally and family as possible. (I certainly have no problem with that either!)

Jenny and Sally have not only survived the turmoil of divorce and the turbulence of adolescence, they've both become caring, intelligent, independent and creative young women.

After a few years of gaining life experience in London, Jenny got a degree in nursing and pursued that career with great success before, before moving up to the role of a clinical practice educator at a major hospital in London, with a delightful sideline as an artist, thus taking that passion of mine into the 21st century. After more than four years of struggle with IVF, she and John at last succeeded in bringing Bella into the world in 2020. They're hoping to resettle in Sweden in the near future.

Sally spent five years in New York, taking advantage of her dual citizenship (no need to apply for residence and work permits or cards of any color, especially green). She began studying human rights (remotely) at Malmö University before returning to Sweden to complete her Master's degree. She worked as a translator for the University of Lund for several years, before switching to computer programming and a new career in web design. She and her partner Jonas have two children: little Allan, born in 2018, and our latest addition, Selma, born this year (2021).

* * * * *

Until the summer of 1983, when the first signs of my asthma began appearing, I'd enjoyed excellent health. The only nights I'd ever spent in the hospital were when I was born in Dallas and when I had my appendectomy in Malmö. The onset of asthma necessitated a week in the hospital in December 1983. Thereafter, a combination of no more smoking, the right medication and vigorous exercise (thanks to about four hours a week of badminton) brought it under control within a couple of years. For nearly two decades I didn't feel particularly limited by it. By 2003, however, the increasing pain in my knee was enough to put an end to my badminton – which had brought the symptoms of my asthma under control.

Nevertheless the pain in my knee intensified and eventually led to two operations for torn cartilage, in the first decade of the new millennium. In connection with the latter operation, it was discovered that my cartilage was not only torn, but missing, worn away: I'd developed arthritis. My arthritis is currently limited to my hip joints, knee joints, feet and toes, early-stage in my hands, and most recently serious compression of the vertebrae in my lower spine.

In the late autumn of 2005. I developed severe pain in my right shoulder, which I would have attributed to a history of excessive badminton and carpentry – had I been right-handed. But I'm *left*-handed, so I went to the district clinic and, after a brief examination, I was given a shot of cortisone. The pain disappeared almost instantly. For a week. When it returned, it had spread to the back of my neck. I was then given two shots of cortisone. The pain was again reduced, but only partially. After about three days it returned to *both* shoulders, the back of my neck *and* my left hip. I knew that pain could radiate out from a source point, but can it *jump* from right shoulder to left hip?! A blood test revealed a bad-ass infection in my body, and I was sent to the emergency clinic at the hospital, where I was given all kinds of blood tests, x-rays, a spinal fluid test, etc. Some of the tests gave instant results, others had to be sent to a lab for analysis. The pain was now excruciating and increasing daily. I could barely raise my arms or walk or sleep. I saw numerous doctors. All my test results came back negative; nobody knew what it was. At the hospital they gave me a strong pain-killer (Citadon, which contains paracetamol and codeine) that helped conceal the worst of the symptoms for a while, but did nothing about the cause. Soon the pain was excruciating enough to keep me awake at night, night after night, for weeks. I could hardly move or do anything. The severe lack of sleep and equally severe pain were running me down.

On December 23rd, as I was leaving the house, struggling to walk the 50 meters to our local pharmacy to get more pain-killers, I saw that our relatively new neighbor (a retired doctor of some kind) directly opposite our house was outside his house putting up a new mailbox. We'd never spoken much beyond polite greetings. He looked up when he saw me struggling. Immediately he stood up and, without taking his eyes off me, came straight over to me in the middle of Korngatan. *"You don't look well!"* he observed sternly, I tried to smile. I nodded in assent. *"May I ask you a few questions?"* I consented. After he'd asked about where I felt pain, for how long, and what had been done about it, he asked if I would permit him to feel my temples and the back of my neck. It sounded odd to me, but I was beyond the few inhibitions I'd ever had about caring about oddness. After examining me right there in the middle of our street, he nodded to himself, straightened up and said he was at least 90% certain about a diagnosis, but wanted to know if he could also have my permission to phone the hospital to hear about my test results, in order to verify his suspicions. Again I consented. *"You see, a lot of these doctors are my former pupils,"* said Anders Gustafsson, my doctor neighbor, who, I soon found out, was also a retired professor of internal medicine. About 20 minutes later, after I'd been to the pharmacy, he knocked on my door. *"I was right! You have polymyalgia rheumatica* [PMR]. *Here's a prescription for prednisolone* [a corticosteroid], *which you need to start taking <u>immediately</u>. You're in imminent danger of irreversible blindness – and much worse!"*

Half an hour later, I took my first dose, 25 mg. That night I slept without pain for the first time in months. It was miraculous!! Anders took it upon himself to become my personal physician. He monitored my progress throughout his successful treatment of my PMR and beyond. He also checked my blood values and treated my borderline diabetes. And he listened to my heart, very carefully. After detecting a very faint heart murmur (no previous medical examination had ever done so), he sent me to a specialist for the first of what would become annual ultrasound cardiac scans, which enabled my defective aortic valve to be replaced – in time – 10 years later. So now I have a new aortic valve courtesy of a Brazilian cow and thanks to Anders' hands-on approach. I feel I owe my life to him.[16]

Anything else? My pulmonary difficulties became exacerbated and developed into COPD in around 2013. "Thanks" to the arthritis, vigorous exercise was

---

16 My painting *Autumn in the Park* (#55) is on permanent loan to Anders, for as long as he lives.

no longer a viable path for mitigating the problems with my lungs. On a New Year's trip with Eva and Christer to Bologna in 2014-15, I had a near-fatal bout of pneumonia that had developed into septicemia. I'm in pain more or less all the time. Walking was becoming increasingly difficult in recent years. But I'm fighting it now, thanks to Karin's enthusiastic support and to the use of a rollator (or wheeled walker), a wonderful (but not patented, intentionally) Swedish invention from 1978.

And yet I feel extremely privileged and fortunate. *Life is wonderful*!! I'm loved by those I love. I'm writing – and in this I've been able to make use of all the creative impulses that once drove me to paint. I hope that what I've written, and what I've painted, will make possible readers think and make you feel. And as long as I'm wishing, I hope that whoever reads *Hindsights* will feel stimulated to think more rationally and feel more compassionately! And that maybe, just maybe, you'll have learned a little more about my art.

* * * * *

Now, in 2021, in the second year of covid-19, it's been 53 years since I lived in the US. I've lived in Sweden for 52 of those years. I've held dual citizenship since 2004, when Swedish law was amended to permit dual citizenship. (The fact that George W. Bush launched another war in Iraq in 2003, a war based on two outright lies and backed by willful ignorance, didn't diminish my motivation to acquire Swedish citizenship!)

Do I still feel American? Do I feel Swedish yet? The answer to the first is *very little*, and to the second is *not entirely*. On my first trip back to the States (in 1974) after coming to Sweden (in 1969), I discovered that half a decade's absence from my homeland had already turned into alienation. That feeling has grown in pace with America's rightward political drift and its bewilderingly religious culture (paradoxically perhaps, the two forces appear to be almost related).

When I left the US in 1968, criticism of US involvement in Vietnam (particularly among people my age) was vocal, uninhibited and widespread. The actions of US troops were questioned – because they were often highly questionable. Sure, the troops were only following orders, but after Nürnberg, is "just following orders" still a viable excuse?!

Afterword

On a flight I made in 2017 from Copenhagen to Seattle, I had to change planes in San Francisco. While waiting for my onward flight, it was announced over the PA system that the incoming flight at the gate next to mine was carrying "heroes" from Iraq, and that everyone should cheer them as they entered the transit hall. Imagine that happening in 1968! In San Francisco! Now it really didn't feel safe to dissent; exercising my freedom to do so might come at a price. (I went to a restroom instead. I was too wiped out after the long flight to take a stand....) I have the feeling that since 9/11, most Americans (or at least a highly vocal minority) automatically regard anybody in a uniform as a hero until proved otherwise. So what word do you save for *real* heroes – those who actually risk or sacrifice their own lives to rescue or protect others, those of singular moral integrity? (And how can anyone claim moral integrity if they are "just following orders"?!)

I got sick of talking to people who proudly claimed that "America is biggest and best" in every respect, yet who know *nothing* about other countries (they often don't even know where other countries are located). Are people from other countries any more knowledgeable about the US than Americans are about them? Not always, but unlike the US and a few other "great" powers, few other countries exert such a high level of financial, military or political pressure on and power over anyone else.

I love many things about Sweden, but I'm critical of others. On the other hand, I *dis*like quite a bit *less* about Sweden than just about any other country (about which I know enough to assess at all).

In chapter 11 of this book, I compared my life to that of a molting crab. Perhaps a better comparison would be the common onion. Like the layers inside the skin of an onion, I carry within me a number of distinct "lives", the epochs of my existence, many of which are sharply demarcated by the jolting changes I've pointed out. I maintain ready access to most of those inner layers, but cutting through the "onion" to gain access may sometimes bring tears. My current self, the tougher outer skin of the onion, is the 76-year-old that people see and react to, while the 26-year-old inside me may be alive and kicking, and may well be the one driving me at any given moment.

In 2016, American voters (*nearly* half of them!) put a perilous buffoon in the White House. During his term in office, he actively made the super-rich even richer and the poorest even more destitute (as Republican presidents have been doing ever since my childhood). He managed to push through strong anti-immigrant legislation in a nation of immigrants. He withdrew the US (historically the world's leading contributor to greenhouse gases) from the Paris Accord to stop climate change by limiting greenhouse gases.

I wish I could feel that mankind has learned some lessons, that the democratic election of someone like Hitler would be unthinkable today. Yes, the American system managed to stave off the reelection of Trump (against fierce attempts by Republicans and other right-wingers to nullify the results). But the threat clearly remains that Trump or those who follow him rabidly could return to power. As I write, fascistic parties are gaining strength and power, even in a number of Western democracies – including Sweden, to my sorrow – and many who basically disagree are merely shrugging it off, closing their eyes, *or just keeping silent*.

Racism continues to thrive and abound (don't ask a *White* person whether that is true!). Women are still being cruelly and often violently suppressed (don't ask a *man* whether that is true!). People are averting their eyes to oppression in the name of "respect" for "cultural diversity". People who are otherwise appalled and angered (rightfully so!) about sexual *discrimination* within Western society often seem to do a double-twist backflip if a minority group is practicing even worse sexual discrimination, simply by claiming it's their *culture*! Some people are less outwardly bothered by wars (as long as they are in someone else's country). Executions, racial discrimination, and gay-bashing produce less of a stir among some than the word *fuck*. Now that is *really* fucked up!

When people have figured out that I am not a believer in any gods, they sometimes ask: "*Don't you believe in anything?*" Of course I do! And here I always think of Bob's lucid retort:

> *Unbelief as I represent it is not a denial of all that is positive,*
> *merely of all that is inauthentic.*

I believe in love and compassion and empathy. I believe that kindness breeds kindness. I believe in the importance of doubt, without which there can be little humility and less open-minded learning; people who claim to know for certain that which can never be known for certain cannot claim any humility at all, nor can they learn if they're convinced they already know. It's inherently dishonest.

I believe in the capacity of the human race for good, despite all the evil and stupidity – the unfortunate parallel capacity – that we demonstrate far too often. I believe in gravity, centrifugal force, thermodynamics, evolution, photosynthesis, anything for which there is convincing evidence. Evidence should not be regarded as convincing unless or until it can be tested, verified and repeated by others independently. That sets the bar pretty high – very high. But until those criteria are met, I believe we do best simply to withhold judgment (to paraphrase Bertrand Russell).

It has taken mankind until all but the last few hundred years to begin to discover real answers to natural phenomena. Many of those answers are partial, first steps, steps in the right direction – perhaps. Others are extremely complicated and may take years of study to comprehend, but any answers they have tend to be supported by evidence. And yet there's always room for doubt. So I believe in none of them *absolutely*; they represent no more than what conclusions we can draw from the currently available evidence. It has been necessary to change the answers in the past, and seems highly likely that we'll need to change them again in the future. Challenging *is challenging*! Merely attributing whatever we don't understand to a god seems to be an incredibly lazy way out, not an answer at all. Nearly everyone I've ever met who claims to "know" there is a god is referring only to his or her *own* god, nobody else's. Thus the most obvious answer to the question "Do you believe in god?" should be "Which one?"

So yes, I do confront religion. I am likely to say, *"Hey, that's only your opinion!"* whenever I hear unverified claims of Truth. I see no reason to let the religionists assume control of the podium or domination of the floor of the world.

I fear I have a troublesome personality defect. I find myself incapable of presenting my arguments dispassionately, at least on any subject I feel strongly about. No matter how solid or unassailable a position I may strive for, I seem to be quite unable just to lay it out there calmly for consideration. People don't realize that I'm not *trying* to be combative (even better: I'm trying *not* to be!), petulant or self-righteous. They don't see that when I'm presenting my position in order for it to be challenged, it's because I want to find out what's wrong with whatever position I hold, so I can get nearer the truth. Thus I put many people off. (Perhaps "piss" would be a better word than "put", a sentence that would be still more accurate without the "Perhaps".)

A few years ago, Karin made a particularly astute observation about me, one that my kids *and* my brothers immediately and spontaneously agreed with: *"You'd make a great trial lawyer, but as a diplomat you'd be a disaster."* I suspect that many others who know me well would also agree. (Unfortunately, so do I.)

I have long held that population control is the single most urgent problem in the world. There have never been anywhere *close* to the number of people inhabiting the earth today – nearly 8 billion as I write this (up from 2.5 billion when I was born). Yes, food production is up, way up – but at the expense of biodiversity. Primeval rain forests are rapidly disappearing to make room for fast-growth crops to feed us all, and to gain access to mineral wealth and slow-growth hardwoods. Such resources will be lost forever. The oceans are being over-fished and over-polluted. The waste products of human endeavors are not only ubiquitous in the seas, they form huge and growing mountains on land.

Consider how dependent our modern world is on high-speed computers for everything from air-traffic control to industrial processes to food production to communications. Consider how many of the essential raw materials for computers and other technological marvels come from rare, non-renewable resources that will soon be depleted at the rate we're consuming them.

Consider our planet's huge growth in energy requirements and our continuing dependency on fossil fuel and what that means for our carbon footprint. Consider what it would mean if we succeeded in reducing our carbon footprint by 10% per capita. (Now, in 2021, we're still trying to limit its growth, with no realistic hope of reducing it!) But also consider how totally meaningless even such an optimistic 10% reduction would be if we at the same time increase the number of *capitas* by 20%!

That's why I feel that population control is *the* big issue. There are two major forces in the world working on it. One is working to reduce population growth, e.g. primarily through the education of women. Generally speaking, the better educated women are, the fewer children they have. They are no longer content simply to bear children and run a household. They gain control of their own bodies and learn about family planning and birth control. The other major force – the opposing force – is religion. "*Ho-hum, back to this!?*" Well, yes. Nearly *all* of the active opposition to the teaching of family planning and birth control is on religious grounds, especially among Christians and Muslims (but even among Orthodox Jews). In far too many countries, religions have far too much clout. Part of their mission derives from ancient injunctions to "multiply and fill the earth". But people have already done that, beyond the breaking point. The other religious reason is to rigidly control sex. For many centuries, the Catholic view was that sex was sinful even in marriage, unless the *intention* was to procreate! No wonder our planet is so fucked up!

* * * * *

Writing *Hindsights* has been an incredible and incredibly arduous journey. The research work behind it has probably taken at least as long as the writing and rewriting and rewriting, etc. Perhaps it's inaccurate to say I've "written" these books; "crafted" would be a better word.

I've done my utmost to be truthful in everything I've written. Does that mean that everything I've written is true? Unfortunately, not at all! It's likely that I've gotten quite a few things wrong. But although I may be *mistaken*, but I haven't *lied* (written something I *know* to be false), nor have I intentionally distorted or exaggerated. I hope that what I've expressed as factual is in fact correct. I also hope that I don't claim that my *opinions* are *factual*, even though I try to base them on what I perceive to be facts.

About 15 years ago, I came up with a simple rule for myself, a formula for making every day worthwhile: Every day I will strive to do two things: *learn something new, and do something kind for someone.* I've long felt (and observed) that pursuing one's own happiness is the wrong way to go. One could make a case that such a pursuit is selfish and narcissistic by definition. If instead one focuses on bringing joy to others (or at least one other person), one's own happiness is almost certain to follow in equal measure.

The more I've learned in life, and about life, the more I understand how little I know. I don't have anywhere close to all questions, let alone the answers, and I have no answers that I claim to be *absolutely* certain. I've lived a full life; in fact, it feels like at least eight lives and lifetimes. I will do my best continue to squeeze every squeezable drop out of what remains, to try to remember to keep learning and to keep trying to show empathy and compassion daily. Empathy might well be a prerequisite for understanding others, and thus for compassion, and thus for showing kindness rather than taking offense.

Some questions may have no answers. Some problems may have no solutions. But it is perhaps better to *consider* that there *might* be – or not be – a solution, than to *conclude* that there *is* no solution – or to conclude that any solution one seems to have found must be *the* solution. Life is more complicated than that.

As I approach the end of the line, it's without fear (although I could do without the pain). I've lived a full life (although it feels like multiple lives). I've got two wonderful and amazing kids, two "bonus" kids and seven lovely and delightful grandkids. And I'm with, and in love with, and loved by my sweet Karin. It all feels like much more than I deserve.

Glimminge, October 10th, 2021

END OF *HINDSIGHTS*

APPENDIX – drawings of our homes

Korngatan 12 in Malmö

My home 1975-2007. My home with Jeanette 1975-77. My home with Lena 1979-88. My home with Karin 1991-2007, and after extensive rebuilding 1989-91 (+ 1994). See *Slings and Arrows* (Book 4), Appendix 1, for drawings of the original restorations of the house.

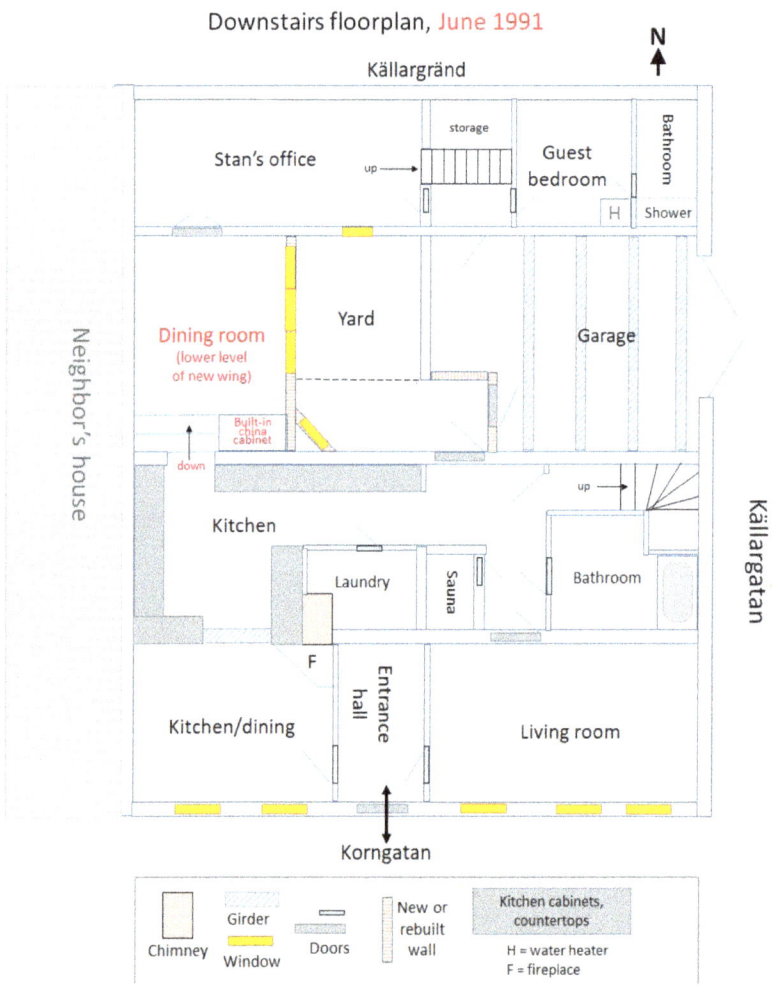

Appendix

Korngatan 12
Upstairs floorplan, June 1994

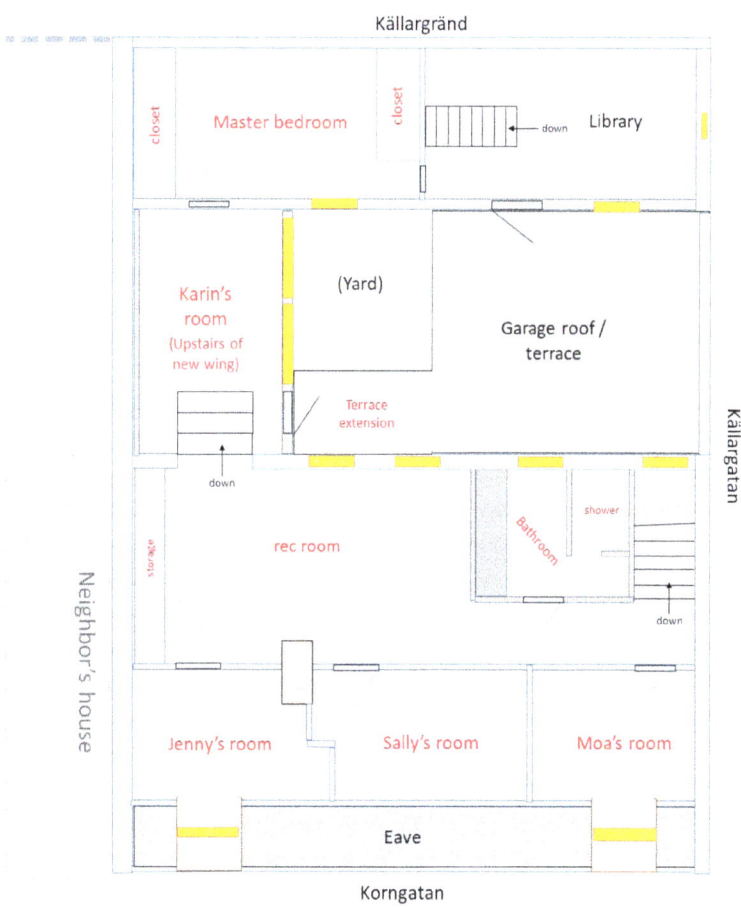

Karin's and Stan's new home in Glimminge Plantering, 2007-date

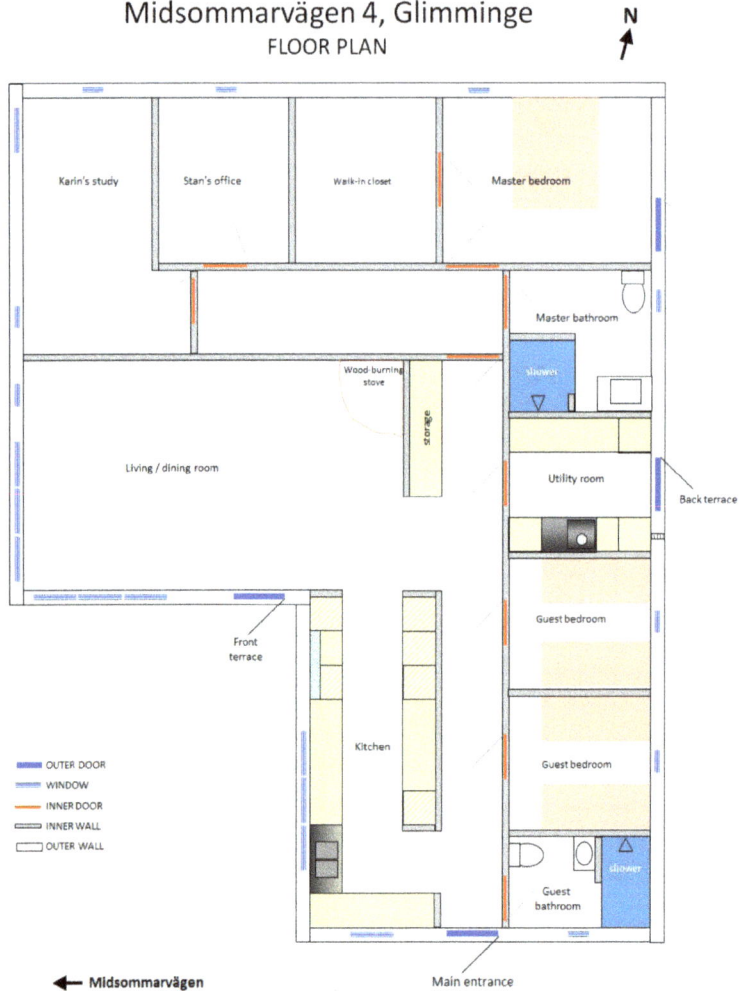

Hindsights
the six-part autobiography of an unknown artist

Book 1
Natural Shocks
by Stan Erisman

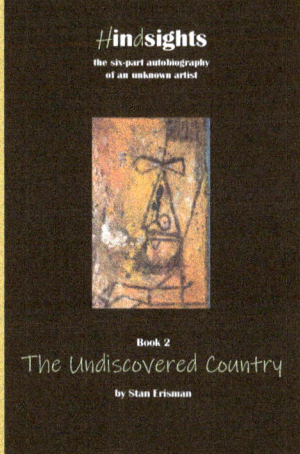

Book 2
The Undiscovered Country
by Stan Erisman

Book 3
No Traveller Returns
by Stan Erisman

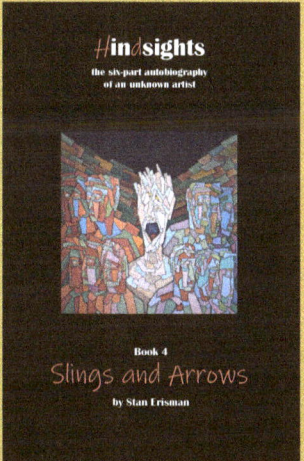

Book 4
Slings and Arrows
by Stan Erisman

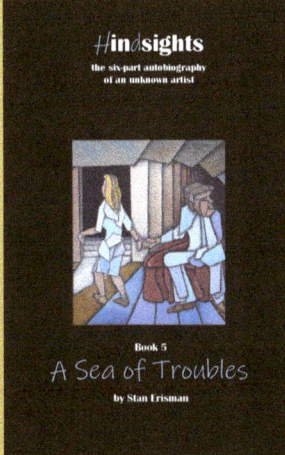

Book 5
A Sea of Troubles
by Stan Erisman

Book 6
Perchance to Dream
by Stan Erisman

www.ingramcontent.com/pod-product-compliance
Lightning Source LLC
Chambersburg PA
CBHW040305170426
43194CB00022B/2901